"This book called me to deeper, more passionate love for our Bridegroom. With intensive research, thoughtful insights and personal experience, Kim Francis makes the Song of Songs come alive. Using contemporary examples ranging from 'do not disturb' signs and overdrawn checking accounts, she makes application to this timeless, and often overlooked, portion of Scripture. The book also provides diagrams, study questions, and book and song resources."

—**Latayne C. Scott**, award-winning author

"A beautifully crafted, in-depth study of the Song of Solomon. A gifted mentor and writer, Kim Francis weaves relatable examples with biblical truths to bring deeper insights into this ultimate love story. I highly recommend this study for those who long for and are ready to seek deeper intimacy with Christ."

—**Carla Stewart**, award-winning author of *Chasing Lilacs* and *Stardust*

"Learning how to receive and experience God's relentless pursuing love is the greatest life-transforming truth we can embrace. *His Banner Over Me Is Pursuing Love* is the most thorough teaching I have ever read on the Song of Solomon from a New Covenant perspective. Kim Francis has written a masterpiece that invites us all to receive, believe, and be transformed by God's pursuing love."

—**Donald Campbell**, Operation 220 Executive Director

"*His Banner Over Me is Pursuing Love* by Kim K. Francis is a very different approach to the Song of Solomon. The author digs deeper than most scholars in that the words are not only between the lovers named in the book, but between the King of Kings and those who love Him and seek after Him. I appreciate the research of Jewish tradition and other sources that bring the Scriptures to our modern-day minds. When you read/study this book, prepare to dig deep and perhaps learn some things about yourself as well as Jesus."

—**Elaine Littau**, author, speaker, humorist (Christian fiction, devotionals, and situational humor)

"I see this as a tender, thought-provoking book in which statements are continually backed up by Scripture. Because of this book, I feel compelled as the bride of Christ to deepen my spiritual union with Him in bearing the fruit of His Spirit. I am challenged to love Him, others, and myself more, the latter being the hardest to do. I am moved by the book's poignant reminders, like how Christ uses my pain as persuasion that I might turn to Him for soothing, or that He jumps for joy over me because I am His! I started to say, "Imagine! Someone like me belongs to someone like Him," but the book candidly stresses that if I keep seeing myself as who I once was, it prevents me from living like who I am now in Him. Finally, my understanding of difficult spiritual concepts is facilitated by the book's vivid analogies. My heart is stronger because of this read!"

—**Sandy Haney**, Christian non-fiction author of *And the Award Goes to ... She Who Shed Hypocrisy* and *Sand Crab Sentiments: A Tide Pool of Poetry*

"Kim Francis brings an inspirational, allegorical approach to the Song of Solomon and provides insight into the fervent love of Christ for His bride, the church. I admire the way she has woven current examples, music and movie references throughout the study to present undeniable truths in a way that are relatable and relevant. This well-researched study can be used as written, or as I enjoyed it, in smaller chunks to let those truths soak in a bit. An incredible journey into Scripture that you will not want to miss!"

—**Linda Boswell**, pastor's wife, mom, illustrator (*Green Grass, Still Waters*)

"Kim reveals from this study of the Song of Solomon and her own experience the truth that Jesus is in love with us and He wants us to personally experience His love. This in-depth study lays bare the revelation of *I am Jesus' one and only true love*. Get this book and enjoy diving deep into Jesus' extravagant love for you."

—**Julie Morris**, Operation 220 Administrator

"Kim has written a book that gives a beautiful visual picture of the love that is ours in Christ. The way she takes apart the story of the Song of Solomon is transforming. She is a prolific, theologically sound and grace-filled writer that I will be happy to recommend for years to come. As a result of my reading this book, I will forever be changed."

—**Wynema Clark**, co-founder and director of *NewCovenantforHousewives.com*

"Intimacy. Gentleness. Passion. Romance. These are just a few of the qualities of Jesus (our Bridegroom) that I experienced in these pages. I love Kim's approach to this Old Testament book. Here you will find a personalized love story, not just about the King and the Shulammite maiden, but between Christ and His bride—which is you and me! By diving deeply into the meanings of the Jewish customs and symbols contained in these verses, she enhances their significance to us. But most meaningful is how the essential truth of both our new identity in Christ and the sweet and loving nature of God are woven throughout this book. Kim lovingly paints for us a new picture of this old story."

—**Lori Fry**, author of *Grace in Brokenness: Hearing God's Heart in Divorce*
and certified biblical life coach and counselor at Scope Ministries, International

HIS BANNER OVER ME IS

Pursuing Love

An intimate, interactive study of the Song of Solomon, Chapters 1 & 2

Kim K. Francis

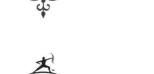

WestBow Press
A DIVISION OF THOMAS NELSON
& ZONDERVAN

Copyright © 2017 Kim K. Francis

All rights reserved. No part of this book may be used or reproduced by any means, graphic, electronic, or mechanical, including photocopying, recording, taping or by any information storage retrieval system without the written permission of the author except in the case of brief quotations embodied in critical articles and reviews.

Unless otherwise indicated, Scripture quotations are from the New American Standard Bible®, NASB®, Copyright © 1960, 1962, 1963, 1968, 1971, 1972, 1973, 1975, 1977, 1995 by The Lockman Foundation. Used by permission. (www.Lockman.org)

Scripture quotations marked (AMPC) are taken from the Amplified® Bible, Classic Edition, Copyright © 1954, 1958, 1962, 1964, 1965, 1987 by The Lockman Foundation. Used by permission. (www.Lockman.org). Scripture quotations marked (CEB) are from the Common English Bible ©2011 Common English Bible. Scripture quotations marked (CEV) are from the Contemporary English Version Copyright © 1991, 1992, 1995 by American Bible Society. Used by Permission. Scripture quotations marked (GNT) are from the Good News Translation in Today's English Version- Second Edition Copyright © 1992 by American Bible Society. Used by Permission. Scripture quotations marked (GW) are taken from GOD'S WORD®, © 1995 God's Word to the Nations. Used by permission of Baker Publishing Group. Scripture quotations marked (HCSB) are taken from Holman Christian Standard Bible® Copyright © 1999, 2000, 2002, 2003, 2009 by Holman Bible Publishers. Used with permission by Holman Bible Publishers, Nashville, Tennessee. All rights reserved. Scripture quotations marked (JUB) are taken from the Jubilee Bible, copyright © 2000, 2001, 2010, 2013 by LIFE SENTENCE Publishing, LLC. Used by permission of LIFE SENTENCE Publishing, LLC, Abbotsford, Wisconsin. All rights reserved. Scripture quotations marked (KJV) are taken from the King James Version of the Bible. Scripture quotations marked (TLB) are taken from *The Living Bible*. Copyright © 1971 by Tyndale House Foundation. Used by permission of Tyndale House Publishers, Inc., Carol Stream, Illinois 60188. All rights reserved. Scripture quotations marked (MSG) are taken from *The Message*. Copyright © 1993, 1994, 1995, 1996, 2000, 2001, 2002. Used by permission of NavPress Publishing Group. Scripture quotations marked (NCV) are taken from the New Century Version®. Copyright © 2005 by Thomas Nelson, Inc. Used by permission. All rights reserved. Scripture quotations marked (NIV) are taken from the HOLY BIBLE, NEW INTERNATIONAL VERSION®, NIV® Copyright © 1973, 1978, 1984, 2011 by Biblica, Inc.® Used by permission. All rights reserved worldwide. Scripture quotations marked (NKJV) are taken from the New King James Version®. Copyright © 1982 by Thomas Nelson, Inc. Used by permission. All rights reserved. Scripture quotations marked (NLT) are taken from the Holy Bible, New Living Translation, copyright © 1996, 2004, 2007 by Tyndale House Foundation. Used by permission of Tyndale House Publishers, Inc., Carol Stream, Illinois 60188. All rights reserved. Scripture quotations marked (TNIV) are taken from the HOLY BIBLE, TODAY'S NEW INTERNATIONAL VERSION®, TNIV® Copyright © 2001, 2005 by Biblica, Inc.® Used by permission. All rights reserved worldwide. Scripture quotations marked (VOICE) are taken from THE VOICE™. Copyright © 2008 by Ecclesia Bible Society. Used by permission. All rights reserved.

All emphasis in Scripture quotations is added by the author.

WestBow Press books may be ordered through booksellers or by contacting:

WestBow Press
A Division of Thomas Nelson & Zondervan
1663 Liberty Drive
Bloomington, IN 47403
www.westbowpress.com
1 (866) 928-1240

Because of the dynamic nature of the Internet, any web addresses or links contained in this book may have changed since publication and may no longer be valid. The views expressed in this work are solely those of the author and do not necessarily reflect the views of the publisher, and the publisher hereby disclaims any responsibility for them.

Any people depicted in stock imagery provided by Thinkstock are models,
and such images are being used for illustrative purposes only.
Certain stock imagery © Thinkstock.

ISBN: 978-1-5127-8518-0 (sc)
ISBN: 978-1-5127-8517-3 (e)

Library of Congress Control Number: 2017906812

Print information available on the last page.

WestBow Press rev. date: 8/31/2017

*To my eternal Bridegroom,
Jesus Christ, and to my
wonderful husband, Steven;
without both unions,
this study would not have been birthed.*

CONTENTS

Foreword ix
Author's Letter to the Bride xi
Author's Background xv
Looking at Scripture through a Bridal Lens xix
Overview of the Song of Solomon xxv

Week 1
This Kiss (Song of Songs 1:1–1:4) 1

Week 2
Flawless (Song of Songs 1:4–1:5) 37

Week 3
You Are More (Song of Songs 1:6–1:9) 77

Week 4
Everything I Do (Song of Songs 1:10–2:2) 125

Week 5
Welcome to the New (Song of Songs 2:3–2:11) 167

Week 6
Remind Me Who I Am (Song of Songs 2:12–2:17) 215

Song List 259
Ancient Jewish Marriage Resource List 261
"Who I Am in Christ IS Who I Am!" Scriptures 263
Leader's Guide 281
Group Covenant 291
Notes 293

FOREWORD

God will totally transform your life as He gently woos you to see Christ as your Spiritual Bridegroom and yourself as the bride of Christ. The Song of Solomon is probably the most misunderstood book in the Bible. Kim Francis carefully lays out a biblical understanding of our oneness with Christ demonstrated in the Song—verse by verse, word by word, and concept by concept. She skillfully weaves together the text with word studies, cross references of Scriptural truth, Jewish customs, stories, personal illustrations, contemporary songs and movies, and practical implications. Step by step, she leads you experientially through a life transformation in Christ that, somewhere in your heart as a believer, you always hoped for and knew would someday come, even if you didn't have the right words for it.

I encourage you to not resist the first part of the book where she speaks of romance and fairy tales. These are simply the ways we have interpreted the deepest longings of our heart to know Christ intimately, and they give us a way to personally remember how very long we have wanted to be overwhelmed by Jesus' redeeming, transcendent, pursuing love.

In case you are male, don't think this book is not for you. The bride of Christ refers to the church. The relationship of the Bridegroom and His bride is the same for women and men. Christ wants us to agree with Him in defining beauty the same way He does, in the hidden person of the new heart He gave us when we believed into Christ.

Even if you have walked in the truths concerning your life in Christ for a long time, this study will pull together resources that will deeply enhance your experiential understanding. She also clears up common misunderstandings of biblical passages too often heard in church.

The Song is often taught as a glorious treatment of physical intimacy in marriage, but this application has only begun in the last 100 years. The Jewish people understood it to apply to God's intense love toward their nation. In our day, we—as individual believers and the church corporately—desperately need to personally comprehend this love that surpasses our own human understanding so that we can be filled up with all the fullness of God in Christ Jesus our Lord unto the glory of God (Ephesians 3).

Isn't it true that we must become better receivers of God's love so we can become better expressers of God's love? You are in for a real adventure if you decide to pick up this book. Just so you know, it is very hard to lay it down!

Penny McAdams
President
Shepherd's Call Counseling and Teaching Ministry, Arlington, TX
Member of Network 220.org

AUTHOR'S LETTER TO THE BRIDE

Beloved bride of Christ:

I am delighted you have decided to join me in this journey toward a greater understanding of our relationship to Christ as His spiritual bride. The bride of Christ is made up of every believer in Christ throughout the ages (John 3:29; 2 Cor. 11:2; Eph. 5:22–32; Rev. 19:7–9; 21:2, 9; 22:17). I believe He has called me, along with many others, to proclaim to the church her identity as *His deeply cherished bride*. He longs for His bride to know who she is, how He feels about her, and her destiny to rule and reign with Him throughout eternity (Rev. 5:10; 20:6).

I first piloted a study I wrote on the entire book of the Song of Solomon with a group of more than forty women. I want to say a special thank-you to all those beautiful ladies with hearts hungry to experience their Spiritual Bridegroom's personal love for them. Your input was priceless and inspiring.

Upon completion of the pilot study, the Lord told me to shelve it and postpone the revision process. While in His waiting room, He impressed on me to adapt this study to minister also to the men in the body of Christ, who are just as much the spiritual bride of Christ as the women. So with much leaning on my Bridegroom, I have depended on Him to give me insight into the hearts of men to help them understand their spiritual marriage to Christ.

I want to say a very special thank-you to my husband, Steven, for prayerfully reading this study and offering a male perspective. Mere words are inadequate to express what your encouragement and support throughout this entire process have meant to me. I love you with all of my heart!

I also want to say thank you to Reann "Pearl" File, a precious sister in Christ who spent hours reading through the study for typos, making sure listed Scriptures were relevant to content, and offering her encouragement, insight, and suggestions. You helped take the "scary" out of self-publishing.

In addition to adapting the study to appeal to men, the Lord impressed on me to more deeply integrate the principles of our spiritual union with Him in His crucifixion, burial, resurrection, and ascension throughout the study. After all, marriage is about *sacred union*. When He revealed my spiritual union (marriage) with Him, it radically changed the way I lived. I have never been the same.

Finally, before beginning the revision process, the Lord directed me to divide the entire study into three parts, titled *His Banner Over Me Is Pursuing Love*, *His Banner Over Me Is Sustaining Love*, and *His Banner Over Me Is Transforming Love*. So what you have before you is the premier study of the Song of Solomon: *His Banner Over Me Is Pursuing Love*. It covers the first two chapters and reveals our Beloved's unrelenting pursuit to capture the affections of His bride … for she has *already* captured His.

It is generally easier for women to picture themselves as the bride of Christ because many are either brides in an earthly marriage or dreaming of someday becoming one. Men, on the other hand, have the advantage of better understanding the role *Christ* plays in relationship to His bride because many are husbands in earthly marriages. In the same way that women have to adjust their thinking when the Bible refers to them as *sons of God*, men also need to adapt their mental perception in order to see themselves as the *spiritual bride of Christ*.

Man (humanity in general) is a spiritual being who lives inside a physical body, not a physical being who houses a spirit. In order to understand our relationship with God, we need to see with spiritual eyes. Being *sons of God* refers to our new birth in Christ (the Son of God) and our role as spiritual children of our Father, God. Being the *bride of Christ*, however, refers to our spiritual union with Christ and our role of experiencing and expressing His cherishing love and exuberant life. Just as a husband and wife in the natural realm share a physical union and bear the fruit of children, Christ and His bride share a spiritual union where He has implanted His bride with His life and, with her cooperation, causes her to manifest the fruit of His Spirit (Rom. 7:4; Gal. 5:22–23; Eph. 5:9).

So, men, don't let it bother you when the words *she* or *her* are used in reference to your relationship to Christ as His bride. Just think of it as a spiritual role rather than a physical relationship. There are also women in the body of Christ who have a difficult time viewing their relationship to Him as intimately as that of a bride. Let me encourage you too to adjust your perception to a spiritual view, rather than an earthly physical view.

Deeply cherished bride of Christ, your Beloved longs for you to understand that you are the love of His life. I could tell you this again and again, sounding like a broken record, but until His Spirit gives you revelation of this truth, it will not affect you personally. You might agree that this is true information because the Bible says Christ's church is His bride, but you will not experience the enjoyment of truly *knowing* you are the object of His extravagant affection until it becomes personal revelation.

So the task at hand is for the objective truth of God's Word (all believers are the brides of Christ) to become subjective truth for you (*I am Christ's bride*). Christ's Spirit is your Teacher (John 14:26). He is the One who causes spiritual truths to become personal through revelation. When we read and meditate on God's Word, we need to have this conviction:

Because You, Lord, have spoken this, I choose to believe it. I agree with You that this is true, regardless of how I feel. Cause me to personally experience the wonders of this truth through Your revelation.

When spiritual truths become personal, they become part of our autopilot—what we believe and act on without consciously thinking about it. When we back our car out of the garage, we don't have to think, *First, I need to press the garage door opener. Then, I need to turn on the ignition while pressing the accelerator. Then, I need to press on the brake while I put the car in reverse. Then, I need to look in the rearview mirror*, and so forth. We automatically do those things because they are deeply ingrained through personal experience—they are habits. When we truly begin to understand and habitually see ourselves as Christ's deeply cherished bride, we will begin to live like who we *already* are.

My prayer is that your personal journey through the Song will help you experience and express Christ's cherishing love and exuberant life. Ask Him to reveal His Bridegroom's heart for you through this study. His greatest desire for His bride is that she would experience *wondrous delight* in intimacy with Him.

The heart who hungers and thirsts for experiential intimacy with Jesus is the heart who will relish this study of the Song of Solomon (Matt. 5:6; Rev. 22:17). I believe you are hungry and thirsty or you would not be giving your precious time to this study. Your increasing desire to experience Christ as your Spiritual Bridegroom will be your greatest asset, because the bottom line is that most people find a way to do what they *want* to do.

If you find that your desire to experience intimacy with Jesus is waning, ask Him to put a greater hunger in you to enjoy His cherishing love and exuberant life. This is a prayer to which He loves to say yes because your desire to experience Him deeply and personally originates within *His* desire for intimacy with you (John 6:44; 1 John 4:19).

Allow your Spiritual Bridegroom to love you unconditionally throughout this study. Hear and respond to His plea in the depths of your being: *My love, let Me show you how much I love you.* Hopefully and prayerfully, by the time you have reached the last page, His Bridegroom love for you will have become personal knowledge. I am looking forward to sharing this noble and romantic quest into the heart of our Bridegroom with you!

Head over heels in love with my Beloved,
Kim

AUTHOR'S BACKGROUND

For the past ten years, Christ has drawn me again and again to the Song of Solomon. I believe He strategically placed this book at the center of the Bible because its message is central to His heart. No other book of the Bible reveals our Bridegroom's extravagant affection for His bride, the church, like this one. It brims with descriptions of the divine romance.

I love romance! I have often wondered why the Lord created me to be such a romantic. At times, I've even thought, *There must be something wrong with me because of my strong desire to be romanced.* My teenage years were spent dreaming of the day when the perfect man would ride into my life on a white stallion, sweep me off my feet, and then whisk me away into the sunset of Happily Ever After.

I really believed that life was supposed to happen like it did in the movies, the Harlequin and Danielle Steel romances, and the soap operas (except for the unbelievable stuff, like people coming back from the dead again and again). Nobody ever told me any different!

I accepted Christ when I was nine but because of not knowing who I was in Him, I sinned greatly and hurt a lot of people in my search for my Mr. Perfect. I have been married three times, so the ministry Christ has called me to in communicating His Bridegroom love to His bride may seem ludicrous to those who have no idea how He has faithfully romanced my heart, causing me to fall head over heels in love with Him. It is amazing how God can take our greatest weakness in the natural, cause us to seek *Him* as the fulfillment of that need, and then use us to help others do the same. Only He can do that.

Most of us can identify people in the Bible with whom we most closely relate. The sinful woman in Luke 7:36–50 is the one with whom I most identify. In fact, I have a Home Interiors' "Tears of Repentance" figurine in my library to serve as a frequent reminder of the pit Jesus brought me out of.

There have also been several Christian songs written about this harlot. I'll never forget the first time I heard CeCe Winans' "Alabaster Box." I was sitting in church one Sunday morning just a couple of years after the Lord brought me out of that shameful lifestyle. I was moved to tears as our worship leader's daughter sang it with incredible passion. Jesus embraced me with His fiery love through the melody and the words. The heart of this song is the thankfulness of someone who has been rescued from a lifestyle of deplorable sin. I completely identified with it, feeling like I could have written the words myself.

Throughout this study, I will share the names of songs and videos that are relevant to the material. I highly recommend that you listen to or watch them, in order to help you experience Jesus' affection for you. You will find a complete song list on page 259. You may even want to create your own playlist of the recommended songs and then add others that have impacted you in your journey with Jesus. Doesn't it make sense that you would want to add music to your study of the *Song of Songs* (another name for the Song of Solomon)?

In Winans' "Alabaster Box," the harlot's name is Mary, but Luke doesn't actually name her. Some believe it is Mary Magdalene, from whom the Lord cast out seven demons (Luke 8:2). But the likelihood of Luke's introducing Mary Magdalene by name for the first time in 8:2 is slim if she were the main character in the Luke 7:36–50 account. She certainly cannot be Mary of Bethany, whose life was characterized by faithfulness (John 12:1–8). I believe this woman was unnamed on purpose. She represents one who realizes the extent of her own sinfulness and her absolute inability to do anything about her condition, apart from the extravagant grace offered through Christ.

If I had to choose one verse that characterizes my life, it would probably be Luke 7:47: "I tell you, her sins—and they are many—have been forgiven, so she has shown me much love. But a person who is forgiven little shows only little love" (NLT). I never want to forget Jesus' faithfulness in pursuing me all of those years, even though I was busy pouring my life—as Winans' song says—into this world's "treasure box."[1]

I realize that some of you can relate to my story and some cannot. If you can say, "I don't have a great testimony of the Lord's delivering me out of a shameful, sinful lifestyle," I think that is nothing short of miraculous, given all the temptations of today's world. Praise the Lord that you were spared the heartache and suffering that come with those choices.

In either case, though, every one of us must come to grips with a vital truth—the truth that we are all born into this world, dead in our trespasses and sins, living in the lusts of our flesh, and are, by nature, children of wrath (Eph. 2:1–3). Whether our sins are despicable or respectable, we must realize that we are as much in need of a Savior as the sinful woman who anointed Jesus' feet, Judas Iscariot (the disciple who betrayed Jesus), and the thief on the cross (Luke 7:36–50; 22:48; 23:39–43).

In 2006, after thirteen years of teaching high school math, the Lord called me, along with my husband, Steven, to found His Heart's Desire Ministries, a ministry dedicated to helping believers in Christ around the globe live loved in Him through understanding their pure, righteous, and holy identity as His bride. And now, after several years of meditating on the Song of Solomon and personally experiencing this divine romance, I am thrilled to be a part of His birthing *His Banner Over Me Is Pursuing Love*.

This intimate, interactive study is my heart's expression of personally experiencing His cherishing love and exuberant life. While I do not claim to be a theologian, scholar, or to have the market cornered on truth, I can say that I am a joyful recipient of my Spiritual Bridegroom's lavish affections.

I have been bless-fully married to Steven Francis for twenty years, all because of my heavenly Husband's great love, grace, and mercy. I will be eternally grateful that He never gave up pursuing an intimate love relationship with me, knowing that someday I would realize that *He* was my Mr. Perfect—always and forever.

LOOKING AT SCRIPTURE THROUGH A BRIDAL LENS

It is no coincidence that we in America and other parts of the world are obsessed with weddings. The dream of finding our one true love is paramount in the hearts and minds of women and men all over the world.

In April 2011, the world was buzzing with excitement over the impending wedding of Great Britain's Prince William, son of Prince Charles and the late Princess Diana—to Kate Middleton, daughter of Michael and Carole Middleton. Unlike Princess Diana, who was the former Lady Diana Spencer of the British aristocracy before she married Prince Charles, Kate was a commoner.

Although Kate's parents were well-to-do, sending her to the finest schools, this is still a Cinderella story because a member of the royal family was joined in holy matrimony to a nonroyal. This is our love story. Once upon a time, we, the bride of Christ, were spiritually separated from God. Now, we are spiritually united to the King of Kings and Lord of Lords! (1 Cor. 6:17). Someday soon, we will reign with Him as coheirs in the kingdom of God (Dan. 7:18, 22, 27; Rev. 5:9–10; 20:4, 6; 22:5).

God, our Father, who transcends time, has written our entire love story—the divine romance. Dwelling in the eternal now, He has seen the end of time since its inception. He didn't look at earthly marriage between a man and his wife and decide, "I think I'll pattern My Son's relationship with His bride, the church, after a human marriage." He patterned earthly marriage after the marriage between His Son, Jesus Christ, and His bride, knowing that history would culminate in the ultimate wedding of all time and eternity. It may surprise you to know that the Word of God *begins* with a wedding—

> So the Lord God caused a deep sleep to fall upon man, and he slept; then He took one of his ribs and closed up the flesh at that place. The Lord God fashioned into a woman the rib which He had taken from the man, and brought her to the man. The man said, "This is now bone of my bones, and flesh of my flesh; she shall be called Woman, because she was taken out of Man." For this reason a man shall leave his father and his mother, and be joined to his wife; and they shall become one flesh. (Gen. 2:21–24)

—and *ends* with a wedding in Revelation 19:7–9.

> Let us be glad and rejoice and give glory to him; for the marriage of the Lamb is come, and his bride has made herself ready. And to her was granted that she should be arrayed in fine linen, clean and bright: for the fine linen is the righteousness of the saints. And he said unto me, Write, Blessed are those who are called unto the marriage supper of the Lamb. And he said unto me, These are the true words of God. (JUB)

Long before He created you in your mother's womb, Father God planned for you to be His Son's eternal bride. In order to vividly capture the scene of this intriguing backstory of your life in Christ, I am enlisting the help of Rhonda Calhoun, a wonderful author, Bible teacher, and cofounder of Harvest Home, Inc. In her audio study of the Song of Solomon, she communicates the story of this "match made in heaven" beautifully. So what follows in the remainder of this section is my attempt to convey what she shared, along with my own personal insight:[1]

> Before time existed, the Holy Trinity—God the Father, God the Son, and God the Spirit—dwelled together in perfect love. Because the nature of love is to give, God desired a family made in His image that He could pour Himself into—vessels who would voluntarily receive and respond to His perfect love. Out of the overflow of His heart's longing, Adam was created. Genesis 2:7 says, "Then the Lord God formed man of dust from the ground, and breathed into his nostrils the breath of life; and man became a living being."
>
> Just think: you were created out of the overflow of God's desire to have someone He could pour Himself—*His love*—into. Can you imagine how different this world would be if every person knew that his or her purpose for existence was to be the object of their Creator's extravagant affection? And it doesn't stop there. Our omniscient God knows that the natural response of each heart lavished with His love is to love Him back and to love others.
>
> Have you ever wondered why God didn't create Eve at the same time He created Adam? The reason is because Adam is a *type* of Christ (Rom. 5:14; 1 Cor. 15:45–49). A *type* is "a symbol of something in the future, as an Old Testament event serving as a prefiguration of a New Testament event."[2] In the same way that Adam had to wait for God to form his bride, Eve, from his rib, Christ had to wait for His bride to be birthed from His resurrection life.
>
> After God created Adam, He planted a beautiful garden where they could walk together in unhindered intimacy (Gen. 2:8). One evening God said to

Adam, "Everything I made is good, except for one thing—the fact that you are alone. You need a life companion, a bride to love, who will love you back" (author's paraphrase of Gen. 2:18). In the same way, God wanted His Son, Jesus, to have a life companion—a bride into whom He could pour His love and life who would voluntarily love Him back.

Next, God instructed Adam to name all the birds and animals He had created. Imagine that Adam, while naming all the creatures, notices that each one has a mate. Deep yearning begins to rise up in his heart for his own counterpart, and in response to Adam's longing, God acts:

> So the Lord God caused a deep sleep to fall upon the man, and he slept; then He took one of his ribs and closed up the flesh at that place. The Lord God fashioned into a woman the rib which He had taken from the man, and brought her to the man. The man said, "This is now bone of my bones, and flesh of my flesh; she shall be called Woman, because she was taken out of Man." For this reason a man shall leave his father and his mother, and be joined to his wife; and they shall become one flesh. (Gen. 2:21–24)

God created Adam from the dust of the ground, but He fashioned Eve from one of Adam's ribs. In order to do this, the shedding of blood was required. God causing Adam to be in a deep sleep as He took a rib from his side foreshadowed the crucifixion and death of Jesus. Throughout Scripture, we find that physical death is referred to as *sleep* (Ps. 13:3; Jer. 51:7; John 11:11; 1 Cor. 15:51). What's more, it is no mere coincidence that a Roman soldier thrust a spear into Jesus' side to ensure that He was dead: "One of the soldiers pierced his side with a spear, and immediately blood and water came out" (John 19:34).

Just as blood and water flow out of a mother's womb when her baby is born, the rib taken from Adam's side to form Eve is a picture of the indestructible life of Christ flowing out of His pierced side to be imparted to His bride. Eve was birthed out of Adam's deep sleep, and Christ's bride was birthed out of His death and ensuing resurrection. The Bible says, "Blessed be the God and Father of our Lord Jesus Christ, who according to His great mercy has caused us to be born again to a living hope through the resurrection of Jesus Christ from the dead" (1 Pet. 1:3). This was God's plan before creation. "He chose us *in Him* before the foundation of the world" (Eph. 1:4). Eve was in Adam just as we were chosen by Father God before the foundation of the world to be *in Christ*.

Can you imagine the look on Adam's face when God presented Eve to him for the first time, declaring, "Therefore shall a man leave his father and his mother, and shall cleave unto his wife: and they shall be one flesh" (Gen. 2:24 KJV)? With his pulse racing and breath taken, Adam was surely held captive by this lovely creature (whose life was made, in part, from his) the moment he laid eyes on her. In the same way, Jesus Christ is enthralled by His gorgeous bride, whose life is found in Him.

Although God is referring to husbands and wives becoming one flesh in an earthly marriage in Genesis 2:24, this verse also foreshadows Jesus' leaving His Father and the Holy Spirit to come to this earth in order to obtain a bride. Paul quotes Genesis 2:24 in his letter to the church at Ephesus, where he compares earthly marriage to the eternal marriage between Christ and the church:

> Wives, be subject to your own husbands, as to the Lord. For the husband is the head of the wife, as Christ also is the head of the church, He Himself, being the Savior of the body. But as the church is subject to Christ, so also the wives ought to be to their husbands in everything. Husbands, love your wives, just as Christ loved the church and gave Himself up for her, so that He might sanctify her, having cleansed her by the washing of water with the word, that He might present to Himself the church in all her glory, having no spot or wrinkle or any such thing; but that she would be holy and blameless. So husbands ought also to love their own wives as their own bodies. He who loves his own wife loves himself; for no one ever hated his own flesh, but nourishes and cherishes it, just as Christ also does the church, because we are members of His body. For this reason *a man shall leave his father and mother and shall be joined to his wife, and the two shall become one flesh. This mystery is great; but I am speaking with reference to Christ and the church.* (Eph. 5:22–32)

Notice that Paul refers to the marriage between Christ and His bride, the church, as a *mystery*. It is a mystery because it is a spiritual union, which cannot be observed with the natural eye. The purpose of this spiritual union is to make the church whole and holy:

> Husbands, go all out in your love for your wives, exactly as Christ did for the church—a loved marked by giving, not getting. Christ's love makes the church whole. His words evoke her beauty. Everything He does and says is designed to bring the best out of her, dressing her in dazzling white silk, radiant with holiness. (Eph. 5:25–27 MSG)

Everything Christ does and says is designed to bring the best out of His bride. When He joined His life to ours in salvation, He gave us everything we need to walk in radiant holiness (1 Cor. 3:16–17; 6:17).

We are betrothed to Christ the moment we say yes to His offer of life. You may be surprised to learn that Jesus followed the ancient Jewish marriage customs in obtaining His bride. Some of these will be mentioned in this study. I enjoy presenting these fascinating customs and their spiritual parallels in detail at our "Your Bridegroom Awaits" women's retreats.[3] If you are interested in learning more about these customs and parallels, please refer to the Ancient Jewish Marriage Resource List on page 261 to help you get started.

Betrothal for the ancient Jewish couple was quite different from today's engagement period. They were considered legally married, even though the marriage process would not be complete until its consummation, one to two years later. Moreover, if a betrothed Jewish man changed his mind and wanted to be released from the marriage, he had to obtain a divorce. We see this custom in the account of Joseph and Mary (Matt. 1:19 NIV). A betrothed Jewish woman, however, didn't have that luxury. She was bound by the betrothal covenant under Jewish law.

As Christ's betrothed bride, we are spiritually married to (united with) Him, even though the marriage process is not yet complete. Our betrothal will one day culminate in the most glorious wedding of all time and eternity.

> Let us be glad and rejoice and give glory to him; for the marriage of the Lamb is come, and his bride has made herself ready. And to her was granted that she should be arrayed in fine linen, clean and bright: for the fine linen is the righteousness of the saints. And he said unto

me, Write, Blessed are those who are called unto the marriage supper of the Lamb. And he said unto me, These are the true words of God. (Rev. 19:7–9 JUB)

The Bible begins with the marriage between Adam and his bride, Eve, and ends with the marriage between Christ and His bride—us! This is who we are! This is who *you* are! You are Jesus' cherished bride—the object of His extravagant affection, the love of His life!

OVERVIEW OF THE SONG OF SOLOMON

The Song of Solomon is one of the thirty-nine books of the Old Testament and was written in Jerusalem around 1000 BC by Solomon during the early years of his reign as king. He also wrote Ecclesiastes and most of the book of Proverbs. All three books are sandwiched between the Psalms and Isaiah, beginning with Proverbs and ending with the Song of Solomon.

Depending on which translation you have, this book is titled the Song of Solomon or the Song of Songs. It is referred to as the Canticles in the Vulgate, the earliest Latin translation of the Bible. In the Jewish Bible (*Tanakh*), it is referred to as the Song of Songs and grouped together with Ruth, Lamentations, Ecclesiastes, and Esther—also known as the Five Megilloth (scrolls). For the purposes of simplification in this study, the book will most generally be referred to as the Song.

This highly symbolic and poetic book has more than one interpretation. Its literal interpretation celebrates love in an earthly marriage and has only existed within the last one hundred years. Many marriages have been strengthened through studies based on the Song's literal interpretation, but earthly marriage is not the focus of this study. The focus of this study is the Song's allegorical interpretation, which, in fact, is its most ancient interpretation.

An *allegory* is "a representation of an abstract or spiritual meaning through concrete or material forms; a figurative treatment of one subject under the guise of another."[1] In its allegorical interpretation, the Song illustrates the epic love story between Christ, the Spiritual Bridegroom, and His bride, the church. Its intent is to launch Christ's bride into the depths of His fiery Bridegroom love as she meditates on it.

The Song of Songs is considered by Orthodox Jews to be an allegory of the love story between Jehovah and His people, Israel, and is read every Sabbath (sundown Friday to sundown Saturday) and every year at Passover. Because of its graphically sensual literal interpretation, it was at one time forbidden reading until the age of thirty. Nonetheless, Rabbi Akiva, a renowned Jewish sage, defended the Song and was instrumental in its inclusion in the Tanakh. His intense passion for the book was expressed when he declared, "Heaven forbid that any man in Israel ever disputed that the Song of Songs is holy. For the whole world is not worth the day on which the Song of Songs was given to Israel, for all the Writings are holy and the Song of Songs is the holy of holies (Mishnah Yadayim 3:5)."[2]

The Song is a unique book of the Bible, composed entirely of dialogue except for the opening verse. Because of this, it is important to keep in mind *who* is speaking. Over the years, there has been some disagreement among translations. Throughout this study, I have trusted the Spirit of Christ to reveal His original intent of the speakers in each verse.

Due to its numerous exchanges of words of affection between King Solomon and the Shulammite maiden, the Song could have been rightly named Terms of Endearment. After teaching math for several years and having a natural interest in numbers, I was curious to find the number of times the two lovers made these endearing interchanges.

The word *love* by itself or used as a root word, appears sixty-two times in this brief poetic book of eight chapters and 117 verses. He calls her …

- beautiful—thirteen times
- my darling—nine times
- my dove—three times
- my love—four times
- lovely—four times
- my perfect one—twice
- my bride—six times
- pure—twice
- "There is no blemish in you"—once

I don't know about you, but if my spouse used these terms of endearment toward me on a regular basis, I would be putty in his hands. One of the ways I feel the most loved is through affirming, encouraging words that are either spoken or written to me, so this book describing my Spiritual Husband's affection for me literally melts my heart when I meditate on it.

In response to King Solomon's outpouring of affectionate love, the Shulammite maiden calls him …

- my Beloved—twenty-six times
- Him whom my soul loves—five times

This love Song is not intended for one who has no interest in an intimate relationship with Jesus. The target audience for this symbolic message is the believer who is seeking a greater understanding and experience of Jesus' personal affections for him or her and is learning to walk in the truths of his or her identity as His beloved bride. Although a description of the believer's salvation experience is included and elaborated on in this study, it is only in retrospect.

The following is a list of character profiles of the individuals and groups of people represented in the Song. Please keep in mind that these are *spiritual* rather than *physical* representations.

They are defined primarily by their spiritual state (believer in Christ or unbeliever in Adam). In addition, the believers in Christ are described secondarily by the extent to which their minds have been renewed with the truths of their identity and the extent to which their true identity is being expressed through their daily lives.

King Solomon represents our Bridegroom King, Jesus Christ, in His glorious resurrection state. Through His finished work on the cross, Jesus established His kingly authority. Solomon's name comes from a word that means peace, and his reign was considered a reign of peace (1 Kings 4:25). Jesus is the Prince of Peace whose eternal kingdom is characterized by righteousness, peace, and joy in the Holy Spirit (Isa. 9:6; Rom. 14:17).

The Shulammite maiden represents the believer in Christ whose mind is in the process of being renewed by the truths of who Christ is and who she is in union with Him. Her soul is being awakened by longings for a fuller experience of Christ's Bridegroom love. These longings have driven her to active pursuit—her magnificent obsession with knowing and enjoying her Beloved through experiential intimacy. She not only loves Christ, but she is falling more deeply *in love* with Him every day.

Maidens represent the group of believers in Christ to which the Shulammite maiden belongs. Because the Song focuses on the individual believer's journey into divine intimacy, the maidens are rarely mentioned. They are understood to be the corporate group of believers whose souls have been awakened by Christ's Bridegroom love and who are each on their own individual journey into divine intimacy.

Daughters of Jerusalem represent the group of believers who are "infants in Christ who cannot digest the solid food of the Word of God" (1 Cor. 3:1–2; Heb. 5:12–13). Their perception is limited to understanding that their eternal destiny is in heaven with Jesus. They have little or no knowledge of the truths of their new identity in Christ. These believers' lives bear little or no fruit because their minds have not been renewed (Rom. 12:1–2). These "baby" believers in Christ are often mistaken for unbelievers because their outward lives closely resemble theirs.

Mother is referred to a total of seven times in the Song. On three of these occasions (1:6; 3:11; 8:1), *mother* refers to Eve, who is the natural mother of all humanity in this earthly realm. Eve is the only mother of a person who has not been regenerated and joined with the Spirit of Christ. In the remaining four references (3:4; 6:9; 8:2, 5) *mother* refers to the "Jerusalem above." Paul writes of her in Galatians 4:26, "But the Jerusalem above is free; she is our mother." The "Jerusalem above" is the heavenly, spiritual realm consisting of all believers in Christ—the corporate bride—who have been regenerated, joined with His Spirit, and are seated with Him in heaven under the new covenant of grace (Eph. 2:6). Ultimately, the "Jerusalem above" will be the New Jerusalem in the new heaven and new earth (John 8:23; Rev. 3:12; 21:1–2; Heb. 12:22).

Mother's sons are referred to only once in the entire Song and represent humanity in general (1:6). The King James Version of the Bible translates this group as "my mother's *children*."

Watchmen, guards, and **shepherds** represent the undershepherds of the Lord in His church who oversee and pastor His flock.

This study is divided into six weeks, each containing five days of perusing the focal Scriptures, reflection, and interaction. Each day you will have opportunities to interact with the study through questions or directives pertaining to the material. Also, at the end of each day's study, you will find the same two questions:

What is your Bridegroom speaking to you through today's study?
How will you respond?

If you need more space than is provided to answer the questions or to follow the directives, feel free to use a writing journal to accompany this study.

When examining individual verses of the Song, we will be using the New American Standard Bible (NASB). This translation is widely regarded as one of the most literal English Bible translations. The focal Scriptures will be centered on the page and bolded. At times throughout the study, other translations will be used to highlight specific concepts in the discussion of the focal Scriptures.

This study of the first two chapters of the Song is titled *His Banner Over Me Is Pursuing Love* because the primary theme of these chapters is the Bridegroom King's passionate pursuit to capture His bride's affections. The week titles are actually the names of songs that were chosen based on important themes contained within that particular week of study.

For those of you who want to delve deeper into the Song, my next six-week study over chapters 3–5 will be titled *His Banner Over Me Is Sustaining Love*, and the last six-week study on chapters 6–8 will be titled *His Banner Over Me Is Transforming Love*. Although we find evidence of our Spiritual Bridegroom's pursuing, sustaining, and transforming love throughout the Song of Solomon, each study is titled this way because of the overriding theme of that section.

Are you ready to dive into the depths of Christ's Bridegroom love for you? I encourage you to begin each day of your study in expectant dependence on your Beloved. Believe that you are who He says you are—His cherished bride—and allow Him to shower you with His extravagant, unconditional affection. When you soak in His lavish love, you will automatically find yourself loving Him, others, and yourself more. Now it's time for you to get in receiving mode and let the divine romance begin!

Week 1

THIS KISS

SONG OF SONGS 1:1–1:4

> "No one can kiss two people
> at the same time.
> A kiss is an expression of a
> personal relationship."
> —Watchman Nee (1903–1972)

Day 1

In the opening line of this divine romance, King Solomon introduces and commends the Song, naming himself as the author:

> **The Song of Songs, which is Solomon's.**
> —Song 1:1

The Song of Songs

King Solomon was a prolific writer, composing three thousand proverbs and 1,005 songs (1 Kings 4:32). In describing this Song as the Song of Songs, he is not merely referring to one of his many ballads. Rather, he is accentuating the most excellent, the ultimate, the crème de la crème of all the songs he has written.

In its literal interpretation, the Song portrays the young king's special love for his Shulammite bride. Even though King Solomon had many wives at the end of his life, it has been said that this poor country shepherdess is the only one he married for love. By God's great design and because of its allegorical interpretation of the love between Christ and His bride, the Song of Solomon was the *only* song written by Solomon that made its way into the Bible.

It should come as no surprise to us that the name of a book portraying the romance of the ultimate couple—Christ and His bride—would be a superlative in the same manner as King of Kings, Lord of Lords, and Holy of Holies. We can be sure of its authenticity because we know that all Scripture finds its source in the very breath of God. The apostle Paul writes, "All Scripture is inspired by God and profitable for teaching, for reproof, for correction, for training in righteousness; so that the man of God may be adequate, equipped for every good work" (2 Tim. 3:16–17).

> ➢ Let's take a trip down memory lane. If you could choose the ultimate love song of all time, what would it be and why? (If you have Internet access, you may want to Google "greatest love songs of all time" to jog your memory.)

Which is Solomon's

Solomon ascribes the authorship of the Song to himself. The root word for Solomon is *shalowm* and means "completeness and peace with God in covenant relationship."[1] You may recognize the Jewish greeting, *shalom*, in this word. Shalom generally means "Peace be unto you" but also carries with it the well wishes of wholeness, wellness, restoration, contentment, and safety. This greeting certainly packs more punch than our typical day-in and day-out exchanges of "Hi, how are you?" "Fine, how are you?"

After Christ's resurrection, Scripture records that He greeted His disciples three times with the phrase "Peace be with you," a translation of shalom (John 20:19, 21, 26). The Greek word used for *peace* in these verses is *eirene*, which means "the tranquil state of a soul assured of its salvation through Christ, and so fearing nothing from God and content with its earthly lot, of whatsoever sort that is."[2]

Christ's first message to His followers after He was raised from the dead assured them of their eternal security and peace with Him. Our peace with God in Christ is all-encompassing and has been completely paid for in advance. Through Christ's finished work on the cross over two thousand years ago and our belief in and acceptance of Him, He completed us, giving us peace with Him—forever.

The Hebrew translation of shalom specifically mentions that our completeness and peace comes through covenant relationship. This is referring to the sacred covenant of marriage. Christ's bride is complete and at peace with Him (Col. 2:10; Rom. 5:1). *Complete* means that—through our eternal union with Christ's Spirit—we possess all we will ever need! We are at peace with the God of the universe because *we are no longer separated from Him.* When we truly understand that He has made us complete through our eternal union with Him, we will want to join with the Shulammite maiden in crying out for the intimate kisses of His mouth.

> **"May he kiss me with the kisses of his mouth!**
> **For your love is better than wine."**
> **—Song 1:2**

May he kiss me with the kisses of his mouth!
The dialogue begins with a passionate declaration from the young Shulammite maiden. This reveals her heart's intense longing for the King to express his personal affection for her. Interestingly, the word *kiss* comes from the Hebrew root word *nasaq*, which means "to kindle, make a fire, burn."[3] Kisses are the most romantic expression of love between two people. In every love story, whether a novel or movie, we can hardly wait for the hero and heroine to share their first kiss.

Now, for the spiritual parallel: the mouth is a symbol for the spoken and written Word of God, so the meaning of this verse for the bride is, "May He express His personal affection for me through the kisses of His Word." Her soul has been awakened to Christ's *exclusive* love and affection for her. Instead of seeing herself among the crowd of *God so loved the world*, she is beginning to see herself standing alone in her Bridegroom's affectionate gaze. Watchman Nee, an influential Chinese Christian author and church leader during the early twentieth century, writes of the kisses between Christ and His bride: "No one can kiss two people at the same time. A kiss is an expression of a personal relationship."[4]

Each one of us needs the personal revelation of *I am Jesus' one and only true love*. Your brain may be going *tilt-tilt* right now, thinking that sounds arrogant and absurd. But I urge you to agree that all things are possible with God (Matt. 19:26). You have utterly and completely captured His heart—forever. To see and experience yourself as Jesus' one and only true love will not puff you up but instead will cause you to fall head over heels in love with the One whose personal kisses continually ignite your heart.

> ➢ When you think about His love for you, do you see yourself standing among a crowd or exclusively His?

One way I experience Jesus' kisses is when I am meditating on His Word and—all of a sudden—it seems to leap off the page and into my heart. I will never forget one of those times. I was reading Galatians 2:20, where the apostle Paul is writing of the believer's union with Christ: "I am crucified with Christ: nevertheless I live; yet not I, but Christ liveth in me: and the life which I now live in the flesh I live by *the faith of the Son of God*, who loved me, and gave himself for me" (KJV).

The phrase "the faith of the Son of God" leapt off the page and into my heart. Christ caused me to realize that because of my spiritual union with Him in His crucifixion and resurrection, I now have *His* faith living in me! I am one spirit with Him (1 Cor. 3:16; 6:17). And if He lives in my spirit, then His attributes, which include His faith, belong to me.

What a kiss! I immediately started bawling like a baby, and in my mind's eye, I saw a picture of Him kissing me all over my face. Now *that's* personal and real. I will never again believe the lie that I do not have enough faith. I will walk by the faith of the One who not only gave His life *for* me but also gave His life *to* me.

A "kiss from the King" communicates a special truth to us, whether it is through meditation on His Word or through any other means He chooses to reveal His personal affection for us.[5] Through Christ's kisses, He causes objective truths to become personal to us. You were kissed by the King when you heard the gospel for the first time and believed in Him. I like to call this love's truest kiss. In the same way that true love's kiss brought Snow White back to life, our salvation (love's truest kiss) is our union with Christ's eternal life.

➤ Briefly describe the time in your life when you personally experienced love's truest kiss.

➤ Briefly describe one or more of your King's most memorable kisses (expressions of His personal affection for you) since your salvation.

I must admit that I am one of those people who will sometimes read the last chapter of a novel because I can't wait to see how it ends. Even though this study does not cover the fifth chapter of the Song, let's take a sneak peek at one of its verses to see how much the Shulammite maiden has grown in her love for the King as a result of personally experiencing the kisses she is asking for in 1:2. I love the paraphrase of *The Message*:

> "His words are kisses, his kisses words.
> Everything about him delights me, thrills me
> through and through!"
> —Song 5:16

These are the words of one who has allowed herself to be loved by a King who is passionately in love with her and, as a result, has fallen head over heels in love with Him. We have a King who wants us to know through personal experience that *He is in love with us*. And it all starts with love's truest kiss—the kiss of salvation by grace through faith, the subject of day 2 of our study.

➤ What is your Bridegroom speaking to you through today's study? How will you respond?

Day 2

In day 1, we found that the Song of Solomon, because of its allegorical interpretation of the divine romance between Christ and His bride, is the only one of King Solomon's songs that found its way into the Holy Scriptures. All romances must have a beginning. Ours started with love's truest kiss—the kiss of our salvation; our eternal union with Christ, our Spiritual Bridegroom.

I love how Jesus sometimes uses movies and songs to communicate His timeless truths to me. Disney's 2007 blockbuster spin on their princesses, *Enchanted*, begins with Giselle telling her forest friends about a vivid dream she had. Through the dream, her heart was awakened with the hope of finding her one true love—the one she was meant to spend Happily Ever After with.

In the opening song of the movie, "True Love's Kiss," we find Giselle imagining the moment in time when she will get to experience true love's kiss for herself. In the last half of the song, Prince Edward appears and begins singing to Giselle, telling her that she's the most beautiful girl he's ever laid eyes on. It is love at first sight, and *both* are convinced that they were made to complete each other.

The last part of the song, where Giselle and Prince Edward are singing to each other, closely resembles the exchanges of love between King Solomon and the young Shulammite maiden in the first two chapters of the Song. As the bride of Christ, our prince is the Prince of Peace, who first awakens our hearts through love's truest kiss—the kiss of salvation by grace through faith in Him. Ephesians 2:8–9 says, "By grace you have been saved through faith; and that not of yourselves, it is the gift of God; not as a result of works, so that no one may boast." *The Message* paraphrases it this way:

> Saving is all his idea, and all his work. All we do is trust him enough to let him do it. It's God's gift from start to finish! We don't play the major role. If we did, we'd probably go around bragging that we'd done the whole thing! No, we neither make nor save ourselves.

Salvation is an incredible gift from the King of Kings to His beloved bride. It can never be earned or deserved but only received through believing in Him. Unbeknownst to most of the bride of Christ, her salvation is actually a triple-crown kiss from the King of Kings.

My husband, Steven, is an avid sports fan. He loves to watch most sports, including all three Thoroughbred horse races here in the United States—the Kentucky Derby, Preakness Stakes, and Belmont Stakes (also known as the Triple Crown). To win all three races in the same year is considered the most prestigious accomplishment in Thoroughbred horse racing. Since its inception in 1919, there have been only twelve Triple Crown winners to date, the most recent being American Pharoah in 2015.

As great and rare an accomplishment as winning the Triple Crown is for a Thoroughbred, its comparison is extremely trivial to the triple-crown kiss of salvation that Jesus secured for His bride through His death and resurrection. Sadly, most of Christ's bride focus on only one aspect of this triple-crown kiss because they are unaware of the other two. The aspect most focused on is our forgiveness. Yet most believers don't even understand the fullness of this gift. As a result, they lack the assurance and confidence the holy bride of the King of Kings should experience in their daily living through their union with Him.

Each of the three aspects of this triple-crown kiss is wonderful in and of itself, but having a personal knowledge of all three will help Christ's bride to consistently experience and express His cherishing love and exuberant life while on this earth. In salvation, Christ's finished work on the cross secured the following for His bride:

- **Complete forgiveness of sins** through His shed blood. Hebrews 9:22 says, "Without shedding of blood there is no forgiveness." Through Christ's one-time offering of Himself on the cross, we have been forgiven *forever* for all the sins of our lifetime—past, present, and future.
- **Complete identity change** through His crucified and resurrected body. Romans 6:6 tells us that "our old self was crucified with Him," and 1 Peter 1:3 says that we were "born again … through the resurrection of Jesus Christ." Second Corinthians 5:17 tells us that we are now brand-new creations in Christ. Through Christ's body, our identity has been forever changed from sinner to saint (Rom. 1:7; 3:7).
- **Complete life change** through His indwelling Spirit. First Corinthians 6:17 says that "the one who joins himself to the Lord is one spirit with Him," and Colossians 3:4 tells us that "Christ … is our life." Through our union with Christ's Spirit, we have been given eternal life. His life *is* our eternal life! (1 John 5:11).

Personal knowledge of this triple-crown kiss has caused the door of my soul to fling wide open to Christ's Bridegroom love and enjoy sweet intimacy with Him. It has given me *permission* to be completely loved by Him. Before Christ's Spirit caused these objective truths to become personal realities for me, I experienced many ups and downs in my daily living. I did not have total assurance that I was completely cleansed. I felt sure that there was something in me that kept Christ from wanting to fully lavish me with His affection. Had I known of this triple-crown kiss when I believed the gospel as a nine-year-old, I daresay my life between the ages of nine and thirty-three would have played out very differently.

Today, we are going to focus on the first aspect of our triple-crown kiss from the King. The following list of Scriptures provides a snapshot of our complete forgiveness through Christ's shed blood on the cross:

- Jesus has forgiven us for the sins of our lifetime (Eph. 1:7; 4:32; Col. 1:13–14; 2:13–14; Heb. 10:18).
- Jesus has taken away our sin (John 1:29; Heb. 9:22, 26; 1 John 3:5).
- Jesus cleansed us and made us perfect forever (Heb. 10:1–3, 11–14; 1 Pet. 3:18).
- Jesus has chosen to forget our sins and will appear a second time without reference to our sin (Heb. 10:14; 9:28).

If you are thinking, *This sounds too good to be true*, I encourage you to look up and write out the above Scriptures for yourself, meditate on them, and trust Christ's indwelling Spirit to confirm the truth of your complete forgiveness in Him. My favorite passage concerning our complete forgiveness is Colossians 2:13–14:

> When you were dead in your transgressions and the uncircumcision of your flesh, He made you alive together with Him, *having forgiven us all our transgressions*, having canceled out the certificate of debt consisting of decrees against us, which was hostile to us; and He has taken it out of the way, having nailed it to the cross.

Some interpret this passage as "He forgave all of our sins up until the moment we got saved, but then after that, we have to make sure we ask forgiveness for every sin we commit." If that is true, then let me ask you an important question: what happens if we forget one?

Imagine that my wealthy earthly husband never wants me to do without anything I need or want, so he deposits a massive sum of money into a savings account to cover every debt I will incur throughout my lifetime. But there's a catch. My checking account has a zero balance. Every time I write a check, I have to tell him what I bought and how much it cost. Then I have to ask him to transfer the exact amount from the savings account to cover my transaction so that I won't overdraw my checking account. While I am extremely thankful my generous husband will always agree to pay each debt, the consequences (overdraft fees, embarrassment) will be costly if I forget even one.

This may sound like a silly example to you, but I lived in fear for years over the possibility that some of my sins would go unforgiven because I couldn't remember them all. You can imagine how thankful I was when I found out my heavenly Husband deposited His unlimited riches into my checking account instead! Now I never have to worry about incurring hefty insufficient funds fees for unconfessed debts. Does this make me any less appreciative for His overwhelming generosity? Of course not! It makes me even more thankful that I can lay my head on my pillow every night and sleep in sweet peace, knowing that I will never have to work to pay off my own sin debt. My heavenly Husband paid it all with the first and only forgiveness deposit the very moment we were joined in sacred union.

To make our ongoing forgiveness contingent on our memory and our asking for it shifts our focus away from what Jesus has *already* accomplished on to what *we must do* to remain in "good standing" with Him. His shed blood and our belief in Him were all that was necessary for us to enjoy our complete once-for-all forgiveness (Heb. 9:22).

If you believe that all of your sins—up until the moment you receive salvation—are forgiven, but the ones you have committed since then aren't forgiven until you confess them, you will not be able to enjoy the assurance and peace Christ died to give to you (Rom. 5:1; 1 John 5:13). This is hardly the kind of life the royal bride of Christ should be living.

It may help you to understand your complete forgiveness by considering the answer to the following questions: How many of your sins did Jesus shed His blood for, and how many of them were in the future when He died for them? *All of them!* We appropriated His complete forgiveness for the sins of our lifetime—past, present, and future—the very yoctosecond (smaller than a nanosecond) we believed in Him.

Opponents of the complete forgiveness doctrine often cite 1 John 1:9 as evidence that we have to keep asking God to forgive our sins to remain cleansed: "If we confess our sins, He is faithful and righteous to forgive us our sins and to cleanse us from all unrighteousness." This verse has been referred to as the Christians' "bar of soap." Thirteen verses later, however, the apostle John writes, "I am writing to you, little children, because *your sins have been forgiven you* for His name's sake" (1 John 2:12).

At first glance, this appears to present a conundrum. The two verses cannot both be true at the same time—*unless* they are addressed to two different audiences. In the first chapter, John was appealing to the Gnostics (those who had infiltrated the early church and believed that they had no sin) to be saved. In contrast, 2:12 is unmistakably addressing believers—little children whose sins *have been forgiven* them.

> ➤ Do you believe that the sins of your entire lifetime—past, present, and future—were forgiven through Jesus' shed blood the moment you believed in Him? If your answer is yes, what difference has it made (or will it make) in your life? If your answer is no or not sure, what is hindering you from believing it? Remember, repetitive exposure to a false concept does not make it any truer.

People who teach that believers have been forgiven for the sins of their lifetime often get accused of giving people a green light to sin. I don't know about you, but I don't recall ever needing anyone to give me a green light! I did a pretty good job of sinning *without* one. But now that I understand what I've been given through Christ's triple-crown kiss, I realize that I really don't *want* to sin. My heart's desire is to express the cherishing love and exuberant life of Christ (Heb. 10:16).

Before I conclude this topic, I would like to clarify a couple of things. First of all, I believe that confession (agreeing with God that we are sinning) and repentance (changing our minds and turning from sin) are healthy and beneficial habits in the life of every believer. When we realize we are sinning, it is important to tell our Beloved we are sorry for not living in complete dependence on Him and to thank Him for the forgiveness that is *already ours* in Him. Nevertheless, our confession and repentance are *not* a means of obtaining more forgiveness. Our initial acceptance of His forgiveness through His shed blood at salvation secured a clean slate for us forever. Christ wants us to believe it and live like we believe it!

Second, our complete forgiveness before God does not shield us from the earthly consequences of our sin and doesn't mean that we don't need to ask for forgiveness from other *people* when we sin against them. In order to maintain healthy relationships, we must be willing to admit our wrongdoing and seek forgiveness from the person we have injured. We also need to be quick to forgive others when they sin against us. We will delve into the importance of forgiving others in week 3.

Jesus wants us to wake up every morning, believing that we stand completely forgiven in Him. This may not be something we fully understand with our minds or feel with our emotions, but we can choose with our will to believe it, regardless of opposing thoughts or feelings. It is much easier to believe our way into a new way of feeling than to try to feel our way into a new way of believing. After all, don't we possess the very *faith* of Christ? Believing that we are completely forgiven for the sins of our lifetime will enable us to receive and enjoy His lavishing affection. That's where the cycle of authentic love in our life begins—by *letting* Him love us unconditionally.

> ➢ If you have trouble allowing yourself to enjoy His unconditional love without thinking you've earned it, ask Him to enable you to in the form of a prayer in the following space. Remember, you don't have to be able to completely wrap your mind around His love in order to experience it.

Today, we focused on the first aspect of our triple-crown kiss of salvation from the King of Kings—our complete forgiveness through His shed blood and our faith in Him. We will cover the other two aspects—our complete identity change and our complete life change—as we progress. Personal knowledge of all three will work together to help us experience sweet intimacy with our Bridegroom and the fulfilling life He died to give us.

In the kingdom of God, our love story, which begins with our salvation, will never end. It will just keep getting sweeter and sweeter as we realize we have *already* been given everything we need for life and godliness (2 Pet.1:3). Sound too good to be true? Maybe in this world but not in His kingdom.

> ➢ What is your Bridegroom speaking to you through today's study? How will you respond?

Day 3

In day 2, we examined the first aspect of our triple-crown kiss of salvation from our Bridegroom King: *We have been completely forgiven for the sins of our lifetime.* There is absolutely nothing we could think, say, or do that could separate us from Him or His love (Rom. 8:38–39). Our Bridegroom longs for us to believe and enjoy His kiss of complete forgiveness. Speaking of His kisses, let's revisit our focal verse from the Song and unpack the second half of it in today's study.

> **"May he kiss me with the kisses of his mouth!**
> **For your love is better than wine."**
> **—Song 1:2**

For your love

The Hebrew word for love is *dowd* and is used in the plural form, expressing relational love. It comes from a word that means "to boil,"[6] which is similar to the previous meaning for *kiss*: "to kindle, to make a fire, to burn." Song 1:2 is a fiery verse, filled with the maiden's intense longing to personally experience the King's ardent affection for her. *Dowd* is also found in an Old Testament passage where God is offering grace to His unfaithful wife, Israel, and reminding her of their betrothal, which was initiated by Him:

> "I came by again and saw you, saw that you were ready for love (*dowd*) and a lover. I took care of you, dressed you and protected you. I promised you my love (*dowd*) and entered into the covenant of marriage with you. I, God, the Master, gave my word. You became mine." (Ezek. 16:8 MSG)

Just as God entered into a sacred covenant of marriage with His wife, Israel, Jesus entered into a sacred marriage covenant with us when we believed in Him (Luke 22:20). The marriage covenants between God and Israel and Jesus and His bride are not merely contracts. A *contract* is a legally binding written agreement between two parties who agree to do their parts. It becomes null and void when either party fails to keep up his or her end of the agreement. You can think of a contract like a handshake. When one person lets go, the agreement is broken.

A *covenant* is also a legally binding written agreement, but it holds more weight than a contract. It cannot be broken unless *both parties fail to do their parts*. The Roman handshake is a wonderful picture of a covenant. Each person grasps the wrist of the other person. If one person lets go, the agreement is still binding because the other party continues holding on to the wrist of the one who let go. Both parties have to let go in order for a covenant to become null and void.

When you believed in Jesus, you entered into a sacred covenant of marriage with Him. Regardless of what *you* have or haven't done since then, *He has never let go of you.* Each of the following verses contains His covenant promise of faithfulness to you:

- "I give eternal life to them, and they will never perish; and no one will snatch them out of My hand" (John 10:28).
- "I will never desert you, nor will I ever forsake you" (Heb. 13:5).
- "If we are faithless, He remains faithful, for He cannot disown Himself" (2 Tim. 2:13 NIV).

The truth is that your Bridegroom will never let go of you, desert you, forsake you, or stop being faithful to you, regardless of what you may think or feel. Let's take a closer look at the last Scripture written by the apostle Paul to Timothy: "If we are faithless, He remains faithful, for *He cannot disown Himself.*" Because of our eternal spiritual union (oneness) with Christ, He cannot disown us, because He cannot disown Himself! This knowledge of our covenant relationship with our Bridegroom is assurance of our eternal security in Him. It doesn't get any better than this! What a faithful and true Bridegroom we have! (Rev. 19:11).

Our Bridegroom reveals His love for us in many different ways. Not only are we kissed by His Word, but we are kissed by Him when we see a beautiful sunrise or sunset, knowing that He hand-painted it to take our breath away at that very moment in time. When I see a beautiful bouquet of flowers, I see His nail-scarred hands holding it and hear Him say, "I made these just for you, Kim—for your pleasure." Christ longs for His bride to take great delight in Him and His kisses (1 Tim. 6:17).

When I hear a favorite love song playing through a store's sound system, I hear my Beloved personally serenading my heart. The most recent song was "I Can't Help Falling in Love with You" by Elvis. I couldn't help but grin when I realized it was a personal kiss from my King. Only *He* could have worked out that timing! Who would have thought something as mundane as buying groceries at my local supermarket could turn into a heartwarming encounter with my divine Lover?

Have you ever been "kissed awake" in the morning with a love song from Jesus? It's not a coincidence; He is singing to you and wants you to recognize that. Just this week, He woke me up at 3:30 in the morning, singing "I'm in the Mood for Love." *I love it when He does that!* It doesn't take me long to hop out of bed and find out what He wants to speak (or sing) to my heart. What a way to start a day! How could anyone deny that our Spiritual Bridegroom is the ultimate Romantic?

The number of different ways a believer can experience Christ and His love are as numerous as there are believers. Dr. Gary Chapman has contributed valuable practical information on how each person is wired differently to receive love from God and each other. In his book *God Speaks Your Love Language: How to Feel and Reflect God's Love*, Dr. Chapman shares five different love languages: words of affirmation, quality time, receiving gifts, acts of service, and physical touch.[7] He also shares how we can determine our primary love language and encourages us to seek God's expressions of love to us in that form. To adapt this to our study, we will focus specifically on experiencing and expressing Christ's Bridegroom love.

We will feel the most loved and cherished by Christ when we experience His love through our primary love language. My primary love language is *words of affirmation*, so I often experience Christ's love through reading books (including the Bible) which affirm His love for me, or when I hear Him telling me in the depths of my heart how much He loves me. For instance, lately I have been finding tiny metallic heart confetti in my carpet (we just held a retreat where we used it). Every time I pick one up, I hear my Beloved say, "You have captured My heart, My sister, My bride" (Song 4:9 HCSB). My love tank fills up fast when He speaks my love language!

My love language that runs a very close second to words of affirmation is *physical touch*. At first glance, one might think it impossible for Christ to communicate His love through this love language because His physical presence is no longer on this earth. Yet He frequently gives me pictures in my mind's eye, where I see Him embracing me, holding my hand, kissing my forehead, or dancing with me. Sometimes I feel a heat come over my head and shoulders that communicates His fiery love to me (and no, I'm not mistaking a hot flash for this).

Through these pictures and physical sensations of warmth, I experience His physical touch and feel His love in ways I've never experienced before. I also experience Christ's love through my husband's physical touch or a hug or touch from another person. If your primary or secondary love language is physical touch, ask Jesus to cause you to recognize when His love is flowing through others to you.

> ➢ If you have Internet access, go to 5lovelanguages.com and click on the words "Discover Your Love Language." Then follow the onscreen instructions to find your personal love language profile. In the following space, please list your scores in order from highest to lowest to discover how you feel the most loved.

For example, mine is 11—words of affirmation, 10—physical touch, 6—acts of service, 2—quality time, and 1—receiving gifts.

Although the personal assessment does not include a "bride of Christ" option, I believe that whether you are single or married, you will feel the most loved by Christ when He communicates His affection for you through your primary and secondary love languages.

Christian author and speaker Gary Thomas has also contributed valuable practical information that helps believers understand how they best relate to Christ. In his book *Sacred Pathways*, Gary shares nine different spiritual temperaments: naturalist, sensate, traditionalist, ascetic, activist, caregiver, enthusiast, contemplative, and intellectual.[8] Understanding our spiritual temperament will help us to see the unique way Christ made each of us to relate to Him. It will also help us not to judge other believers, just because they have a different way of connecting with Him than we do.

> ➤ If you have Internet access and would like to find your spiritual temperament, go to http://www.focusonthefamily.com/marriage/growing-together-spiritually/differing-faith-expressions/your-spiritual-temperament-quiz and take the Spiritual Temperament Quiz. After I completed the quiz, I found that I am a contemplative–ascetic–intellectual–enthusiast–naturalist–sensate–caregiver–activist–traditionalist in that order. Please list your spiritual temperaments from most dominant to least dominant in order to understand how you best relate to your Bridegroom.

Knowing my primary love language and dominant spiritual temperament has helped me understand how I relate best to my Spiritual Bridegroom. This knowledge has also helped me to realize that just because I relate to Him differently than others, that doesn't make me weird or better than someone else. He loves our individuality! Understanding and accepting that we are all unique will help us experience greater intimacy with Him and greater unity with each other.

Our Bridegroom knows better than anyone what makes us tick. He knows exactly how to communicate His love to us to capture our attention. In the Song, the Shulammite maiden has allowed herself to be intoxicated by the King's love and compares its effects to that of earthly wine.

Is better than wine

In Scripture, *wine* symbolizes celebration and great joy. I don't think it's a coincidence that Jesus' first recorded miracle was turning water into wine at a wedding (John 2:1–11). Marriage, in Hebrew thought, is considered the pinnacle of earthly joys. I'm intrigued by the fact that every Hebrew and Greek word in the Bible has a number attached to it that communicates an even richer layer of meaning:

> The number attached to *wine* or *yayin* is seventy. At the time of King Solomon's reign, there were seventy nations that existed in the known world. When the Shulammite says, "for your love is better than wine," she is saying, "Your love is better than anything this world has to offer!"⁹

In Song 1:2, when the maiden says, *For your love is better than wine*, she is declaring that His love is more intoxicating than any other worldly pleasure. She's right. Once you have personally experienced the exhilaration of Jesus' Bridegroom love, there is nothing in this world that can even come close to it.

Several years ago, a slogan for a popular candy bar communicated the message that, unless you actually tasted and swallowed the candy bar, you would never know how satisfying it was. It's the same with Jesus' Bridegroom love. You will never know how satisfying and intoxicating it is until you experience His exclusive love for you, His cherished bride. "O, taste and see that the Lord is good!" (Ps. 34:8).

One day, during a particularly sweet season of Jesus' wooing my heart in His Bridegroom love, I was perusing the CDs of love songs at one of our local discount stores. I enjoy listening to music to fan the flame of love in my heart for Him, so when I discovered several CDs filled with classic romantic ballads, I immediately bought them (they were cheap) and couldn't wait to get home to start listening to them. Well, you can imagine my disappointment as I opened each one, played it, and realized it was not done by the original singers. It just wasn't the same! I wanted the real deal, and all I got was a lot of cheap substitutes. Every kind of worldly love is a cheap substitute when compared to the unconditional, fiery love of our Spiritual Bridegroom.

Jesus is so good to use earthly examples to drive deep biblical truths in my mind. For instance, many people today use artificial sweeteners in place of real sugar in order to cut calories but still enjoy the sweet taste. I watched a spot on the *700 Club* one day that grabbed my attention. They were discussing different sugar substitutes, saying that even though the products may taste like sugar, your body still knows it's not getting the real thing. You will continue to crave real sugar even after you consume the substitutes. I thought, *It's the same with earthly loves.* When we try to get our need for love met through any other means than a vibrant love relationship with Christ, we will always come up short.

Jesus' Bridegroom love for us far surpasses even the beautiful, committed love of married couples. Every great love affair eventually gets past the first-love feelings of the relationship, but Jesus *never* gets over His lovesickness for us. Bottom line: Christ never intended for our earthly mate to completely fulfill us. That's something only *He* can do (Col. 2:10).

> ➤ Take a few moments to think about all the loves in your life that Jesus' love is better than. Fill in the blank: Jesus, Your love for me is better than _____.

Jude's epistle urges us to keep ourselves in the love of God (verse 21). In other words, "keep the home fires burning." In Christ's message given to the apostle John for the church at Ephesus, He rebukes them, saying, "You do not love me now as you did at first" (Rev. 2:4 GNT). Then, in the next verse, he urges them to change their minds about the most important aspect of their relationship. One translation says, "It's time to rethink and change your ways" (Rev. 2:5 VOICE). He's essentially saying, "The secret to loving is living loved in Me. If everything you do does not come from the foundation of My love, it means nothing. It all begins with letting Me love you."

I was watching a movie one evening when a statement by a wholesome small-town lawyer caught my attention. Someone was trying to give him a gift, and he responded by saying that he couldn't receive anything he hadn't earned. Sadly, that mind-set is often as prevalent in believers as it is in unbelievers. Believers who know that there is absolutely nothing they could do to earn heaven, mistakenly (and often subconsciously) believe that they have to work for everything else in their daily living before they will receive and enjoy it, just like the lawyer

(Gal. 3:3). I find it interesting that he was an expert in the law. In more ways than one. He had law-based living mastered.

Because we live in a world where we are programmed to think that we have to earn or somehow deserve love, it can be difficult for us to allow Jesus to lavish us with His unconditional love. Dennis Jernigan has written and composed a beautiful song called "Let Me Love You," which expresses Christ's intense longing for His bride to let Him love her. You can find it in iTunes. I believe listening to it could help you better experience and enjoy His unconditional Bridegroom love for you.

In today's study, we learned that Christ's fiery Bridegroom love for us exists within a sacred covenant of marriage, where He remains faithful even when we are faithless. We also looked at how understanding our primary love language and dominant spiritual temperament can help us experience greater intimacy in our relationship with Him.

In day 4, we will focus on our Bridegroom's affections for us in the first part of Song 1:3 and then explore some rich Old Testament symbolism, which pointed to Christ hundreds of years before He made His appearance on planet earth. We will also discuss the night-and-day difference between living under the bondage of the law and living in the exhilarating freedom of grace.

> ➤ What is your Bridegroom speaking to you through today's study? How will you respond?

Day 4

My hope for you by this day of your first week of study is that you have begun to experience your Bridegroom's cherishing love for you in real, personal ways. Today, we are going to learn more about His affections for His bride and examine the stark contrast between living under law and living in grace. We will also probe the rich symbolism found in the ingredients of the fragrant incense and holy anointing oil used by the Levitical priests of Moses' day, all of which point toward the fragrant attributes of our Bridegroom, Jesus Christ. Let's begin with our focal verse.

> **"Your oils have a pleasing fragrance,**
> **Your name is like purified oil;**
> **Therefore the maidens love you."**
> **—Song 1:3**

Your oils

The maiden continues to praise her King by referring to His fragrant oils. In order to discover what these oils represent, let's take a look at Psalm 45, a messianic psalm closely related to the Song of Solomon. Titled "A Song Celebrating the King's Marriage—A Song of Love," this psalm foreshadows the wedding celebration of Christ and His bride. The key difference between the Song of Solomon and Psalm 45 is that the Song of Solomon refers to the *individual* believer's journey as Christ's bride, whereas Psalm 45 portrays the bride of Christ in the *corporate* sense.

This prophetic wedding psalm opens with the declaration of a heart overflowing with praise to the Bridegroom King: "My heart bursts it banks, spilling beauty and goodness. I pour it out in a poem to the king, shaping the river into words" (MSG).

➤ Read Psalm 45:1–7. What type of oil was Christ anointed with?

The oil of joy or gladness in Psalm 45:7 refers to the emotion of joy or gladness. Likewise, the oils referred to in Song 1:3 represent the full spectrum of Christ's emotions for His bride—His heart's affections for her.

One morning while I was spending focused time with Jesus, a strong desire rose up within me to experience His affections. I picked up Mike Bickle's book *The Pleasures of Loving God* and turned to the chapter that describes the longings of the bride of Christ. The following is a paraphrase of what I read:

> Something powerful is awakened in us when we truly know and feel our Bridegroom's enjoyment of us, and we respond in abandonment to Him. Even a little knowledge of how much He enjoys us goes a very long way. Our love for Jesus rests on the assurance that we are not only wanted and pursued by Him, but that He also enjoys and delights in us.[10]

Hmmm ... I am *wanted, pursued, enjoyed,* and *delighted in* by Jesus. My heart was stirred as I read this, and the thought went through my mind, *The only way we can truly enjoy our relationship with Jesus is to experience His enjoyment of us.* This led me to pray, "Lord, cause me to experience Your emotions for me. I want to feel what You feel for me." Have you ever heard the expression, "Be careful what you ask for because you just might get it"? I was totally unprepared for the kiss I was about to receive from my affectionate Bridegroom.

I turned on some beautiful music, got on my knees, and just sat at His feet, worshipping Him. I was moved to tears, and in my mind's eye I could see them wetting His nail-scarred feet. All of a sudden, this overwhelming emotion came over me. I saw Jesus (also in my mind's eye) clothed in the royal garments of a prince, much like we see in movies set in medieval times. He was trying to get to me so that He could lavish me with His love. But something was holding Him back.

I began to realize that the barrier was not a *something* but a *Someone*. It was the hand of Father God. I wondered why He was restraining Jesus. In response to my unspoken thought, I heard a gentle voice in my mind, *If I allowed My Son to lavish you with His full affection while you are in your mortal body, you wouldn't be able to bear it*. Even now, as I reflect on this vision, it brings tears to my eyes. Although we will not be able to experience the fullness of His intense affection for us until we are clothed with our glorified bodies, it doesn't hurt to ask Him to cause us to experience as much of it as possible while we are on this earth (1 Cor. 15:50–55). Go ahead, ask! You won't be disappointed.

Not long after that personal revelation of the magnitude of Jesus' affections for me, I shared this experience with a close friend of mine, who also has a heart for the romance of our Bridegroom. Later that evening, along with our good friends, Ben & Jerry, we were watching a remake of the Cinderella story called *Ever After*. At the end of the movie, Prince Henry of France has just left his botched arranged wedding to a Spanish princess, where they both realized that their hearts would not allow them to go through with the ceremony. Each of them was in love with a commoner. In this scene, Henry has just arrived at the brooding castle where Danielle, the peasant girl he has fallen in love with, is being held captive by a sinister villain.

Danielle manages to escape at the same time Henry rides up on his horse. As he dismounts and walks toward her, she bows her head in shame, painfully aware of her soiled appearance. With an orphan shoe in his hand, Henry drops to one knee, declares that she is his match in every way, and asks her to be his wife.

As I watched this tender scene (which, by the way, is *our* love story), I realized that Prince Henry's attire was the same as what Jesus was wearing in the vision He had given me. I told my friend this, and her face lit up as she grinned and said, "Those are his *wedding* garments!" I understood then that the vision had an even richer meaning: It is the Bridegroom love that our physical bodies would not be able to endure if we were to fully experience it while on this earth. *Oh, how He loves us!*

> Have you personally experienced Jesus' affection for you, where you could actually feel what He was feeling? If so, describe that experience and don't forget to thank Him for it. If not, and you would like to feel what He feels for you, pen a prayer in the following space, expressing your desire. And then share how He answers it.

Now back to our focal verse. Not only do Jesus' oils represent the full spectrum of His emotions for His bride, but oil is a symbol of His Spirit throughout Scripture. Christ's Spirit is referred to as the *Spirit of grace* (Heb. 10:29). Christ was filled with grace (John 1:14). Simply put, Jesus is grace personified. Any effort to fully define grace would be like an ant attempting to create an Intel microchip. Not going to happen. Nevertheless, I'm going to give it my best shot.

Simply put, grace is the unprovoked favor and kindness of God toward man in the Person of Jesus Christ. There is nothing greater that Father God could do *for* us than to make the life of His Son available *to* us. For unbelievers, grace is Christ's life available for the asking; it's a gift that is received through believing in Him (John 3:16). If you've been a Christian for very long, you have likely seen the well-known acronym for grace: "God's Riches At Christ's Expense." That pretty well sums it up. Through Christ's sacrifice on the cross, His eternal resurrection life is available as a gift for anyone who is willing to receive it.

For believers in Christ, grace is the twenty-four/seven availability of His life to be enjoyed by us and expressed through us. John 1:16 tells us that we have received the fullness of His grace. *Fullness* means "fullness." When we believe (consciously or subconsciously) that we are lacking anything we need or that we have to earn or deserve what we receive from Christ, we are erroneously living under a law-based system rather than grace (Rom. 6:14–15). That's like a royal choosing to live as a homeless person on the streets.

Through Moses, God gave the Israelites the law as a standard for living, a way to define sin, and (unbeknownst to them) to ultimately cause all who were living under it to throw up their hands in utter frustration because they could not keep it perfectly (Matt. 5:48; Gal. 3:10; James 2:10). Perfection is the law's standard, and no one except Jesus lived a perfect, sinless life.

So why give the law in the first place if it was humanly impossible to keep it? Hundreds of years later, the apostle Paul states its purpose in his letter to the church at Galatia: "*The law was our guardian leading us to Christ* so that we could be made right with God through *faith*" (Gal.

3:24 NCV). The law was given to the Israelites to show them that in and of themselves, they were completely incapable of achieving righteousness based on their behavior. It was given to show them their desperate need for *Someone who was not them* to deliver them from that performance-based hamster wheel. Even though the law wasn't given to the Gentiles (non-Israelites), everyone who tries to achieve righteousness through what they do or don't do is still living under his or her own self-imposed law-based system (Lev. 26:46; Ps. 147:19–20; Rom. 2:14).

This may lead you to wonder, *Is the law bad?* No. In Matthew 5:17, Jesus said that He did not come to do away with the law, but to *fulfill* it. And fulfill it He did—on a bloody cross. The One who lived a sinless life made it possible for us to obtain the righteousness of faith (Rom. 4:13; Gal. 3:29). Paul writes, "But now apart from the Law the righteousness of God has been manifested … even the *righteousness of God through faith* in Jesus Christ for all those who believe" (Rom. 3:21–22).

Through faith in Jesus, believers have been made the "righteousness of God in Him" (2 Cor. 5:21). Take time to let that sink in. In his letter to the church at Rome, Paul wrote, "For *Christ is the end of the law for righteousness* to everyone who believes" (Rom. 10:4). Christ puts an end to our futile attempts to earn righteousness and imparts His righteousness as a gift the moment we believe in Him.

Heartbreakingly, many believers are still living under a law-based system today. Born into a world saturated with performance-based standards, they still believe they have to do something for God in order to stay in "right" relationship with Him and earn His affections. This belief and the behavior that follows it completely disregard the work of the cross in their lives. In short, law causes a believer to focus on his or her performance for Jesus; grace causes a believer to focus on Jesus' perfect performance for him or her on the cross and to live from His abundant life.

> ➣ Which system would you say you most generally live under, law or grace? If your answer is law, ask Jesus to cause you to live from the twenty-four/seven availability of His life. If your answer is grace, praise Him for the exhilarating awareness of His indwelling life, and ask Him to cause you to remember to continue to live *from Him*.

The believer in Christ who fails to understand grace will inevitably experience bondage to a performance-based lifestyle, trying to earn or deserve the blessings and favor of God. This is as ridiculous as trying to walk into a room you are *already* in. It's impossible because you are *already* there! Ephesians 1:3 says, "Blessed be the God and Father of our Lord Jesus Christ, who *has blessed us with every spiritual blessing* in the heavenly places in Christ." Can you believe that? You no longer have to ask for spiritual blessings because you *already* have the Spirit of Christ, Mr. Grace, living in you! And boy, does He smell good, as we will see in the next part of our focal verse.

Have a pleasing fragrance

The Shulammite is drawn to the sweet fragrance of her King's gracious affections (oils) for her. The New Living Translation says, "How fragrant your *cologne*." Everyone with a working sense of smell understands the power of fragrance in attraction. There may be nothing that attracts you to a particular person, but when he or she walks into a room wearing your favorite cologne or perfume, you are instantly drawn to that person.

The high priest who ministered in the tabernacle of Moses' day and later in Solomon's temple understood that even God Himself was drawn by fragrance. Under God's specific direction, he burned fragrant incense continuously at the altar of incense. God gave Moses the recipe for it in Exodus 30:34–35:

> Then the Lord said to Moses, "Take for yourself spices, stacte and onycha and galbanum, spices with pure frankincense; there shall be an equal part of each. With it you shall make incense, a perfume, the work of a perfumer, salted, pure, and holy."

Each of these ingredients specifically symbolizes the rich and fragrant attributes of Christ:

> **Stacte**—an aromatic gum resin obtained from balsam wood. *Stacte* comes from the Hebrew root word *nataph*, which means "to gently fall in drops, prophesy, or preach."[11] Revelation 19:10 says, "The testimony of Jesus is the spirit of prophecy." Stacte points to Christ's truth and mercy.

> **Onycha**—a mollusk membrane that reduces the evaporation rate of the other ingredients. *Onycha* comes from the Hebrew root word *shacal*, which means "lion."[12] The resurrected Christ is "the Lion … from the tribe of Judah" (Rev. 5:5). *Lion* speaks of Christ's eternal kingly authority.

Galbanum—an aromatic gum resin obtained from a Persian plant. *Galbanum* comes from the Hebrew root word *cheleb*, which means "fat; the best or most excellent of any kind."[13] Fat from animal sacrifices symbolized the most excellent offering to God. Galbanum symbolized Christ's most excellent offering of His life on the cross, which took away our sins (Heb. 10:12).

Frankincense—an aromatic gum resin obtained by slashing the bark of a Boswellia tree, causing its white resin to bleed out and harden. *Frankincense* comes from the Hebrew root word *laban*, which means "to become white, purify."[14] Frankincense was one of the gifts of the magi given to Jesus as a child, foreshadowing the purity of His sacrifice on the cross.

➤ Use one or two words to help you remember the attributes of Christ in each of the following ingredients of the fragrant incense:

stacte:

onycha:

galbanum:

frankincense:

It's mind-boggling to think that every one of these ingredients pointed to the glorious attributes of One who was scheduled to show up on planet earth over a millennium later to be the ultimate, once-for-all sacrifice for humankind!

In Ephesians 5:2, Paul speaks of Christ's offering using an old covenant metaphor: "Christ also loved you and gave Himself up for us, an offering and a sacrifice to God as a fragrant aroma." Because God was completely satisfied with Christ's sacrifice on our behalf, and His Spirit now lives in us, we can manifest His sweet aroma everywhere we go. "But thanks be to God, who always leads us in triumph in Christ, and manifests through us the sweet aroma of the knowledge of Him in every place. For we are a fragrance of Christ to God among those who are being saved and among those who are perishing" (2 Cor. 2:14–15). You, dear bride, are a fragrance of Christ to God.

In addition to the recipe for the fragrant incense, God also gave Moses the directions for making the holy anointing oil to be used in the tabernacle. Exodus 30:23–25 says,

Moreover, the Lord spoke to Moses, saying, "Take also for yourself the finest of spices: of flowing myrrh five hundred shekels, and of fragrant cinnamon half as much, two hundred and fifty, and of fragrant cane (calamus) two hundred fifty, and of cassia five hundred, according to the shekel of the sanctuary, and of olive oil a hin. "You shall make of these a holy anointing oil, a perfume mixture, the work of a perfumer; it shall be a holy anointing oil."

Let's look at the symbolism found in each of the ingredients of the holy anointing oil, which also point to the rich and fragrant attributes of Christ:

Myrrh—an aromatic gum resin obtained from bleeding the bark of Commiphora trees. *Myrrh* comes from the Hebrew root word *marar*, which means "bitter"[15] and is commonly used as a burial spice. Myrrh, like frankincense, was also one of the gifts of the magi given to Jesus as a child, foreshadowing His death. Myrrh is most expensive in its liquid form and symbolizes Christ's life being poured out unto death on the cross.

Cinnamon—a fragrant spice obtained from the inner bark of Cinnamomum trees. *Cinnamon* comes from the Hebrew word *qinnamown*, which means "to erect, stand upright,"[16] and symbolizes the righteousness and holiness of Christ.

Calamus—a spice obtained by cutting and drying the stalk of the tall, marshy Calamus plant and then reducing it to powder. *Calamus* comes from the Hebrew root word *qanah*, which means "to redeem"[17] and symbolizes Christ's redemption (purchase) of His bride through His sacrifice on the cross.

Cassia—a spice (related to but less fragrant than cinnamon) obtained from the inner bark of trees from the Cinnamomum family. *Cassia* comes from the Hebrew root word *qadad*, which means "to bow down"[18] and signifies Christ's humility and submission in His death. Cassia was also used to repel insects and snakes.

Olive oil is made from crushing and expelling the oil of olives and symbolizes the Spirit of the resurrected Christ.

➤ Use one or two words to help you remember the attributes of Christ in each of the following spices contained in the holy anointing oil:

myrrh:

cinnamon:

calamus:

cassia:

After God told Moses how to make the holy anointing oil, He instructed him to use it to anoint the tabernacle, all its furniture and utensils, and the priests who would minister there (Ex. 30:26–28, 30). What was God's purpose in covering everything and everyone with this special oil? The answer is found in Exodus 30:29: "You shall also *consecrate* them, that they may be most holy; whatever touches them shall be holy."

The purpose of the holy anointing oil was to consecrate—set apart for holy use—everything and everyone that it touched. The holy anointing oil painted a beautiful portrait of the indwelling life of Christ. In fact, the word *Christ* actually means "anointed."[19] Just as the tabernacle, its contents, and the priests were anointed with the holy anointing oil to signify their being set apart for God's holy use, believers in Christ are *already* anointed and made holy by His indwelling Spirit. First Corinthians 3:16–17 says, "Do you not know that you are a temple of God and that the Spirit of God dwells in you? … for the temple of God is holy, and that is what you are."

Dear bride of Christ, do you realize that *you have already been made holy* in Him? If you equate holiness only with godly behavior, you are putting the cart before the horse. *Who we are is not determined by what we do.* Holy living is predicated on knowing that we are holy.

➤ Do you have a difficult time believing you are holy? The more you believe this amazing truth, the more your *do* will begin to line up with your holy *who*.

A lot of truth was covered in today's study, from understanding the fervency of Christ's emotions for His bride, to the night-and-day difference between law- and grace-based living, to the rich symbolism found in the ingredients of the fragrant incense and holy anointing oil used in Moses' day—all of which pointed to and found its fulfillment in Christ. I hope you feel like you've enjoyed a rich meal.

In our final day of our first week of study, we will wrap up our discussion of Song 1:3 and unpack the first part of the next verse.

> ➤ What is your Bridegroom speaking to you through today's study? How will you respond?

Day 5

Today, we are going to conclude our first week of study. Now that the maiden has begun to experience the King's personal affections for her, she is hooked! She is forever ruined for ordinary pleasures. In the next phrase of verse 3, she responds to His extravagant kisses by extolling His name.

> **"Your oils have a pleasing fragrance,**
> **Your name is like purified oil;**
> **Therefore the maidens love you."**
> **—Song 1:3**

Your name

Name refers to "one's reputation, fame, or glory."[20] It represents all that a person is and has accomplished. King Solomon's reputation preceded him, being famous for his unmatched wisdom. Scripture tells us that Solomon's wisdom was, in fact, God's own wisdom (1 Kings 3:28). Because Solomon's reputation was connected to the name of the Lord, the queen of Sheba sought him out and "came to test him with difficult questions" (1 Kings 10:1). Even though Solomon had a renowned reputation for operating in the wisdom of God, believers in Christ have it far better. The indwelling Christ Himself is our wisdom:

> But God has brought you into union with Christ Jesus, and *God has made Christ to be our wisdom*. By him we are put right with God; we become God's holy people and are set free. (1 Cor. 1:30 GNT)

Have you ever noticed how we sometimes name-drop to impress others in an effort to build our own reputation? As the bride of Christ, the only name we will ever need to name-drop is the precious and powerful name of Jesus. In the same way a wife acquires her husband's last name in marriage, we acquired Jesus' name when we believed in Him (Christian). What's more, we are joint heirs with Him, which means that everything He has also belongs to us (Gal. 4:7; Rom. 8:17).

Because we are in Him, Jesus instructs us to pray to Father God in His name (John 14:13, 15:16, 16:23, 26). When we pray in the name of Jesus, we are praying as if Jesus Himself were doing the praying. We are praying a prayer that Jesus can sign His name to—a prayer in accordance with His will, which will always bring glory to His Father (John 14:13). So when we pray in Jesus' name, it is important to pray His will revealed in His written Word. There may be times when it is difficult to discern His will due to the nature of the situation. If that is the case, it is always a good idea to seal your prayer with, "Above all, Father, I pray Your will be done in Jesus' name."

Not only are we to pray in Jesus' name, but we are instructed to do *everything* we do in His name: "Whatever you do in word or deed, do *all* in the name of the Lord Jesus, giving thanks through Him to God the Father" (Col. 3:17). This simply means that we are to walk by His Spirit—to live from the inside out; to live Christ (Phil.1:2).

Many in the world today don't have a clue how matchless the name of Jesus is. Some speak His name in vain or curse it, as if it has little or no value. We can take heart that someday, every knee will bow at the name that is above every name:

> For this reason also, God highly exalted Him, and bestowed on Him the name which is above every name, so that *at the name of Jesus every knee will bow*, of those who are in heaven and on earth and under the earth, and that every tongue will confess that Jesus Christ is Lord, to the glory of God the Father. (Phil. 2:9–11)

Every knee means "every knee"—no exceptions. I can hardly wait for the day when the fullness of His glory is revealed, and every knee is bowed and every tongue acknowledges the Lordship of Jesus Christ, our eternal Bridegroom.

Is like purified oil

The maiden compares His name—who He is—to purified oil. The word *purified* means "to empty or pour out."[21] In fact, our English word *pour* comes from the Latin *purare*, which means "to purify."[22]

In the previous section we found that oil, in general, signifies Christ's Spirit. The maiden's words—Your name is like purified oil—paints a beautiful picture of Christ's life being poured out for us on the cross so that it could be poured into us the moment we believe in Him, thus purifying us forever. God's riches at Christ's expense.

Although this study is on the first two chapters of the Song, I can't help but point out that our Spiritual Bridegroom specifically describes us, His bride, as *pure* twice in the sixth chapter:

> "But my dove, my perfect one, is unique:
> She is her mother's only daughter;
> She is the *pure* child of the one who bore her.
> The maidens saw her and called her blessed,
> The queens and the concubines also, and they praised her saying,
> 'Who is this that grows like the dawn,
> As beautiful as the full moon,
> As *pure* as the sun,
> As awesome as an army with banners?'"
> —Song 6:9–10

Therefore the maidens love you

Any time we see the word *therefore* in Scripture, we need to take notice. What comes after *therefore* is connected to what was written prior to that. The maidens love the King because of His affectionate grace (oils) and His great reputation (name) for pouring His life (purified oil) into those who will receive it, thus purifying them.

This is the first occurrence of the word *maidens* in the Song and the only time that the Shulammite refers to this group. Here, she is declaring, "I am not the only one who loves You. Because of all Your wonderful qualities, the maidens cannot help but love You too."

In the New American Standard Bible, the English word *maidens* is found a total of four times in the Song. However, two different words are used. *Almah* is found in Song 1:3 and 6:8 and means "virgins of marriageable age."[23] *Bath* occurs in Song 2:2 and 6:9 and has a different meaning than *almah*. We will uncover it in week 4 of our study.

Let's revisit the character profile for the maidens (based on *almah*) found at the beginning of our study in the section titled "Overview of the Song of Solomon":

> **Maidens** represent the group of believers in Christ to which the Shulammite maiden belongs. Because the Song focuses on the individual believer's journey into divine intimacy, the maidens are rarely mentioned. They are understood to be the corporate group of believers whose souls have been awakened by Christ's Bridegroom love and who are each on their own individual journey into divine intimacy.

You, dear reader, are most likely part of this group, or you wouldn't be taking this study. You have literally been "kissed awake" by your Bridegroom's love for you. Watchman Nee shares the prerequisite for this awakening in his commentary on the Song: "The beginning of love in everyone toward the Lord is a vision of His person."[24]

The Lord longs to reveal Himself as an affectionate Bridegroom to His bride. Ask Him to more fully reveal Himself to you in this way and expect Him to answer you. Because we all get caught up in the busyness of everyday life, we have to be intentional if we want to experience intimacy in our earthly relationships. It's no different in our spiritual relationship with Christ.

> ➤ Schedule an appointment (write it on your calendar) to spend focused time with Jesus and then keep it. Put on some of your favorite worship music (mine is instrumental), and ask Him to cause you to hear His voice and experience His cherishing love. To help you stay focused, you can journal as you spend time with Him, writing down what you want to say to Him. I find that while I am writing, I often hear His response. Be sure to write down what you hear Him say. This way, you will have a written record of your time spent together. Use the page titled "My Focused Time with Jesus" at the end of this week of the study, a separate sheet of paper, or your journal to do this.

I believe you will be so blessed by your focused time with Jesus that you will want to intentionally schedule more times where you can just be with Him, share what's on your heart, and listen for His response.

Now that the Shulammite maiden has begun to experience intimacy with the King, she can't seem to get enough of His affectionate love. (This reminds me of a popular potato chip slogan.) We know this because of what she says to Him in the first part of the next verse in the Song.

> **"Draw me after you and let us run together!**
> **The king has brought me into his chambers."**
> **"We will rejoice in you and be glad;**
> **We will extol your love more than wine.**
> **Rightly do they love you."**
> **—Song 1:4**

Draw me after you

In the same way that necessity is the mother of invention, dissatisfaction with our current experience of Christ's affections is the springboard of our pursuit to enjoy His personal love for us. We will not pursue intimate experiences with our King unless we are dissatisfied with our current level of intimacy. According to Nee,

> Spiritual edification can never be separated from a pursuit that is based on hunger and thirst. If the Holy Spirit has not put *a real dissatisfaction with a general relationship* and *a pursuit for personal affection* within a believer, he can never expect to have an intimate experience of the Lord.[25]

One of the greatest gifts Christ can give us is dissatisfaction with our lack of experiential intimacy with Him. This will spur us to pursue Him to satisfy that longing. This principle of spiritual hunger and thirst has been tried and true in my own life.

In 2004, Christ impressed me to begin praying, "Stir up a firestorm of hunger in me to experience Your love." I knew that if He did not give me a desire to experience His affectionate love, I would not faithfully pursue Him. Our Bridegroom loves to answer our cry for greater hunger because He knows that hunger leads to pursuit, and pursuit ultimately leads to satisfaction.

During that time, Jesus used grace-filled books by authors who were enjoying His personal affection to increase my longing. Through that process—and much to my delight and surprise—Christ revealed to me that the source of my dissatisfaction and longing was actually His longing for experiential intimacy with me. He wanted me first!

In John 6:44, Jesus says, "No one can come to Me unless the Father who sent Me draws him." Jesus is referring to *salvation* here, but the spiritual principle applies to our ongoing experiential intimacy with Him. Every time we think about Jesus, every time our hearts feel love for Him, it is actually a response to the magnetic pull of His great desire for us to enjoy real experiences *of* His love. Every time you feel love for Christ, remember where it originated, and thank Him for loving and wanting you first.

> ➢ If you long for a greater hunger and thirst to pursue experiential intimacy with Jesus, personalize your desire in the form of a prayer in the following space. Then, every time you sense that longing rise up within you, acknowledge that it originated in *His longing* for you. And finally, by all means, obey that desire!

And let us run together!

Us in this part of the verse is referring to the Shulammite and the maidens, not the Shulammite and the King. Because this could easily be misinterpreted, I believe the first part of verse 4 in the King James Version is more accurate: "Draw me, we will run after thee."

As the Shulammite testifies of how the King has communicated His affectionate love to her, hunger naturally rises up within those who are watching and listening to have their own personal experiences of His love. "We will run after thee" means the Shulammite and her companions will continue to respond to His drawing love. Psalm 45 also illustrates the principle of "influencing many by drawing one":

> "The King's daughter is all glorious within;
> Her clothing is interwoven with gold.
> She will be led to the King in embroidered work;
> *The virgins, her companions who follow her,*
> *Will be brought to You.*
> They will be led forth with gladness and rejoicing;
> They will enter the King's palace" (verses 13–14).

Several years ago, Jesus directed my attention to the phrase, *The virgins, her companions who follow her, will be brought to You.* He said to me, "I am calling you as a forerunner to declare to My church her true identity and destiny as My beloved bride."

A forerunner is a person who is sent ahead of another to announce his or her soon coming. John the Baptist spoke of his role as a forerunner of Christ in John 3:28: "You yourselves are my witnesses that I said, 'I am not the Christ,' but, *'I have been sent ahead of Him.'*" Christ is calling forerunners from around the world to herald the church's identity and her destiny as His bride to rule and reign with Him throughout eternity. Who knows? He may be calling you too.

This closes the first week of our study. I hope it has whetted your appetite to continue your own personal pursuit to experience your Bridegroom's affections and to find out what's next for the Shulammite maiden and her King. In week 2, we will finish unpacking verse 4 along with verse 5 and concentrate on our new identity as Christ's pure, righteous, and holy bride. We will also look at how the flesh can interfere with our living from our true identity and what we can do to consistently express Christ's cherishing love and exuberant life in this world.

> ➢ What is your Bridegroom speaking to you through today's study? How will you respond?

My Focused Time with Jesus

Week 2

FLAWLESS

SONG OF SONGS 1:4–1:5

"Like a hero who takes the stage when
we're on the edge of our seats saying it's too late
well let me introduce you to amazing grace."
—MercyMe, "Flawless"

Day 1

In this week of our study of the Song, we will finish unpacking verse 4 along with verse 5. It may seem to you that we are moving at a snail's pace through these verses. There is a good reason for this: we are building a solid foundation for experiential intimacy with our Spiritual Bridegroom, Jesus Christ. Unless the bride of Christ understands and sees herself as the new—pure, righteous, and holy—creation she *already is* in Him, she will have a difficult time enjoying His cherishing love for her.

> **"Draw me after you and let us run together!**
> **The king has brought me into his chambers."**
> **"We will rejoice in you and be glad;**
> **We will extol your love more than wine.**
> **Rightly do they love you."**
> **—Song 1:4**

The king has brought me

This is the first of two places in the Song where the maiden refers to Him as "the king" (1:4; 1:12). We don't want to miss the important spiritual principle found within her use of this title. Watchman Nee writes,

> The use of the word "King" here shows that before we come to recognize the Lord as the beloved Bridegroom of our souls we must first recognize Him as the reigning King. Complete dedication to His rule and authority always precedes a life of intimate love and devotion.[1]

The last sentence bears repeating: *Complete dedication to His rule and authority always precedes a life of intimate love and devotion.* After reflecting on this statement as it pertains to my own life, I wholeheartedly agree. I accepted Jesus as my Savior when I was nine years old, yet I did not *recognize* Him as the reigning King of my life until I was thirty-three. Please notice that I did *not* say that Jesus *became* my reigning King at thirty-three. Jesus is the reigning King of Kings and Lord of Lords, whether we recognize it or not.

In June 1997, my only child, Wesley, told me he wanted to go live with his dad. He had lived with me for the first five years following our divorce. Although I was shocked and devastated when he shared the news, I understood his need to be with his dad. (A twelve-year-old should never have to choose between his parents.)

When school started in August, I felt lost. I was Wesley's mom. That's what I did. That's who I was. Or so I thought. My whole world, up until that time, revolved around taking care of him and, of course, trying to get my needs and wants met. By November, I felt myself slipping into depression and was desperate *not* to revisit that horrible place. I had gone down that debilitating road a few years earlier, where I couldn't eat or sleep and didn't want to live, and I was fearful of returning there.

One early morning as I was flipping through the TV channels, I came across a woman Bible teacher who was sharing how to practically apply biblical truths in our everyday living. I was mesmerized by what she was saying because I had very little knowledge of Scripture. I watched her program every day and—with my Bible open, pen-in-hand, and spiral notebook—began the process of renewing my mind with God's Word. I felt like someone who had been starving her whole life and found a banquet spread for royalty.

Doing life *my* way for my entire life had resulted in nothing but emptiness. I could certainly relate to the words of Solomon after he had lived off the world's pleasures for years: "'Meaningless! Meaningless!' says the Teacher. 'Everything is meaningless!'" (Eccl. 12:8 TNIV). Solomon is saying that if you go through this very brief time on earth without an eternal perspective, you will live in futility. And that is exactly what I had done up to that point in my life.

When I began to understand that Jesus was not only my Savior but also my Lord and reigning King, He surprised me with His wooing love. I realize now that He had actually been wooing me all along; I just didn't recognize it in the midst of all the heartache and suffering I had put myself and those who were closest to me through.

A few years after Wesley went to live with his dad, I was reading a passage penned by the Old Testament prophet Isaiah. One sentence seemed to describe perfectly what had happened in my life: "In the year of King Uzziah's death I saw the Lord sitting on a throne, lofty and exalted, with the train of His robe filling the temple" (Isa. 6:1).

King Uzziah reigned from 791 BC until his death in 740 BC. He had a reputation for being one of the most godly and powerful kings of Judah. In spite of that, he was stricken with leprosy after disobeying God by burning incense in the temple—a charge given by the Lord to the Levitical priesthood. Sadly, King Uzziah remained leprous until his death.

Uzziah was the only king that Isaiah—an impressionable young Hebrew—had ever known. Because Uzziah's reign was characterized by great feats, prosperity, and peace, Isaiah likely held him in high esteem. Other than the earthly throne King Uzziah sat on, it is probable that he occupied a pedestal in Isaiah's heart. That is, until the year of King Uzziah's death.

Please notice in Isaiah 6:1 that Isaiah saw the Lord the same year that King Uzziah died.

The first time I read this, the Lord immediately spoke to my heart, "In the year that Wesley left, you finally recognized Me as Lord and King of your life." In His great love for us, Jesus will use the painful circumstances in our lives to motivate us to seek Him as the sole source of our relief. Sometimes, the Lord is difficult to see, apart from suffering.

It is easy to unintentionally place people—earthly kings, presidents, movie stars, sports figures, pastors, teachers, spouses, children, family, and friends—on a pedestal. That is what I had done with Wesley. He had occupied a place in my heart that Jesus alone was meant to fill.

> ➢ Do my and Isaiah's stories ring true in your own life? If yes, briefly describe the details in the following space. If no, do you know someone who has a similar story?

Let's go back to the last line of Nee's quote in the beginning of this section: "Complete dedication to His rule and authority always precedes a life of intimate love and devotion." As previously mentioned, this statement has been proven true in my own life. But I would be remiss if I stopped there. Although completely dedicated to Him, I was *still* not experiencing the intimacy with Him that I longed for. Can you relate? Have you recognized Jesus as Lord and King but believe there has to be *more* than what you are currently experiencing in your relationship with Him?

I am convinced that the answer to experiencing greater intimacy with our Bridegroom lies largely in our understanding the fullness of the triple-crown kiss of salvation we received when we believed in Him. In day 2 of our first week of study, we focused on the first aspect of our triple-crown kiss—the complete forgiveness of all of our sins, past, present, and future—and the freedom that comes from understanding and walking in that truth. The other two aspects of our triple-crown kiss are as equally important. When we believed in Jesus, we also experienced a complete identity change and a complete life change—the subject of the remainder of today's study.

It wasn't until Jesus revealed my pure, holy, and righteous identity to me that I began to experience wondrous delight in intimacy with Him. Just think about it. If you see yourself as a dirty rotten sinner, chances are you won't be too excited about asking a holy God to cause you to experience His affection. In our discussion of the next phrase in the Song and through the accompanying diagrams, my hope is that you will begin to see yourself as the pure, holy, and righteous bride of Christ you *already* are in Him.

Into his chambers

Just as the human physical heart has chambers, the King's chambers symbolize His heart. When we describe the heart of a person, we are speaking of who the person essentially is. In John 4:24, Jesus describes Himself to a Samaritan woman at a well: "God is spirit." When we speak of Jesus' heart, we are referring to who He is, which is Spirit.

Immediately after the Shulammite maiden implores the King for a greater experience of His affections, He answers her request by bringing her into His chambers. A king's chambers were his private quarters, reserved for his personal and sometimes intimate affairs. So the King's chambers represent a place of intimacy.

Our experiential intimacy with our Spiritual Bridegroom King would be impossible, if not for the initial event that launched us into a personal love relationship with Him. I am speaking here of our spiritual union with Christ's Spirit at salvation (John 14:16–17; 1 Cor. 6:17).

Because man is made in God's image, man is a spiritual being—a spiritual heart. Man is not a physical being who has a spiritual heart but a spiritual heart who has a soul and lives in a physical body (1 Thess. 5:23; Heb. 4:12). Every person born into this world is a spiritual heart separated from the life (Spirit) of God because of the fall of Adam in the garden of Eden. The Bible describes this separation from God as being *dead in Adam*: "For as in Adam all die, so also in Christ all will be made alive" (1 Cor. 15:22). Let's look at a picture of *Man in Adam*:

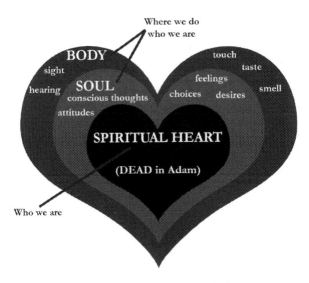

Figure 1: Man in Adam

God told Adam and Eve that on the day they ate from the forbidden tree they would "surely die" (Gen. 2:17). When they disobeyed God, they did not die physically; they died spiritually. Please notice that God defined them by their spiritual hearts. The Greek word for death is defined and explained by *Vine's Dictionary* as:

The separation of man from God; Adam died on the day he disobeyed God, and hence all mankind are born in the same spiritual condition, from which, however, those who believe in Christ are delivered. "Death" is the opposite of life; it never denotes non-existence. As spiritual life is "conscious existence in communion with God," so spiritual "death" is "conscious existence in separation from God."[2]

Simply put,

- *spiritual life* is conscious existence in communion (union) with God, and
- *spiritual death* is conscious existence in separation from God.

After eating the forbidden fruit, Adam and Eve's spirits became separated from God's life. Every person is either separated from God's life or in union with God's life. There are only two spiritual locations: *in Adam* or *in Christ*. At this moment, you are either spiritually dead in Adam or spiritually alive in Christ. There is no in-between spiritual state. It's that simple.

Our spiritual heart is the essence of our being; it is who we are. Our soul is where we experience conscious thoughts, attitudes, feelings, desires, and choices. These, in turn, influence our actions. Our body is our physical house—where we experience this world through our five senses of sight, hearing, touch, taste, and smell, and express action. Simply put,

- our *spiritual heart* is who we are, and
- our *soul* and *body* are where we do who we are.

God's greatest desire is to give everyone born into this world a new spiritual heart. Once we receive a new spiritual heart, He then desires that our souls and bodies (where we experience and express conscious thoughts, attitudes, feelings, desires, choices, and actions) be continually filled with and animated by His Spirit (life), from the inside out.

God spoke of this new spiritual heart through the prophet Ezekiel, six hundred years before Christ's crucifixion. In this Old Testament passage, He tells us what He is going to accomplish through Christ's death and resurrection:

> "I'll give you a new (spiritual) heart, put a new spirit (identity change) in you. I'll remove the stone heart from your body and replace it with a heart that's God-willed, not self-willed. I'll put my Spirit in you (life change) and make it possible for you to do what I tell you and live by my commands." (Ezek. 36:26–27 MSG)

Our new spiritual hearts are our new spirits (identity change) united with Christ's Spirit (life change)—it is who we are. The New Testament clearly tells us that in order for this identity and life change to take place, we must believe in Jesus. How is this accomplished in the spiritual realm? Let's begin by looking at the conversation between Jesus and an inquisitive Pharisee named Nicodemus:

> Jesus replied, "I tell you the truth, unless you are born again, you cannot see the kingdom of God."
>
> "What do you mean?" exclaimed Nicodemus. "How can an old man go back into his mother's womb and be born again?"
>
> Jesus replied, "I assure you, no one can enter the Kingdom of God without being born of water and the Spirit. Humans can reproduce only human life, but the Holy Spirit gives birth to spiritual life." (John 3:3–6 NLT)

Jesus told Nicodemus that man had to experience a spiritual rebirth in order to enter the kingdom of God. *Born of water* is speaking of our physical birth. *Born of the Spirit* is speaking of our spiritual rebirth in Him. Later, in verse 16, Jesus told Nicodemus how this spiritual rebirth occurs: "For God loved the world so much that he gave his one and only Son, so that everyone who believes in him will not perish but have eternal life" (NLT).

Everyone who believes in Jesus has eternal life. Believing in Jesus is not the same as believing Jesus. To believe Him simply means to believe that what He says is true is an objective fact. Believing *in* Jesus (Greek *into*) takes believing a step further. It means that not only do we believe that we are born spiritually dead in Adam—separated from Jesus' life—but we do something about it. We *choose* to be joined to His life, to be made alive by believing *into* Him.

As a nine-year-old, I interpreted this as asking Jesus to come live in my heart. But if you think about it, we are actually made alive by being placed into His life. The moment we believe in Jesus, Father God takes us out of Adam and puts us *into* Christ, uniting us with His Spirit (Col. 1:13; 1 Cor. 6:17). Because of our spiritual union with Christ, we instantaneously become the righteousness of God: "He made Him who knew no sin to be sin on our behalf, so that we might become the righteousness of God in Him" (2 Cor. 5:21).

Notice that this Scripture does not say that we *receive* the righteousness of God; it says that we *become* the righteousness of God in Christ. While Jesus hung on the cross, He literally became sin so that we could become the righteousness of God by believing into Him. The following excerpt from Rhonda Calhoun's book *The Great I AM* is a beautiful illustration of the exchange that took place when we believed in (into) Jesus:

> I see Jesus standing in a doorway. His arms are extended so I run to Him expecting to be embraced. I am surprised when I run into Him and through

Him. I am traveling at what seems to be the speed of light through a glorious white Light. Laser beams of light are going through me and gold is being formed within my being. I am filled with perfect love.

Suddenly I come out the other side. I look around and see a blinding throne of light but, surprisingly, it doesn't hurt my eyes. I look down and see that I am nothing but beautiful, glorious, wonderful light, perfect in every way. There is no darkness in me. I am elated beyond words! Pure love and pure joy floods me! I have nothing dark within me.

I turn and look behind me. I see Jesus still standing in the doorway; His back is to me. I can see through Him. I gasp because I can see my flesh, my impurities, my sin, and my weaknesses within this perfect Man. He has taken on my filth that I might take on His righteousness!

I exclaim, "Now I understand, now I know how You can say that I am without spot or wrinkle or blemish. This is how You can say that I am as beautiful as the full moon, as pure as the sun. It is because I am hidden with Christ in God! It is because You took my sins as Your own that I can stand before you clean, pure, and desirable! I am free! I am complete! I am perfect! I am acceptable because You took all that would keep me from You! Oh, thank You for the cross! Thank You for becoming sin in my place!"[3]

When a person believes in (into) Jesus, his or her identity is instantly changed and united with Christ's Spirit (life). Please note the differences in the previous diagram of *Man in Adam* and the following diagram of *Man in Christ*.

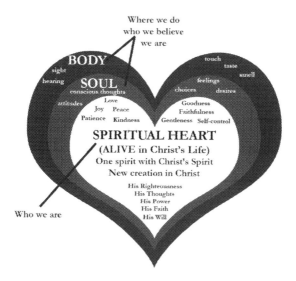

Figure 2: Man in Christ

Man in Christ is a new spiritual heart, alive because of his or her union with Christ's life. First John 1:5 says, "God is Light, and in Him there is no darkness at all." As you can see in Figure 2, *Man in Christ* has no darkness at all. The soul and body of *Man in Christ* are where this new life is either expressed by faith or suppressed by sin (Rom. 14:23).

Because the spiritual realm is unseen and unfelt with the physical senses, the degree to which believers in Christ live out of their true identity (new spiritual heart) will be the degree to which they live out *who they believe they are*, rather than simply *who they are*.

When we express our new spiritual hearts, this is what the Bible refers to as being "filled with the Spirit" (Eph. 5:18). When we suppress our new spiritual hearts, this is what the Bible refers to as "quenching the Spirit" (1 Thess. 5:19). These two ways of living will be elaborated on in the rest of this week's study.

Let's zoom in on the new spiritual heart so we can see who we are and what we have because of Christ's life in us:

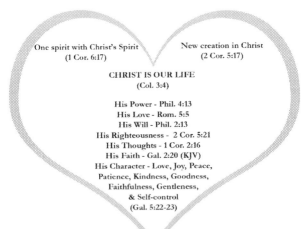

Figure 3: New Spiritual Heart
(Ezekiel 36:26-27)

First Corinthians 6:17 says, "The one who joins himself to the Lord is one spirit with Him." Second Corinthians 5:17 says, "If anyone is in Christ, he is a new creature; the old things passed away; behold, new things have come." Colossians 3:4 tells us that Christ is literally now our life: "When Christ, *who is our life*, is revealed, then you also will be revealed with Him in glory."

We now have His power because Philippians 4:13 says, "I can do all things through Him who strengthens me." We have His love because Romans 5:5 says, "The love of God has been poured out within our hearts through the Holy Spirit who was given to us." We want what

He wants because Philippians 2:13 says, "It is God who is at work in you, both to will and to work for His good pleasure." We are the righteousness of God because 2 Corinthians 5:21 says, "He made Him who knew no sin to be sin on our behalf, so that we might become the righteousness of God in Him."

We have His thoughts because 1 Corinthians 2:16 says, "We have the mind of Christ." We have the very faith of Christ within us because Galatians 2:20 says, "I am crucified with Christ: nevertheless I live; yet not I, but Christ liveth in me: and the life which I now live in the flesh I live by *the faith of the Son of God*, who loved me, and gave himself for me" (KJV). We have His love, joy, peace, patience, kindness, goodness, faithfulness, gentleness, and self-control because His Spirit lives in us (Gal. 5:22–23). We now have all of these attributes of Christ *by grace through faith*:

> For by grace you have been saved through faith; and that not of yourselves, it is the gift of God; not as a result of works, so that no one may boast. (Eph. 2:8-9)

Our triple-crown kiss of salvation is the gift of God. It is not merely a gift *from* God but the gift *of* God in the person of Jesus Christ. Jesus is our triple-crown kiss! In Him we have complete forgiveness, a complete identity change, and a complete life change. Our faith (believing *into* Christ) was "the hand that received Him."

We did absolutely nothing to earn or deserve Him; therefore, there is absolutely nothing we can do to *unearn* or *undeserve* Him. In Him, we are eternally secure. Because of what Christ has done for us and in us, we can experience and express His cherishing love and exuberant life in this world.

I would like to ask you, dear reader, the two most important questions to which you will ever need to know the correct answers: (1) Are you in Adam or are you in Christ?; and (2) if you are in Christ, how do you know you are in Him?

Which of the following would best reflect your answer to the second question?

- I am basically a good person who has done more good than bad.
- I realized I was dead in Adam, separated from God, and asked Him to give me His life.

If you are trusting in the things you have done (your self-righteousness or good works) to earn salvation, you have not understood the gospel (it's called the *good news* because Christ did all of the work!). But if you have realized your complete helplessness to save yourself and asked Him to save you by giving you His life (by being placed into His life), you have been saved. You have been rescued from the domain of darkness—from being *in Adam*—and transferred into the kingdom of God's beloved Son, to being *in Christ* (Col. 1:13). You are eternally united to Christ's Spirit and *already* are seated with Him in the heavenly places (Eph. 2:6). The only thing keeping you from being in the physical presence of Jesus is your mortal, physical body (2 Cor. 5:8).

If your answer to the first question above is, "I am in Adam," and you want to be eternally united with Jesus—you want to be *in Christ*—you can pray the prayer below to receive His life:

> Dear God,
> I realize that I am spiritually dead in Adam,
> separated from Your life.
> I believe that Your Son, Jesus, died and was resurrected
> so that I could be born again—made alive in Him.
> I want to be born again and joined with His life.
> Right now, by faith, I receive His life
> in exchange for my old life in Adam.
> Thank You, Father, for giving me eternal life,
> which is the very life of Christ Himself.
> In His name I pray,
> amen.

If you have received new life in Christ through sincerely praying this prayer, you are now in Him—forever. Rejoice! Celebrate! Your eternal destiny (spiritual location) has been changed! Who you are is a brand-new creation in Christ Jesus! Hallelujah!

Whether you just became a new believer or you have been in Christ for years, it is very important for you to understand that you aren't going to feel like a brand-new person twenty-four/seven. Feelings are in the realm of the soul and body, both of which are subject to the influences of the world in which we live. Your new birth is in your spiritual heart and involves faith—believing in the unseen or the unfelt. Even though you may not see or feel the truth that your identity has changed, you can *know* it through believing God's Word. Bottom line: your new birth is reality because God says it is.

Because the King has brought you into His chambers (eternal spiritual union with Him), you can ask Him to cause you to experience greater intimacy with Him, just as the Shulammite did at the beginning of our focal verse ("Draw me after you"). This comes from focusing on His continual indwelling presence, speaking to Him, and listening for His voice in response.

There is no greater joy on earth or in heaven than the joy that comes from knowing that we dwell eternally in the chambers of our King's heart, that we are pure, holy, and righteous new creations in Him, and that He longs for us to experience wondrous delight in our intimacy with Him. As we will see in the remainder of our study on verse 4 in day 2, joy is the exuberant response of a heart that realizes it was once dead in Adam and now understands that it has been forever made alive in Christ.

> ➢ What is your Bridegroom speaking to you through today's study? How will you respond?

Day 2

In day 1, the gospel was clearly presented. Every person is born into this world spiritually dead in Adam, separated from the life of Christ. Therefore, our greatest need is to be made spiritually alive through believing in (into) Him. The reality of Jesus' finished work on the cross for all of mankind is not just *good* news. It is the *best* and *most important* news anyone will ever hear.

If you have responded to the gospel by receiving the exuberant life of Christ and have begun to experience His cherishing love, joy will automatically be expressed through your life, just as it was through the Shulammite and the other maidens.

> **"Draw me after you and let us run together!**
> **The king has brought me into his chambers."**
> **"We will rejoice in you and be glad;**
> **We will extol your love more than wine.**
> **Rightly do they love you."**
> **—Song 1:4**

We will rejoice in you and be glad
Immediately after being brought into the King's chambers (His heart) and experiencing His intimate love, the Shulammite declares that she and the other maidens will rejoice in Him and be glad. The words *rejoice* and *glad* are paired together over twenty times throughout Scripture. One well-known verse that combines these two words is Psalm 118:24: "This is the day which

the Lord has made; let us *rejoice* and be *glad* in it" (ESV). We sing a popular praise chorus based on this verse in our church services today. Can you hear it?

In almost every instance where the two words occur, they are referring to God's people rejoicing and being glad in Him—in His strength, salvation, loving-kindness, and all of the great things He has done. We find a passage in Isaiah, however, that not only speaks of God's desire for His people to be glad and rejoice forever but also speaks of God's rejoicing and gladness in His people:

> "Be glad and rejoice forever in what I create; for behold, I create Jerusalem for rejoicing and her people for gladness. *I will also rejoice in Jerusalem and be glad in My people*; and there will no longer be heard in her the voice of weeping and the sound of crying." (Isa. 65:18–19)

God created His people for the purpose of taking great pleasure in them and their taking great pleasure in Him in response (Ps. 149:4; 37:4). When looking at Old Testament Scriptures referring to Jerusalem and her people, Israel, it is important to realize that all believers in Christ are considered *spiritual* Israel: "If you belong to Christ, then you are Abraham's descendants, heirs according to promise" (Gal. 3:29).

Father God gave us great cause for rejoicing and being glad in Him when He re-created us in His Son, Jesus Christ (Eph. 2:10). What's even more wonderful to try to wrap our minds around is that Christ is continually rejoicing over those who belong to Him with joy. We all need a personal revelation of the intensity of Christ's joy over us, just because we are in Him. I love the way the Amplified Bible, Classic Edition expresses this:

> The Lord your God is in the midst of you, a Mighty One, a Savior [Who saves]! He will rejoice over you with joy; He will rest [in silent satisfaction] and in His love He will be silent and make no mention [of past sins, or even recall them]; He will exult over you with singing. (Zeph. 3:17)

Having wiped our sin slate forever clean, making us brand-new and giving us His life, our King is completely satisfied with us. He is so thrilled with our saying yes to His invitation to enter into this divine romance that He never stops rejoicing over us with joy and exulting over us with singing.

Exult means "to show or feel a lively or triumphant joy; rejoice exceedingly; to leap, especially for joy."[4] The last time I was so happy that I was leaping and expressing triumphant joy was when my son's six-man football team upset the number-one-ranked, defending state champion, advancing them to the regional quarter finals. That was the most exciting victory

I had ever witnessed. I was so pumped for Wesley and his teammates that it took me a long time to calm down. I still get excited when I remember that Friday night under those bright stadium lights in Happy, Texas.

As exciting and joyous an occasion as that victory was, that was almost fifteen years ago. They lost their next game by only a few points, ending their season. None of those boys went on to play college football. Most are now husbands and fathers, making a decent living for their families. While that momentous win will live on in their memories, it doesn't hold a candle to the eternal triumph that our Bridegroom secured for us on the cross.

Right now—at this very moment in time—our mighty Victor is leaping, springing, and expressing triumphant joy over us (He's singing too!) because we belong to Him forever! His feelings of joy over us will never change based on what we do or don't do.

Many of us, because of living for years in this performance-based world's system, have a faulty paradigm that needs to change if we want to regularly experience His passionate affection for us. We must realize that Christ's kingdom (the spiritual realm in which we now live) is *identity*-based, not *works*-based. When we experience the personal revelation that He is continually rejoicing over us because of who we are in Him, we will join with the Shulammite and the other maidens in rejoicing in Him and being glad.

In Song 1:4, *rejoice* refers to an outward joy expressed through words and actions, such as praise and dancing (including exulting). On a more tranquil note, the phrase *be glad* indicates an inward joy reflected in the countenance. When the Shulammite says, "We will rejoice in you and be glad," she is saying that she and the other maidens are joyful, inside and out.

If we are honest with ourselves and each other, we must admit that rejoicing comes rather easily when we sense and experience His fervent love for us. In difficult times, where we don't have the accompanying warm fuzzies, rejoicing is a more deliberate choice of the will. As the bride of Christ, we aren't restricted to making choices based on the feelings we experience in the realm of the soul and body. Because we truly want what God wants, and we possess His power, we are fully equipped to make choices based on who we are in our new spiritual hearts (Phil. 2:13; 4:13).

Feelings are fickle. They can change on a dime. We can feel twenty (or more) different ways about the same thing on any given day. Jesus told us that, living in this fallen world, we *would* have trouble, not *might* have trouble (John 16:33). In the face of adversity, making the choice to act on what is true rather than how we feel is important.

The apostle Paul tells us there are only two ways for the believer in Christ to live—by the Spirit or by the flesh: "But I say, *walk by the Spirit*, and you will not carry out the desire of *the flesh*" (Gal. 5:16). We can choose to walk by His Spirit from the inside out or to be controlled from the outside in by fleshly desires experienced in the soul and body. When we focus on our true identity in Christ and His continual gladness in and rejoicing over us, we will be much less likely to walk by the flesh. In day 4 of this week's study, we will define *the flesh* and discuss the difference in walking by the Spirit and walking by the flesh in greater detail.

We will extol your love
As a result of experiencing intimacy with Him, the Shulammite and the other maidens not only are rejoicing and being glad in Him, but they also are *extolling* His love. *Extol* means "to remember, recall, call to mind."[5] Just like rejoicing, extolling His love is easy to do when He makes us aware of His affection for us but difficult when we are just not feelin' the love. In the same way that we choose to rejoice in Him and be glad without the warm fuzzies, we also can choose to remember (think about on purpose) His love for us.

One way that we can remember Christ's love for us in dry times is through personalizing Scriptures. For instance, let's personalize Isaiah 43:4, where God is saying to His people, "You are precious in My sight … you are honored and I love you." Insert your name, as if He were speaking these words directly to you (because He is): "[Your name], you are precious in My sight. [Your name], you are honored and I love you."

Next, picture Jesus standing before you or sitting beside you while you listen to Him speak these words to you. This is not make-believe. He *is* speaking these words to you, and He loves it when you own them. Picturing and hearing Jesus speak truth to us is walking by faith.

You can also take Scriptures that speak of His love for you and form them into prayers of thankfulness: "Lord Jesus, thank You for making me precious in Your sight. Thank You for giving me honor and for loving me unconditionally."

Below you will find more "love notes" from Jesus. Be careful not to read through them too quickly. Take time to personalize and savor each one:

- "I've never quit loving you and never will. Expect love, love, and more love!" (Jer. 31:3 MSG).
- "God so loved the world, that He gave His only begotten Son, that whoever believes in Him shall not perish, but have eternal life" (John 3:16).
- "Greater love has no one than this, that one lay down his life for his friends" (John 15:13).
- "The love of God has been poured out within our hearts through the Holy Spirit who was given to us" (Rom. 5:5).
- "God demonstrates His own love toward us, in that while we were yet sinners, Christ died for us" (Rom. 5:8).

- "I am convinced that neither death, nor life, nor angels, nor principalities, nor things present, nor things to come, nor powers, nor height, nor depth, nor any other created thing, will be able to separate us from the love of God, which is in Christ Jesus our Lord" (Rom. 8:38–39).
- "The love of Christ controls us, having concluded this, that one died for all, therefore all died" (2 Cor. 5:14).
- "He chose us in Him before the foundation of the world, that we would be holy and blameless before Him. In love He predestined us to adoption as sons through Jesus Christ to Himself, according to the kind intention of His will" (Eph. 1:4–5).
- "God, being rich in mercy, because of His great love with which He loved us, even when we were dead in our transgressions, made us alive together with Christ (by grace you have been saved), and raised us up with Him, and seated us with Him in the heavenly places in Christ Jesus, so that in the ages to come He might show the surpassing riches of His grace in kindness toward us in Christ Jesus" (Eph. 2:4–6).
- "That He would grant you, according to the riches of His glory, to be strengthened with power through His Spirit in the inner man, so that Christ may dwell in your hearts through faith; and that you, being rooted and grounded in love, may be able to comprehend with all the saints what is the breadth and length and height and depth, and to know the love of Christ which surpasses knowledge, that you may be filled up to all the fullness of God. Now to Him who is able to do far more abundantly beyond all that we ask or think, according to the power that works within us, to Him be the glory in the church and in Christ Jesus to all generations forever and ever. Amen" (Eph. 3:16–21).
- "See how great a love the Father has bestowed on us, that we would be called children of God; and such we are. For this reason the world does not know us, because it did not know Him" (1 John 3:1).

You may be able to recall some love notes from Jesus that are meaningful to you that aren't on this brief list. We can find a rich tapestry of verses strewn throughout the Bible that speak of God's great love for us.

As you begin the process of extolling His love for you by personalizing Scriptures, you will find that sometimes it is helpful to use a translation different from the one you normally use. When something is familiar, it has a tendency to lose its "spark." I use the website

BibleGateway.com because it has a large variety of translations to choose from. Often I find that a Scripture worded in a different way gives me a fresh perspective on it.

Another way you can extol His love for you is to bring to mind all of the ways He has shown His love to you in the past. If you don't want to forget how Jesus personally reveals His love for you, journaling is a great way to preserve your love story with Him. I've been journaling since 1995 at the suggestion of a close friend and am so glad that I have a written record of the last two decades of my romance with Him.

Whichever way you choose to extol His love, the importance of meditating on His personal words of affection for you cannot be overstated. When we focus on and fill our minds with truth, something supernatural happens. Christ's indwelling Spirit ignites those truths with fire, and personal revelation is birthed. This is how truths that begin as mere words or mental concepts find their fruition as burning realities within. They become living, flaming knowledge—knowledge that transcends thinking.

> ➢ Write a letter to yourself from Jesus in the following space, using a few of your favorite Scriptures that communicate His cherishing love for you.

More than wine

In verse 2, the Shulammite compared her King's love to the intoxicating effects of wine, declaring that it was better than every other type of worldly pleasure. In this phrase, she is saying that she and the other maidens will think and talk about (extol) His love more than any other temporary worldly pleasure. We can experience great enjoyment by keeping Christ and His love for us at the forefront of our minds.

Although we have an eternity ahead of us where we will continually experience the delights of His cherishing Bridegroom love for us, we don't have to wait until our physical death or His return for us (whichever comes first) to enjoy it. There's no time like the present to experience His presence!

Rightly do they love you

The Shulammite diverts her attention from her joint participation with the maidens ("We will") in rejoicing in and extolling their King's love and places it squarely on them. One might think at first that she only means, *Of course they are going to love You, after all You've done for them*. But I believe the King James Version zeroes in on the specific reason why the maidens love Him so much: "We will be glad and rejoice in thee, we will remember thy love more than wine: the *upright* love thee."

In Scripture, *upright* and *righteous* mean the same thing (Ps. 32:11). The maidens love Him so much because He has forever made them righteous. We've already learned that a believer is "the righteousness of God in Christ" (2 Cor. 5:21). Still, to many this is a foreign concept. They continue to look to their feelings and behavior to decide whether or not they are righteous, rather than believing the Word of God. Because believers are *already* righteous, we should take God at His word and act like He's telling the truth.

It deeply pains me to hear a Bible teacher or preacher telling believers that they need to "get right with God." This is like telling a person to sit in a chair in which he or she is *already* sitting. It's impossible to do! Our being right with God has nothing to do with what we have or have not done but refers to our justification in Him.

Justified means that we stand before Christ "just-as-if-I'd" never sinned. We are justified by faith (believing into Jesus) and now have peace with God through Christ (Rom. 5:1). The spiritual kingdom of God (where we live) is "righteousness and peace and joy in the Holy Spirit" (Rom. 14:17). I don't believe the order of those terms is coincidental. When we know that we are "the righteousness of God in Christ," we will enjoy peace with Him, and joy will naturally exude from our lives. And that's not all; genuine love will flow from our hearts to the One who made us righteous in Him.

➤ What is your Bridegroom speaking to you through today's study? How will you respond?

Day 3

Beloved bride of Christ, how I pray you are beginning to see yourself as you truly are in Him through the pages of this study. Understanding your identity in Christ will help you experience the divine romance of His cherishing love for you. If you are having a difficult time believing you are Christ's pure, holy, and righteous bride, take heart. After years of viewing yourself through a natural earthly perspective, seeing yourself through an eternal spiritual perspective takes time. Your feelings and behavior will begin to line up with the truth of your new identity as you continually renew your mind. In the next verse of the Song, it appears that the Shulammite maiden is also having a difficult time seeing the fullness of who she truly is.

> **"I am black but lovely,**
> **O daughters of Jerusalem,**
> **Like the tents of Kedar,**
> **Like the curtains of Solomon."**
> **—Song 1:5**

I am black but lovely, O daughters of Jerusalem

An unknown amount of time has passed between the Shulammite and the other maidens' rejoicing in and extolling the love of their King in verses 2–4 and this verse. In verse 5, her focus has turned onto herself, and she is now addressing a new group that has emerged onto the scene—the daughters of Jerusalem. We want to be careful not to confuse this group of believers with the maidens—those who are faithfully pursuing their King in response to their longing for greater experiential intimacy with Him. Let's revisit the character profile for the daughters of Jerusalem from the overview found at the beginning of this study to get better acquainted with them.

Daughters of Jerusalem represent the group of believers who are "infants in Christ who cannot digest the solid food of the Word of God" (1 Cor. 3:1–2; Heb. 5:12–13). Their perception is limited to understanding that their eternal destiny is in heaven with Jesus. They have little or no knowledge of the truths of their new identity in Christ. These believers' lives bear little or no fruit because their minds have not been renewed (Rom. 12:1–2). These "baby" believers in Christ are often mistaken for unbelievers because their outward lives closely resemble theirs.

Paul addresses believers like these in his letter to the Corinthians: "I gave you milk to drink, not solid food; for you were not yet able to receive it. Indeed, even now you are not yet able, for you are still fleshly" (1 Cor. 3:2–3). The author of Hebrews also describes this type of believer: "For everyone who partakes only of milk is not accustomed to the word of righteousness, for he is an infant" (Heb. 5:13).

Believers who are "unaccustomed to the word of righteousness" are ignorant (lacking knowledge) of their pure, holy, and righteous identity in Jesus Christ (2 Cor. 5:21). Although they have believed in (into) Jesus and understood that their eternal destination is heaven, the renewal of their minds concerning who they are either hit a stalemate or never really began, for whatever reason.

The maiden too was a daughter of Jerusalem when she first believed. But something happened within her that has not yet happened in them. That something was *desire*. A longing rose up within her to know Him more deeply. In her pursuit of greater intimacy with Him and knowledge of the truth, she has come to understand that His Spirit actually lives *in* her. She now has a "Christ-in-me" consciousness. Before going to the cross, Jesus promised His disciples that one day His Spirit would live *in* them:

> "I will ask the Father, and He will give you another Helper, that He may be with you forever; that is the Spirit of truth, whom the world cannot receive, because it does not see Him or know Him, but you know Him because *He abides with you and will be in you.*" (John 14:16–17)

Jesus wanted to assure His disciples that even though His physical presence would no longer abide (live) *with* them, His coming Spirit would forever *indwell* them. He promised them that they would not be unaware of this, but they would know He indwelt them. "In that day you will know that I am in My Father, and *you in Me*, and *I in you*" (John 14:20). Did you notice in this verse that He also told them they would know that they were also in Him? Not just He in them but they in Him. You in Christ, and Christ in you. I love the way author and Bible teacher Bill Gillham describes this spiritual union:

> Salvation is similar to a coin in that it has two sides: "Christ in you" (heads), and you "in Christ" (tails). Every Christian knows the heads side (Jesus in me), but to many believers the tails side (I am in Christ) remains a mystery, mere rows of black print on white paper. When some brothers ... showed me what it means to be "in Christ" ... it launched me on a fresh, new walk with the Lord. I ultimately counted all of the "tails side" verses (in Christ, in Him, in Jesus Christ, in Christ Jesus, in whom, etc.) in the New Testament, which I then compared with the Christ-in-you-verses (heads). For every Christ-in-you verse, there are *ten* you-in-Christ verses! That's right. A ten-to-one ratio of you *in Christ* over Christ *in you*. If this realization impacts you like it did me, and you've embraced only the "heads" side of the coin, you're already asking God to show you what you're missing. *God wishes all Christians understood and walked in the truth of being "in Christ."* That's how we become saints![6]

Please don't miss the last sentence of the quote: *That's how we become saints!* Because our new spirit is completely immersed into Christ's Spirit, we are one spirit with Him and made complete in Him (1 Cor. 6:17; Col. 2:10).

We can infer from the maiden's first statement in Song 1:5—*I am black but lovely*—that she has an imperfect understanding of who she is. She does not primarily see herself as a lovely spiritual being indwelling an imperfect physical body. Instead, she sees herself as a sinful (black) physical being who happens to have a lovely spirit (because Christ lives there). She does not understand that her new spiritual heart is *who she is* and that Christ's Spirit has completely permeated her.

The Shulammite's description of herself as "black but lovely" is the first statement of how she sees herself—her self-image. At this point in the Song, she has likely fallen into some type of habitual sin because of her primary focus on her blackness. Her feelings and behavior have taken center stage in her vision, rather than God's truth. She has yet to realize that though her feelings can be great followers of realized truths, they are lousy leaders.

In general, believers will see themselves in one of three ways after salvation:[7]

Self-image 1: "I am a sinner saved by grace. I have been forgiven and am going to heaven when I die, but I am still the same person I was before salvation (John 3:16). At the core of my being is a sin-nature. God's desires and my desires are polar opposites most of the time."

Self-image 2: "Second Peter 1:4 says I received a new nature in salvation, but my feelings and behavior indicate that my old nature is still very much alive. Therefore, it is apparent that I now have two natures—the good, new me *and* the bad, old me."

Self-image 3: "I am a saint who sometimes acts like a sinner. Not only did I receive forgiveness and a new nature at salvation, but the bad, old me—my sin nature—was crucified with Christ on the cross (Rom. 6:6; Gal. 2:20). I am a new creation because I am in Christ (2 Cor. 5:17). The desire of my new heart is *not* to sin, even though sometimes I still do."

➢ Which self-image is closest to the one you currently hold of yourself?

Please notice that each self-image is directly proportional to the extent the believer's mind has been renewed with the truths of his or her new identity in Christ. The maiden is most likely holding self-image 2 at this point in her journey. She believes she has two natures, basing her evaluation on her feelings and behavior. She feels like a "house divided."

On June 16, 1858, Abraham Lincoln gave a famous acceptance speech upon his nomination for the Illinois Republican Party's US Senate seat. He called it "The House Divided Speech." It became one of the best-known speeches of his career because it created a lasting image of the dangers of the disunion of his country due to human slavery issues. Perhaps the most remembered part of this speech was, "A house divided against itself cannot stand. I believe this government cannot endure, permanently, half slave and half free."[8] Lincoln actually borrowed the words of Jesus to make his point that a country divided over the issue of slavery could not survive:

"If a house is divided against itself, that house will not be able to stand" (Mark 3:25).

This was Jesus' response to those who were accusing Him of being possessed by Satan. In saying that a house divided against itself wouldn't be able to stand, He meant that a man could not be of Satan's kingdom and cast out demons at the same time because of the obvious conflict of interest.

After reading Jesus' statement, do you think that He would purposely set you up to fail by creating you half good and half bad—a house divided? I hope your answer resounds in loud agreement with mine: *No way!* How could anyone who "lives and moves and exists" in Christ be anything other than good? (Acts 17:28).

The maiden's problem is the same problem that multitudes of believers have experienced throughout the ages and still experience today: her lack of knowledge of her new identity in Christ. One of the reasons we are so bewildered by the truth of our new nature is because we cannot feel spiritual reality with our natural senses:

> You can feel both your body and your soul. If I put my hand on your shoulder, you'd know that I touched you … By speaking to your soul, I can make you glad, sad, or mad … It's easy to know how you feel in your body and soul because you're constantly in touch with them!
>
> However, your spirit cannot be accessed in any natural way. Jesus declared, "That which is born of the flesh is flesh; and that which is born of the Spirit is spirit" (John 3:6). He meant there's no direct connection between the two … You simply cannot contact your spirit through your emotions or your physical body. Herein lies one of the great problems of the Christian life!
>
> If you don't understand that spiritual reality can't be felt, then you'll be confused when God's Word declares that you have the same power that raised Jesus from the dead (Eph. 1:18–20). If you think truth can be discerned through your natural senses, then you'll be baffled when the Bible says that you're a brand–new creature … (2 Cor. 5:17).
>
> Understanding spirit, soul, and body unlocks the spirit realm so you can experience who you are and what you have in Christ! Since the spirit realm can't be naturally seen or felt, the only way to accurately perceive spiritual truth is through the Bible. Simply take God's Word and believe it![9]

In order to accurately perceive spiritual truth, we need to simply take God's Word and believe it. Don't count on your feelings to convey spiritual truth—unless, of course, they are feelings that are responding to the truths of your new identity in Christ.

Not only does the maiden have a limited understanding of her pure, holy, and righteous identity in Christ, but she is also confusing what she does with who she is. Have you ever noticed that when you first meet someone, right after you tell the person your name you then tell what you do for a living? In this world's system, the prevalent attitude is that what we do is who we are. But that is not the way it works in God's kingdom. God wants us to believe what He says about who we are and "walk by faith, not by sight" (2 Cor. 5:7).

A similar passage can be found in Paul's letter to the church in Galatia, where he is speaking of two different ways a believer can choose to live (walk). We touched on this in day 2 of this week's study:

> Walk by *the Spirit*, and you will not carry out the desire of *the flesh*. For *the flesh* sets its desire against *the Spirit*, and *the Spirit* against *the flesh*; for these are in opposition to one another, so that you may not do the things that you please. (Gal. 5:16–17)

"Walking by the Spirit" can be equated to walking by faith, and walking by the flesh to walking by sight. When we trust Christ to live His life through us, depending on Him moment by moment, we are walking by the Spirit. But what does it mean to walk by the flesh? Specifically, what is the flesh, and how does it influence us?

First, let's clarify what the flesh is *not*: The flesh is not our unregenerate spiritual heart, our old man, or our sin nature. These are all terms for the person we were before we believed in Jesus. Scripture clearly tells us that our old self died with Christ when He died on the cross:

- "Our old self was crucified with Him" (Rom. 6:6).
- "I have been crucified with Christ; and it is no longer I who live, but Christ lives in me" (Gal. 2:20).

I hope by this point in our study, you are beginning to understand that who you were before you were born again in Christ is dead and gone—nonexistent. You no longer have a sin nature; it is not in your holy nature to sin.

Now, you may be scratching your head, thinking, *Okay, I see in Scripture that my old self is dead, so it can't be my old man that is influencing me to sin. If it's not my old man, then who or what is it? What is the flesh?* In day 4, we will define the flesh and take a closer look at the role it plays in the life of a new creation in Christ.

> ➤ What is your Bridegroom speaking to you through today's study? How will you respond?

Day 4

In day 3, we were introduced to a new group in the audience of the Shulammite's life—the daughters of Jerusalem. Then, we began looking at the maiden's first statement of self-image (how she views herself) in her journey of divine intimacy with her King.

> **"I am black but lovely,**
> **O daughters of Jerusalem,**
> **Like the tents of Kedar,**
> **Like the curtains of Solomon."**
> **—Song 1:5**

I am black but lovely, O daughters of Jerusalem

In describing herself as "black but lovely," it is apparent that the maiden has only a partial understanding of her pure, holy, and righteous identity in Christ. This is because she is basing her knowledge on her feelings and behavior, rather than what God says is true about her. Because we still live in this fallen world inside earthly, human bodies (I like to call it our mobile home), we have to deal with the influence of the flesh. Day 3's study ended with the question, "What is the flesh?"

We clarified that the flesh is not our unregenerate spiritual heart, also known as the *old man* or *sin nature* (which, by the way, is dead and gone). The term *flesh* comes from the Greek word *sarx*, which can have different meanings according to its context. *Flesh* can refer to man's natural physical body, but that is not our primary focus in this section.

The popular New International Version of the Bible, from 1973 until it was revised in 2011, unfortunately interpreted *the flesh* as the *sin nature* in crucial passages that speak of the believer's identity in Christ. However, the revision reflects the much-needed changes, making it clear that the flesh and the sin nature are not one and the same. Let's compare Galatians 5:16–17 in both versions, along with the New American Standard Bible (the translation most used in this study), in order to recognize the importance of not equating the two terms:

> **NIV (1973)**: So I say, live by the Spirit, and you will not gratify the desires of *the sinful nature*. For *the sinful nature* desires what is contrary to the Spirit, and the Spirit what is contrary to *the sinful nature*. They are in conflict with each other, so that you do not do what you want.

> **NIV (2011):** So I say, walk by the Spirit, and you will not gratify the desires of *the flesh*. For *the flesh* desires what is contrary to the Spirit, and the Spirit what is contrary to *the flesh*. They are in conflict with each other, so that you are not to do whatever you want.

> **NASB:** But I say, walk by the Spirit, and you will not carry out the desire of *the flesh*. For *the flesh* sets its desire against the Spirit, and the Spirit against *the flesh*; for these are in opposition to one another, so that you may not do the things that you please.

The NIV (2011) and NASB basically say the same thing—the flesh and the sinful nature are not the same thing. Also, please notice in the last part of both translations that *the Spirit* and *the flesh* are in conflict with each other, so that "you are not to do whatever you want," or so that "you may not do the things that you please." This is *not* saying that Christ's Spirit is trying to keep us from doing the bad things we innately want to do. That wouldn't make sense in light of the truths of our new identity.

It *is* saying that the flesh is a way of living that interferes with our new heart's desire to walk by His Spirit. When we walk by His Spirit, we are doing the things we innately want to do because we are one spirit with Him. On the contrary, when we walk by the flesh, we are not living in accordance with the desire of our new hearts.

> ➤ Beloved bride of Christ, do you believe that the desire of your new spiritual heart is to walk by His Spirit? Why or why not?

If we interpret the flesh as our sin nature, it will undermine the very foundation by which we are to live as a new creation in Christ (2 Cor. 5:17). How could we see ourselves as pure, holy, and righteous, if we have a sin nature at the core of our being? Every time we sin, we will think, *Well, it's just my nature to sin. I'm a dirty rotten sinner, saved by grace.* If we believe this lie, our lives will be characterized by defeat, and we will be powerless (because of ignorance) to overcome sin in our lives.

Walking by the flesh is a way of living in this world that is rooted in the deception of

Satan—the deception that who we are was not changed at salvation and that we can get our needs met apart from Christ. In other words, we can do it ourselves.

When we are walking by the flesh, we are living just as if we are not one spirit with Christ's Spirit (1 Cor. 6:17). The heart of all sin is independence from God. Any time believers choose to walk by the sufficiency of the flesh, they are relying on their limited physical strength and the "self-sufficient" habit patterns stored in their earthly brains, rather than depending on Christ's life in and through them.

Let's look at a list of common flesh patterns that interfere with walking by the Spirit. Please keep in mind that this list is just a sampling of all the different flesh patterns believers can express:

Sampling of Flesh Patterns a Believer Can Experience

Angry	Anxious	Argumentative	Bitter
Bossy	Body-conscious	Complacent	Codependent
Controlling	Critical	Defensive	Depressed
Envious	Easily-offended	Fearful	Feelings-based
Greedy	Guilty	Hateful	Headstrong
Insecure	Impulsive	Jealous	Judgmental
Lazy	Lustful	Manipulating	Materialistic
Negative	Nervous	Obsessive/Compulsive	Opinionated
Prideful	Perfectionist	Performance-based self-acceptance	
Performance-based acceptance of others		Rejection	Rebellious
Selfish	Sexual lust	Suspicious	Temperamental
Time-conscious	Unbelief	Unforgiving	Unlovely

As previously stated, these habit patterns are stored in the brain, which is part of the physical body. Let's add the flesh to our figure of *Man in Christ* from day 1 of this week's study:

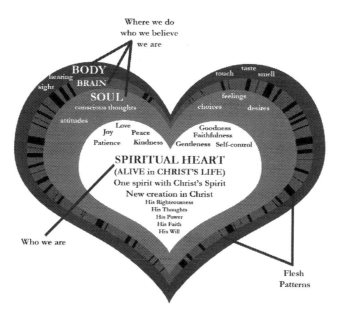

Figure 4: The Flesh

Please notice in Figure 4: The Flesh, that these flesh patterns are not located in the new man—who we are. Our brain is like a computer that receives and stores information. As long as we live in these earthly bodies, we will be influenced by the flesh patterns installed in our brains.

In the figure, the thicker lines indicate stronger patterns, whereas the thinner lines indicate weaker patterns. We need to be aware of these flesh patterns in order to understand where we are most likely to try to get our needs met apart from Christ. However, it is important for us to realize that God does not define us by the flesh patterns stored in our earthly brains. The flesh is not who we are! Second Corinthians 5:16–17 says,

> So we have stopped evaluating others by what the world thinks about them. Once I mistakenly thought of Christ that way, as though he were merely a human being. How differently I think about him now! What this means is that *those who become Christians become new persons*. They are not the same anymore, for *the old life is gone. A new life has begun!* (NLT).

The following diagram shows the top ten flesh patterns in my brain that exhibit the strongest influence in my life. They may be similar to yours, or they may not be. We are all different. Let's look at Figure 5: Top Ten Flesh Patterns That Influence Kim:

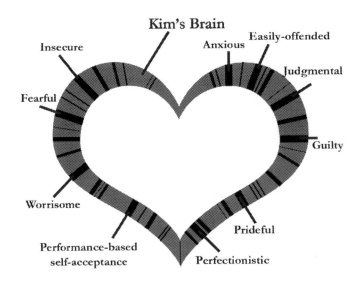

Figure 5: Top Ten Flesh Patterns That Influence Kim

Please notice there are lines that aren't labeled. Time and space do not permit me to go over every single flesh pattern (that I'm aware of) and the strength with which it influences my life. My goal here is to give you a general picture of the strongest patterns that influence the conscious thoughts, attitudes, feelings, desires, choices, and actions I experience when I am walking by the flesh.

I also want to point out the importance of not owning the flesh. Notice that I did not label Figure 5 as "Kim's Top Ten Flesh Patterns" but "Top Ten Flesh Patterns That Influence Kim." To own the flesh would be to say that it is part of who we are, which is not true. Yes, it does influence us in the same way that the environment in which we live affects us. But who we are eternally are our new spiritual hearts—our new spirit men joined with the life of Christ.

> Which top ten flesh patterns from the previous chart exhibit the strongest influence in your life? (If one of your patterns for getting your needs met apart from Christ is not listed, feel free to add it here.) How will being aware of the flesh patterns that influence you benefit you?

What can we do as new creations in Christ in order to consistently walk by the Spirit instead of the flesh? The apostle Paul gives us valuable insight in his letter to the church at Rome: "Do not be *conformed* to this world, but be *transformed* by the renewing of your mind, so that you may prove what the will of God is, that which is good and acceptable and perfect" (Rom. 12:2). At first glance, the two words *conformed* and *transformed* look very similar, but they are, in fact, very different.

> The word *conformed* in the original language means "take an outward form which is inconsistent with who you really are on the inside." The word *transformed* is the opposite. It means "take an outward form which is consistent with who you really are on the inside." So basically, Romans 12:2 is saying, "Quit acting like someone you're not, and start acting like your true self."[10]

Quit acting like someone you're not, and start acting like your true self. In order to do this, we have to know who we really are on the inside in order for our outward behavior to match. One of the greatest deterrents to making our outside match our inside lies in the realm of the soul—feelings we experience that don't line up with our true identities. We must continually allow the Word of God and the indwelling Spirit of Christ to take the driver's seat in our lives, rather than our feelings. Hannah Whithall Smith writes:

> [Formerly] what the Bible said was altogether a secondary consideration to what I might feel; indeed, as far as I can recollect, I did not consider the Bible at all. "How do I feel?" not "What does God say?" was my daily cry. I was trying to feel before I knew; and instead of basing my feelings upon knowledge, I was seeking to base my knowledge upon my feelings.
>
> I could not possibly feel glad that I had a fortune in the bank, unless I knew that it was really there. [When] I learned that the facts were far more important that my feelings about these facts, and consequently gave up looking at my feelings, and sought only to discover the facts, I became always happy in my [walk with God]. It was no longer "How do I feel?" but always "What does God say?" And He said such delightful things, that to find them out became my supreme delight.[11]

We will experience supreme delight when we allow God's Word, rather than our feelings, to drive us. That said, we need to honestly admit that it can be very difficult to change the way we feel about something lickety-split (that's Texan for "real fast"). We must change the way we think about it first. Feelings can't be programmed directly because they are "responders" to whatever we are thinking about. We can change ungodly feelings by reprogramming the thought patterns that are causing them.

We began our discussion with the two different ways in which believers can choose to walk: by the Spirit or the flesh. The apostle Paul writes in Galatians 5:16, "If we walk by the Spirit, we will not carry out the desire of the flesh." He also writes in Romans 8:6 that it all begins with our mind-set—what we choose to focus on. "For the mind set on the flesh is death, but the mind set on the Spirit is life and peace." Focus is everything.

Let's look at diagrams of the two different ways we can choose to walk. Please notice what happens in Figure 6: Walking by the Spirit, when the mind is set on the Spirit:

"LIFE and PEACE"

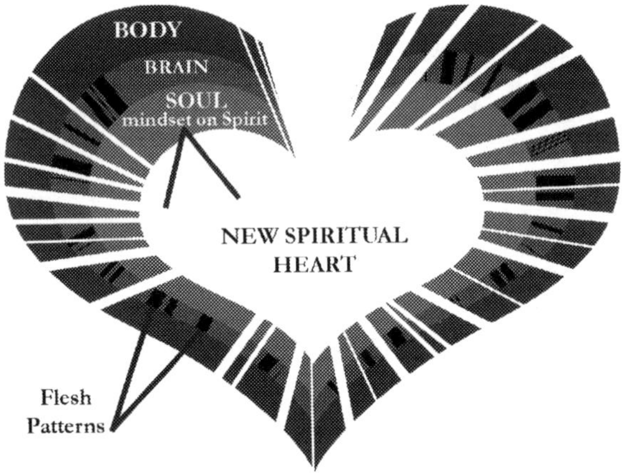

Figure 6: Walking by the Spirit
(Galatians 5:17 & Romans 8:6)

We walk by the Spirit when we focus on and believe the truths in God's Word concerning our new identities, trusting Him to live through our lives. Walking by the Spirit releases the flow of Christ's life into the soul and the body of the believer. This is what Paul meant in Ephesians 5:18 when he wrote, "Be filled with the Spirit." When believers walk by the Spirit, they look a lot different from the rest of the world.

In stark contrast, notice what happens in Figure 7: Walking by the Flesh, when the mind is set on the flesh:

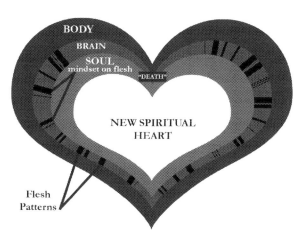

Figure 7: Walking by the Flesh
(Galatians 5:17 & Romans 8:6)

We walk by the flesh when we believe we are the same persons we were before salvation. We focus on our feelings and behavior, trust in the sufficiency of the flesh, and live just as we did before we were recreated in Christ. In a nutshell, we live *just as if* we were not in union with Christ's Spirit. The life of Christ is hindered (looks like a shut door) from flowing out into the soul and body of the believer. When believers walk by the flesh, they look no different from the rest of the world.

Please understand that the choice is up to us. When we renew our minds with the truths of our new identities in Christ found in God's Word, we will live out of our new spiritual hearts, as shown in Figure 6: Walking by the Spirit. When we do not renew our minds with His truth, and we continue to walk by the flesh, we will live just as if we never received new hearts, and Christ's life will be hindered from being expressed through our lives, as shown in Figure 7: Walking by the Flesh. Whatever we focus on will control our lives. That is so important; it bears repeating: whatever we focus on will control our lives.

> ➢ Do you find the statement, "Whatever we focus on will control our lives," to be true in your own life? If so, give a recent example where what you focused on ended up controlling you.

You may be wondering, *What can I do when I realize I am walking by the flesh instead of by Christ's Spirit?* How can we stop walking by the flesh and start walking by the Spirit? I have found that when I apply CPR, it helps to change the way I'm walking. No, not the kind you learn in first-aid training to revive a person's physical heart but the kind we learn from the Word of God which activates our new spiritual hearts. I like to use the letters CPR to remind me what to do: Confess—Praise—Repent. *Confession* is agreeing with the Lord that you are walking by the flesh instead of His Spirit. *Praise* is appreciating Him for giving you everything you need to walk by His Spirit (namely, His indwelling Spirit). *Repentance* means to change your focus from depending on your natural strength (self-effort) to depending on Christ's supernatural strength in and through you.

When we walk by the Spirit, we don't have to try *not* to walk by the flesh (Gal. 5:16). It's just like smiling. When we smile because we're happy, we aren't trying not to frown. We're happy and we know it, and our faces will surely show it. (You'll have to excuse me for having a childlike moment there.) When you begin to believe that you are the pure, holy, and righteous bride of the King of Kings, your life will surely show it!

> ➤ What is your Bridegroom speaking to you through today's study? How will you respond?

In the first four days of week 2, we covered a lot of foundational truths through examining

- the gospel (the best and most important news anyone will ever hear),
- the importance of remembering our Bridegroom's love for us by personalizing Scripture,
- the believer's pure, righteous, and holy identity in Christ, and
- the difference between walking by the flesh and walking by the Spirit.

In our final day of this week's study, we will finish unpacking verse 5, where we will find that the root of the Shulammite's struggle is her erroneous belief that she is part bad and part good.

> **"I am black but lovely,**
> **O daughters of Jerusalem,**
> **Like the tents of Kedar,**
> **Like the curtains of Solomon."**
> **—Song 1:5**

Like the tents of Kedar

The maiden compares her blackness to the tents of Kedar. Kedar was Abraham's grandson—Ishmael's second-born son. When Abraham (he was actually named Abram at the time) was seventy-five years old, God told him to leave his home (Haran) and go to a land that He would show him. He promised Abram that He would make him a great nation with descendants too numerous to count (Gen. 12:1–4). At that time, Abram and his wife, Sarai, ten years his junior, were childless.

Abram agreed to leave all he had ever known—all that was familiar to him—and he and Sarai ended up in Canaan. Several years passed, and Abram and Sarai remained childless. Sarai got tired of waiting on God to provide Abram with a son through her own womb. She took matters into her own hands, deciding that her handmaid, Hagar, should sleep with Abram. Abram, also weary of waiting on God to fulfill His promise, listened to Sarai and slept with Hagar. As a result, Hagar conceived and gave birth to a son, Ishmael, when Abram was eighty-six years old (Gen. 16:1–16).

When Abram was ninety-nine years old, the Lord reminded him of His covenant promise to make him the father of a multitude of nations through Sarai's womb. At that time, he changed Abram's name to Abraham, Sarai's name to Sarah, and established the covenant of circumcision. Circumcision would be the sign that set Abraham and his descendants apart as "God's very own people" and was a foreshadowing of the new birth in Christ. Shortly afterward, when Abraham was one hundred years old and Sarah was ninety, their son, Isaac, was born.

Although God kept His promise, Abram and Sarai's acting independently of Him years earlier was not without major repercussions. The conflict between the descendants of Ishmael (Arabs) and the descendants of Isaac (Israelites) continues to present day. In his letter to the church at Galatia, the apostle Paul used the two-thousand-year-old example of Abram and Sarai to remind them that no good can come from walking by the flesh. "But the son by the bondwoman was born according to the flesh, and the son by the freewoman through the promise" (Gal. 4:23). Ishmael was born according to the flesh to Abram and Sarai; Isaac was born through the promise of God to Abraham and Sarah.

Since Kedar was Ishmael's son, he represents the flesh in our focal verse. The tents of Kedar were made from black goatskins and symbolize "walking by the flesh." These dwelling places were continually exposed to the harsh elements of living in the hot, arid desert regions. In like manner, believers still live in their unredeemed physical bodies under the harsh conditions of this fallen world and are vulnerable to being deceived and tempted into walking by the flesh. Because flesh patterns are embedded in the physical brain, they do not magically disappear when we are born again. Even though we can reprogram these patterns through the Word of God and dependence on Christ's Spirit, we will (to some extent) have to deal with the flesh as long as we live in these earthly bodies.

- ➤ Every believer has suffered repercussions from walking by the flesh at some point in his or her life. Describe an instance from your own life and what you learned from it.

The Shulammite is mistaken when she describes herself as "black, like the tents of Kedar." She is describing her behavior rather than who she is. Based on what we've learned so far, a more accurate statement of her self-image would be, "Even though my words and actions are sometimes sinful (black), who I really am in Christ is lovely. Because of my lack of knowledge (which influences my choices), my *do* does not always line up with my *true who*." Throughout her journey, the maiden will progressively come to understand that she is not defined by her behavior but by who she is in Christ. And as a result, she will increasingly live out of her new identity—by His Spirit.

Like the curtains of Solomon
In contrast to the black tents of Kedar, the maiden compares her loveliness to the *curtains of Solomon* in this phrase. These curtains are actually a reference to the exquisite veil found inside Solomon's temple that separated the Holy Place from the Holy of Holies (Exod. 26:31–35; 2 Chron. 3:14). This veil symbolized the barrier between man and God under old covenant law. Unlike the black tents of Kedar, which were out in the open and visible to anyone, these

curtains were hidden from the public eye, seen only by the priests who ministered in the temple.

When Christ yielded up His Spirit on the cross and breathed his last, this veil was split in two from top to bottom by the hand of God Himself (Matt. 27:51). This torn veil signified Christ's flesh being torn unto death as the way for man to be united with God. The barrier between God and man was obliterated forever by Jesus' death on the cross, thus initiating the new covenant of grace for the Israelites and the only covenant between God and the Gentiles (Lev. 26:46; Ps. 147:19–20; Rom. 2:14).

Just as we found the fragrant attributes of Christ in the rich symbolism of the ingredients of the incense and the holy anointing oil, we also can find Christ's loveliness in every detail of this veil. "You shall make a veil of blue and purple and scarlet material and fine twisted linen; it shall be made with cherubim, the work of a skillful workman" (Exod. 26:31):[12]

- **blue**—the color of Christ's heavenly origin and His deity as the Son of God
- **scarlet**—the color of Christ's earthly origin in His humanity as the Son of Man, specifically the color of His blood, shed for the forgiveness of sins
- **purple**—the color of Christ's royalty; the mixing of blue and scarlet, representing the God-Man who was both King of Kings and the King of the Jews
- **fine twisted linen**—Christ's spotless righteousness (Rev. 19:7–8)
- **cherubim**—celestial beings woven into the linen with gold thread, which represented Christ's holiness

Because the bride of Christ is spiritually united with Him, she is

- of heavenly origin, seated with Him in heavenly places (Eph. 2:6),
- royalty, as the future wife of the King of Kings (Rev. 21:9),
- the righteousness of God (2 Cor. 5:21), and
- holy (1 Cor. 3:17).

Please notice that as Christ's bride, we share in His loveliness in all of the attributes except for the color of His blood, *shed for us* in His perfect humanity.

When the maiden compares her loveliness to the exquisite beauty of Solomon's curtains, she is continuing to speak of her outward behavior, rather than her inward identity. She is wrongly equating her *who* with her *do*. Interestingly enough, she doesn't realize that even though her behavior may look good on the outside, if it has not originated from dependence on Christ's life within, she is still walking by the flesh (John 15:5).

In contrast to the tents of Kedar, which symbolize "walking by the flesh," the curtains of

Solomon in this verse signify "walking by the Spirit." We find another reference to the *fine linen* from which these curtains are made in the New Testament:

> Let us be glad and rejoice and give glory to him; for the marriage of the Lamb is come, and his bride has made herself ready. And to her was granted that she should be arrayed in fine linen, clean and bright: for *the fine linen is the righteousness of the saints*. (Rev. 19:7–8 JUB)

These verses are speaking of the marriage of the Lamb that will occur sometime after Christ returns for His bride (John 14:2–3; 1 Cor. 15:50–57; 1 Thess. 4:13–18). (We will discuss end-time events in greater detail in day 3 of week 5.) Verse 8 says that this bright, clean fine linen represents the bride's righteousness and was given to her to wear. Second Corinthians 5:21 tells us that this righteousness is "the righteousness of God in Christ." So we can think of wearing a wedding dress as living out our true identities and equate it with walking by the Spirit. (Okay, you guys can think of it as a radiant white robe!)

We can't flip through our television channels without noticing the world's fascination (or obsession) with weddings. I recently watched a movie called *The Wedding Dress*, which depicted how one special dress touched the lives of five different couples. The women who put it on seemed to be forever changed just by wearing it. When we put on Christ, allowing Him to live His life through us, our outward lives are transformed.

The Learning Channel has a program called *Say Yes to the Dress*. It's all about the bride-to-be's search for the perfect wedding dress. I love the title. For the bride of Christ, we *already* possess the perfect dress—the life of Christ. Saying yes to the dress simply means choosing to walk by His Spirit instead of the flesh.

In April 2011, the countdown to the royal wedding between Great Britain's Prince William of Wales and commoner Kate Middleton had begun. You may remember the media frenzy that took place. On almost every show I watched, people were speculating about what food they would be serving at the reception, who would be attending (and what they would be wearing), what the cake would look like, and so on. But the biggest question on everyone's mind was, what will Kate's dress look like?

According to ancient Jewish marriage customs, once a Jewish bridegroom and his bride were legally betrothed, they began to prepare for the final phase of their marriage—their consummation. The Jewish bridegroom would go back to his father's house to begin building on a room where the consummation would take place and where he and his bride would live together as a married couple. The Jewish bride would begin preparing her trousseau, which of course included her wedding dress. As the bride sensed the time of her bridegroom's return drawing near, she would even begin wearing her wedding dress to bed. She didn't want to waste any time putting it on if her beloved came to steal her away in the middle of the night.

Fortunately, for the bride of Christ, it will not be a question of how beautiful our dress is or whether or not we will be wearing it (walking by the Spirit) when the Lord Himself descends from heaven to meet us in the air (1 Thess. 4:16–17). In that moment, our mortal bodies will be exchanged with immortal bodies, saturated with the glorious life of Christ (1 Cor. 15:53). Death will be swallowed up into victory, and the flesh will be no more! (1 Cor. 15:54). "Thanks be to God, who gives us the victory through our Lord Jesus Christ" (1 Cor. 15:57).

> ➤ Take a few moments to write an expression of your thanks to God, who has *already* given you the victory in the person of Jesus Christ.

Our time left on this earth is our only opportunity to choose between walking by His Spirit and walking by the flesh. Walking by the Spirit can also be equated with "putting on the new self," as seen in the following Scriptures:

- "In reference to your former manner of life … lay aside the old self, which is being corrupted in accordance with the lusts of deceit, and … be renewed in the spirit of your mind, and *put on the new self*, which in the likeness of God has been created in righteousness and holiness of the truth" (Eph. 4:22–24).
- "Do not lie to one another, since you laid aside the old self with its evil practices, and have *put on the new self* who is being renewed to a true knowledge according to the image of the One who created him—a renewal in which there is no distinction between Greek and Jew, circumcised and uncircumcised, barbarian, Scythian, slave and freeman, but Christ is all, and in all. So, as those who have been chosen of God, holy and beloved, *put on* a heart of compassion, kindness, humility, gentleness and patience; bearing with one another, and forgiving each other, whoever has a complaint against anyone; just as the Lord forgave you, so also should you. Beyond all things *put on* love, which is the perfect bond of unity" (Col. 3:9–14).

In both of these passages, Paul refers to the catalyst for putting on the new self—*the renewal of the mind*. We will put on the new self to the extent that we renew our minds with the truth of who we *already* are and allow His Spirit to be expressed through our attitudes, words, and actions.

Our second week of study has now drawn to a close. This week was filled with the truths of our identity in Christ and how we are to live on this earth as new creations. You may have even forgotten that you're doing a study of the Song of Solomon, due to all the foundational truths that have been covered.

In week 3, we will look at the continued dialogue between the Shulammite and the daughters of Jerusalem, and for the first time in the Song, the King will begin to speak. This week is going to be extra-special because we will get to soak in the King's grace-filled responses to the maiden's requests. There is nothing more thrilling than hearing the voice of our Bridegroom King!

We will also discuss common snares of the flesh and the appropriate biblical response to each. This knowledge will help us to avoid those traps and live lives that consistently glorify Christ.

> What is your Bridegroom speaking to you through today's study? How will you respond?

Week 3

YOU ARE MORE

SONG OF SONGS 1:6–1:9

"This is not about what you've done,
But what's been done for you.
This is not about where you've been,
But where your brokenness brings you to."
—Tenth Avenue North, "You Are More"

Day 1

It's hard to believe we are one-third of the way through our study. So far, we've looked at vital foundational truths that will be elaborated on as we continue peering into the Shulammite's journey of divine intimacy with her King. The following is a brief summary of those truths:

- The gospel—Jesus Christ was crucified, buried, resurrected, and ascended so that whosoever believes in Him will experience the triple-crown kiss of salvation.
- In salvation, the bride of Christ has been forgiven for the sins of her entire lifetime—past, present, and future.
- In salvation, the bride of Christ has been given a pure, holy, and righteous identity in Him.
- In salvation, the bride of Christ has been eternally united with His Spirit. Christ *is* her life!
- At present, the bride of Christ lives inside a mortal, physical body on this earth, so she contends daily with the flesh—the patterns of self-sufficient independence in her brain.
- At present, the bride of Christ is joined in union with His Spirit, so she can choose to live from His life in complete dependence on Him.

It is important to keep in mind that the Shulammite's journey is the result of her King's *pursuing love* for her—the underlying theme of this entire study. Where would any of us be if it were not for His desire for us to experience and express His cherishing love and His exuberant life?

With the exception of King Solomon's opening verse in the first chapter, the Shulammite has done all of the talking so far. In verses 2–4, she is focused on her King, praising His wonderful attributes. In verse 5, however, her attention is diverted to herself and the daughters of Jerusalem.

She describes herself to the daughters as part bad (black) and part good (lovely), basing her evaluation on her behavior. Until she learns to separate her *do* from her *true who*, her self-image will be faulty. God's design is that we first get a clear picture of who we are in Christ, and then our *do* will begin to issue from our lovely new *who*—our new spiritual heart.

It will soon be apparent that the catalyst for this change in the Shulammite's self-image will be the *voice of her King*. As she turns to Him for answers, listens, and then chooses to believe Him over the clamor of all the other worldly voices attempting to define her, her behavior will change (Song 1:7–9).

In this week's study, we are going to look at some common snares of the flesh and ways we can steer clear of these. Today, we are going to focus on the fleshly traps of judgment, anger, frustration, and blame—and our responsibility when we find ourselves caught in the midst of them.

In Song 1:6, the Shulammite maiden continues her conversation with the daughters of Jerusalem.

> **"Do not stare at me because I am swarthy,**
> **For the sun has burned me.**
> **My mother's sons were angry with me;**
> **They made me caretaker of the vineyards,**
> **But I have not taken care of my own vineyard."**
> **—Song 1:6**

Do not stare at me because I am swarthy

After ignorantly describing herself to the daughters of Jerusalem, basing her evaluation on her imperfect behavior rather than her pure, holy, and righteous identity in Christ, the maiden shouldn't be surprised to find them staring at her. They too are now focusing on her imperfect behavior. She pleads with them not to stare at her in judgment but in the same breath describes herself as *swarthy*, which means "blackness." As long as she judges herself on the basis of her behavior, how can she expect the daughters to do less?

Judgment is an all-too-common snare of the flesh. For the purposes of our discussion, I want to clarify that the type of judgment I am referring to is *a negative focus on the visible flaws in others' outward appearances and behaviors*. When we judge others, we are eating from the tree of the knowledge of good and evil, deciding whether they are good (right) or bad (wrong) based on their outward appearances and actions (Gen. 2:9, 17). To put it simply, we are evaluating them according to the flesh (2 Cor. 5:16–17). When we judge another person, what we are really doing is math—subtracting from their worth to add to ours (because we don't know where our true worth comes from):

> Every one of our judgments prevents us from agreeing with God that each person we encounter has unsurpassable worth, as evidenced by the fact that Jesus died for them. Instead of ascribing worth to others, at cost to ourselves, we tend to feed our hungry souls by ascribing worth to ourselves, at cost to

others. What we see when we judge another are the things we judge rather than a human being whom God was willing to die for. Our judgment prevents us from seeing their unsurpassable worth.[1]

What we see when we judge another person are externals, rather than an internal heart with unsurpassable worth. Jesus gave every one of us unsurpassable worth by dying on the cross for us. *Unsurpassable worth* means "a worth that cannot be exceeded in value." We will never be worth more than we are at this moment. Take a minute to think about that statement.

Here's something else to chew on: Do you realize that it is impossible to *judge* someone and *love* that person at the same time? Judgment and love are mutually exclusive. Simply put, if we are judging, we are not loving.

We would also do well to remember that judging *ourselves* on the basis of outward appearance and actions is just as wrong as judging another person. That's what the Shulammite is doing in Song 1:5–6. When we find ourselves steeped in judging others and ourselves, it is an obvious symptom of a root problem—our lack of knowledge of the unsurpassable worth Christ has *already* given each one of us. When we focus on Christ (eat from the tree of life), acknowledging and enjoying the unsurpassable worth He has given us, regardless of our outward appearances and actions, our hungry souls will be satisfied, and we will have little appetite for judging others.

> ➤ Do you find yourself more often judging, rather than loving others and yourself? If your answer is yes, please understand that trying hard *not* to judge will only exacerbate the problem because of your negative focus. The way to get free from the snare of judgment is to immerse yourself in the unconditional love of Jesus and to understand the unsurpassable worth He has *already* given you by dying for you. Write a prayer from your heart, asking Jesus to cause you to understand the unsurpassable worth He has given to you and to experience the unconditional love He has for you. As He does this, judgment toward yourself and others will greatly diminish.

For the sun has burned me

Immediately after the Shulammite tells the daughters of Jerusalem not to judge her, she begins to cite the reasons for her imperfect behavior, the first of which is being burned by the sun. Here, she is referring to the harsh effects she has suffered from living and working in this world. The repeated theme in Ecclesiastes (King Solomon also authored) is that all of man's labor under the sun (in this fallen world), done apart from the inspiration of God, is *futile*.

Since the fall of man in the garden of Eden, we have lived in a world that is under the dominion of Satan (1 John 5:19). This was not God's original purpose for His creation. He created every human being with an intrinsic need to be unconditionally loved, valued, and accepted, knowing that complete union with and dependence on Him would meet these needs perfectly. Sadly, from the cradle to the coffin, from taking our first steps to our last breath, we are conditioned in this world to *earn* our love, value, and acceptance by living on a performance-based treadmill.

> Our hunger causes us to search for people who will love us. Our desire for acceptance pressures us to perform to gain praise from others. We strive for success, driving our minds and bodies harder and further, hoping that because of our sweat and sacrifice others will appreciate us more.
>
> But the man or woman who lives only for the love and attention of others is never satisfied—at least, not for long. Despite our efforts, we will never find lasting, fulfilling peace if we must continually prove ourselves to others. Our desire to be loved and accepted is a symptom of a deeper need—the need that frequently governs our behavior and is the primary source of our emotional pain. Often unrecognized, this is our need for self-worth.[2]

Our need for self-worth goes far beyond a humanistic need to feel good about ourselves. In order to have a biblical self-image, we need to understand where our need for love, value, and acceptance comes from and how those needs can be met:

> What a waste to attempt to change behavior without truly understanding the driving needs that cause such behavior! Yet millions of people spend a lifetime searching for love, acceptance, and success without understanding the need that compels them. We must understand that this hunger for self-worth is God-given and can only be satisfied by Him. Our value is not dependent on our ability to earn the fickle acceptance of people, but rather, its true source is the love and acceptance of God. He created us. He alone knows how to fulfill all of our needs.[3]

Our hunger for self-worth is God-given and can only be satisfied by Him. Because our Creator alone knows how to perfectly fulfill all of our needs, any time we look to a source outside of Him, we will get burned. The burns caused by trying to get our needs met from this world—rather than the One who has *already* given us unsurpassable worth—are the resulting flesh patterns installed in our physical brains.

These patterns can appear attractive, average, or repulsive, depending on the eye of the beholder. For instance, in Figure 5: Top Ten Flesh Patterns That Influence Kim, found on page 66, the performance-based self-acceptance and the perfectionistic flesh patterns would probably look attractive to this world because of their pleasing surface results. The insecure, fearful, worrisome, anxious, and guilty flesh patterns might look average because they seem to be the norm in most people's lives today. The prideful, judgmental, and easily offended patterns would likely be repulsive to the ordinary observer.

Regardless of whether the flesh patterns are attractive, average, or repulsive to the human eye, they are *all* repulsive to Christ because they find their source in self-sufficient independence, rather than in complete dependence on Him to meet all of our needs.

Even though the flesh patterns we commonly exhibit are repulsive to and grieve Christ's Spirit, this does not mean that *we* are repulsive to Him. He perfectly separates our *true who* from our *do* and wants us to realize that we are not defined by the flesh patterns we exhibit. He redefined us (re-created us) at salvation and joined His life (Spirit) to our new spirit, giving us a pure, righteous, and holy identity. Because of this, we can progressively choose to replace repulsive, self-sufficient flesh patterns with faith-filled Spirit patterns—patterns that find their source in the One who lived a life of perfect dependence on His Father to meet all of His needs while clothed in human flesh on this earth (John 5:19; Rom. 12:2).

> ➤ Look back at page 66, where you listed the top ten flesh patterns that exhibit the strongest influence in your life. List the ones you think would be considered attractive, average, and repulsive below. The purpose of this exercise is to reinforce the idea that no matter what type of flesh we exhibit, it does not define us. Who we are in Christ *is* who we are! We can choose to walk by His Spirit, rather than these patterns.

Attractive:

Average:

Repulsive:

My mother's sons were angry with me
The Shulammite continues to cite the reasons for her imperfect behavior to the daughters of Jerusalem, bringing up two new people groups: her mother and her mother's sons. Let's first revisit the character profile for mother found at the beginning of our study to find out who she represents:

> **Mother** is referred to a total of seven times in the Song. On three of these occasions (1:6; 3:11; 8:1), *mother* refers to Eve, who is the natural mother of all humanity in this earthly realm. Eve is the only mother of a person who has not been regenerated and joined with the Spirit of Christ. In the remaining four references (3:4; 6:9; 8:2, 5) *mother* refers to the "Jerusalem above." Paul writes of her in Galatians 4:26, "But the Jerusalem above is free; she is our mother." The "Jerusalem above" is the heavenly, spiritual realm consisting of all believers in Christ—the corporate bride—who have been regenerated, joined with His Spirit, and seated with Him in heaven under the new covenant of grace (Eph. 2:6). Ultimately, the "Jerusalem above" will be the New Jerusalem in the new heaven and new earth (John 8:23; Rev. 3:12; 21:1–2; Heb. 12:22).

Please notice that the *only* mother mentioned in this study of the Song of Solomon 1–2 is Eve, the natural mother of all humanity in this earthly realm. The Shulammite has yet to fully see herself as a new spiritual heart through an eternal spiritual lens. She still sees herself clumped together with the rest of humanity in this world.

She doesn't understand that she is *already* joined to Christ and seated with Him in heaven, while at the same time walking on this earth (Eph. 2:6). She is currently limiting her view of herself to a natural earthly perspective, basing her observations on what can be seen with the human eye—namely, her behavior. In Song 1:6, she appears to be blaming her mother's sons, pointing the finger at them for the burns she has received from living in this world. Let's find out what people group they represent.

> **Mother's sons** are referred to only once in the entire Song and represent humanity in general (1:6). The King James Version of the Bible translates this group as "my mother's *children*."

Mother's sons aren't merely referring to the males in this world but to humanity in general. The Shulammite is saying in this verse that humanity is angry with her. Can you relate to that statement? Have you ever felt like the world was angry with you? Have *you* ever felt angry at the world? If you answered yes to any or all of these questions, you are in good company. Welcome to planet earth. It seems that the society in which we live is becoming angrier each day.

Let's not be naïve. It isn't just unbelievers who are spewing their wrath; believers walking by angry flesh can be found on every street corner. The intensity of anger in this world for Christians and non-Christians alike has grown to the degree that it now has a new name—*rage*. Road rage, air rage, bike rage, computer rage, narcissistic rage, shopping cart rage, and wrap rage, just to name a few. Go ahead and Google "wrap rage." You know you want to.

Why are so many people angry? Think about the last time you got angry. Okay, I guess it's time to get personal. The last time I got angry and frustrated (frustration is a close cousin to anger), it was at Facebook (I wouldn't go as far as to call it *Facebook rage*, though). I was trying to create an album by uploading about sixty pictures and was only able to upload part of them. My goal was to create an album, but the limitations of Facebook were blocking my goal. What was wrong with my goal? I had adopted a goal outside of my control.

The anger I felt when Facebook was blocking my goal was not nearly as intense as the anger I felt toward some important people in my life for their unwillingness (due to their inability to understand) to support an important decision I had made. My goal was for them to understand and support my decision, but *they blocked it* by misunderstanding and not supporting me.

What was wrong with my goal? My goal was to get other people to *do something*, but they weren't budging. Still aren't. Might not ever. You have to admit, when *people*, rather than inanimate things like social media, block our goals, the level of anger and frustration seems to increase exponentially.

If you think about it, most (if not all) of our anger and frustration is caused by blocked goals.[4] When we set goals outside of our control, we will inevitably experience anger and frustration. We cannot control the actions of others. We can only control our behavior; therefore, we should only set goals within our control.

For instance, if my goals in writing this study are to help my readers fall in love with Jesus and to gain their praise and acceptance as a respectable Christian author, I could be sorely disappointed. I cannot control the response of anyone who participates in this study. On the other hand, if my goal is to write this study in complete dependence on my Bridegroom, I am assured of success. Reliance on Christ is a choice I can make which always pleases Him. And pleasing Him is all that really matters.

> ➤ Are you currently experiencing anger and frustration? If your answer is yes, is it because you have adopted goals outside of your control? Briefly describe

the situation (without mentioning names) and relinquish any self-perceived control you think you might have. Rest in the knowledge that you can control what *you* do, in dependence on Christ.

Much like the Shulammite, we often blame others for "causing" us to feel or act a certain way. But the truth is, regardless of what they've done to us, our response is our responsibility:

> Responsibility means "response ability"—the ability to choose our own responses. If I say, "You make me so mad!" I am really saying, "You are controlling not only what you do, but also how I respond to you!" Put in those terms, my assertion is obviously ridiculous. I am denying that I have "response ability." I have deluded myself into thinking that you are controlling my responses. No wonder I feel like screaming! We must not assume people have power over us that they really do not have. They are responsible to God for what they do, while we are responsible for our responses.[5]

We *must not* assume people have power over us that they really do not have. If we could get this revelation, it would totally transform the way we interact with other people. Victor Frankl, a Jewish psychiatrist imprisoned in the Nazi death camps during World War II, is one man we can all learn from in this area.

> Frankl's parents, brother, and wife died in the camps or were murdered in gas ovens. Of his immediate family, only his sister survived the camps. Frankl himself suffered torture and innumerable indignities, never knowing from one moment to the next if his captors would send him to the ovens or leave him among those who were "saved" and left with the task of removing the bodies or shoveling out the ashes of those who had been cremated while they were still alive.
>
> One day, naked and alone in a small room, Frankl began to become aware of what he later called "the last of the human freedoms"—the one freedom his Nazi captors could not take away. Frankl openly acknowledged that the Nazis

could control his entire environment and do what they wanted with his body. They could not, however, destroy his inner identity. He saw himself as a self-aware human being who had an ability to be a somewhat objective observer of his situation. He still had the power within himself to determine how his outer circumstances and the Nazis' treatment of him were going to affect his inner self. He saw that there was a gap between what happened to him (the stimulus) and his reaction to the stimulus (response), and that in that gap lay the freedom or power to choose a response.[6]

Regardless of what comes at us from the outside, we can choose on the inside how we're going to let it affect us. This is something we need to remember every day. As long as we live in this fallen world, circumstances will continue to require our responses. Rather than reacting impulsively (allowing our feelings to be in the driver's seat) to negative situations, let's take responsibility for our responses and choose wisely.

Before wrapping up our discussion on this topic, an important point needs to be made. While Frankl's example is admirable in that it emphasizes our freedom to choose our responses, it disregards one very important part of the equation in the believer's life—the power of Christ's indwelling Spirit to enable us to do so. After all, self-control is a fruit of the Spirit (Gal. 5:22–23).

If we leave Christ out of the equation in choosing the appropriate response, we are *still* walking by the flesh. We can choose to respond by the flesh, trusting in our natural strength and abilities, or we can choose to respond by the Spirit, acknowledging our union with Him and depending on His power in and through us. This way, *He* gets all the glory.

➢ Is there a situation in your life where you've blamed someone else for the way you are feeling and acting? What are you going to do now that you understand that your response is *your* responsibility?

Today we examined the fleshly traps of judgment, anger, frustration, and blame—and our responsibility when we find ourselves caught in the midst of them. In day 2, we will finish unpacking Song 1:6 by looking at the fleshly traps of unforgiveness and performance-based acceptance. We will also examine the importance of understanding the difference between forgiveness and tolerance.

> ➢ What is your Bridegroom speaking to you through today's study? How will you respond?

Day 2

In day 1, we looked at several different reasons the Shulammite maiden gave to the daughters of Jerusalem for her imperfect behavior. She blamed this fallen world and the people who live in it, rather than taking full responsibility for her own attitudes and actions. No matter what excuses we make for walking by the flesh, they are still *excuses*—lies masquerading as valid reasons. The truth is, we have the power of Christ's indwelling Spirit available to us twenty-four/seven to enable us to walk in His supernatural strength and abilities, instead of our measly natural strength and abilities.

Today we are going to wrap up our discussion of Song 1:6 by focusing on the fleshly traps of unforgiveness and performance-based acceptance. We are also going to see what the Shulammite does when she realizes she has been looking to the wrong sources to find her worth and value and turns to the only One who can give her the answers she seeks.

> **"Do not stare at me because I am swarthy,**
> **For the sun has burned me.**
> **My mother's sons were angry with me;**
> **They made me caretaker of the vineyards,**
> **But I have not taken care of my own vineyard."**
> **—Song 1:6**

My mother's sons were angry with me
Closely related to and intermingled with judgment, anger, frustration, and blame is one of the most damaging fleshly traps known to mankind—unforgiveness toward someone who has hurt us.

A refusal to forgive someone usually begins with an event where the person either purposely or unknowingly causes us pain. Whether we realize it or not, we make a choice soon after the wounding occurs. We either decide to lock up the person in an imagined debtor's prison until he or she apologizes and/or we stop feeling hurt (a common response), or we immediately release the person from the debt owed to us by offering him or her the gift of forgiveness (an uncommon response).

If we don't quickly forgive our offender, it will ultimately manifest in anger, bitterness, and resentment toward him or her. Drinking from this multilayered cup of flesh is like drinking poison and expecting the one who wounded us to get sick. As long as we justify our refusal to forgive the one who wounded us, we will remain in our misery.

It isn't someone else's sin against us that makes us miserable; it's our own sin of refusing to forgive the person. (If you are like me, you may need to read that again.) Getting a revelation of this one truth will cause us to take full responsibility for our self-inflicted misery and resolutely choose to forgive our offender. If we live long enough, we will have *many* opportunities to forgive others, so we might as well make up our minds right now to be quick forgivers and enjoy our lives, regardless of what other people may or may not do.

You may be thinking, *But you don't know what this person did to me. He [or she] doesn't deserve my forgiveness!* You're right; *I* don't know, but *God* does, and He has forgiven you for the sins of your entire lifetime. And you didn't deserve it either. None of us deserves His forgiveness. That's why grace made its grand entrance into this world in the Person of Jesus Christ.

Even if you don't think any of your sins are as bad as the ones committed against you, granting forgiveness to your offender is still necessary if you want to consistently live a Christ-glorifying life. God commands us to forgive others in the same way He has forgiven us—completely:

- "Be kind to one another, tender-hearted, forgiving each other, *just as God in Christ also has forgiven you*" (Eph. 4:32).
- "So, as those who have been chosen of God, holy and beloved, put on a heart of compassion, kindness, humility, gentleness and patience; bearing with one another, and forgiving each other, whoever has a complaint against anyone; *just as the Lord forgave you, so also should you*" (Col. 3:12–13).

Many people wrongly believe (as I did) that they have to *feel* like forgiving someone who has wronged them before they can actually do it. This lie from the pit of hell will enslave us if we believe it. Forgiveness is not a feeling; it is a *determined decision* of the will. We can choose to forgive because we are in union with the ultimate Forgiver, and we can do all things through Him who gives us strength (Phil. 4:13).

Before concluding the topic of forgiveness, I would be remiss if I did not address the rampant epidemic of refusing to forgive *ourselves* for the things we have done wrong. Plain and simple, when we refuse to forgive ourselves for something Jesus has freely and completely forgiven, we are saying that we know better than He does. In effect, we are devaluing the shed blood of Christ that secured our complete forgiveness forever.

In my own life, when I began to realize and own the totality of my forgiveness in Christ, I found it much easier to forgive myself and others. When you think about it, how can we offer anyone what we ourselves have refused to experience? Until you own Christ's *complete forgiveness*, I daresay you will find it difficult to freely forgive yourself and others who have wounded you.

> There is no time like the present to stop drinking the poison that is making you sick and miserable. Obey Christ by first releasing *yourself* from your imagined debtor's prison. Then, release everyone else you are keeping locked up. It is important and healthy to talk to Christ about the pain you are feeling, caused by the inflicted wounds. Christ doesn't want you to pretend that the event didn't hurt you, as if it wasn't real; He wants to rub His healing salve into the *real* wound. Then say, "Regardless of my feelings and upon Your command to forgive, I choose to forgive by the power of Your Spirit." Picture yourself inside a prison cell, walking up to its unlocked door. Open it and walk through it, saying, "I forgive myself for [name of the offense/offenses]." Then, one at a time, motion each person you have held captive to walk through the door as you say, "I forgive you, [name of perpetrator], for [name of the offense/offenses], and I release you from the debt you owe me. You are free to go." Then watch them walk through the open door. For each prisoner you release, write his or her name (start with yours), the offense, and the date and time you forgave them in the following space.

When the enemy tempts you to believe that you have not forgiven others or yourself (and believe me, he will), revisit this page (earmark it), and praise Jesus that you are free from unforgiveness.

One final note on forgiving others: there is a difference between tolerance and forgiveness.

While it is necessary to forgive our offender if we want to consistently live Christ-glorifying lives, we do not have to continue to put ourselves in situations where we allow that person to hurt us. It's that simple.

Now, we are going to look at the last part of verse 6 and listen to the final reason the Shulammite gives for her failings. Then we will see the epiphany she experiences, which causes her to stop making excuses.

They made me caretaker of the vineyards
The maiden continues to speak of humanity (they), now blaming them for making her take care of the vineyards. The plural *vineyards* symbolize man's plans for his work.[7] In this instance, the Shulammite is saying that others forced her to work in a profession she did not choose.

Although she has not yet realized it, her hunger for self-acceptance and the acceptance of others has been the driving force in the decisions she has made concerning her life's work. She could have said no when they told her to take care of the vineyards. Whether our choice of profession comes from the influence of others or from our own hunger to "be important" or "make a difference," things can (and often will) go awry when we try to find our acceptance in *what we do*, rather than in *who we are in Christ*.

When I enrolled in college and began pursuing my education degree, I had not recognized Jesus as my Lord. I was pretty sure that I was going to spend eternity in heaven with Him when I died, but that was all I understood about my salvation. Because of my spiritual amnesia (not knowing who I was in Christ), I followed the trappings of this world in order to make a name for myself.

School was something I had always been good at. I often received high praise for high grades. From as early as fourth grade, my only desire was to be a teacher. Because I loved learning, I wanted to help others to learn.

One of the first classes I took in college was algebra. I loved it because it came so easily to me and I made straight A's. I felt really good about myself and even tutored others who were struggling. So, I decided to change my major from elementary education to secondary math education.

Looking back, I realize that I attached my worth and value to my ability to do and teach math well. That's called *performance-based self-acceptance*. I also found acceptance from others because of my math abilities. People are going to like you when you help them pass their math test!

Christ is so incredibly kind. He made sure that I got burned out teaching remedial math at my second teaching job. It seemed like no matter what I did, no matter how many hours I put in, I was never a "good enough" (*perfectionist* flesh pattern) teacher. In my eyes,

I was a failure because not every student of mine passed the state-mandated test. By that time, I had done life my own way for so long that I almost had a nervous breakdown. I was also in the middle of a very shaky second marriage, and my plan for my life was clearly headed south.

But Jesus knew exactly what He was doing. He saw to it that all my fleshly attempts at attaining love, value, and acceptance failed. Utterly. Although it was one of the most painful times in my life, Jesus used it to get my attention. I completely agree with C. S. Lewis when he said, "God whispers to us in our pleasures, speaks to us in our conscience, but shouts in our pains: It is His megaphone to rouse a deaf world."[8]

The pain that both I and the Shulammite were experiencing was the direct result of trying to milk our love, value, and acceptance from this world—with no success. Thankfully, at just the right time (God's timing is perfect), the light began to dawn ... for both of us.

But I have not taken care of my own vineyard

At some point between the comma after *vineyards* and the *But* in this line, the Shulammite had what we might call "a light bulb moment." She is now taking full responsibility for the choices she has made ("*I have not taken care of my vineyard*.") This statement is the beginning of the maiden's repentance. Godly repentance is simply changing our minds to agree with Him.

For the maiden, *repentance* means to stop trying to milk her acceptance through what she did and start looking to Christ to get that need met. That's exactly what I did too. I took a break from teaching, got a job as a loan secretary, fell in love with Steven, and then I fell in love with Jesus. Through Jesus' unconditional love and acceptance of me, I began to realize that my significance did not come from my works but from *Him* alone. That revelation was liberating and life-changing for me!

> ➢ Is there anything that you are doing in an attempt to gain love and acceptance from yourself, others, or Christ? If so, you need to repent (agree with Jesus that you are *already* completely loved and accepted in Him) and begin living in that liberating awareness.

In contrast to the plural *vineyards*, the singular *vineyard* signifies the Lord's plan for man's work.[9] You may be as surprised as I was to learn that the only work the Lord requires from each one of us is that we respond to the gospel of grace by *believing* in Him:

> Therefore they said to Him, "What shall we do, so that we may work the works of God?" Jesus answered and said to them, "This is the work of God, that *you believe in Him* whom He has sent." (John 6:28–29)

Wow! That's pretty simple, huh? The only work that God requires from us is to believe in (into) His Son, Jesus. If you think I'm promoting a passive lifestyle, let me assure that I am not. Once we are in Christ, *He* will do the good works "He planned for us to walk in" *through us* as we trust Him (Eph. 2:10).

Even though the Shulammite had already believed in her King, she had not acknowledged her complete acceptance in Him through her faith—that is, until now. She turns from speaking to the daughters of Jerusalem and puts her attention squarely on the One who loves her unconditionally and has made her completely acceptable in Him, saying,

> **"Tell me, O you whom my soul loves,**
> **Where do you pasture your flock,**
> **Where do you make it lie down at noon?**
> **For why should I be like one who veils herself**
> **Beside the flocks of your companions?"**
> **—Song 1:7**

Tell me

Now that the maiden realizes *He alone* is the source of everything she needs, she implores Him for direction in her life. We need to pay attention here. How many times do we run to other people or the plethora of humanistic, self-help methods saturating the Internet for answers, rather than to the One who has (and is) the answer to every question?

When the maiden cries, *Tell me*, she is placing the highest and most urgent priority on hearing His voice. The indwelling Spirit of Christ—the Word of God—is continually speaking. We can trust Him to enable us to hear His voice, whether we are sitting in the quiet of the morning with our Bibles open, or we are going through the ordinary activities of our daily lives.

In John's gospel, Jesus describes Himself as a Shepherd who leads His sheep by speaking to them: "The sheep hear his voice and he calls his own sheep by name and leads them out … he goes ahead of them, and the sheep follow him because they know his voice" (John 10:3–4).

Notice that Jesus didn't say, "The sheep hear his voice when they get still enough to listen." Most sheep are just mindin' their own business when the voice of their master causes their ears to perk up. Then, they follow wherever his voice leads (unless they get distracted by something or someone else).

We need to be careful not to make a "law" out of listening, where hearing from Jesus is dependent on what *we do*. I am not minimizing the importance of quiet times, where we ask Jesus to speak to us and then tune in to His voice. I love these intimate moments with Him and am thankful that I get to enjoy these often. The point I'm trying to make is that He can cause us to hear His voice, whether we are listening or not. And let's be honest. The largest percent of the time, our conscious focus is on what we are doing, rather than intently listening for His voice.

Jesus can speak to us through a myriad of ways. Because His Spirit indwells us, He can speak to us and guide us through His written Word; specifically, new covenant teaching. While the entire Word of God was written for us, not all of it is directly addressed to believers in Christ. It's vitally important that we distinguish between the two if we are going to walk in the liberating truths of the gospel—the finished work of Christ.

Jesus can also speak to us through thoughts and impressions (which will always agree with new covenant teaching), through desires (which find their source in His desires), through the circumstances (good and bad) of our lives, and through other people. Whatever mode of communication He uses, He is faithful to cause us to hear His voice at just the right time.

O you whom my soul loves

This is the first of a total of five times throughout the Song that the Shulammite refers to her King as the One whom her soul loves. It is the only occurrence in this premier study. We will find that, as she progressively allows Him to love her unconditionally and meet her every need, she falls more deeply in love with Him and addresses Him more intimately.

The verb *loves* means "to desire, to breathe after."[10] The maiden is overcome with desire to hear the voice of the One her soul loves, knowing that He alone can bring refreshing restoration to her withered, weary soul. The word *desperate* might aptly describe her state at this point in the Song.

Desperate comes from the word *despair*, which means "to lose, give up, or be without hope."[11] We will temporarily lose hope when we focus on our painful circumstances, rather than looking at the unseen eternal realities of Christ's supernatural kingdom in which we live (Rom. 8:24; Eph. 2:6). At times, He allows us to despair in our earthly circumstances because His goal is to sharpen our *spiritual* eyesight. He wants us to learn to fix our hope solely in Him. In fact, the apostle Paul refers to Him as *the God of our hope*.

May the God of your hope so fill you with all joy and peace in believing [through the experience of your faith] that by the power of the Holy Spirit you may abound and be overflowing (bubbling over) with hope (Rom. 15:13 AMPC).

> ➤ Look at Romans 15:13 carefully. What is the catalyst for our being filled with all joy and peace? By what power will we abound with hope?

When we believed in Jesus, we received His life. Furthermore, when we believe what His Word says about who we are and what we have in Him, we open the door of our new spiritual hearts (our new spirits united with Christ's Spirit) and allow His life to be expressed through our souls and bodies (in the form of thoughts, feelings, attitudes, desires, and actions). We experience joy and peace through *believing* and, consequently, abound in *hope* by the power of Christ's Spirit.

I love the spin that *The Message* gives to this effervescent verse: "Oh! May the God of green hope fill you up with joy, fill you up with peace, so that your believing lives, filled with the life-giving energy of the Holy Spirit, will brim over with hope!" Isn't that awesome? I feel energized just reading it.

When we realize that we possess the indwelling, life-giving energy of Christ's Spirit, we will experience joy and peace, and overflow with abounding hope—hope that the unseen world is eternal and glorious, and the temporary painful circumstances of this fallen world won't last forever (2 Cor. 4:18).

Where do you pasture your flock, where do you make it lie down at noon?
For the first of four times in the Song, the Shulammite uses shepherding language to describe the One her soul loves in a role other than that of King (Song 2:16; 6:2, 3). Interestingly, she describes His role as a shepherd in the same breath that she is asking Him to speak to her (John 10:3–4).

In addition to protecting their sheep from predators, the most important aspects of a shepherd's job description is to lead the sheep to proper nourishment (pasture your flock) and to cause them to rest (make it lie down at noon). In this line of Song 1:7, you might say that the maiden is searching for the Good Shepherd's Bed and Breakfast. We can find similar language in Psalm 23:1–3, where Jesus is also described as a shepherd: "The Lord is my shepherd, I shall not want. He makes me lie down in green pastures; He leads me beside quiet waters. He restores my soul."

The maiden would not be looking to the One her soul loves for spiritual nourishment and rest unless she was convinced that He was a *good* Shepherd. *Good* means "beautiful, handsome, surpassing, and precious."[12] In John's gospel, Jesus describes Himself and His role as the good shepherd. "I am the good shepherd; the good shepherd lays down His life for the sheep ... I am the good shepherd, and I know My own and My own know Me" (John 10:11, 14).

Over six hundred years earlier, God spoke through the prophet Ezekiel concerning the good Shepherd's coming. "Then I will set over them one shepherd, My servant David, and he will feed them himself and be their shepherd" (Ezek. 34:23). *My servant David* is pointing toward Christ, who is both the eternal Shepherd of His flock and King of His people. In this verse, God promised His people that one day they would no longer be guided by prophets and priests but would be nourished and cared for by Jesus Himself (Heb. 1:1–2).

The author of Hebrews goes a step further in describing our good Shepherd as the *great Shepherd* of *the sheep*: "The God of peace, who brought up from the dead the great Shepherd of the sheep through the blood of the eternal covenant, even Jesus our Lord" (Heb. 13:20). The Greek word for *great* is *megas* and means "eminent ability, virtue, authority, and power; excellent; splendid."[13] This is where we get our prefix *mega*, which means "extremely good, great, or successful."[14] What a joy for Christ's flock to be shepherded by the most successful, powerful, virtuous, and splendidly excellent Shepherd of all the ages!

In Song 1:7, the Shulammite has confidence in her great Shepherd's ability to lead her to the best nourishment possible. She believes He will feed her with His Word, fully satisfying her and giving her much-needed rest (Ezek. 34:15). He will cause her to lie down at the time of day when the sun's rays are most intense (noon).

After a shepherd leads his sheep to green pastures for their morning feed, he causes them to lie down and rest so they can get the most benefit from what they just ate. Sheep are *ruminates*. After they chew their food and swallow it, they regurgitate and chew it again and again in order to get the maximum amount of nourishment possible from their food. I find it interesting that the verb *ruminate* means "to meditate on; ponder."[15] When we meditate on the words of our great Shepherd, our souls are greatly nourished.

The New Testament book of Hebrews contains some of the most concentrated nourishment for Jesus' flock found in the entire Word of God. Its contents can be likened to the green food powders people add to their diets to maximize their physical health. Since our topic is "resting in order to get the maximum benefit from our food," let's look at a passage in Hebrews that describes God's Sabbath rest for the believer:

> For we who have believed enter that rest … So there remains a Sabbath rest for the people of God. For the one who has entered His rest has himself also rested from his works (Heb. 4:3, 9–10).

Because of Christ's finished work on the cross, He is now our resting place—our *Sabbath rest*. When we believed in Him, we admitted that we could not save ourselves through our self-righteous works. We needed the gift of His righteousness to save us (Rom. 5:17). The Sabbath rest is not a day of the week when the bride of Christ rests from her work; it is a continual state of being, where she rests in His finished work on her behalf.

At this point in the Song, the Shulammite is in an optimal place to receive the personal revelation that her great Shepherd is her resting place. She is completely worn out from trying to do life in her natural strength and is primed and ready to receive the revelation that she no longer has to work (perform) for His or others' acceptance.

Understanding and experiencing Jesus as our Sabbath rest is serious business, according to the apostle Paul. He sharply rebuked the Galatian Christians, who were influenced by false teachers to add works to their gift of salvation.

> Let me put this question to you: How did your new life begin? Was it by working your heads off to please God? Or was it by responding to God's Message to you? Are you going to continue this craziness? For only crazy people would think they could complete by their own efforts what was begun by God. If you weren't smart enough or strong enough to begin it, how do you suppose you could perfect it? Did you go through this whole painful learning process for nothing? It is not yet a total loss, but it certainly will be if you keep this up! (Galatians 3:2–4 MSG)

➤ Have you been influenced to add works to the gift of your salvation—your Sabbath rest in Christ? Do you see the absurdity in trying to work for something you *already* possess? In the form of a prayer in the following space, ask Christ to cause you to realize when you are performing to earn His and others' acceptance. And when He does, repent—change your mind—by acknowledging that you are resting in His finished work on the cross.

Today, we examined the fleshly traps of unforgiveness and performance-based acceptance and the biblical, Christ-glorifying response to each. Furthermore, we discovered that the maiden's King is also a Shepherd who speaks to her and leads her to nourishment and rest. Because of her great Shepherd-King's finished work on the cross, she can rest and revel in His complete forgiveness and acceptance of her and, in turn, offer it to others.

In day 3 of our study, we will hear the final question that the Shulammite asks the One her soul loves, and we will listen to the beginning of His grace-filled response.

➤ What is your Bridegroom speaking to you through today's study? How will you respond?

Day 3

Living in a world inundated with judgment, frustration, anger, unforgiveness, bitterness, resentment, and performance-based acceptance can be painful and wearisome. In Song 1:7, the Shulammite is desperately seeking her great Shepherd's direction in order to find much-needed nourishment and rest.

Today, we are going to look at two more prevalent fleshly traps as we unpack the maiden's last question to the One whom her soul loves.

> "Tell me, O you whom my soul loves,
> Where do you pasture your flock,
> Where do you make it lie down at noon?
> For why should I be like one who veils herself
> Beside the flocks of your companions?"
> —Song 1:7

For why should I be like one who veils herself
In the first half of this rhetorical question, the Shulammite is saying, "Does what I've done wrong merit hiding behind a veil of guilt and shame for the rest of my life?" A common human

response to wrongdoing is to feel guilt and shame and to want to go into hiding. When Adam and Eve disobeyed God in the garden of Eden, their eyes were opened to what they had done wrong. They saw their own nakedness (their separation from God's presence) and immediately covered themselves with fig leaves. For the first time in their lives, they felt the piercing pain of sin's consequences, specifically *guilt* and *shame* (see Genesis 3).

Guilt and shame are so closely related it can be difficult to distinguish between the two. While *guilt* says, "I feel bad about what I've done wrong," *shame* goes a step further, saying, "Because I've done wrong, *I* must be a bad person." Both the guilt and the shame that Adam and Eve experienced when they disobeyed God were valid because their wrongdoing resulted in their separation from Him. Before they sinned, Adam and Eve were in perfect union with God's life—they were "right with God" because they were joined to Him. When they sinned, they were immediately separated from His life and experienced spiritual death.

Every unbeliever has valid reasons to experience both guilt and shame. Yet for Christ's bride, there is no biblical basis to experience either in the realm of spiritual accounting. Let's look at what God says about casting a guilty verdict on a believer in Christ.

The biblical definition for *guilt* is "to owe a debt."[16] After absorbing the sin of the world and before taking His last breath, Jesus cried out, "It is finished!" (John 19:30). *Finished* means "to bring to a close, to end, to pay."[17] The moment we believed in Him for salvation, we cashed in on His entire payment for our personal sin debt. As a result, we are declared "not guilty" in the eternal spiritual realm. And as for *shame*, our wrongdoing can never change our forever state of right-being (2 Corinthians 5:21). Believers are right with God for all time and eternity because of Jesus' finished work (John 10:28, 2 Tim. 2:13; Heb. 13:5).

Please don't misinterpret my words as my taking a light view on sin. Christ suffered unspeakable torture on our behalf because of sin. Sin is ugly and can cause massive collateral damage. It is also important to point out that even though Christ has obliterated our guilt as far as the eternal spiritual realm goes, it does not mean we are shielded from the earthly convictions of "guilty" when we wound another person or break the law of the land. Depending on the severity of the sin, we may even have to pay our debt to society by spending time in prison.

Since we are on the subject of guilt, I would like to address a common misconception among believers concerning the Spirit's role in the conviction of sin. Since the verb *convict* means "to declare someone guilty of an offense,"[18] it is erroneous to say that Christ's Spirit *convicts* (declares "guilty") believers when they sin. There is only one place in the entire Word of God that speaks of the Spirit's role in conviction, and the recipients are not believers in Christ:

> "And He, when He comes, will convict *the world* concerning sin and righteousness and judgment." (John 16:8)

Please notice that those being convicted by the Spirit are people who have not been made the righteousness of God in Christ (the world). It is true that we carry a guilt conviction from the moment we are born *until* the moment we are born again in Christ. But at that moment, Christ wipes our personal sin record clean—forever. We can never again in the spiritual realm be convicted for the wrong that we do.

Now you may be wondering, *If it's not the conviction of the Spirit that grabs my gut when I sin, then what is it?* The answer is found in the apostle Paul's second letter to the church at Corinth, where he speaks of a godly sorrow over our sins, which leads to true repentance—a change of mind and actions (2 Cor. 7:9–10). A genuine godly sorrow is God-given and results when He causes us to realize that sin doesn't fit who we are in Him.

Although painful, I am thankful for the gift of godly sorrow when I sin and usually say something like the following to the Lord in response:

> "I'm so sorry, Lord. Thank You for causing me to realize that my behavior doesn't reflect who I am. Thank You for paying my sin debt in full, so that I wouldn't have to. Cause me to live out my true identity in You."

In light of the foregoing discussion, I hope that you now realize that Christ's Spirit does not *convict* a believer. Before going to the cross, Jesus told His disciples of the major role that His coming Spirit would play in their lives. "When He, the Spirit of truth, comes, He will guide you into all the truth" (John 16:13). The primary way Christ's Spirit relates to His bride is to guide her into all truth. He will let her know when she is not living out her true identity and will lovingly prompt her to walk in truth.

There are those who might think it unnecessary to distinguish between the Spirit's conviction of unbelievers and the godly sorrow given to believers by the Spirit when they sin, saying that it's merely semantics. I would have to strongly disagree. Words are incredibly powerful motivators, for good or bad. I didn't begin to enjoy the intimacy I now share with Christ until I stopped believing some of the erroneous teaching that well-meaning Bible teachers were (and, sadly, still are) teaching and began immersing myself in the fullness of Christ's finished work on the cross.

Now, when I hear believers mistakenly referring to the "conviction of God" in their lives—saying things like, "He nailed me! He really got me this time!"—my soul aches for them. Our Bridegroom is not holding a hammer, waiting to "nail" His bride every time she messes up. Think about it. It makes no sense at all for the One who wiped out our sin record forever to "nail" us for the sin that we commit.

The next time you, dear bride, experience godly sorrow over your ungodly attitudes or actions through the guidance of your Bridegroom's indwelling Spirit, thank Him for this wonderful gift that He uses to motivate you to stop sinning. And please, please acknowledge that He is not "convicting" or "nailing" you. Your guilty, old man was nailed to the cross and crucified with Him over two thousand years ago (Rom. 6:6; Gal. 2:20; Col. 3:3). Once was enough.

> ➤ Write a prayer of thankfulness to God for your eternal state of being "not guilty."

Beside the flocks of your companions?
In the last phrase of Song 1:7, the Shulammite is speaking of the place where she is most susceptible to taking on a sentence of guilt and shame: beside the flocks of the great Shepherd's companions. Who comprises the great Shepherd's companions and their flocks? His *companions* specifically refer to those who minister to His people, and their *flocks* consist of the people to whom they minister.

Please don't hear me as saying that guilt and shame are used to motivate believers in all Christian churches and gatherings, because I am not. But it is most unfortunately happening in some places where the finished work of Christ, the gospel of grace, is not regularly and clearly communicated.

I witnessed this one afternoon while I was riding my exercise bike and flipping through the television channels. I stopped on a Christian station where a popular political figure was giving a message. The gist of his message was that the reason America is in the shape it's in is because Americans are not adhering to the laws of God. He used an Old Testament prophetic warning to Israel to make his point. In short, he was using guilt and shame to motivate the church to "get their act together and make God proud." His message, though well-meaning, reeked of legalism—the system by which man tries to gain favor with God based on what he does or doesn't do.

While some would agree that Americans, as a whole, have a reputation for being spoiled and materialistic, I had to disagree with the speaker when he said that our (he also wrongly equated the terms *American* and *Christian*) core problem was a behavior issue. The Old Testament prophet Hosea and the apostle Paul both told us that our core problem was our lack of knowledge of the truth (Hos. 4:6; Rom. 12:2).

Behavior is a surface issue. Always has been. Always will be. The lack of knowledge Paul is referring to in Romans is our lack of knowledge of the pure, holy, and righteous identity we *already* possess because of the finished work of Christ. If all believers totally immersed themselves in the gospel of grace, unbelievers (and believers who have stopped attending church) would flock to churches and Christian gatherings in droves to find out how they could experience the same.

I changed the channel. Although the speaker could have ended his message on a grace note (I don't know), what I did hear was the perfect example of why unbelievers and some believers refuse to step foot in a church building—the use of guilt and shame to motivate godly behavior.

I love the Shulammite's gumption when she says, *Why should I be like one who veils herself beside the flocks of your companions?* It appears that she is now bucking the legalistic system, saying, *Why should I miss out on the wonders of God's grace, just because my behavior isn't always perfect?* We could all use a little more gumption when it comes to reveling in and sharing God's grace. Gumption is just a Southern word for courage.

Throughout our discussion of Song 1:6–7, we have examined many fleshly traps in which believers can find themselves ensnared, largely through the ignorance of their new identities in Christ. We've also discussed biblical, Christ-glorifying responses in each case. Jesus told us that knowing truth would set us free (John 8:32). I hope you have begun to experience more freedom and intimacy with Christ as a result of meditating on His Word and seeing your true identity in Him.

We have now reached the end of the maiden's six-verse discourse. She is about to receive answers to her heart's desperate cry for nourishment and rest, and they are far better than she could have ever imagined in her wildest dreams (Eph. 3:20). Let's listen carefully to the grace-filled response from the One her soul loves.

> **"If you yourself do not know,**
> **Most beautiful among women,**
> **Go forth on the trail of the flock**
> **And pasture your young goats**
> **By the tents of the shepherds."**
> **—Song 1:8**

If you yourself do not know

As indicated by her great Shepherd's first words to her, the maiden's foremost problem has been her lack of knowledge (*if you … do not know*). He is specifically referring to her lack of experiential knowledge, as opposed to her lack of general head knowledge because He says, "If you yourself do not know."

Let's fast-forward about three thousand years to the year 2010. A young woman wakes up in a motel room after a long weekend of partying. She is a believer, and she is absolutely overcome with self-loathing as she recalls the details of the weekend. As her soul fills with anguish, tears begin to burn her already bloodshot eyes. She whispers, "I'm so sorry, Lord. I'm so sorry."

As quickly as she can, she gets up and gets dressed, washes her face, grabs her purse, and gets in her car. Feelings of guilt and shame overwhelm her. She truly believes that this time she has gone too far. She starts her car and hits the "Seek" button on the radio, hoping she will find something to listen to that will drown out the condemning voices in her head. It stops on a Christian radio station, and she is blown away by the words from Tenth Avenue North's "You Are More." The heart of this song is that we are more than our sins and failures and that God is never going to stop loving us, no matter what we've done. (You can go to YouTube.com and type in "Tenth Avenue North You Are More" to watch the music video.)

Blinded by a sudden rush of tears, she lays her head on the steering wheel while hanging on every word of the lyrics. When the song finishes, she blows her nose, wipes her eyes, and thinks to herself, *He knows what I've done, and He still loves me. I haven't outsinned His love! Thank You, Lord! Thank You! Thank You! I love You, Lord. Thank You for loving me unconditionally.*

Now, rewind three thousand years back to the Song. It is just as important to notice what the great Shepherd does *not* say to the Shulammite maiden as what He *does* say to her. He does not rebuke her by telling her everything she did wrong, but He gently begins to speak truth to her heart, reminding her who she is. Not a single time throughout this Song will you find the great Shepherd focusing on her failures, weaknesses, or sin.

When we believers are made aware of our sin, we often feel dirty and distant from Christ. Because emotions are such strong motivators, we end up doing a mental disconnect from Him and convince ourselves that He has left us. *After all,* we reason, *how could a perfect and holy God stand to be in the presence of one who has failed so miserably?*

This is another unfortunate misconception, because our clean and close union with Him can never be changed by our behavior. We cannot get any cleaner or closer than being "one spirit with Him" in holy matrimony (1 Cor. 3:17, 6:17). The amazing truth is that when we sin, our Bridegroom is right there in our new heart, doing what He does best—unconditionally loving us and empowering us to turn away from it as we look to Him.

He never changes, regardless of what we do or don't do. But as long as we believe the lie that He turns His heart away from us or leaves us when we sin, by what power will we be able to stop sinning? If we fall victim to the detrimental lie that we are somehow separated from His empowering presence when we sin, we will be unable to consistently experience victory over that sin and the joy that true intimacy with Him can bring.

Some of us automatically do a mental disconnect with Jesus—because we make Him out to be like our earthly parents or other rigid authority figures who criticized us when we messed up or hardly ever praised us for a job well done. These stern authoritarians will often use negative reinforcement, such as scare tactics and demeaning words like, "You can't do anything right!" in order to evoke positive changes in their subordinate's behavior. That might work in animals and short term for some people, but *never* in the long run. Christ knows better than anyone the power of positive reinforcement, and He is committed to speaking truth to those of us who belong to Him. He knows that reminders of who we are in Him will evoke the needed positive changes in our attitudes and actions.

> ➤ Have your parents or other authority figures in your life ever used negative reinforcement in order to evoke positive changes in your attitudes and actions? If yes, did it work, and was it lasting? Have you ever used negative reinforcement to evoke positive change in others? If yes, did it work, and was it lasting?

Most beautiful among women

Okay, now you guys are going to have to do some mental tweaking in order to get the most benefit from this section. Being described as beautiful just isn't natural to most men. It may help you to understand that beautiful, in this context, comes from a word that means "to be bright, handsome, and fair."[19] And regardless of whether our physical gender is male or female, "women" here refers to a spiritual, rather than physical, role. The Lord defines true beauty by looking at the core of our being—our new spiritual hearts, not our outward appearance or behavior (1 Sam. 16:7).

The great Shepherd doesn't waste any time in telling the maiden how beautiful she is in Him. And who she is in Him *is* who she truly is! He doesn't have to wear rose-colored glasses when he looks at her. He defines her solely by her new spiritual heart—her new spirit joined in union with His Spirit. He longs for her to see the truth that she is most beautiful among women. He knows that when she believes the truth concerning her identity in Him, she will begin to *act* like the beautiful new creation she *already* is.

When He calls her *most beautiful among women*, He is not saying that she is more beautiful to Him than all the other believers. All believers are equally beautiful to Christ. However, when our Bridegroom personally relates to each one of us, calling us *most beautiful*, it is just as if we are the only two people in existence. I stand before Him as the sole object of His lavish affection. You stand before Him as His one and only true love. When He speaks to you personally, He doesn't have someone else on His mind; you truly are the most beautiful among women to Him. In a sense, you are the only one on His radar.

When I was a senior in high school, our class voted on the male and female students who were most likely to succeed, most intelligent, most athletic, most friendly, most handsome, most beautiful, and so forth. Since I was such a bookworm (driven by performance-based acceptance), it came as no surprise when I was voted "Most Intelligent" and "Most Likely to Succeed." You would think I'd be satisfied with those honors, but I wasn't. I already knew that everyone thought I was the smartest girl in my class.

All women, young and old, can relate to me when I say the honor I longed for most was that of Most Beautiful. Not that I ever thought I would get it, because I didn't. But a girl can dream, can't she? The funny thing about the honor of being named Most Beautiful was that most of the time, the girl who was awarded it was born with natural outward beauty. She didn't have to work hard at being beautiful; she just was. In the same way, the bride of Christ doesn't have to work hard at being beautiful—we are reborn that way in Christ.

Christ wants us to agree with Him and define beauty the same way He does—by looking at the heart (Amos 3:3). If we could really see our true beauty and feel His emotions when He gazes on us, we would live very different lives. We would also see that He is deeply grieved when we define ourselves by the world's *what-you-see-is-what-you-get* standards instead of His.

Choose to believe by faith—at this very moment—that you are beautiful. He thinks you're wonderful and longs for you to enjoy Him as much as He enjoys the beautiful new creation of you.

One day, as I was driving to Amarillo, Texas, listening to a Christian radio station, Jesus began serenading my heart in order to solidify the truth of my eternal beauty in Him. The song that was playing was "You Call Me Yours," performed by Prelude. I was moved to tears as I allowed the words of the One my soul loves to penetrate my emotions, telling me how beautiful, righteous, holy, forgiven, and pure I was in Him.

For you guys, MercyMe's song "Flawless," from their album *Welcome to the New*, may better minister this truth to you. (I personally love both songs.) You can go to YouTube.com and type in "MercyMe Flawless Story Behind the Song" to hear lead singer Bart Millard's personal testimony of coming to understand his flawlessness in Christ.

The first time I heard both of these songs I knew that Jesus was speaking directly through the lyrics to me, personally. I hope that you too, through this study, are beginning to see your true beauty in Christ.

➢ What is your Bridegroom speaking to you through today's study? How will you respond?

Day 4

In day 3, we started unpacking the great Shepherd's response to the Shulammite maiden's desperate plea for direction in finding nourishment and rest. He began by addressing her as most beautiful among women—"the fairest of them all." That phrase might bring to mind the words spoken by the evil queen in the Snow White fairy tale. Every day, she would look into an enchanted mirror and ask it to tell her who was the fairest of them all. If the mirror's answer was anyone other than the queen, that poor girl was quickly eliminated.

Thankfully, as Jesus' future queen, the bride of Christ doesn't have to live in that kind of plaguing insecurity, looking to a magic mirror to tell her truth. We have the mirror of God's Word to gaze into in order to see our true beauty in Him—one of the themes found in today's study.

> **"If you yourself do not know,**
> **Most beautiful among women,**
> **Go forth on the trail of the flock**
> **And pasture your young goats**
> **By the tents of the shepherds."**
> **—Song 1:8**

Go forth on the trail of the flock
After reminding the maiden who she is, the great Shepherd is now giving her direction, telling her to go forth on the trail of the flock. He is basically telling her to follow the path trod by the faithful men and women of God who have gone before her. These are members of the Lord's flock who consistently walked in truth and joy, following a path illuminated by His Word (Ps. 119:105). Notice that Solomon's father, King David, described this path as *the path of life* in Psalm 16:11:

> "You will make known to me the path of life;
> In Your presence is fullness of joy;
> In Your right hand there are pleasures forever."

In addition to King David—one who experienced great joy on the path of life that led him into the presence of the Lord—we can find many great men and women of the Bible who blazed a trail of faith for us.

The eleventh chapter of Hebrews is often referred to as the Faith Hall of Fame because it lists several Old Testament saints who had one thing in common—they trusted and believed God. We find the definition of *faith* in the opening verse of the chapter: "Faith means being sure of the things we hope for and knowing that something is real even if we do not see it" (Heb. 11:1 NCV).

Let's zoom in on the last part of that definition—knowing that something is real even if we do not see it. Even though we have never laid eyes on the resurrected Jesus, we know that He is real, that His Spirit lives in us, and that He can be completely relied on. I love the definition for faith found in 2 Timothy 1:5 in the Amplified Bible, Classic Edition: "the leaning of your entire personality on God in Christ in absolute trust and confidence in His power, wisdom, and goodness."

By directing the maiden to go forth on the trail of the flock, the great Shepherd is saying, "Take the same path of faith as those who have gone before you. Lean entirely upon Me in absolute trust and confidence in My power, My wisdom, and My goodness." What a great path to follow.

Joseph is one of my personal favorites of God's flock from the Old Testament because he persevered under trial and had a forgiving heart. He was unjustly treated by his brothers, sold into Egyptian slavery, and imprisoned for thirteen years before Pharaoh made him second-in-command over all of Egypt (Genesis, chapters 37–50).

Joseph's understanding of God's sovereignty gave him peace in the midst of harsh circumstances. When famine drove his brothers to Egypt, uniting them once again, Joseph told them that God worked his imprisonment out for the good of many people (Gen. 50:20). Rather than nursing his wounds and becoming bitter, Joseph forgave his brothers and focused on the good that God brought out of his adversity. What a great path to follow.

My favorites of God's flock from the New Testament are the apostles John and Paul. John knew in the core of his being that Jesus loved him. He even refers to himself four times in his gospel as *the disciple whom Jesus loved* (John 19:26; 20:2; 21:7, 20). He truly believed he was Jesus' favorite disciple. Sound arrogant? I don't think so. John experienced a deep sense of security in knowing how much he was loved by Jesus through his personal relationship with Him. What a great path to follow.

Because of the revelation given to the apostle Paul concerning our identity in Christ, I clearly see that *I am not who I was* when I was born into this world. I became a brand-new creation when I believed in (into) Jesus. Paul wasn't taught by men; the resurrected Christ personally downloaded him with the precious truths concerning the believer's identity (Gal. 1:11–12). In most of Paul's letters to the churches, he begins by reminding them who they are in order to evoke positive behavioral changes. What a great path to follow.

There are many great men and women of faith (trailblazers) who are not mentioned in the Bible. I recently attended the funeral of a friend's mother-in-law. Rather than giving a traditional message, the pastor spent the service reading tributes from several members of her family. In almost every one of the testimonials, the family members describe themselves as her *favorite* son, grandchild, daughter-in-law, and so on. This woman of faith left a wonderful legacy of making each one of her loved ones believe that he or she was her favorite. No, she wasn't misleading them or pretending. When she spent one-on-one time with them, they each were her favorite. What a great path to follow.

At just the right time in my life, my home church hosted a Freedom in Christ conference where Jamie Lash, Bible teacher and director of student development at Dallas Baptist University, passionately and powerfully communicated the truths of the believer's new identity in Christ. Through his message, titled "The New Creature," I began to understand that, at salvation, Christ didn't just come into my life, but He literally *became* my life.

I felt like Dorothy being swept away from the dull black-and-white landscape of Kansas to the bright, panoramic spectrum of Oz. And I'm still in Oz over fifteen years later. Through Jamie's faithfulness in blazing a trail to Perryton, Texas, my course of religious rule-keeping was changed forever, and I was set on a joy-filled, grace-illuminated path. What a great path to follow.

During his conference, Jamie shared quotes from trailblazers who had inspired him. Hungry for these truths to go deep, I began devouring every book I could find by these authors, which eventually led me to Bill and Anabel Gillham's books. Bill and Anabel have left an incredible legacy of communicating the truths of our new life in Christ in simple and practical ways. Although both are now present with the Lord, the ministry they founded—Lifetime Ministries—continues to reach others with the liberating truths of our new life in Christ. What a great path to follow.

Finally, the most recent trailblazer who has impacted my life is best-selling author and West Texas pastor, Andrew Farley. His simple, straightforward teaching style is helping people better understand the grace of God and enjoy the freedom that Christ died to give them. Farley wears many other grace-directed hats—all of which point people to the simplicity of the gospel. What a great path to follow.

> Which Bible characters, pastors, teachers, authors, mentors, family members, and friends have blazed a trail of faith for you, influencing your life in positive ways?

After several years of walking on a grace-illuminated path in the liberating truths of our new life in Christ, I steer clear of legalistic teachers and authors who profess that believers still have a sin nature or wicked and deceitful hearts. Although they may be sincere and well-meaning, they are sincerely *wrong*. The believer's new heart—the union of our new spirit and Christ's Spirit—is the wellspring of the authentic Christian life (Prov. 4:23; John 7:38). Now, when I hear or read something that contradicts the truth of my new identity in Christ, I immediately discount it.

It is *vital* that we fill our minds with truths concerning who we are in Him. As we meditate on the Word of God, read books by Christian authors who communicate the gospel of grace, and watch or listen to sound, new-covenant teaching, we will be endued with an unshakeable trust in the Man who is the Path and the Plan—"the Way, the Truth, and the Life" (John 14:6). He lives in our hearts and will cause us to go the distance on the unique course He has laid out for each one of our lives—as we look to Him (2 Tim. 4:7).

After the great Shepherd points the maiden in the direction of the "faith-trodden" trail of the flock in Song 1:8, He gives her critical counsel in her next course of action.

And pasture your young goats

Young goats have a tendency to lead sheep astray. The *young goats* the great Shepherd is referring to here are the maiden's undisciplined emotions, which have a strong propensity to steer her off course (to influence her to walk by the flesh).

Throughout this study, we have looked at the role feelings should play in the life of the believer. Because they are such powerful motivators, daily reminders are helpful.

- It is much easier to believe our way into a new way of feeling than to try to feel our way into a new way of believing.
- Feelings are in the realm of the soul and body, which are both subject to the influences of the world in which we live.

- Feelings are fickle. They can change on a dime. We can feel twenty (or more) different ways about the same thing on any given day.
- Although feelings can be great followers of realized truths, they are lousy leaders.
- Don't count on your feelings to convey spiritual truth, unless they are feelings that are responding to the truths of your new identity in Christ.
- We must continually allow the Word of God and the indwelling Spirit of Christ to take the driver's seat in our lives, rather than our feelings.
- Feelings can't be programmed directly because they are "responders" to whatever we are thinking about. We can change ungodly feelings by reprogramming the thought patterns that are causing them.

Undisciplined emotions are the by-products of a wrong focus. They are a natural result of stinkin' thinkin', as we in the panhandle of Texas say. Have you ever tried to stop feeling lousy after dwelling on lousy thoughts? Good luck. Although we can't change our emotions directly, we *can* change our focus. Paul gives us the prescription for experiencing godly emotions in his letter to the Philippian church: "Fix your thoughts on what is true and good and right. Think about things that are pure and lovely, and dwell on the fine, good things in others. Think about all you can praise God for and be glad about" (Phil. 4:8 TLB).

In the last line of Song 1:8, the great Shepherd specifically tells the maiden *where* to feed her malnourished, undisciplined emotions:

By the tents of the shepherds

We have already established that these shepherds are those who minister to God's people (the flock). Their tents are their "dwelling places"—where they live. King David wanted to live out his days on this earth in the tabernacle, the house of the Lord. He also referred to it as the secret place.

> "One thing I have asked from the Lord, that I shall seek:
> That *I may dwell in the house of the Lord* all the days of my life,
> To behold the beauty of the Lord
> And to meditate in His temple.
> For in the day of trouble He will conceal me in His tabernacle;
> In *the secret place* of His tent He will hide me;
> He will lift me up on a rock" (Ps. 27:4–5).

The ninety-first psalm also refers to the dwelling place of the Most High as *the secret place*:

"He who dwells in the secret place of the Most High
Shall abide under the shadow of the Almighty" (Ps. 91:1 NKJV).

Both of these Old Testament passages are prophetically pointing to "the place" where all believers will someday dwell—*in Christ*. By directing the maiden to pasture her young goats by the tents of the shepherds, the great Shepherd is telling her that meditating (chewing) on the powerful truths of her new identity in Christ will lessen the likelihood of her being led astray by undisciplined emotions.

There are many Scriptures that speak of our being *in Christ, in Him, in Jesus,* and so on. One of my favorite passages concerning our identity in Christ is found in Paul's first letter to the Corinthian church.

> By His doing *you are in Christ Jesus*, who became to us wisdom from God, and righteousness and sanctification, and redemption, so that, just as it is written, "Let him who boasts, boast in the Lord." (1 Cor. 1:30–31)

In Christ, we have everything we need to live lives that glorify Him! He is our wisdom from God, our righteousness, our sanctification, and our redemption. Father God made us brand-new creations (new spiritual hearts) in Christ at salvation. We are *literally* someone we were not before we believed in Jesus. The key to experiencing and expressing Christ's cherishing love and exuberant life is getting our minds renewed with the truths of our new identities.

Chances are you have heard Christians say, "I just need this truth to get from my head to my heart." I used to say it. What I *meant* when I said it was that I wanted that truth to become real and experiential in my life. But when you think about it (I will probably be accused of nit-picking here), what we *really* need is for the truths of our new spiritual hearts (who we *already* are) to get to our heads (renewal of the mind). Then we can experience transformation from the *inside out*.

Believers can undergo an extreme mental and emotional makeover by meditating on and believing the truths of their new identities and trusting Christ's Spirit to live through their lives. This makeover will cause the believer's inward beauty in Christ to gradually become his or her outward beauty (Rom. 12:2; 2 Cor. 3:18).

The New Testament is jam-packed with truths concerning the believer's identity in Christ. On pages 263–279, you will find a list of Scriptures, titled "Who I Am in Christ IS Who I Am!" These Scriptures describe who you are now and forever as a new creation in Christ Jesus. For each Scripture, I chose the translation that I believe best reflects the spiritual truths of our union with Christ in His crucifixion, burial, resurrection, and ascension.

Let's face it. If we don't have tangible daily reminders of who we are, we will experience "spiritual amnesia" on a regular basis and fail to live out of our true identities. The Hallmark Hall of Fame movie *Remember Sunday* reflects the important idea of being reminded of who we are. In the movie, a young man in the prime of his life experienced a brain aneurysm, which caused him to lose his short-term memory. He didn't have any trouble remembering the events of his life that occurred prior to the aneurysm. However, every night as he slept, his memories of everything that had happened *after* his aneurysm disappeared.

In an effort to help him remember who he was, his concerned and loving sister put sticky notes all over his house. Each morning upon waking, he read the notes, trusted what they said, and let them guide his day.

We need to do the same thing! We don't have any trouble walking in the habit patterns we formed before we were made new in Christ (or the ones we formed as believers walking by the flesh). What we often have difficulty grasping are the truths of our pure, righteous, and holy identities in Christ.

Even though walking by the flesh may seem to be the most natural way to live, it is our responsibility to daily remind ourselves of who we are in Christ and walk by His Spirit instead. *No one else can do this for us.* If we expect our outward lives to change without renewing our minds with truth, we will be disappointed—to say the least. There's no time like the present to begin our extreme mental and emotional makeover. Because I am a visual/kinesthetic learner, I like to use ruled note cards to do this.

1. Second Corinthians 5:17 is a good place to start. Write 2 Corinthians 5:17 and the Scripture (from your favorite translation) on the front of your note card. "Anyone who is joined to Christ is a new being; the old is gone, the new has come" (GNT).
2. On the back, personalize the Scripture in your own words. "I am joined to Christ. I am a new being. Who I used to be is gone!" Envision what you look like living as a brand-new person in Christ.
3. Give your note card hands and feet by *acting* like the new person you *already* are, trusting Christ to live through you.

If you are an auditory learner, you can do this exercise by recording (you could even sing) and listening to these truths on a regular basis. I believe there's something special about hearing your own voice—rather than the voice of a stranger—tell you the truth about who you are.

In the movie *Remember Sunday*, the young man used a digital recorder to record what he wanted to remember about his present day and would listen to it the next day. He had no trouble believing what he heard because the voice on the recorder was his. In the same way, when we listen to ourselves tell ourselves the truth about who we are, we aren't just hearing our own voice in English with our regional accent. We are hearing the voice of God resonating through ours.

> ➤ Pick three or more Scriptures from the group of "Who I Am in Christ IS Who I Am!" verses on pages 263–279 and begin your extreme mental and emotional makeover today by renewing your mind in the way that you learn best.

When you begin the process of renewing your mind with the truths of your new identity in Christ—whether you use sticky notes, ruled cards, audio recordings, or another method that works best for you—healthy, godly emotions will naturally result. You will be following the direction of the great Shepherd (pasturing your young goats by the tents of the shepherds), and your outward life will undergo radical transformation.

> ➤ What is your Bridegroom speaking to you through today's study? How will you respond?

Day 5

In the first part of the great Shepherd's response to the Shulammite's plea for direction in finding spiritual nourishment and rest, He speaks of her true beauty and tells her to follow the path of the faithful men and women who have gone before her. He also instructs her to feed on the truths of her identity in Christ in order to keep from being led astray by undisciplined emotions.

All throughout the Song, we will find that the Shepherd-King is tender, kind, and loving toward the maiden—not harsh, hard, or critical. Never once will we see Him pointing a bony finger at her when she messes up, telling her to get her act together.

In our final day of this week's study, we will continue to look at His endearing and encouraging reply as He describes her true identity.

> **"To me, my darling, you are like
> My mare among the chariots of Pharaoh."**
> —Song 1:9

To me, my darling

Directly on the heels of addressing the maiden as *most beautiful among women* (verse 8), the gracious Shepherd-King now refers to her as *my darling*. The Song of Solomon is the only book in the entire Bible where Christ addresses His bride as *my darling*. And He doesn't just say it once or twice, but *nine* times! For a "words of affirmation" person, this is better than cake and ice cream!

If we're not careful, we could easily skip over one tiny word in this term of endearment—*my*. The Shepherd-King uses this pronoun a total of thirty-three times in the Song to refer to His possession of the maiden. He wants her to know that she is *His* darling. That she belongs to Him alone. The apostle Paul reinforces this simple yet profound truth when he tells the church, "You belong to Christ" (1 Cor. 3:23).

Darling means "beloved female companion."[20] (Guys, please remember this is a *spiritual* role.) The King James Version renders the phrase *my darling* as *my love*. I can't help but hear Lionel Richie singing his classic romantic ballad "My Love" every time I see that phrase.

Dictionary.com defines *darling* as "one dearly loved; favorite; cherished."[21] When the Shepherd-King addresses the maiden as *my darling*, He is saying, *You are My favorite companion; I love and cherish you dearly*. And that is what He is saying to you, dear bride, at this very moment. Can you hear Him?

You are like my mare among the chariots of Pharaoh

The first time I read this part of Song 1:9, I thought, *How could being compared to a horse possibly be a compliment?* After further research, I was delighted to find that the King's mare is most likely an exquisite Arabian. Let's take a look at some fascinating facts about these horses:

- one of the most celebrated, beautiful, and favorite breeds in the world
- known for its gentle disposition, loyalty, patience, sense of direction, and desire to please
- known for its alertness, speed, stamina, intelligence, and courage
- known for its ability to carry weight out of proportion to its size for extended periods of time
- the most common choice of kings

In light of all of these wonderful characteristics of the Arabian horse, I'm definitely beginning to warm up to the idea of being compared to one.

A note on Song 1:9 from a popular study Bible also lauds the beauty of the King's darling: "Her beauty attracts attention the way a mare would among the Egyptian chariot stallions."[22] When the King likens the maiden to *my mare among the chariots of Pharaoh*, He is saying, "You are exquisite, one of a kind. You stand out among all the unbelievers of the world. You alone have captured My heart." He wants us to understand that we belong to Him, we are not of this world, and we have His undivided attention (John 15:19; 17:14). Although He loves all of His creation, He is *in love* with His bride.

King Solomon purchased his horses from the king of Egypt at a high price (1 Kings 10:28). Living in Egypt is symbolic of belonging to the spiritual realm of Adam—in bondage to sin. Our King, Jesus, purchased us at the highest possible price (His life), bringing us out of Adam and uniting us to Him, forever freeing us from bondage to sin (Rom. 6:18, 22).

Since we are on the subject of the king's horses and the chariots of Pharaoh, I can't help but remember the demise of the Egyptians who were plunged to certain death in the Red Sea while in hot pursuit to destroy the Israelites. Horse-drawn chariots were commonly used in battle, hunting, and racing in ancient times. In Scripture, they symbolize the natural strength of the things of this world (which includes the strength of men), as opposed to God's strength: "Some boast in chariots and some in horses, but we will boast in the name of the Lord, our God" (Ps. 20:7).

It's not uncommon at funerals to hear people speak admirably of the deceased as a "strong" person. Although some are references to the person's "strength in the Lord," most refer to the person's natural bent or strength. This saddens my heart, because the Lord is not impressed with our natural strength. You may be as surprised as I was to learn that He actually detests it. No, He doesn't detest our physical strength in and of itself, but He detests it when it gets in the way of our depending on *His strength* (Hab. 1:11; 2 Cor. 12:9).

When believers live out of their natural strength—*by the flesh*—they hinder the flow of Christ's life through them. (They also miss out on the joy of experiential union with Him.) Walking by the flesh holds no eternal value, regardless of the temporary applause it receives in the natural realm.

You might ask, "How do I know when I'm living out of my natural strength and when I'm trusting in the Lord's strength through me?" That's a good question. It is an attitude of the soul. Each day upon waking, ask the Lord to cause you to remember to depend on Him to live His life through you, rather than you living in your natural strength. He wants us to do everything in intimate partnership with Him. Our part is to trust Him to live His life through us; His part is to do it *all* through us and for us. The apostle Paul understood the value of trusting Christ to live through him: "For I will not presume to speak of anything except what Christ has accomplished through me" (Rom. 15:18).

This is walking by faith, not by sight or feelings. In the same way that we trusted Christ for our salvation, we need to trust Him to live through us each day. Because this occurs in the spiritual realm, we are not necessarily going to *feel* His life coursing through our veins as we walk by faith. Although there have been times when I have strongly sensed Him living through me, most of the time I don't. But I still believe that He is doing it. Think about it. If we consistently felt His power through us, we wouldn't need to walk by faith, would we?

Here's a suggestion: throughout the day, practice trusting Christ to do all your tasks through you, even the ones you think you can handle in your natural strength. This way, *trusting Christ as your life* can become part of your autopilot—your habit patterns. If we develop this practice of trusting Christ to do *everything* through us and for us, we will be "all practiced-up" to trust Him to handle the difficult circumstances—which, by the way, will invariably come our way as we live in this world (John 16:33).

There may be times when you trust Christ to live through you, and the results don't turn out the way you think they should have. When this happens, it is important to remember that we are not responsible for the outcome; our only responsibility is to trust Christ. What may look like a failure in the natural realm is a success in the spiritual realm, if what we did was done in dependence on Christ.

> ➤ Have you ever sincerely trusted Christ to do something through you, and the results didn't turn out like you thought they should have? If so, briefly describe the situation. Then, affirm the truth that, regardless of the results, the act was a success because of your dependence on Christ.

In light of our discussion on the importance of dependence on Christ, I would like to comment on one of the previous descriptions of the Arabian horse: *known for its ability to carry weight out of proportion to its size for extended periods of time.* Some believers take pride in their natural ability to bear burdens. We often hear them say, "The Lord never puts more on us than we can bear." When they say this, they are usually referring to 1 Corinthians 10:13, taking it completely out of context.

No temptation has overtaken you except what is common to us all. And God is faithful; he will not let you be tempted beyond what you can bear. But *when you are tempted*, he will also provide a way out so that you can endure it. (TNIV)

In this verse, the apostle Paul is referring to God's faithfulness in providing believers who are experiencing the *temptation to sin* with a way out, not our natural ability to bear burdens.

The next time you think that God will never put more on you than you can bear in your natural strength, you would be wise to stop believing that. In his second letter to the church at Corinth, the apostle Paul wrote of circumstances in his life that were beyond his natural ability to bear.

We do not want you to be unaware, brethren, of our affliction which came to us in Asia, that *we were burdened excessively, beyond our strength*, so that we despaired even of life; indeed, we had the sentence of death within ourselves *so that we would not trust in ourselves, but in God* who raises the dead. (2 Cor. 1:8)

Notice that Paul states the reason he was burdened beyond his strength was so that he would not trust in himself, but in God. The truth is, the Lord will allow circumstances in our lives that are more than we can handle, so that we will learn to stop relying on our natural strength and trust in His strength instead. Sadly, most of us will not learn this, apart from going through circumstances where our natural resources are utterly exhausted. I didn't. Christ taught me the powerful principle of learning to trust Him as my life during one of the most painful seasons I've ever experienced.

In the summer of 2002, I was at the altar during an evening church service, asking the Lord how He wanted to use my life for His glory. He showed me (by flashing a picture through my mind) that someday I would be teaching His Word instead of high school math.

I'm not saying that the Lord didn't use me for His glory while I was teaching high school math because I believe He did. He was just showing me that He was about to change the vocation through which He would reveal His glory through me. But first (and unbeknownst to me), He needed to do a major "mental overhaul" in the way I viewed the Christian life.

Not long after the Lord gave me that picture, I was lying on my face on our bedroom floor, asking Him *when* I was going to get to stop teaching math and start teaching His Word. After a while, I heard Him speak (in the form of a thought going through my mind).

"But those who wait on the Lord
Shall renew their strength;
They shall mount up with wings like eagles,

> They shall run and not be weary,
> They shall walk and not faint" (Isa. 40:31 NKJV).

Out of this entire Scripture, the only word I really heard was *wait*, and the impatient flesh pattern in my brain instantly rose up in rebuke. I was disappointed that I wasn't going to start teaching His Word right away.

That summer, I had been taking good care of myself, working out, and eating right. When school started in the fall, I remember telling a good friend of mine that I had never felt stronger in my life after she commented on how well I looked. While there is nothing wrong with good nutrition and exercise habits, I took it to an extreme and became proud without realizing it. My focus was on me, and what I was doing to make myself healthy and strong. My physical strength was my chariot—what I was trusting in, rather than Christ.

In the months that followed, I began having problems with my colon. I had never had colon issues before and began to worry that something was seriously wrong. A word of advice if you are having health issues: don't try to diagnose yourself through the Internet. Because of what I read, fear compounded my colon issues.

I made an appointment with a gastroenterologist and had a colonoscopy. It revealed that I had irritable bowel syndrome, which could be controlled with diet and stress reduction. Nothing too serious. I was so relieved that I didn't have cancer.

One morning not long after that, I swallowed a handful of vitamins and aspirin with some orange juice. It felt like one of the vitamins had permanently lodged in my esophagus. In the days that followed, I experienced a chronic sore throat. (This is a severe hiccup for someone who teaches school.) By the end of every workday, I was so exhausted all I wanted to do was go to bed.

I went to a couple of different specialists, one of whom diagnosed me with acid reflux and put me on medicine to treat those symptoms. The medicine didn't help at all because I didn't have acid reflux. I still had a chronic sore throat, though—along with the irritable bowel syndrome.

After suffering through almost two years of this—going from doctor to doctor, praying healing Scriptures, and believing God, I threw up my hands and told the Lord, "I have done everything I know to do, and nothing is working. If anything good is going to come out of this, You are going to have to do it. I quit!"

One month later, I went through three weeks of testing at the Mayo Clinic in Rochester, Minnesota. I was diagnosed with esophageal nerve damage and prescribed a low-dose medication to help relieve the chronic pain. Today, I'm happy to report that after almost ten years of being on that medication, the chronic sore throat is gone, and I no longer have to take it.

While I am very grateful that the Lord healed me, *I am more thankful that He did not do it right away.* Yes, that's right. He taught me so much through that painful two-year process. Up until that time, I had begun to understand that Christ lived in me, but I viewed Him as a "helper" when I got stuck in a hard place that I couldn't get out of on my own. In other words, His power remained dormant in me until I thought I needed it.

All of my efforts had to be completely exhausted before I finally understood that He didn't want to just "help me" live my life—He wanted me to realize that *He was my Life*, and apart from trusting dependence on Him, I could do nothing of eternal value (John 15:5). Looking back at the moment when I gave up, I believe He must have grinned a mile wide and said, "Good! Now *I* can do something."

Remember that great "wait" Scripture the Lord gave me from Isaiah? After understanding my spiritual union with Him, He took me back to it, this time in a different translation:

> "Yet those who wait for the Lord
> Will *gain new strength*;
> They will mount up with wings like eagles,
> They will run and not get tired,
> They will walk and not become weary" (Isa. 40:31 NASB).

The first two lines of the previous translation said,

> "But those who wait on the Lord
> Shall *renew their strength*" (Isa. 40:31 NKJV).

Immediately, the words *new strength* from the New American Standard Bible jumped off the page and into my heart! What a kiss! *His strength* was the new strength!

What's even more fascinating is that the word *wait* actually means "to bind together."[23] When we recognize that our spirit and Christ's Spirit are eternally bound together, we will begin to understand that we have no life apart from Him. And get this: the word *gain* signifies "a substitution or interchange—an exchange of His supernatural strength for our natural strength."[24] In light of my new understanding, the following is my personal paraphrase of the first part of this verse:

> Those who understand and acknowledge their spiritual union with the Lord
> will exchange their natural strength for His supernatural strength
> by trusting Him to live His life through them.

When we stop relying on our natural strength and begin trusting Him to live through us, we can't go wrong! But just like everything else in His kingdom, we must do this *by faith*.

We began our discussion on this topic by examining the false statement, "God will not put anything on us we can't bear." I hope by now that you understand that He *will* lovingly allow us to go through painful circumstances where our natural resources are depleted, in order to teach us complete dependence on His indwelling life.

If you are having a difficult time understanding how you can learn to trust Christ to live His life through you, I believe an inspiring video about Dick and Rick Hoyt—a father/son Ironman triathlon team—may help you. It's not just any team; Rick has cerebral palsy. Go to YouTube.com and type in "A father's love—the world's strongest dad" to watch it.

Did you catch what Rick said in the video? "When *I'm* running my disability disappears." He gets it. He sees himself and his father as one—Dick pulling, pedaling, pushing, and carrying him, and Rick trusting him to do it all.

> ➢ Are you tired of living life in your own strength, falsely believing that you are only to rely on Christ's strength when your natural resources run out?

When we live life in our own strength, we are taking on a burden that Christ never intended for us to bear. He doesn't merely *suggest* that we cast our burdens on Him; He *commands* it. "Cast your burden upon the Lord and He will sustain you; He will never allow the righteous to be shaken" (Ps. 55:22).

> ➢ Would you like to give up living your life in your natural strength and cast that burden—along with all of the other burdens you are carrying—on the Lord?

Though many sincere believers understand that the Lord commands us to cast our burdens on Him, we often take the burden back soon after we give it to Him. In her wonderful book *The Confident Woman*, Anabel Gillham shares a seeing-is-believing, burden-releasing exercise that I (along with many others) have found most helpful in giving burdens to the Lord and *leaving* them with Him.

1. Get a watch, a felt-tipped pen, a piece of paper, a pencil, an envelope, and a half brick (or something around the same weight and size).
2. Go to the nearest store that sells helium balloons and buy a plump one.

3. With all your paraphernalia, go to a field, a vacant lot, the football stadium, the park—anywhere spacious without trees or buildings.
4. With your felt-tipped pen, write as many details of your circumstance as you need to on the balloon in order to identify it with your problems.
5. Now, hold your brick and the string to the balloon in your hand, lifting your arm straight out in front of you. As you do this, begin talking to the Lord about your burden. Tell Him every detail! Tell Him you can't carry this burden any longer. Tell Him how angry you are, how hurt, how tired—tell Him *everything*. Hold that brick and balloon up until your arm is hurting so badly you don't know if you're crying over your burden or because of the pain in your arm.
6. When you can't hold your arm up another second, with the command for "casting your burden on the Lord" in your heart and mind, and praying and thanking Him for His concern, His power, and His love for you, *drop the brick and set your balloon free*, releasing your burden and easing your pain. Watch it climb, see it disappear into the very dwelling place of God.
7. Take your paper and record the date and time with this statement: "On _____ [date], at _____ [time], I gave my burden to the Lord." Now write this: "And He took it." Look for the balloon. Can you see it? A tiny speck? Fold your paper and put it in your envelope. Seal it and print "God" and the date and time on the front. Don't lose that envelope; you will pick it up many times and thank God for what He did for you on this day.
8. Thank Him. When you get home, get three index cards and write "God" and the date and time on each one. Put those cards someplace where you will see them often (over the sink, in the medicine cabinet, on the dash of your car). Every time you glance at a card, visualize that speck in the sky—the burden, out of your control and in the arms of God.

It's a simple exercise, yet it will be much like an altar erected in remembrance, reminding you of what God has done. Does this mean you will never cry again? No. Does it mean your emotions will never rocket to the top again? Of course not. Will you want desperately to take the burden back at times? Yes. There has been only one decisive change: *The burden is no longer yours.*[25]

If you want to cast the heavy burden of living your life on the Lord, along with all the other burdens you have been carrying, go buy your balloon, and don't waste another minute carrying that heavy load!

> ➤ What is your Bridegroom speaking to you through today's study? How will you respond?

Week 4

EVERYTHING I DO

SONG OF SONGS 1:10–2:2

"For the love of Christ controls us,
having concluded this,
that one died for all, therefore, all died."
—2 Corinthians 5:14

Day 1

We begin the fourth week of our study of the Song in the middle of the Shepherd-King's response to the Shulammite's plea for guidance in finding nourishment and rest. After calling her *most beautiful among women* and *my darling*, He continues to lavish her with the refreshing truths of her pure, holy, and righteous identity in Him, which, we will see, has a transforming effect on her as she begins to believe what He is saying:

> **"Your cheeks are lovely with ornaments,**
> **Your neck with strings of beads."**
> —Song 1:10

Your cheeks are lovely with ornaments

This verse is a continuation of the previous verse where the Shepherd-King compares the maiden's loveliness to His exquisite Arabian mare. Owners of Arabian show horses prepare them for events by adorning them with jeweled halters similar to the way that women from various Middle Eastern countries wear their jewelry. You can go to Google Images and type in "Arabian horse show halters" and then do a separate search on "jewelry for Indian women" to find many stunning examples where both the horses' and women's natural beauty are accentuated by jewelry elegantly framing their faces.

In describing the maiden's cheeks, the Shepherd-King refers to the "seat of her beauty,"[1] the place where her beauty is reflected to the world. When someone refers to another person's outward beauty, most of the time he or she is describing the person's facial features. Our cheeks are one of the most expressive parts of our faces, showcasing our emotions. When we are joyful and smiling, our cheeks are raised; when we are downcast and frowning, they are lowered.

The Shepherd-King specifically describes her cheeks as *lovely with ornaments*. *Lovely* means "comely, beautiful, befitting,"[2] and the word *ornaments* comes from the Hebrew root word *tuwr*, which means "to seek, search out, explore."[3] In describing her cheeks this way, He is delighted that the maiden is looking to Him to meet her emotional needs. He is showing her a picture of the godly emotions that reside in her new spiritual heart and are expressed as she wholeheartedly seeks Him and His guidance (Ps. 105:3; 1 Chron. 16:11).

When we fix our eyes on Jesus and meditate on the truth concerning our pure, holy, and righteous identity, we will experience and express godly emotions. On the contrary, when we focus on the flesh and unpleasant circumstances, we will experience and express ungodly emotions (Rom. 8:6). It's that simple.

After speaking of the maiden's emotional beauty, the Shepherd-King describes yet another one of her lovely attributes.

Your neck with strings of beads

In Scripture, the neck often represents a person's will. People known for their stubborn and rebellious will are commonly described as "stiff-necked," whereas people who easily bow the neck are known for their submissive will. Our will is our "chooser," and the strings of beads signify the moment-by-moment choices we make. It's mind-boggling to think of the number of choices the average person makes each day. From what we wear to what we will eat for breakfast to whether or not we will make a particular purchase, we make thousands of decisions every day.

We can think of our will as a swinging door connecting our new hearts (our spiritual union with Christ) and our souls (where we experience conscious thoughts, attitudes, feelings, desires, and choices). When we make conscious choices in dependence on Christ—walking by His Spirit—the door swings outward, releasing the flow of His life into our souls and then our bodies (actions). (See Figure 6: Walking by the Spirit, page 68).

On the other hand, when we choose to depend on our natural resources (physical strength, talent)—walking by the flesh—the swinging door remains stationary, stopping the flow of Christ's life through our souls and bodies. (See Figure 7: Walking by the Flesh, page 69).

The driving force of our choices is desire. Our desires are either Spirit- or flesh-inspired, depending on our focus (Rom. 8:6; Gal. 5:17). Whether we are aware of it or not, when we were spiritually united with Christ at salvation, His heart's desires became our heart's desires:

- "I'll give you a new heart, put a new spirit in you. I'll remove the stone heart from your body and replace it with a heart that's God-willed, not self-willed" (Ezek. 36:26 MSG).
- "[Not in your own strength] for it is God Who is all the while effectually at work in you [energizing and creating in you the power and desire], both to will and to work for His good pleasure and satisfaction and delight" (Phil. 2:13 AMPC).
- "This time I'm writing out the plan in them, carving it on the lining of their hearts" (Heb. 8:10 MSG).

Because of our union with Christ, our new hearts possess and agree with His thoughts, feelings, and desires. If we don't realize this, we will mistake desires fueled by the flesh for our new hearts' desires:

A new creature in Christ no longer desires or craves to live a sinful life. That's why Christians find such a life deeply unrewarding. Granted, it feels good to get your needs met, but when you sin to accomplish this, you feel rotten. The reason for this is that God has given us the heart transplant that He prophesied in Ezekiel 36:26–27 and fulfilled in us through our deaths and re-creations in Christ. This isn't bypass surgery, gang. He *removed* that old, lost, rebellious, desperately sick heart and replaced it with a heart of love for Him. We must consistently remind ourselves (and one another) of this fact instead of talking about how "desperately wicked" our hearts are. That is the Old Testament description of the unregenerated heart in Jeremiah 17:9.[4]

When we renew our minds with the truth that *we want what Christ wants* and focus on Him, our emotions will respond positively and influence us to make godly choices. Although Christ's Spirit will always influence us to make godly choices, He will not override our decision-making process. If He made our decisions for us, we would be like mindless drones with no free will. As long as we fill our minds with the truths concerning our new identities in Christ and see ourselves as *those who want what Christ wants*, we will be encouraged to walk by His Spirit rather than the flesh.

I love it when Jesus uses scenes from movies to solidify spiritual truth in my mind. One day, while I was watching the latest film adaptation of Jane Austen's classic novel, *Pride and Prejudice*, He lavished me with an unexpected kiss. In this particular scene, Mr. Bingley got down on one knee and proposed marriage to Jane, the eldest of the Bennett sisters. Overcome with extreme happiness, she responded by saying yes over and over again.

Jesus immediately spoke to me (through a thought in my mind): *This is a picture of your new will in Me.* I was thrilled to hear His affirmation that my new heart (who I am) really wants what He wants. While I certainly do not walk by the Spirit all of the time, He knows that my heart's desires are *His heart's desires*. And your heart's desires, dear bride of Christ, are also in complete agreement with His. You just need to believe it and act like He is telling the truth!

➤ Act like Jesus is telling the truth by declaring (write it out) that your heart's desires are one with His heart's desires:

To summarize Song 1:10, the Shepherd-King is telling His darling maiden that He is delighted she is seeking Him and focusing on the truth, rather than the things of this world, in order to get her emotional needs met. He is also taking great pleasure in her moment-by-moment choices to depend on Him to live His life through her. She is beginning to enjoy the sweetness which comes from understanding that her heart's desires are, in fact, His heart's desires. She can trust her new heart in Him. What joy and freedom is found in this revelation!

After affirming her, the Shepherd-King—for the first and *only* time in the Song—speaks of Himself in the *plural* form:

> **"We will make for you ornaments of gold**
> **With beads of silver."**
> —Song 1:11

We will make for you

When He says, *We will make for you*, He is referring to the entire Godhead—the Trinity—who dwells in Him: "For in Him all the fullness of deity dwells in bodily form" (Col. 2:9). This means that the Father, Son, and Holy Spirit are fully united and embodied in Christ. And because we are in Christ, we are included in this holy embrace of the Godhead (John 14:20).

In this part of Song 1:11, the Shepherd-King is promising the maiden that He, His Father, and His Spirit will continue to work together on her behalf as she trusts in and depends on Him. (I find it interesting that the numerical location of this verse that speaks of the Trinity is 1:11, don't you?)

Ornaments of gold with beads of silver

Ornaments refer to "circular pieces of jewelry."[5] A circle represents the eternal (no beginning and no end) life of the Godhead. *Gold* symbolizes "divine (holy) attributes,"[6] and *silver* signifies "eternal redemption."[7] To *redeem* something means to "buy it back."[8] Silver was a primary medium of exchange in the Scriptures. Judas Iscariot, one of Jesus' disciples, was paid thirty pieces of silver in exchange for betraying Jesus into the hands of the chief Sanhedrin priests (Matt. 26:15; 27:3, 9).

Redemption was one of the first words spoken out of the mouth of Zacharias, eight days after his son, John the Baptist, was born. "Blessed be the Lord God of Israel, for He has visited us and accomplished *redemption* for His people" (Luke 1:68). Zacharias had finally believed what the angel Gabriel had told him over nine months earlier about his son being a forerunner of the soon-coming Messiah (who would also happen to be John's younger cousin) (Luke 1:5–23). Because of Zacharias' unbelief, he had been unable to speak until the time came for them to circumcise and name John (Luke 1:59–64).

The redemption that Jesus accomplished was his buying mankind back from the kingdom of darkness (bondage to sin) through His finished work on the cross:

> Through His own blood, He entered the holy place once for all, having obtained eternal *redemption*. (Heb. 9:12)

One translation says, "He ... offered this sacrifice once and for all to *free us forever*" (GW). The redemption that Jesus accomplished would forever free those who believed in (into) Him.

Another wonderful passage of Scripture that speaks of our redemption in Christ is Colossians 1:13–14: "For he has rescued us from the kingdom of darkness and transferred us into the Kingdom of his dear Son, who *purchased our freedom* and forgave our sins" (NLT).

The beads of silver represent our choices of dependence on Christ, which all have at their foundation our eternal redemption in Christ. We could not walk by faith apart from our union with Him. So when Jesus is saying that the Godhead will make ornaments of gold with beads of silver for the maiden, He means that as she chooses to depend on Him, His eternally divine attributes will be expressed through her life, exquisitely adorning her.

The price Jesus paid for us was, in fact, a bridal price, or *mohar* in Hebrew. In the ancient Jewish marriage customs, a prospective groom was required to offer a *mohar* to the father of the girl he had chosen to be his bride. The bridal price is specifically mentioned in the Old Testament. Shechem loved Dinah so much he was willing to pay her father whatever price he exacted—no matter how high (Gen. 34:11–12). The asking price for Michal, King Saul's daughter, was one hundred Philistine foreskins. Zealous to secure her as his bride, David brought two hundred foreskins instead (1 Sam. 18:25–27).

Sometimes the bridal price was paid in the form of service. Jacob served Rachel's father, Laban, for seven years to obtain her as his bride. At the end of that time, Laban tricked Jacob into marrying Rachel's older sister, Leah, instead. Because of Jacob's great love for Rachel, he ended up serving another seven years for her (Gen. 29:1–30). Fourteen years of wages back then would amount to around $700,000 in today's economy. Now that's a high price to pay for a bride!

Even though the following example of a bridal price is not found in the Bible, it illustrates what can happen when someone is willing to pay an exorbitant price in order to have and to hold another:

> The story is told of a primitive culture where brides were purchased from their parents using cattle as an exchange medium. An average woman might merit the bride-price of two cattle; an exceptional woman might bring three; while a less desirable woman's family would receive one cow.

Into this society, the story goes, a rich and attractive suitor came, looking for a wife. All the families paraded their eligible daughters before him. Everyone was surprised when he announced his intention to negotiate with the family of a young woman who was unattractive and clumsy.

Perhaps it's a bargain he's after, the townspeople speculated, wondering if perhaps he would offer chickens instead of cows. To everyone's amazement, he offered the girl's family six cows for their daughter and quickly whisked her away for a long honeymoon.

When they returned, months later, no one recognized the new bride. Gone were the slumping shoulders and dull eyes. It was as if she were a new person, radiating beauty and confidence.

No, her husband had not bought her beauty treatments or a facelift. He had begun their relationship by showing her in a tangible way that he thought she was important and valuable. She had begun to act the part, to see herself as he saw her, and the rest of her life she was viewed with awe by all her friends—a six-cow woman.[9]

The price this winsome suitor paid for his bride caused her to see how much he loved and valued her, and she began *living* like the loved and valued bride she was! The bridal price Jesus paid for His bride was the highest price a bridegroom could ever pay for a bride and reflects our unsurpassable worth and value. Several verses in the New Testament mention this price.

- "Knowing that you were not *redeemed* with perishable things like silver or gold …, but with precious blood, as of a lamb unblemished and spotless, the blood of Christ" (1 Pet. 1:18–19).
- "He has *purchased* us to be his own people" (Eph. 1:14 NLT).
- "You have been *bought* with a price" (1 Cor. 6:20).

➤ Bride of Christ, do you understand that your unsurpassable worth and value is reflected in the price your Bridegroom, Jesus Christ, paid for you? There is nothing more valuable than His life—given *for* you and *to* you—through His death and resurrection. Write a prayer of thankfulness for the unsurpassable worth and value given to you through His redemption.

We've come to the end of the Shepherd-King's four-verse response to the maiden's desperate cry for guidance in finding refreshing nourishment and rest. In summary, He does not harshly rebuke her for her failings (walking by the flesh) but tenderly reminds her who she is in Him. He tells her to feed on His Word in order to renew her mind with the truth of her pure, holy, and righteous identity in Him. He speaks of the lovely emotions and desires she now possesses because of her union with Him and promises that He, His Father, and His Spirit will work together to adorn her with divine attributes as she depends on Him.

In day 2 of this week's study, the Shepherd-King will continue to deepen the Shulammite's understanding of her eternal redemption in Him through personal revelation, as she looks to Him to meet all of her needs.

> What is your Bridegroom speaking to you through today's study? How will you respond?

Day 2

In today's study, we will look at the first line of the maiden's response after listening to her Shepherd-King's endearing and encouraging words to her. It's possible that the daughters of Jerusalem are still part of her audience, since we have no evidence of their leaving the scene.

Her words aren't spoken directly to Him as they were in verse 7 but are a description of what she sees and what happens to her as He more fully reveals Himself and His finished work on the cross.

> **"While the king was at his table,**
> **My perfume gave forth its fragrance."**
> **—Song 1:12**

While the king was at his table

The last time the maiden referred to Him as *the king* was in Song 1:4, where the reference was to His chambers. There, we discussed our spiritual union with Him by believing in (into) Him. This occurrence in verse 12 also speaks of our union.

The King James Version translates the first part of this verse as *While the king sitteth at his table*. The word *sitteth* conveys the wonderful truth that Jesus' work of redeeming mankind is *finished*—a done deal. He is now seated at the right hand of His Father, and we are *literally* seated with Him (Mark 16:19; Col. 3:1; Eph. 2:6; Heb. 1:3; 8:1; 10:12; 12:2; Rev. 3:21; 20:4). Who we are *is* our new spiritual heart, and we are *already* sitting down in heaven with Jesus!

The word *table* comes from the Hebrew word *mecab*, which means "to encompass or surround."[10] Because of Jesus' finished work, we are in union with His Spirit, fully encompassed by His love and presence.

Up to this point in the Song, the maiden's struggle has largely been due to her incomplete understanding of her identity in Christ. In our discussion of Song 1:5, where the maiden describes herself as "black but lovely," we looked at three different descriptions of self-image that most believers commonly hold after salvation. Let's revisit those.

> **Self-image 1:** "I am a sinner saved by grace. I have been forgiven and am going to heaven when I die, but I am still the same person I was before salvation (John 3:16). At the core of my being is a sin-nature. God's desires and my desires are polar opposites most of the time."
>
> **Self-image 2:** "Second Peter 1:4 says I received a new nature in salvation, but my feelings and behavior indicate that my old nature is still very much alive. Therefore, it is apparent that I now have two natures—the good, new me *and* the bad, old me."
>
> **Self-image 3:** "I am a saint who sometimes acts like a sinner. Not only did I receive forgiveness and a new nature at salvation, but the bad, old me—my sin nature—was crucified with Christ on the cross (Rom. 6:6; Gal. 2:20). I am a new creation because I am in Christ (2 Cor. 5:17). The desire of my new heart is *not* to sin, even though sometimes I still do."

We surmised in our discussion of Song 1:5 that the maiden most likely held self-image 2, because she described herself as both black and lovely. She believed that she had two natures—a sin nature and Christ nature—living inside her at the same time.

In an effort to correct her false self-image, the King tells His darling maiden that she is *already* beautiful, and as she focuses on and believes Him, this beauty will be expressed in and through her life (verses 8–11).

In Song 1:12 (our focal verse), the King will cause her to see the origin of her beauty—what happened to her the moment she believed in Him—in order to deepen her understanding of her new identity and union with Him.

In our church services today, we sometimes refer to our King's table as the *table of communion*. The communion table commemorates Jesus' death on the cross—the price He paid so that we could partake of His life. Let's look at a passage in John's gospel where Jesus speaks of two aspects of His life.

> "I am the bread of life. Your fathers ate the manna in the wilderness, and they died. This is the bread (one version calls it *the man*) which comes down out of heaven, so that one may eat of it and not die. I am the living bread that came down out of heaven; if anyone eats of this bread, he will live forever; and the bread also which I will give for the life of the world is My flesh."
>
> Then the Jews began to argue with one another, saying, "How can this man give us His flesh to eat?"
>
> So Jesus said to them, "Truly, truly, I say to you, unless you eat the flesh of the Son of Man and drink His blood, you have no life in yourselves. He who eats My flesh and drinks My blood has eternal life, and I will raise him up on the last day. For My flesh is true food, and My blood is true drink. He who eats My flesh and drinks My blood abides in Me, and I in him. As the living Father sent Me, and I live because of the Father, so he who eats Me, he also will live because of Me. This is the bread which came down out of heaven; not as the fathers ate and died; he who eats this bread will live forever." (John 6:48–58)

Obviously, Jesus is not speaking of our eating His physical flesh or drinking His actual blood. He is referring to our receiving His eternal life (His Spirit), so that we can live forever joined to Him (1 Cor. 6:19). When we partake of communion, we are symbolically celebrating our receipt of two aspects of His life.

- **Drinking the wine or juice** symbolizes our receiving the gift of forgiveness for the sins of our lifetime through His blood poured out on the cross for us (Matt. 26:28; Eph. 1:7; Heb. 9:22).
- **Eating the bread** symbolizes our receiving the gift of a new heart (our new spirit joined with Christ's Spirit), a new identity, through His body crucified on the cross (Ezek. 36:26–27; 2 Cor. 5:21; Col. 1:22; Heb. 10:10).

Through Christ's blood and body given for us on the cross, we now have everything we need for life and godliness (2 Pet. 1:3).

You may be wondering, "If this is true, then why aren't we seeing more of the cherishing love and exuberant life of Christ being expressed through His body—the church?" The answer is simple. It is because of the church's lack of knowledge of its identity change at salvation (Hos. 4:6; Rom. 12:2).

We hear again and again of the believer's forgiveness through the shed blood of Jesus, but how often do we hear that we become a brand-new person at salvation? I must admit that we hear of our new identity in Christ more often now than we did while I was growing up. But still, the meaning of our newness is vague and hardly ever elaborated.

In this section, we are going to examine the spiritual principles of *substitution* and *identification* in order to gain a greater understanding of what actually (not theoretically) happened to us when we believed in (into) Christ.

In *substitution*, Christ died *for* us—as a substitute in our place—on the cross. Let's look at some Scriptures that illustrate this truth.

- "He was pierced through for our transgressions, He was crushed for our iniquities; the chastening for our well-being fell upon Him, and by His scourging we are healed" (Isa. 53:5).
- "All of us like sheep have gone astray, each of us has turned to his own way; but the Lord has caused the iniquity of us all to fall on Him" (Isa. 53:6).
- "God demonstrates His own love toward us, in that while we were yet sinners, Christ died for us" (Rom. 5:8).
- "The love of Christ controls us, having concluded this, that one died for all, therefore all died" (2 Cor. 5:14).
- "God has not destined us for wrath, but for obtaining salvation through our Lord Jesus Christ, who died for us, so that whether we are awake or asleep, we will live together with Him" (1 Thess. 5:9–10).

- "He Himself bore our sins in His body on the cross, so that we might die to sin and live to righteousness; for by His wounds you were healed" (1 Pet. 2:24).

All of the foregoing Scriptures show that Christ—in His fleshly body—underwent a horrifying, excruciating death in our place, so that our physical bodies (where we live) wouldn't have to be subjected to an actual crucifixion.

When we say that we *identify* with another person, we are saying that we share something in common with that person. In *identification*, we (our spirit man—who we are) literally shared the entire experience of Christ's crucifixion, burial, resurrection, and ascension with Him. Our old self (our sin nature) died with Him on the cross and was buried with Him (burial shows the finality of death). Then, we were born again in His resurrection (we now have a pure, righteous, and holy nature) and are now seated with Him in heaven. Let's look at some Scriptures that illustrate this truth.

- "Our old self was crucified with Him, in order that our body of sin might be done away with, so that we would no longer be slaves to sin for he who has died is freed from sin" (Rom. 6:6–7).
- "The love of Christ controls us, having concluded this, that one died for all, therefore all died" (2 Cor. 5:14).
- "I have been crucified with Christ; it is no longer I who live, but Christ lives in me; and the life which I now live in the flesh I live by faith in the Son of God, who loved me and gave Himself for me" (Gal. 2:20 NKJV).
- "God, being rich in mercy, because of His great love with which He loved us, even when we were dead in our transgressions, made us alive together with Christ (by grace you have been saved), and raised us up with Him, and seated us with Him in the heavenly places in Christ Jesus" (Eph. 2:4–6).
- "He has now reconciled you in His fleshly body through death, in order to present you before Him holy and blameless and beyond reproach" (Col. 1:22).
- "Having been buried with Him in baptism, in which you were also raised up with Him through faith in the working of God, who raised Him from the dead. When you were dead in your transgressions and the uncircumcision of your flesh, He made you alive together with Him, having forgiven us all our transgressions" (Col. 2:12–13).
- "If you have been raised up with Christ, keep seeking the things above, where Christ is, seated at the right hand of God. Set your mind on the things above, not on the things that are on earth. For you have died and your life is hidden

with Christ in God. When Christ, who is our life, is revealed, then you also will be revealed with Him in glory" (Col. 3:1–4).
- "Blessed be the God and Father of our Lord Jesus Christ, who according to His great mercy has caused us to be born again to a living hope through the resurrection of Jesus Christ from the dead" (1 Pet. 1:3).
- "He Himself bore our sins in His body on the cross, so that we might die to sin and live to righteousness; for by His wounds you were healed" (1 Pet. 2:24).

Please notice that 2 Corinthians 5:14 and 1 Peter 2:24 illustrate both principles of substitution and identification. Although the spiritual principle of identification is rarely taught, the abundance of Scriptures provided in support of it cannot be denied.

If I would have experienced the revelation as a nine-year-old "newbie" in Christ that not only did He die for me, but the bad me died with Him and the good me was born again in His resurrection, I believe my life would have gone down an entirely different path.

Knowledge of our true identities in Christ will positively influence us to live like who we *know* we are. The following story about an eagle who thought he was a chicken illustrates this principle.

> Did you hear the story of the baby eagle that was hatched into a family of chickens? His whole life he grew up believing he was a chicken. After all, he lived in a chicken house, ate chicken food, and played chicken games.
>
> One day, while a fellow eagle was soaring through the air, he spotted the earthbound eagle scratching in the dirt with the other chickens below. He immediately flew down and, upon landing, asked him why he lived with and acted like the chickens, when he was, in fact, an eagle.
>
> The earthbound eagle was stunned to hear this news. If this were true, his whole life up to that point had been based on a lie! However, something deep inside of him made him *want* to believe that he was an eagle. *So he did.*
>
> Immediately, his fellow eagle began to show him how to glide above the clouds and teach him the natural ways of an eagle. It wasn't difficult for him to learn, because *this was the life he was born to live!*[11]

Are you ready to ditch that old way of life and begin to consistently live out the truth of your pure, holy, and righteous identity in Christ? Go ahead! You were reborn to fly, not to scratch around in the dirt.

If we fully understood the truth of our complete forgiveness and identification with Christ in His crucifixion, burial, resurrection, and ascension, Easter (Resurrection Sunday) would mean much, much more to us. It wasn't just three people who died that day at Golgotha; every believer in Christ died with Him. And three days later, when He was resurrected from the tomb, everyone who died with Him was reborn in His resurrection. Take some time to let that amazing truth sink in.

In Song 1:12, the King more fully reveals to the maiden what happened to her in the eternal spiritual realm through His crucifixion, burial, resurrection, and ascension. He longs for her to continually see herself as she truly is in Him—to hold self-image 3.

> "I am a saint who sometimes acts like a sinner. Not only did I receive forgiveness and a new nature at salvation, but the bad, old me—my sin nature—was crucified with Christ on the cross (Rom. 6:6; Gal. 2:20). I am a new creation because I am in Christ (2 Cor. 5:17). The desire of my new heart is *not* to sin, even though sometimes I still do."

He knows that as she acknowledges the truth of her new life in Him, she will begin to experience many more moments soaring above the difficulties of this world than she will scratching around in the dirt. And maybe—just maybe—she will be able to encourage the other eagles who believe they are chickens to do the same.

> ➢ Practically speaking, how do you plan to help yourself remain aware of your complete forgiveness and new identity in Christ?

The communion table also represents the place where the betrothal cup sits as negotiations take place between the prospective groom and the bride's father in the ancient Jewish marriage customs. Once the terms of the marriage contract were agreed to, the bride's father handed an empty cup to the groom. The groom then poured wine into the cup and drank from it, signifying his "I do." In our spiritual betrothal to Jesus, Father God offered this cup to Him in the garden of Gethsemane.

> He went a little beyond them, and fell on His face and prayed, saying, "My Father, if it is possible, let this cup pass from Me; yet not as I will, but as You will." (Matt. 26:39)

Jesus willingly drank from the betrothal cup, saying "I do" when He poured out His life on the cross for us.

After the Jewish bridegroom drank from the cup, he placed it in front of the girl he wanted to marry. With his heart pounding in his chest and his breath taken, the question utmost in his mind was, *Will she pick up the cup and drink from it?*

If she did not drink from the cup, this meant she refused to be his wife, and the marriage process ended there. If, however, she picked up the cup and drank from it, this signified her acceptance of his offer of marriage—her "I do." Even though many believers are unaware that Christ's offer of eternal life is a marriage proposal, we are saying "I do" and drinking from the betrothal cup when we receive His life at salvation.

Communion is a beautiful symbol of Christ's proposal to us and our reception of His life when we believe in (into) Him. Each time we partake of the bread and the juice, we can commemorate our first saying yes to Him.

When you eat the bread, remember that it symbolizes your identification with Christ in His crucifixion, burial, resurrection, and ascension. When you drink the juice, remember that it not only symbolizes the complete forgiveness you have through His shed blood, but it also symbolizes your saying yes to His proposal of marriage. In short, the communion table is a place where we can remember and celebrate our forever life in Him!

One way that helps me to appreciate the fullness of what Christ did for me is to watch Mel Gibson's 2003 epic motion picture, *The Passion of the Christ*. This movie could have been titled *The Man Who Gave All for Love*. Watch it when you want to fan the flame of love in your heart for your Spiritual Bridegroom. This movie poignantly portrays the lengths He went to in order to capture our hearts and secure us as His eternal bride.

There is something about movies and music that can touch places in our emotions where mere words cannot. A classic secular song that could have been on the soundtrack of Gibson's movie is "(Everything I Do) I Do It for You," first performed by Bryan Adams in the 1991 feature film, *Robin Hood: Prince of Thieves*. Its lyrics reflect the heart of a man who was willing to do anything—including dying—for the love of his life. And that is exactly what Jesus did to secure us as His eternal bride.

My perfume gave forth its fragrance

As the King reveals the fullness of His finished work on the cross—the maiden's complete forgiveness and identification with Him in His death, burial, resurrection, and ascension—her perfume gave forth its fragrance. What is her perfume and what fragrance does it emit?

The Hebrew word for *perfume* is *nerd* and refers to a costly and precious spice obtained from crushing and distilling the underground stems of the spikenard plant into a thick aromatic oil.¹² Spikenard is expensive because it is harvested from the Himalayan Mountains at altitudes between ten thousand and sixteen thousand feet.¹³

The word *fragrance* first occurred in Song 1:3 and referred to the King's aromatic affections (oils) for the Shulammite. He was crushed to the point of death so that she could experience His cherishing love and exuberant life forever (Isa. 53:5). When she realizes and experiences the fullness of His love and life through intimacy with His indwelling Spirit, she cannot help but express His fragrance through her life (2 Cor. 2:14–15). Endued with His love, she can now love Him, herself, and others. First John 4:19 says, "We love, because He first loved us."

The words of Song 1:12 could serve as a prophetic title for the passage in John's gospel where Mary of Bethany anoints Jesus just days before His crucifixion.

While the King Was at His Table, My Perfume Gave Forth Its Fragrance

> Jesus, therefore, six days before the Passover, came to Bethany where Lazarus was, whom Jesus had raised from the dead. So they made Him a supper there, and Martha was serving; but Lazarus was one of those reclining at the table with Him. Mary then took a pound of very costly perfume of pure nard, and anointed the feet of Jesus and wiped His feet with her hair; and the house was filled with the fragrance of the perfume. But Judas Iscariot, one of His disciples, who was intending to betray Him, said, "Why was this perfume not sold for three hundred denarii and given to poor people?" Now he said this, not because he was concerned about the poor, but because he was a thief, and as he had the money box, he used to pilfer what was put into it. Therefore Jesus said, "Let her alone, so that she may keep it for the day of My burial. For you always have the poor with you, but you do not always have Me." (John 12:1–8)

In Jesus' day, a pound of pure nard was worth three hundred denarii, approximately a year's wages. For a young girl of thirteen or fourteen to be in possession of such a costly item likely meant that this was Mary's dowry—all that she would take into her earthly marriage. The fact that she "wasted it" (in the eyes of Judas) on Jesus could be an indication that she knew *He* would be her eternal Spiritual Husband. Another strong indicator that Mary may have known this truth was that her head was uncovered, exposing her hair. In ancient Jewish culture, women's hair was considered sensual; therefore, they only removed their head covering in the presence of their husbands.

Although Scripture does not actually record Jesus telling Mary of Bethany to anoint

Him for burial, I believe it's possible that He could have shared the intimate details of His imminent death with her as she spent hours at His feet, hanging on His every word (Luke 10:38–42).

Song 1:12 could be summarized in this way: the Shulammite maiden is overwhelmed by the King's revelation of His communion table. In salvation, He forgave the sins of her lifetime through the shedding of His blood and caused her to be a coparticipant in the death, burial, resurrection, and ascension of His body—giving her a brand-new eternal identity. When we, like the maiden, experience these amazing truths as personal revelation, we will not be able to keep from exuding His fragrance—His cherishing love and exuberant life—affecting everyone we come into contact with.

In day 3 of our study, the maiden will begin to describe her Shepherd-King more intimately as a result of this revelation of her identification (union) with Him in His crucifixion, burial, resurrection, and ascension.

> ➢ What is your Bridegroom speaking to you through today's study? How will you respond?

Day 3

Through her Shepherd-King's gentle encouragement, endearing words of affection, and His revelation of her complete forgiveness, identity change, and eternal union with Him, the maiden has fallen head over heels in love with Him. The One whose heart she has captured has now unequivocally captured hers. How could she *not* be in love with the One who gave His life for her so that she could be His forever?

Now, let's look at today's focal verse to see how experiencing His intense love for her changes the way she describes Him:

> **"My beloved is to me a pouch of myrrh**
> **Which lies all night between my breasts."**
> **—Song 1:13**

My beloved is to me

This is the first of twenty-six times in the entire Song that the maiden refers to her Shepherd-King as *my Beloved*, and the first of nine times in this study. It is also the first time she describes Him as "belonging to her" through the use of the personal possessive *my*. No wonder this brief book of the Bible has been described as the "divine romance of Christ and His bride"!

When people are in love, they can't help but talk about their beloved to anyone with ears to listen. The Hebrew word for *beloved* is *dowd*. The word used to describe the King's love for the maiden in verses 2 and 4 is the same word that she uses to describe "His person" in this verse. His love is who He is and what He does (1 John 4:8, 16). Love *loves*.

As stated earlier in our discussion of Song 1:2, *dowd* comes from a word that means "to boil." When the maiden refers to her Shepherd-King as *my Beloved*, she is saying, "He is the One whose heart burns for me!"

She referred to Him as *the king* in verses 4 and 12 and indirectly referred to Him as a *shepherd* in verse 7. It is no coincidence that she does not refer to Him as *my Beloved* until after He calls her *most beautiful among women*, *My darling*, and *lovely*. How could we refer to Jesus as *my Beloved*—the One whose heart burns for me—unless we have first personally embraced His burning heart for us?

Sadly, most of us will not allow ourselves to experience His lavishing love unless we believe we have earned it. Extravagant affection poured out on one so undeserving flies in the face of performance-based flesh. We need to *know that we know that we know* that we can never earn His passionate love. It is a free gift from our Beloved to be opened, enjoyed, and celebrated (Rom. 3:24; 5:15–17; 6:23).

Aren't the best gifts the ones given for no other reason than "just because I love you"? We need to ask our Beloved to open our eyes to the extravagant love He showers on us every moment of every day because we are in Him, and He is perfect love.

If we only allow ourselves to embrace His love when we feel like we've done something to deserve it, we are living under the law of works instead of the law of grace:

> The law of works means relating to God on the basis of what we do. When we live under this law of works, the more condemned we are in our weakness, the more proud we will be in our victory. The more our weakness wipes out our confidence, the more our success will build up our pride. We cannot measure our success by our own works and ride the roller coaster of legalism—down into condemnation and up into pride. He wants us to stand before Him knowing that we only stand secure because of what He did and who He is. That is true grace.

The law of grace means relating to God on the basis of who we are in His heart. There is nothing a human heart can do in the context of works, actions, or holiness to motivate God to enjoy them. There is no righteousness you can add to yourself to promote His kindness toward you. The more we find God's enjoyment of us in the midst of our weakness, the more protected we will be in the midst of our promotion. The more confident we are before God in our weakness, the more gratitude and humility we will have in our victory. The reason for this is that when we are confident in the midst of weakness, it reflects the fact that our confidence is truly anchored in God's grace and not in our own strength.[14]

When we live under the law of works, the more condemned we are in our weakness, the more proud we will be in our victory. Why is that? Because we mistakenly believe it is all about our performance. When we truly get a revelation of His grace, we will see that there is nothing we can *do* to add to our righteousness or motivate our Beloved to enjoy us. He has *already* made us completely righteous and enjoyable!

You may need to meditate on this excerpt on a regular basis to remind yourself that your confidence and security are found in the finished work of Christ (grace) and not what you do or don't do (law). Please don't wait until you feel like you have earned or deserved His love to embrace and enjoy it. He loves and delights in you in the same degree at all times, whether you are experiencing great victory or miserable defeat.

> ➢ Ask your Beloved to cause you to embrace His love for and enjoyment of you—regardless of what you do or don't do—so that these truths can become part of your autopilot. Then, keep your spiritual eyes and ears peeled, and record your experiences in the following space.

A pouch of myrrh

The maiden's Shepherd-King used the language of metaphor in comparing her to His exquisite mare in verse 9. Now, in verses 13–14, the maiden uses metaphors to convey what He means to her.

In our study of verse 3, we found that the Hebrew meaning of *myrrh* was "bitter" and its Greek meaning was "burial spice." With the images of His bitter suffering and death on the cross freshly painted on her mind—through His revelation of the communion table—she likens her Beloved to a pouch of myrrh.

The word *pouch* comes from the Hebrew root word *tsarar*, which means "to bind together."[15] The apostle Paul wrote that believers are "always carrying about in the body the dying of Jesus, so that the life of Jesus also may be manifested in our body" (2 Cor. 4:10). We were bound together with Christ in His death (co-crucifixion) so that we could be raised to new life in His resurrection and allow Him to express His life through ours (Rom. 6:6; Gal. 2:20; 1 Pet. 1:3).

Pouch also refers to "a bundle." A *bundle* is "a number of things considered together."[16] So, a pouch of myrrh signifies the abundance of benefits available for us to enjoy because of our Beloved's bitter suffering and death on the cross.

Which lies all night

If we had lived during Solomon's reign (970 BC–931 BC), we would better understand the advantages of wearing a pouch of myrrh around our necks for refreshment. In that era, people didn't bathe or wash every day. They would sometimes wear a pouch of myrrh to bed so that its fragrance would mask their body odor and refresh them during the night as they slept. Aren't you glad that God didn't choose for you to live during that time period? (Acts 17:26).

Night is symbolic of our Beloved's bodily absence. Because we have not yet laid eyes on His physical presence, this walk of faith on earth can often feel like nighttime. Still, we can take heart because His indwelling presence never leaves us. First Peter 1:8 says, "You love him even though you have never seen him. Though you do not see him now, you trust him; and you rejoice with a glorious, inexpressible joy" (NLT). If we will acknowledge our Beloved's indwelling presence and meditate on spiritual truth at all times (both the good times and the dark), we will consistently experience and express His cherishing love and exuberant life.

Between my breasts

The maiden's breasts in the last phrase of verse 13 symbolize the "faith and love" she now possesses through union with her Beloved. *Faith* and *love* are mentioned six times throughout the Song: twice by her (1:13; 8:10), three times by her Beloved (4:5; 7:7; 7:8), and once by the daughters of Jerusalem (7:3). There must be a strong correlation between faith and love because these two words occur together in twenty-six verses in the New Testament. Let's take a look at some of these:

- "If I have the gift of prophecy, and know all mysteries and all knowledge; and if I have all faith, so as to remove mountains, but do not have love, I am nothing" (1 Cor. 13:2).

- "In Christ Jesus neither circumcision nor uncircumcision means anything, but faith working through love" (Gal. 5:6).
- "But since we are of the day, let us be sober, having put on the breastplate of faith and love" (1 Thess. 5:8).
- "The grace of our Lord was more than abundant, with the faith and love which are found in Christ Jesus" (1 Tim. 1:14).

These verses show us that faith without love means nothing, faith works through love, faith and love together form a breastplate, and faith and love are found in Christ Jesus. Faith and love go together. You can't express one without the other when you are expressing Christ.

Did you happen to notice in 1 Thessalonians 5:8 that the apostle Paul tells us that we are *of the day*? This means that even though we live in the night of this world—the absence of Jesus' physical presence—we are not *of* the night. We belong to the Morning Star (2 Pet. 1:19). We have all the faith and love we need to walk through the night of this world because of our Beloved's indwelling presence.

Colossians 1:4 is another wonderful Scripture where we find faith and love connected:

> We have heard of your *faith* in Christ Jesus, *the leaning of your entire human personality on Him in absolute trust and confidence in His power, wisdom, and goodness*, and of the *love* which you have and show for all the saints, God's consecrated ones. (AMPC)

Here we find that wonderful definition of faith again: "the leaning of your entire human personality on Him in absolute trust and confidence in His power, wisdom, and goodness." If we are exercising the faith He has given us through His indwelling Spirit—leaning on Him in absolute trust and confidence in His power, wisdom, and goodness—we will experience His cherishing *love* for us and express it to others.

- ➤ If you are not regularly experiencing His refreshing presence and expressing love to others, ask yourself, "Am I consistently leaning on Him in absolute trust and confidence in His power, His wisdom, and His goodness?" If your answer is no, ask Him to enable you to in the form of a prayer in the following space. Then, don't forget to record how He faithfully answers your prayer.

In the third and final study of the Song, we will find that the maiden has become very adept at leaning on her Beloved's refreshing, indwelling Spirit through much practice (Song 8:5). The more we learn to lean on our Beloved in every circumstance of our lives, the more He proves Himself to be everything we could ever need or want.

In the next verse, the maiden continues to use metaphorical language to describe yet another wonderful aspect of her Beloved.

> **"My beloved is to me a cluster of henna blossoms**
> **In the vineyards of Engedi."**
> —Song 1:14

My beloved is to me a cluster of henna blossoms

In Solomon's day, the Hebrew people used the word *cluster* to describe a man of eminent virtue and knowledge. When the maiden describes her Beloved as *a cluster of henna blossoms*, she is saying, "This is a man that has all things in him."[17] I love that! Our Beloved is our All in All, our Everything. The apostle John expressed this well in his gospel.

> In the beginning was the Word, and the Word was with God, and the Word was God. He was in the beginning with God. All things came into being through Him, and apart from Him nothing came into being that has come into being. In Him was life, and the life was the Light of men. (John 1:1–4)

Through our Beloved, all things came into being. Let's chew on that for a minute. This *Man in whom is everything* now lives *in us* because of His finished work on the cross. Amazing. Grace.

Henna means "price of a life, ransom."[18] A rich red dye is made from crushing the leaves of the henna plant. The symbolism here is as plain as the noses on our faces. As a result of the crushing our Beloved received, His precious blood was poured out as our ransom price—the price He paid to obtain us as His bride (Isa. 53:5).

It is customary for a bride from Pakistan, India, Africa, or the Middle East to apply henna dye as a paste to the palms of her hands and the soles of her feet on the night before her wedding. Through this tradition, the bride is declaring that there is an eternal blood bond between herself and her bridegroom. She is saying, *I belong to him forever!*

The leaves of the henna plant weren't the only part of the plant that represented Christ:

> The Henna flowers are heavy with fragrance and hang in beautiful cream white clusters against their bright green leaves. The flowers and leaves present such richness of perfume, and the diversity of color and beauty, as are a fitting emblem of Christ, who embraces all the power and wonderful attributes of the Godhead. 'For in Him dwells all the fullness of the Godhead bodily.' Just as the myrrh was hidden away in the bosom and perfumed the person from within, so the henna flowers were used by oriental women to deck and adorn their persons without. The fragrance of the myrrh is perceptible to others, but they neither see nor know what it is nor where it is hidden. The henna flowers are not only smelled, but seen and admired by all.
>
> The Beloved, as the cluster of Henna flowers, is that decking and ornamenting of ourselves with His attributes in our daily walk, which is seen, recognized and enjoyed by all about us. But before we can be adorned with this outward adorning, He must become to us as the little bundle of Myrrh. As we partake of His death and feed upon Him, then we are able to put on these Henna flowers through His ransom price. The world will judge our Christ by the way we look, and by what they see in you and me.[19]

What beautiful imagery we find in this excerpt: "The Beloved, as the cluster of Henna flowers, is that decking and ornamenting of ourselves with His attributes in our daily walk, which is seen, recognized and enjoyed by all about us."

While the pouch of myrrh signifies the abundance of benefits the maiden derives from experiencing her Beloved's "indwelling" life; the cluster of henna blossoms signifies the abundance of benefits that others enjoy through the "outward expression" of His life through hers.

Whether we realize it or not, people who know we are Christians judge our Beloved by our outward lives. While living in this world, we have the tremendous honor and privilege of allowing the fragrant attributes of His indwelling life to be expressed through us. Let's not take it for granted; let's bring glory to His name in all that we say and do! (1 Cor. 6:20; 7:23).

In the last phrase of Song 1:14, we find the geographical location of the aromatic henna blossoms.

In the vineyards of Engedi

En Gedi is an oasis in Israel, located along the west coast of the Dead Sea, thirty-five miles southeast of Jerusalem. En Gedi's warm springs give birth to its rich vegetation. Israel's only naturally occurring waterfall is found in this oasis; therefore, it should come as no surprise that *Engedi* means "fountain of the lamb."[20]

Experiencing Christ's cherishing love and exuberant life in the midst of the harsh difficulties of this world is like drinking deeply of and immersing ourselves in a refreshing oasis in the middle of a hot, dry desert region. You've probably seen the commercial where the guy is walking through the desert, eyes a vending machine filled with iced tea, takes a drink of it, and is immediately plunged into a pool of crystal blue water. Ahhh! Nothing compares to the enjoyment of Christ's thirst-quenching, rejuvenating presence when you are parched.

At the time of Solomon's writing, En Gedi was populated with vineyards surrounded by short hedges of henna trees. These dense, thorny hedges protected the vineyard's soil against wind erosion and the valuable grape crops from hungry animals. Christ as *a cluster of henna blossoms in the vineyards of Engedi* represents His refreshing protection of our hearts while we live in this world. Regardless of our circumstances, we are forever sealed and protected in Him (2 Cor. 1:22; Eph. 1:13; 4:30).

➤ Describe a time in your life when you experienced Christ as "a cluster of henna blossoms in the vineyards of Engedi."

Through the maiden's descriptions of her Beloved, it is evident that He is causing her to experience for herself (verse 13) and express to the world around her (verse 14) His cherishing love and exuberant life. Elated that she is seeking Him alone to meet her needs and growing in her knowledge of who He is in her and who she is in Him, the beloved Shepherd-King responds to the maiden with an even greater intensity than before.

> **"How beautiful you are, my darling,**
> **How beautiful you are!**
> **Your eyes are like doves."**
> — **Song 1:15**

How beautiful you are, my darling, How beautiful you are!
These are the words of a man in love! He is overcome by His darling maiden's beauty, calling her *beautiful* twice in the same breath. He is telling her that her inward beauty—the beauty of her new heart—is now being outwardly manifested in her words and actions. In our discussion of Song 1:8, we found that *beautiful* means "to be bright, handsome, and fair." She is absolutely radiant!

What has caused this change in her outward appearance? In verses 5–7, she was downcast and focused on her failures, pleading with her Shepherd-King for His guidance. He responded to her in verses 8–12 by describing her beauty in Him and directing her to fill her mind with the truths of her new identity. He revealed the basis for her inward beauty—her union with Him in His crucifixion, burial, resurrection, and ascension. Her outward radiance is the result of seeking Him and seeing her inward beauty in Him. Psalm 34:5 says, "They looked to Him and were radiant, and their faces will never be ashamed."

In the Sunday morning service at our church, the lights are almost always dimmed during the prayer time. A young boy, three rows up and to the left of where I was sitting, recently caught my attention. He was looking down, and his face was glowing. No, he wasn't having a spiritual experience, if that's what you were thinking. He was looking at his smartphone and was radiant. I was confident he was looking at Scripture, though—he was sitting right next to his mother! When I saw him, I immediately thought of Psalm 34:5 and grinned. I love our Beloved's sense of humor.

As I approached the big five-oh, I could hardly believe it. It wasn't that long ago when I thought someone in his or her fifties was *ancient*. With the exception of experiencing a few aches and pains every now and then, I didn't feel anywhere near fifty. I said, "I didn't *feel* anywhere near fifty." I didn't say I didn't look it.

Just ask the sales lady at the counter of one of our local department stores. While I was doing some holiday shopping a few years ago, she asked me if I had the special discount card for people who were fifty and older. Having recently turned forty-eight, I smiled and politely responded, "I'm not fifty yet but getting close." No, I'm not holding a grudge. No, *really*. All kidding aside, with each passing year in my Beloved, life just keeps getting sweeter and sweeter. The apostle Paul speaks of the believer's *internal* fountain of youth in his second letter to the church at Corinth: "Therefore we do not lose heart, but though our outer man is decaying, yet our inner man is being renewed day by day" (2 Cor. 4:16).

As evidenced by the store clerk's assumption about my age, wrinkles have popped up all over my face (like uninvited guests) in the past few years. I am beginning to understand why all the fuss about creams, chemical peels, Botox, and plastic surgery, and asking my Beloved to cause me to age *gracefully* and *gratefully*.

Wouldn't it be wonderful if we could find a picture of how we wanted to look and just stare at it until we were magically transformed into that image? I'm dreaming again, I know, but do you realize that we have a promise greater than that of physical transformation? The only thing it costs us is our time and focus. The Word of God tells us that as we gaze upon His glory, we are being transformed into His same image. This principle of being "transformed by beholding" comes from 2 Corinthians 3:18:

> Now all of us, with our faces unveiled, reflect the glory of the Lord as if we are mirrors; and so we are being transformed, metamorphosed, into His same image from one radiance of glory to another, just as the Spirit of the Lord accomplishes it. (VOICE)

Even though we cannot yet see our Beloved face to face, we *can* gaze on His glorious person by spending focused time with Him and meditating on what His Word says about who He is in us and who we are in Him. As we do this, our lives will become a radiant reflection of Him.

Physical beauty will continue to fade as we age and become more gravitationally challenged, but spiritual transformation lasts forever. Great hope and comfort can be found in knowing this.

Oh, and by the way, one day we will experience the complete package of our salvation when we get our glorified bodies—bodies saturated with divine, life-giving energy that will live forever in perfect union with Jesus (1 Cor. 15:51–57). Doesn't that sound wonderful? The older I get, the more I appreciate and look forward to the fulfillment of this incredible promise.

In day 4 of this week's study, we will look at one particular aspect of the maiden's beauty that appears to overwhelm her beloved Shepherd-King—and her swooning response when He tells her what it is.

> ➤ What is your Bridegroom speaking to you through today's study? How will you respond?

Day 4

We begin today's study in the middle of Song 1:15. Here we find the beloved Shepherd-King responding to the maiden's description of Him after He revealed to her the fullness of His finished work on the cross and her lovely new identity in Him. In the two opening lines, He first spoke of her inward beauty and then of the outward manifestation of her inward beauty. In the last line, He reveals the catalyst for this transformation.

> **"How beautiful you are, my darling,**
> **How beautiful you are!**
> **Your eyes are like doves."**
> **—Song 1:15**

Your eyes are like doves
This is the first of two occurrences in the Song where He tells His darling maiden that her eyes are like doves (see also Song 4:1). In three additional places in the Song, He extends the description by addressing her as my dove (Song 2:14; 5:2; 6:9). With this many references comparing His bride to a dove in this short book of the Bible, it is important for us to understand what the beloved Shepherd-King means when He says that we have *eyes like doves*.

All species of doves are generally seen in pairs because they mate for life—'til death do they part. This is why doves are often called "love birds" and are a common symbol used in wedding announcements, favors, and other memorabilia.

Have you ever had the experience of seeing a pair of these loyal lovers in the middle of the highway, gazing at each other, totally oblivious to the fact that you are approximately three seconds away from rocking their world? I have. And I remember thinking, *If they don't get out of the way* … Sad to say, that particular love story didn't end in Happily Ever After.

Because vision is a bird's most acute sense, you would think this would aid in their survival rate. While it is true that doves have a wide vision span due to their eyes being on both sides of their heads, when they are using both eyes together to focus on what's right in front of them (binocular vision), they cannot see in their periphery—they cannot focus on two things at the same time. When the love of their life is right in front of them, you can be sure that the rest of the world is completely shut out. The saying, "Love is blind" takes on a whole new meaning for doves.

Can you imagine being so enamored with your Beloved that even when outward circumstances rock your world, you can still say, "It is well with my soul"? Horatio Spafford was … and did. Horatio was a prominent American lawyer in Chicago during the 1860s. He and his wife, Anna, were supporters and close friends of the well-known evangelist Dwight L. Moody.

Beginning in 1870 with the death of their four-year-old son to pneumonia, a series of tragic events unfolded in the Spaffords' lives. A year later, the Great Chicago Fire destroyed most of their real estate investments when the city was reduced to ashes. Those events alone would have been enough to shake the foundation of anyone's faith.

In the fall of 1873, the family planned to leave by steamship on a European vacation. Horatio was unexpectedly delayed by business and sent his wife and four daughters, ages two to eleven, ahead of him, planning to join them later. On November 2, within hours of setting sail, the luxury steamer was accidentally rammed by an iron British sailing ship.

The steamer sank within twelve minutes and 226 of the 313 passengers and crew drowned. All four of the Spaffords' daughters were among those who died. Anna was found floating unconscious on a plank of wood and was rescued by the crew of the British ship. Nine days later, after landing in Cardiff, Wales, Anna sent her husband a Western Union telegram that read, in part, "Saved alone. What shall I do …"[21] A pastor and fellow survivor with Anna recalled her saying afterward, "God gave me four daughters. Now they have been taken from me. Someday I will understand why."[22]

After receiving Anna's telegram, Horatio left immediately by ship from Chicago to be with her. While crossing the Atlantic, the captain of the ship called Horatio to his cabin to tell him they were passing over the area where his four daughters drowned. (My soul aches as I imagine that sacred moment in time.)

Later, Horatio wrote to Anna's half-sister, Rachel: "On Thursday last we passed over the spot where she went down, in mid-ocean, the waters three miles deep. But I do not think of our dear ones there. They are safe, folded, the dear lambs."[23] Soon after that, in memory of his four daughters, Horatio penned "It Is Well with My Soul"—one of the most influential and enduring Christian hymns ever known. The song reflects one who is unwavering in his faith, even when everything in his world falls apart.

Both Horatio and Anna kept their eyes firmly fixed on Jesus throughout the tragic events of their lives. To have that kind of undistracted devotion is awe-inspiring. No matter what we go through while living on planet earth in this temporary time realm, it is possible to remain hopefully confident with *eyes like doves* on our Beloved (Matt. 19:26).

Earlier in our discussion of Song 1:8, we found that Solomon's father, King David, also had eyes like doves for the Lord.

> If you have Internet access, go to BibleGateway.com, find Psalm 27:4 from *The Message*, and write it in the following space.

King David longed to live continually with the Lord, contemplate His beauty, and study at His feet. Unlike David, believers in Christ are *never* without the Lord. But if we don't acknowledge that truth, contemplate His beauty, and study at His feet, we won't enjoy the benefits of His continual presence.

One of the greatest challenges facing believers in this world of multitasking and constant distraction is keeping our focus on Jesus. The author of Hebrews encourages us to lay aside everything that would keep us from gazing on the One who embraced His cross—so that He could embrace His bride forever (Heb. 12:1–2).

Brother Lawrence, a seventeenth-century Franciscan monk, was another saint who had *eyes like doves* for the Lord. He is still inspiring many in the body of Christ through his timeless classic, *The Practice of the Presence of God*. In this small book, he shares how he developed the habit of remaining aware of God's presence with him in every part of his life, from his daily prayers to cooking and cleaning to repairing sandals. He reminds us that not one aspect of our lives is mundane as long as we recognize God's presence with us at all times. The following is one of my favorite quotes from this tiny treasure:

> There is not in the world a kind of life more sweet and delightful than that of continual conversation with God. Those only can comprehend it who practice and experience it.[24]

Those only can comprehend it who practice and experience it. Continual conversation with God. Doesn't that sound inviting? Our focus will determine what we experience. There's no time like the present to begin practicing our Beloved's presence! Let's join the Shulammite, the Spaffords, King David, Brother Lawrence, and countless other believers throughout the ages who had eyes like doves for the Lord and learn how to enjoy the sweet and delightful life we have in Him.

> Ask your Beloved to cause you to enjoy His presence as you go about your day, conversing with Him and trusting Him to accomplish all your tasks—whether

large or small—through you. When you get distracted and realize you've taken your focus off of Him, don't beat yourself up. Thank Him for the gentle nudge and continue to enjoy His presence.

Have you ever given someone a compliment and before the last word rolls off your tongue, that person is complimenting you in return? That is exactly what is happening in the next verse of the Song. After the beloved Shepherd-King tells the dove-eyed maiden she is beautiful inside and out, she ardently responds,

> **"How handsome you are, my beloved,**
> **And so pleasant!**
> **Indeed, our couch is luxuriant!"**
> **—Song 1:16**

How handsome you are, my beloved, And so pleasant!
This is the first of five times throughout the Song that the maiden directly addresses Him as *my Beloved*. If this dialogue were to occur in a public place, we would likely hear, "Get a room, will ya?" from an annoyed observer. The exchanges between the maiden and her Beloved are definitely getting more intimate.

When the maiden tells her Beloved how handsome He is, she is saying, "Your beauty made me beautiful." Enraptured by His beauty, she adds as an afterthought, "And so pleasant!" The word *pleasant* comes from the Hebrew root word *naem*, which means "delightful, sweet, lovely, and agreeable."[25] She is taking great pleasure in the intimacy she is experiencing with Him.

As Christ's bride, we would do well to remember that we cannot take great pleasure in Him unless we first understand and experience the great pleasure He takes in us. If you need a refreshing reminder of how much your Beloved enjoys you, just ask Him! He delights in revealing His pleasure in you (Zeph. 3:17).

Indeed, our couch is luxuriant!
This declaration is evidence that her Beloved has fulfilled the cry of her heart from verse 7: "Where do you feed your flock and *where do you make it lie down at noon?*" When referring to *our couch*, she is speaking of their place of rest and intimacy. At this moment, Christ's bride is sitting with Him on a celestial sofa (Eph. 2:6). (I'd like to call it a *loveseat*.)

Luxuriant means "fresh, green, and flourishing."[26] Green is the color of new life—the life of Christ being lived through our lives. At this point in the Song, the maiden is experiencing His cherishing love and exuberant life and expressing her love for Him in response.

➤ Are you regularly enjoying Christ's cherishing love and exuberant life? If yes, use the following space to give some specific examples. If no, do you know why you aren't? Write a prayer that expresses the desire of your heart to enjoy Him more fully.

In the final verse of the first chapter of the Song, the maiden goes from describing their couch—their place of shared rest and intimacy—to depicting the very foundation on which it sits *and* its protective covering.

> **"The beams of our houses are cedars,**
> **Our rafters, cypresses."**
> **—Song 1:17**

The beams of our houses are cedars

Most translations use the singular *house* instead of *houses*. The house she is referring to is the place where she and her Beloved dwell together in intimacy—her *new heart*. This would not have been possible, had her Beloved not come to this earth to live as a man in human flesh.

Humans are sometimes compared to trees in the Word of God (Ps. 1:3; Jer. 17:8; Isa. 61:3). The tree of life in the garden of Eden in Genesis and the New Jerusalem in Revelation both symbolize Christ's perfect humanity.

The maiden describes the beams of the house that she and her Beloved share as being made from cedar. A cedar tree is one of the strongest, most fragrant, rot-resistant, bug-repelling trees in the world. Because of its hardy qualities, most of the wood in Solomon's temple came from these trees (see 1 Kings 6). Interestingly, throughout the temple the cedar was overlaid with gold, signifying both the humanity (cedar) and divinity (gold) of Jesus.

The beams of a house are the heavy timbers that form the foundation and hold up its superstructure. The cedar beams in the Song speak of "Jesus' perfect Manhood."[27] In order to redeem fallen man, Jesus came to earth in the flesh and lived a sinless life. His perfect humanity laid the foundation for our new life in Him. In his first letter to the Corinthians, Paul wrote, "For no man can lay a foundation other than the one which is laid, which is Jesus Christ" (3:11).

Our rafters, cypresses

These cypress rafters are the timbers that form the framework of the roof of a house. This wood is also very hard, fragrant, and durable. Cypress trees have dark and gloomy evergreen foliage and are commonly found in Judean graveyards. The cypress rafters in the Song symbolize "Jesus' death on the cross."[28] If it were not for the perfect manhood (cedars) and death (cypresses) of Jesus, this maiden could not enjoy intimate union with her Beloved within her new heart.

When framing a house, the foundational beams go on first and the rafters of the roof go on last. Jesus became the God-Man first (cedar beams), before He died on the cross (cypress rafters), in order to give us new life in His resurrection (1 Pet. 1:3). The symbolism found in the Song is fascinating!

While we are on the subject of building houses, before Jesus went to the cross He told His disciples that He was going away to prepare a dwelling place for them in His Father's house.

> "In My Father's house are many dwelling places; if it were not so, I would have told you; for I go to prepare a place for you. If I go and prepare a place for you, I will come again and receive you to Myself, that where I am, there you may be also." (John 14:2–3)

As mentioned previously, in the ancient Jewish marriage customs, the prospective groom left his bride as soon as their betrothal was official and went back to his father's house to begin building a room onto it. This is where their marriage would one day be consummated and where they would live together as husband and wife.

Interestingly enough, the groom didn't get to decide when this room was ready for his new bride. It was up to his father to determine when it was completely finished. Then, he would tell his son that he could go get his bride and bring her home. This paints a beautiful picture of our betrothal to Christ at salvation. Our Beloved (His actual, physical presence) has gone away to prepare a place for us to live with Him in eternal wedded bliss (in the spiritual sense, we already do). He will return for us when Father God says it is time (Matt. 24:36; Mark 13:32).

A few years ago, I was at the checkout counter of one of my favorite downtown shops, visiting with the couple who owned it. They are believers, so we usually end up talking about the Lord. The husband began to describe a shape that he had seen in the sky earlier that week, saying it was "fascinating and perfectly sculpted." He had never before laid eyes on anything like it and was sure God was speaking through His celestial handiwork.

When he drew what he'd seen on a piece of paper, I said, "That looks like a rooftop. You know, Jesus has gone to prepare a place for His bride. Maybe God is trying to tell us something." A couple of months later, I shared this with our ministry team at a meeting, and one of the ladies said, "Well, you know, the *roof* is the last thing to go on." Immediately, I realized that the Lord's message was, *It won't be long before I send My Son to get His bride* (1 Thess. 4:17). About a week later, I came across this passage of Scripture:

> The heavens proclaim the glory of God. The skies display his craftsmanship. Day after day they continue to speak; night after night they make him known. They speak without a sound or word; their voice is never heard. Yet their message has gone throughout the earth, and their words to all the world. God has made a home in the heavens for the sun. It bursts forth like a radiant bridegroom after his wedding. (Ps. 19:1–5 NLT)

I love how the *sun* (Son) is compared to a radiant bridegroom in this passage. The older I get, the closer I am to seeing the face of my Bridegroom—the resurrected God-Man in all His glory! If I had my druthers, I would still be living on planet earth when Jesus returns in the air to meet His bride and take her home with Him to heaven. There are times, though, when I have such an overwhelming desire to be with Him (in His physical presence) I can hardly stand it.

One cold, damp November day, while I was pulling into one of our local dollar stores, this longing caught me by surprise. It was a good thing I was parking because I started bawling like a baby when the melody and words of a song on the radio caused that desire to surface.

It reminded me of a time when I was missing my mom (she went to be with Jesus in 2006), and I experienced what the pamphlet from the funeral home called a "grief-burst." This fresh flood of tears was a combination of my missing Jesus and feeling His missing me at the same time. The song that was playing was "Finally Home" by Kerrie Roberts. Its lyrics describe how good it feels to go home where you are loved unconditionally and how our ultimate home in heaven with Jesus will be far better than that. Beautiful. I still cry every time I hear it because I sense Jesus' strong desire to be face to face with His bride. And His desire for me makes me long to see Him even more.

God's Word tells us that He has given humanity an awareness of eternity, even though we can't fully comprehend it (Eccl. 3:11). I can only begin to imagine what heaven will be like. Although I am sure that heaven will be breathtaking, I'm convinced that it won't be the *place* that captures my heart; it will be a *Person*. Everything else will fade into the background of His radiant face. My Beloved will be my eternal home: "I saw no temple in it, for the Lord God the Almighty and the Lamb are its temple" (Rev. 21:22).

We have now reached the end of the first chapter of the Song. How I hope and pray that you are beginning to experience your Beloved's cherishing love and exuberant life in very personal ways.

In the last day of our study this week, we will unpack the first two verses of chapter 2. There, we will hear more evidence that the maiden's mind is being renewed with the truths of her lovely new identity in Christ. We will also get to hear more life-giving, encouraging words from her Beloved as He continues to tell her who she is.

> ➤ What is your Bridegroom speaking to you through today's study? How will you respond?

Day 5

The maiden has begun to experience the exhilarating fulfillment that comes from listening to the voice of her Beloved. Shared intimacy with Him is beginning to change the way she sees herself. She is growing in her awareness of His finished work on the cross—what He has *already* accomplished *for* her and *in* her. She has been completely forgiven for the sins of her lifetime and has been given a brand-new, righteousness-of-God identity (1 Cor. 6:17; 2 Cor. 5:17, 21). She really is who He says she is. Most beautiful among women. His darling. Lovely. Eyes like doves. These endearing, affirming words coming from a trustworthy suitor would melt the heart of any girl. (Guys, do the mental tweaking here—*spiritual role*, not physical gender.)

The maiden's response to her Beloved began in Song 1:16–17 and continues into the first verse of the second chapter.

> **"I am the rose of Sharon,**
> **The lily of the valleys."**
> **—Song 2:1**

When studying the Bible, it is important to keep in mind that the system of dividing it into chapter and verse was *man's* doing—not the original Author's. God wasn't up in heaven saying, "Solomon, we need to end this verse here and start a new one. And we need to close chapter 1 right here and begin chapter 2 with these words."

Unfortunately, Song 2:1 has been misinterpreted in some translations and commentaries as being spoken by Jesus (maybe because it is the start of a new chapter). As a result, various hymns, writings, and works of art have mistakenly referred to Him as being the rose of Sharon and the lily of the valley.

In this verse, we have proof that the Shulammite is beginning to see herself as she truly is because she describes herself quite differently from the previous roller-coaster adjectives of black—then lovely—then swarthy (Song 1:5–6). For the first time in this divine romance, the maiden affirms the truth of her new identity *out loud*:

I am the rose of Sharon

I recently watched the 1940 film adaptation of Steinbeck's novel, *The Grapes of Wrath*, for the first time. I couldn't help but grin when I heard the name of the eldest daughter of the Joad family. It was Rose of Sharon and pronounced "Rosasharn" by the other family members.

Rose of Sharon was the daughter of a poor Oklahoma sharecropper during the Great Depression. At the beginning of the movie, the entire twelve-member Joad family and an ex-preacher load up in a dilapidated 1926 Hudson sedan and head to California to look for work.

Rose of Sharon was a frail young woman, expecting her first child. Her husband, Connie, was overwhelmed by the responsibilities of marriage and impending fatherhood and abandoned her and their unborn baby not long after they arrived in California. His leaving literally broke her heart. In the novel, their baby is born dead—in all likelihood due to Rose of Sharon's loss of the will to live, coupled with her extreme malnutrition. Her dismal life actually lies in stark contrast to the *real* meaning of the rose of Sharon in the Song.

When the Shulammite maiden describes herself as the rose of Sharon, she is not referring to what we typically think of as a rose but to a sand lily. We know this because she gives it another name in her next breath: "I am the rose of Sharon, the lily of the valleys." This sand lily is not the lily of the valley of today—a small white, bell-shaped flower we commonly see in wedding arrangements. They are two different flowers.

The rose of Sharon, or sand lily, is found on the Sharon Plain, the sandy coastland of Israel. This piece of land stretches about ten miles wide between the Mediterranean Sea on the west and the mountains of Samaria on the east. From north to south, it runs about thirty miles in length from modern-day Haifa and Mount Carmel to the Yarkon River (which lies at the edge of the present city of Tel-Aviv). The port city of Caesarea is also located on the Sharon Plain. Today, this coastal plain is the most densely populated region of Israel.

The lily of the valleys

Lily comes from the Hebrew word *shuwshan*, which means "white, from the root."[29] In describing herself as a lily, the maiden is saying that her new heart (root) is pure (white). She is beginning to see herself as new and pure. Clean—not dirty.

The word *lily* is found thirteen times in the Old Testament, eight of which are in the Song (2:1–2, 16; 4:5; 5:13; 6:2–3; 7:2). Its frequent occurrence in this brief book highlights how important it is to our Beloved that we have an accurate view of our new, pure heart in Him.

Oh, how it pains me when I hear Christ's bride describing herself as "wicked and deceitful," while at the same time *trying* to be "holy." It is preposterous to think that we could consistently live a life that is inconsistent with the way we perceive ourselves! Please, please take Christ at His Word and believe that you are His pure, righteous, and holy bride.

The symbolism found in the sand lily is amazing. If you would like to see a photo of this lovely flower, search Google Images for "sand lily." Its flower is pure white and shaped like a crown. Notice also how its stem is bent as if it was bowing in humility. The full-grown sand lily can withstand extreme conditions because of its deep root system. Its fragrance is subtly sweet and exotic, blooming at the end of summer. This signifies "the flowering of the desolate land."[30]

In this description of the sand lily, we can see the once downcast Shulammite maiden blossoming into the beauty she was created to be, during the most difficult season of her life (Song 1:6). Because she is deeply rooted and grounded in her identity in Him, she can withstand the harsh circumstances of this world in His strength (John 16:33; Phil. 4:13). She will wear a crown in eternity because her Beloved wore a crown of thorns for her. In humility, she understands that the origin of her beauty is the union of her beautiful new spirit with His Spirit—both of which she received as grace gifts from her Beloved.

Some people sincerely believe that viewing themselves as lowly worms is true humility. I beg to differ. True humility is seeing ourselves the same way our Beloved sees us—as new creations united with His Spirit, equipped with everything we need to live a holy life. True humility is an understanding that *we are nothing apart from Him*, but at the same time realizing *we are not apart from Him*. Nor will we ever be. We live this life, all the while understanding that our Beloved is living through us as we trust Him (Rom. 8:11).

Until we understand who we are in Christ, we will have a tendency to focus on our natural inadequacies. If we belittle ourselves by dwelling on the shortcomings and failures of the flesh, it will ultimately lead to more walking by the flesh. What we focus on will develop in our lives.

It's just like taking a picture with a Polaroid instant camera. Remember those? Although their pictures weren't as clear as the ones we get with the digital cameras of today, we still got a picture of the bowl of fruit we were focusing on when we pressed the red button. *What we focus on will develop in our lives.* We would do well to remember that.

Christ longs for us to live out of an awareness and acknowledgment of our new identity in Him. When we do this, we take our minds off the insufficiency of the flesh and put our focus where it rightly belongs—the complete sufficiency of the One who indwells our new heart.

The Shulammite's description of herself as *the rose of Sharon, the lily of the valley* bears no resemblance to Rose of Sharon's bleak view of herself in Steinbeck's novel. This vulnerable young woman allowed her husband's abandonment of her to define her worth and value. She viewed herself as worthless, lost the will to live, and forfeited the life of their unborn child. Likewise, when the bride of Christ accepts a view of herself other than that of her Beloved's, spiritual fruit is sadly forfeited in her life. Love, joy, peace, patience, kindness, goodness, faithfulness, gentleness, and self-control are aborted when we do not affirm the truth of who we truly are in Him (Gal. 5:22–23).

> ➤ Are you beginning to see yourself through the eyes of your Beloved? If you are still accepting a false view of yourself, spiritual fruit is being aborted in your life. Ask Jesus to cause you to affirm your new identity in Him so that His fruit will be consistently expressed through your life.

As mentioned before, music can move us in ways that words by themselves cannot. "More Than Ashes" is a beautiful, inspiring song written by Tim Reimherr (performed by the Merchant Band) that could be the theme song for this section of the Song. It is penned from the maiden's perspective and expresses the heart of one who realizes who she is and who is looking forward to her majestic wedding day—when she will finally marry her Beloved.

After the maiden sees and affirms the truth of who she is in her Beloved, He elaborates on her description of herself, encouraging her all the more.

> **"Like a lily among thorns,**
> **So is my darling among the maidens."**
> **—Song 2:2**

Like a lily among thorns, so is my darling among the maidens

He contrasts His darling lily with the thorny maidens in this verse. As we discussed earlier in our section on Song 1:3, the Hebrew word for maidens in Song 2:2 is not the same word used for maidens in Song 1:3.

In the New American Standard Bible, the English word *maidens* is found a total of four times in the Song. However, there are two different Hebrew words given. *Almah* is found in Song 1:3 and 6:8 and means "virgins of marriageable age."[31] *Bath* is found in Song 2:2 and 6:9 and is the same word used for the daughters of Jerusalem throughout the Song.[32] I believe this was an oversight in the translation and should have read, "Like a lily among thorns, so is my darling among the *daughters of Jerusalem*."

Remember, the daughters of Jerusalem have not been awakened to divine intimacy with Christ. They are infants in Him, with little or no knowledge of their new identity. Their minds have not been renewed with the truth.

The beloved Shepherd-King is not contrasting His darling maiden's identity with that of the daughters of Jerusalem in this verse. They have the same identity (spiritual location)—they are both *in Christ*. Rather, He is contrasting their daily living. *Thorns* represent "man's independence from God, living in their natural strength."[33] He is saying that while the maiden is learning to live in dependence on Him—walking by His Spirit—the daughters' daily living continues to be characterized as walking by the flesh.

Song 2:2 has special significance to me, reminding me of something very precious that my Beloved spoke to me one morning while I was journaling. Some of my friends had been talking about the Lord giving them a new name like He did when he changed Abram's name to Abraham, Jacob's to Israel, Saul's to Paul, and so on. I remember thinking *and* saying to Him, "I want to know what my new name is." He immediately lavished me with a kiss by directing my attention to one of my favorite Thomas Kinkade prints called *The Garden of Prayer*.

This print captivated my heart the first time I saw it. I was immediately drawn into it. In this secret place of rendezvous, a stream of water runs alongside a beautifully ornate gazebo. Many times, my Beloved has given me pictures of us dancing there together. But there was one part of the picture I had never really noticed before.

That morning, He drew my attention to the white calla lilies strewn along the water's edge. I remembered then that most flowers have a specific meaning attached to them. So I did what every inquiring mind does today when they want to know something—I Googled it. I found the meaning of calla lily to be better than any name I could have imagined for myself: "magnificent beauty."[34] I heard my Beloved whisper to my heart, *Your new name is Magnificent Beauty*. What an amazing kiss! Now, every time I see a calla lily, I'm reminded of my new name.

➤ Has your Beloved given you a new name? If yes, what is it? If no, don't be afraid to ask Him what it is. Then listen to His response. He wants to speak to you.

I understand that my Beloved is not referring to physical beauty when He calls me by my new name. He is referring to the beauty of my new heart. While the world cherishes outward beauty that fades with time, our Beloved cherishes the inward spiritual beauty that never fades.

Lest you think I might get a "big head" when my Beloved so affectionately kisses my heart, think again. We have enough negative voices in this world working hard to tear us down, notch by notch. In the math world, one positive cancels out one negative. In the real world, it simply doesn't work that way:

> Studies have shown that, in the average home, for every positive statement, a child receives ten negative statements. The school environment is only slightly better; students hear seven negative statements from their teachers for every one positive statement. No wonder so many children are growing up feeling that they are losers. Parents and teachers are conveying the perception every day in how they talk to their children.
>
> These studies go on to point out that it takes four positive statements to negate the effect of one negative statement. You probably verify that finding every time you wear a new suit or dress. A number of your friends may say, "Oh, what a good-looking outfit." But it only takes one comment like "It's really not you" to send you scurrying back to the store for a refund.[35]

It takes four positive statements to negate the effect of one negative statement. Think about it. The bad stuff is easier to believe because we live in a fallen world. Our enemy works overtime trying to get us to buy lies about who we are. And way too many times we take the bait—hook, line, and sinker.

We need to understand that negative thoughts often will feel true because they are so familiar. Hear this! *The volume and frequency of lies don't make them any truer.* A lie is a lie, whether it is heard and believed once or a thousand times.

The bottom line is that we feel the way we feel because we think the way we think. If we meditate on lies, the feelings that respond to those lies are both invalid and unreliable.

➤ What negative feelings do you deal with on a regular basis?

➤ Ask your Beloved to enable you to pinpoint the ungodly thoughts that are causing these negative feelings, and write them word for word, exactly as you hear them in your mind. *Please do not skip this exercise. Your answers will be used in week 6 to expose the primary strategy the enemy uses in the daily battle going on in your thought life.*

➤ Do these thoughts reflect a pure, righteous, and holy heart in Christ?

We have a choice. We can believe a God who cannot lie, or we can believe all the deceptive messages we are receiving from the world, the flesh, and Satan. It has to be an intentional choice, though—an act of our will.

As believers, we have the two greatest weapons (which are not of this world) available to us to use against Satan's lies: our sword of truth (the *Word of God*) and the indwelling *Spirit of Christ*. It is vital that we fill our minds with truth—the truth of who we are in Christ and the truth that He is our life. This is a very effective strategy in winning the daily battle going on in our thought life.

Week 4 closes on a positive note. The Shulammite is beginning to believe and walk in the truths of her new identity. As a result, she is experiencing greater intimacy with her Beloved. In week 5, we are going to look at her deepening devotion for Him (Song 2:3–7) and His invitation to her to step out of her comfort zone and join Him in unfamiliar, even scary, places (Song 2:8–11). In week 6, we will discuss in greater depth the specific strategies Satan uses in his warfare against our minds and how being armed with this knowledge will enable us to consistently walk by Christ's Spirit.

- ➢ What is your Bridegroom speaking to you through today's study? How will you respond?

Week 5

WELCOME TO THE NEW SONG OF SONGS 2:3–2:11

"There is no better test as to whether a man is really preaching the New Testament gospel of salvation than this, that some people might misunderstand it and misinterpret it to mean that it really amounts to this, that because you are saved by grace alone it does not matter at all what you do; you can go on sinning as much as you like because it will redound all the more to the glory of grace. That is a very good test of gospel preaching. If my preaching and presentation of the gospel of salvation does not expose it to that misunderstanding, then it is not the gospel."
—D. M. Lloyd-Jones, *Romans: The New Man*

Day 1

With two weeks left in our study on the first two chapters of the Song, we have several verses to cover. Now that a solid foundation has been laid for our pure, holy, and righteous identity in Christ, we will be moving more quickly through the dialogue between the Shulammite maiden, her Beloved, and the daughters of Jerusalem.

In Song 2:2, the beloved Shepherd-King compared His darling lily with the thorny daughters—believers whose outward lives closely resemble those of unbelievers. Although the maiden and the daughters have the same core identity, the maiden's lifestyle is beginning to look quite different from the daughters' lifestyles. She is getting her mind renewed with the truth about who she is, allowing herself to experience His cherishing love and exuberant life, and is now beginning to express His love and life. What goes in eventually comes out. What we focus on develops in our lives. You get the point.

Overwhelmed by the abundance of her Beloved's affirming and endearing words, the maiden turns her focus back to Him.

> **"Like an apple tree among the trees of the forest,**
> **So is my beloved among the young men.**
> **In his shade I took great delight and sat down,**
> **And his fruit was sweet to my taste."**
> **—Song 2:3**

Like an apple tree among the trees of the forest, so is my beloved among young men.
In the same way that her Beloved compared her lifestyle to that of the daughters of Jerusalem, she is now comparing His provision (apple tree) to that of the young men of this world (trees of the forest).

In our discussion of Song 1:17, we found that trees commonly symbolize humanity throughout Scripture. In describing her Beloved as an apple tree, the maiden is actually referring to the "citron tree"[1]—a type of evergreen citrus tree that bears lovely golden citrons. Citrons have a rare fragrance and taste like tangerines with a hint of lemon. The citron tree was likely translated apple tree in this verse because the ancient Greeks often referred to its fruit as the Median or Persian apple.[2]

The citron is the fruit King Solomon is referring to in his well-known proverb: "Like *golden apples* in silver settings, so is a word spoken at the right time" (Prov. 25:11 GW). This verse paints a beautiful picture of our Beloved's divine (golden) words spoken in His perfect timing to those He has redeemed (silver). These timely spoken words are often referred to as "words in due season." At this point in the Song, the maiden's Beloved has been speaking life-giving words in due season to her.

It is interesting to note that most of the trees in the forests of the Middle East are non-fruit-bearing evergreens. When the maiden likens her Beloved to the *young men* of this world, she is comparing His ability to meet her needs to that of other people. She is saying, "The nourishment you provide through the words you speak far surpasses what another human being could supply! I'm going to stop depending on the ordinary words (words that aren't truth) of other people to strengthen me and look to You as my primary source for nourishment."

In response to her request for direction in finding nourishment, her Beloved simply spoke words of truth to her (Song 1:7–11, 15; 2:2). When we experience our Beloved's timely spoken words through reading the Bible, Bible-based books, prayer, other people, or circumstances, they enrich our souls much like nutrient-dense foods provide the nourishment our bodies need.

In the New Testament, the apostle Paul describes a "good servant of Christ Jesus" as one who has been "constantly nourished on the words of the faith and of the sound doctrine which you have been following" (1 Tim. 4:6). In referring to the words of the faith and the sound doctrine, Paul is speaking specifically of the gospel—the good news of the new covenant of grace—as opposed to old covenant law.

In the early church, there were those who felt it necessary to mix law and grace to be made right with God. It's no different today. Sadly, many believers think their righteous standing with God hinges on what they do for Him, rather than what He has *already* accomplished for them and in them.

In his shade

Unlike most fruit-bearing trees that lose their leaves, healthy evergreen citron trees provide year-round shade. The maiden takes great delight in resting from her works in the cool shade of His grace—*all because of His finished work on the cross.*

The cool refreshment of His shade lies in stark contrast to her years of living unprotected in this performance-saturated world system under the hot sun (Song 1:6). What a vast difference there is between the sweat that comes from *trying* to be good enough to earn right standing with our Beloved and the refreshment resulting from *trusting* that His goodness has *already* made us the righteousness of God in Him (2 Cor. 5:21)!

If you find yourself still trying to achieve a works-based righteousness (law-based living), rather than resting in your faith-based righteousness (grace-based living), I implore you to carefully examine the abundance of Scriptural evidence that says the two ways of living are mutually exclusive (have nothing in common):

- "Christ is the end of the law for righteousness to everyone who believes" (Rom. 10:4).
- "Sin shall not be master over you, for you are not under law but under grace" (Rom. 6:14).
- "No one can ever be made right with God by doing what the law commands" (Rom. 3:20 NLT).
- "God's righteousness has been revealed apart from the Law, which is confirmed by the Law and the Prophets. God's righteousness comes through the faithfulness of Jesus Christ for all who have faith in him. There's no distinction" (Rom. 3:21–22 CEB).
- "We are made right with God through faith and not by obeying the law" (Rom. 3:28 NLT).
- "The promise to Abraham and to his descendants, that he would inherit the world, didn't come through the Law but through the righteousness that comes from faith" (Rom. 4:13 CEB).
- "We know that a person isn't made righteous by the works of the Law but rather through the faithfulness of Jesus Christ. We ourselves believed in Christ Jesus so that we could be made righteous by the faithfulness of Christ and not by the works of the Law—because no one will be made righteous by the works of the Law" (Gal. 2:16 CEB).
- "If we can be acceptable to God by obeying the Law, it was useless for Christ to die" (Gal. 2:21 CEV).
- "Whoever seeks to be righteous by following certain works of the law actually falls under the law's curse. I'm giving it to you straight from Scripture because it is as true now as when it was written: 'Cursed is everyone who doesn't live by and do all that is written in the law'" (Gal. 3:10).
- "If a law had been given which was able to impart life, then righteousness would indeed have been based on law" (Gal. 3:21 VOICE).
- "The old rule is now set aside, because it was weak and useless. The law of Moses could not make anything perfect. But now a better hope has been given to us, and with this hope we can come near to God" (Heb. 7:18–19 NCV).
- "If the first covenant had been faultless, there would have been no need for a second covenant to replace it" (Heb. 8:7 NLT).
- "When God speaks of a 'new' covenant, it means he has made the first one obsolete. It is now out of date" (Heb. 8:13 NLT).

Also, let me remind you that the old covenant law of Moses was exclusively between God and the Israelites—not the Gentiles (Lev. 26:46; Ps. 147:19–20; Rom. 2:14; Eph. 2:11–12). Before Jesus died, Gentiles were excluded from a covenant relationship with God. The *only* covenant that has ever been offered by God to the Gentiles is the *new covenant*—the covenant of righteousness based on faith in Jesus Christ alone (Rom. 3:21–22, 28; 4:13; 10:6; Phil. 3:9).

> ➤ After reading the list of Scriptures comparing the two mutually exclusive covenants, which one speaks the loudest to you, and why?

Many believers in Christ fear that this teaching of living in the glorious shade of our Beloved's grace will lead to laziness and licentiousness. The apostle Paul anticipated that this misconception would arise from his teaching that *righteousness is obtained through faith in Christ alone* and not through works of the law. In his letter to the church at Rome, after clearly presenting the gospel of grace in chapters 3–5, he begins chapter 6 by asking the rhetorical question, "What shall we say then? Are we to continue in sin so that grace may increase?" I appreciate D. M. Lloyd-Jones's comments on this verse:

> There is no better test as to whether a man is really preaching the New Testament gospel of salvation than this, that some people might misunderstand it and misinterpret it to mean that it really amounts to this, that because you are saved by grace alone it does not matter at all what you do; you can go on sinning as much as you like because it will redound all the more to the glory of grace. That is a very good test of gospel preaching. If my preaching and presentation of the gospel of salvation does not expose it to that misunderstanding, then it is not the gospel.[3]

"If my preaching and presentation of the gospel of salvation does not expose it to the misunderstanding that it doesn't matter what I do, then it is not the gospel." As an avid proponent of the gospel of grace, this quote thrills my heart! Every time I share this life-changing, liberating message with someone, the most common response is, *Are you saying that I can sin all I want, and it won't make any difference?* My answer is, "It won't make a difference in your eternal destiny.

When you believed in (into) Jesus, you became a brand-new creation, sealed in Him forever. It will, however, make a difference in your daily living. You weren't re-created in Christ for sinning, but for *good works* (Eph. 2:10). You will be absolutely miserable living a lifestyle of habitual sin because it doesn't fit who you are."

Paul sums up the end result of sinning quite well in Romans 6:21 when he says, "What did you gain from doing the things that you are now ashamed of?" (GNT). When I choose to walk by the flesh rather than His Spirit, I experience painful remorse (godly sorrow) over my ungodly behavior because it is not an expression of my true identity. It goes against the true grain of my new heart. Now that I understand that my heart's desire is not to sin, I have experienced incredible freedom. That's right. *I don't want to sin.* And neither do you, dear bride.

I know people whose constant companion is misery because they are clueless of the spiritual heart transplant they received when they believed in Jesus. Their minds have not gotten the memo: *You have a new heart with godly desires! You don't want to sin at all!* (Ezek. 36:25–27; Rom. 12:2; Heb. 10:15–16). Sometimes, it takes a while for believers to be convinced of this truth. After peeling away layers of deeply rooted flesh patterns and meditating on the truth of their new identity, most end up seeing the truth and agreeing that they don't want to sin—*they want what He wants!*

To clear up any misconceptions that may arise concerning Paul's question in Romans 6:1, he emphatically (and immediately) answers it in the very next verse: "May it never be! How shall we who died to sin still live in it?" (Rom. 6:2). He describes the believer in Christ as *one who has died to sin.*

Please recall from week 2 that *spiritual death* means "separation from the life of God" and *spiritual life* means "united with or joined to the life of God." When Paul speaks of the believer as one who has died to sin, he means that the believer's spirit is no longer *in Adam*, under sin's rule and reign, but is *in Christ*, under the reign of grace (Rom. 5:21). Am I suggesting that we will no longer be influenced to sin when we live under grace? No, I am not. What I am saying is that when a believer sins, it brings nothing but misery. Amen?

I am going to step onto a soapbox for a couple of paragraphs in order to clear up a major misunderstanding that somehow has evolved from the phrase *die to sin*. The phrase I'm speaking of is *die to self*. I challenge you to do a biblical search for the phrase. Although you won't find it in the original Greek and Aramaic languages, the use of the word is epidemic in Christian circles.

On the surface, the phrase may seem harmless. But for a new creature in Christ, it presents a whopping problem. It begs the response, *If I'm supposed to die to self, then that must mean that who I am is a bad person.* While well-informed believers may be able to do the mental translation by saying that the phrase die to self simply means to "die to the flesh" (walk by the Spirit instead of the flesh), the less-informed Christian will experience an underlying disease every time they hear the phrase. The phrase die to self—when used to refer to Christian living—will bring nothing but confusion. And "God is not the author of confusion but of peace" (1 Cor. 14:33 NKJV). (I'm stepping off the soapbox now.)

Now, let's get back to our discussion on the mistaken notion that grace teaching will encourage people to sin. In Paul's letter to Titus, he clears up this misconception by stating the true purpose of grace:

> For *the grace of God* has appeared, bringing salvation to all men, *instructing us to deny ungodliness and worldly desires and to live sensibly, righteously and godly* in the present age, looking for the blessed hope and the appearing of the glory of our great God and Savior, Christ Jesus, who gave Himself for us to redeem us from every lawless deed, and to purify for Himself a people for His own possession, zealous for good deeds. (Titus 2:11–14)

Everyone I know who has been adequately instructed in grace is convinced that his or her heart's desire is "to deny ungodliness and worldly desires and to live sensibly, righteously, and godly." Christ's bride has been redeemed from every lawless deed, purified, and made His own, zealous for good deeds. That's the gospel truth. That's good news! No, that's the *best news* you will ever hear! When you rest in the shade of the gospel of His grace, good works will ooze out of your life.

I took great delight

The maiden is now experiencing *great delight* because of understanding the extraordinary night-and-day difference between living under the law (from *do, do, do*) and living under grace (to *be, be, be*). She is enjoying the exhilarating pleasure of resting in her Beloved's presence. Life in Christ is good!

- ➤ Do you believe that your Beloved wants you to enjoy your life in Him to the fullest? If you aren't currently experiencing enjoyment in your relationship with Him, what do you think is hindering you?

Jesus wants us to enjoy life. His Word tells us that He "richly supplies us with all things to enjoy" (1 Tim. 6:17). What's more, He wants us to realize that *He is our life* and the source of our greatest enjoyment. The *Westminster Shorter Catechism* states that man's chief purpose in life is "to glorify God and enjoy Him forever."[4] We enjoy and glorify our Beloved when we experience and express His cherishing love and exuberant life.

As the bride of Christ, we need to learn how to master the art of taking great delight in Him. Just as Julia Child mastered the art of French cooking, wouldn't it be wonderful if we could master the art of enjoying Jesus? I want to experience and enjoy Him as much as possible this side of eternity. I want *joy* to be the marrow that courses through my veins. I want to come to the end of my life on this earth (if Jesus tarries) and be able to say that I truly lived—because I intimately knew *life* Himself. I want my first gaze into my Beloved's eyes to be familiar, not foreign.

In my attempt to communicate to the bride of Christ how knowing her identity will enable her to experience and express His cherishing love and exuberant life, I'm reminded of a quote by theologian Dr. Howard Hendricks: "A mist in the pulpit is a fog in the pews."[5] If we don't understand and practice what we preach, how can we effectively teach others? No one wants to read a book on how to bake the perfect cherry pie unless he or she knows the author makes delicious cherry pies! Likewise, no one wants to read a book or listen to a message about how to enjoy Jesus unless the author or speaker consistently shows forth the fruit of delighting in Him.

For over ten years now, I have been on a journey of learning to rest in the shade of my Beloved's grace and delighting in Him as I allow myself to experience His unconditional love. While I cannot claim that I have mastered the art of enjoying Him, I will say that I *am* in hot pursuit.

The most important thing I've learned is something I've said before (in different ways) and will keep saying: the key to delighting in Jesus is to personally experience His delight in you. He delights in and celebrates you at all times—simply because you are His. Our Beloved is a Master at separating our *who* from our *do*. He is filled with compassion for us in our struggles. He's not holding a hammer, ready to nail us if we don't get our act together. We can rest entirely in Him—in His love, power, goodness, and wisdom.

And sat down

Rather than "In his shade, I took great delight and sat down," I believe the more accurate order of the phrase we are unpacking is "I sat down in His shade and took great delight." How could we *possibly* experience great pleasure in our Beloved unless we first knew that we did not have to earn His love and acceptance through good works?

Sitting implies resting. This doesn't mean we lie on the couch all day, watching television, eating potato chips and doughnuts. While it is true that much of Christ's bride would greatly benefit from slowing down and resting physically, the phrase "sat down" refers to the spiritual rest of the new covenant—the rest that says "the work of our righteousness is finished in Christ" (see Hebrews 4).

One piece of furniture you would never find in the ancient tabernacle or temple of God is a chair. The Levitical priests were forbidden to sit down while offering sacrifices for their own sins and the sins of their people. Hebrews 10:11 says, "Every priest *stands* daily ministering and offering time after time the same sacrifices, which can never take away sins." The blood sacrifices offered by the Levitical priests year after year on the Day of Atonement could never completely take away the people's sins; they merely covered them from year to year. If you don't think there is a difference in the two terms, you might want to think again.

Imagine that I am preparing to entertain some important guests in my home one weekend. I spend the week before they arrive having the white carpet in my living room cleaned and planning the meals I'm going to serve. The weekend arrives, and my doorbell rings. As I'm walking to the door with a glass of grape juice in my hand, I trip and accidentally spill it on my white carpet.

Oh no! I don't want my company to see the mess I've made, so I go into another room to get a large area rug to cover up the stain until they leave on Sunday afternoon. Has the stain been taken away? Of course not! It has merely been covered up. It's out of sight but definitely not out of my mind. I'm very aware of the mess I'm going to have to deal with after my guests leave.

Although the sins of the Hebrew people were covered by their year-after-year sacrifices on the Day of Atonement, their relief was only temporary, not permanent. They would be back in Jerusalem at the same time next year to get their sins covered once again:

> The law is only an unclear picture of the good things coming in the future; it is not the real thing. The people under the law offer the same sacrifices every year, but these sacrifices *can never make perfect* those who come near to worship God. If the law could make them perfect, the sacrifices would have already stopped. The worshipers would be made clean, and they would no longer have a sense of sin. (Heb. 10:1–2 NCV)

The clear implication of this passage in Hebrews is that the sacrifice of Jesus—our high priest—was perfect and made us clean forever. We don't have to live with a sin consciousness! Instead, we can focus on Jesus—the Lamb of God, who *took away* all of our sins:

> But He, having offered one sacrifice for sins for all time, sat down at the right hand of God, waiting from that time onward until His enemies be made a footstool for His feet. For by one offering *He has perfected for all time those who are sanctified.* (Heb. 10:12–14)

Please, please don't skim over this passage. By offering Himself *once as a sacrifice for sins for all time*, Jesus has *perfected for all time those who are sanctified*. Who are "those who are sanctified"? Believers in Christ—His bride. Paul writes, "But you were washed, but you were *sanctified*, but you were justified in the name of the Lord Jesus Christ and in the Spirit of our God" (1 Cor. 6:11). Did you notice the verb tense? Past tense. *Fait accompli.* Beloved bride, Jesus Christ has perfected you for all time. You can experience delight-filled rest in that knowledge—*if you will own it.*

You may be surprised to learn (as I was) that Jesus never even would have qualified for the Levitical priesthood because He was from the tribe of Judah (Heb. 4:14; Rev. 5:5). This was further evidence that His new covenant of grace (which took away our sins) had nothing to do with the Mosaic Law (Rom. 11:27; 1 John 3:5; Heb. 9:26).

Jesus' sacrifice was made *one time for all people* before He sat down at the right hand of His Father. Several verses in the New Testament speak of Jesus' *sitting down* at His Father's right hand after finishing His work of redemption on the cross (Mark 16:19; Heb. 1:3; 10:12; 12:2). And guess what? Because we are in Him—and He is sitting down—we are resting with Him! *The Message* communicates this truth beautifully:

> Immense in mercy and with an incredible love, He embraced us. He took our sin-dead lives and made us alive in Christ. He did all this on His own, with no help from us! Then *He picked us up and set us down in highest heaven in company with Jesus, our Messiah.* Now God has us where He wants us, with all the time in this world and the next to shower grace and kindness upon us in Christ Jesus. Saving is all His idea, and all His work. All we do is trust Him enough to let Him do it. It's God's gift from start to finish! We don't play a major role. If we did, we'd probably go around bragging that we'd done the whole thing. No, we neither make nor save ourselves. God does both the making and saving. (Eph. 2:4–9)

Don't miss this: *Now God has us where He wants us, with all the time in this world and the next to shower grace and kindness upon us in Christ Jesus.* Take time to savor those words. The only part we played in our salvation was hearing the gospel message and owning it through believing in (into) Christ. And the only part we play in our daily living is to trust Him to live His life through ours. Wow! What an incredibly kind and gracious God we serve!

The maiden is in a wonderful place, resting in her Beloved's finished work and enjoying Him. In day 2, we will wrap up our discussion of Song 2:3 and look at some practical ways in which we can take great delight in our Beloved.

> ➢ What is your Bridegroom speaking to you through today's study? How will you respond?

Day 2

At the close of day 1, we were unpacking the phrase "and sat down" from Song 2:3. We compared the mutually exclusive old and new covenant systems for dealing with sin. Under the old, the high priests who offered blood sacrifices year after year to atone for their own sins and the sins of the Hebrew people weren't allowed to sit down on the job. Under the new, Jesus (our High Priest) sat down beside His Father after finishing the work of redeeming mankind, and everyone *in Him* sat down with Him in His rest. There is no contest. There is no comparison. The old way is bondage. The new way is freedom (John 14:6)—not freedom *to sin* but freedom *from sin* (Rom. 6:7, 18, 22).

Today, we are going to wrap up our discussion of our focal verse:

> **"Like an apple tree among the trees of the forest,**
> **So is my beloved among the young men.**
> **In his shade I took great delight and sat down,**
> **And his fruit was sweet to my taste."**
> **—Song 2:3**

The Hebrew phrase *sat down* means "to dwell, remain, to be inhabited, abide."[6] To *dwell* somewhere simply means to live there. The word *abide* is a word we commonly hear in Christian circles. In the past, I ignorantly used the word to refer to whether or not I was trusting in or depending on Jesus at any given moment in time (*I'm abiding in Christ* or *I haven't been abiding in Him*). In other words, *abiding* was just another word for walking by the Spirit. I was thrilled to learn that *abiding* is not something *I do* but an *eternal state of being that Christ caused*.

Shortly before going to the cross, we find Jesus standing in the middle of a vineyard with His disciples, speaking of a time in the near future when He would no longer be physically present with them. Instead, He would be living *in* them. Pointing to a vine (the trunk) and its branches, Jesus said,

> *Abide in Me*, and *I in you*. As the branch cannot bear fruit of itself unless it abides in the vine, so neither can you unless you *abide in Me*. I am the vine, you are the branches; he who *abides in Me* and *I in him*, he bears much fruit, for apart from Me you can do nothing. (John 15:4–5)

Before the new covenant became effective through the death of Jesus, the Spirit of God did not inhabit (abide in) His people (Heb. 9:15–17). Instead, He would come *upon* them at specific times to enable them to accomplish His purposes. In this passage, *abide* means "to live, to remain continually, to be held, to be kept."[7] Jesus was saying to His disciples, "I want you to live continually in Me and I in you. I want to hold you and keep you forever."

Up to that point, Jesus had been doing life *with* His disciples for about three years. Their brains must have been going *tilt-tilt* when He told them of His desire "to live in them" and for them to "live in Him." Strange—to say the least.

But this wasn't the first time Jesus used that kind of language. If we back up a few verses to the previous chapter, we find Him speaking of a day in the future where they would understand this mysterious union. "In that day, *you will know* that *I am in My Father*, and *you in Me*, and *I in you*" (John 14:20).

You can just imagine the difficult time the disciples must have had understanding what He was saying without enlightened spiritual ears and eyes. He obviously wasn't talking about the physical realm that could be seen with the natural eye but the eternal, invisible *spiritual* realm.

In instructing His disciples to abide in Him, Jesus was prophesying of the time after His death and resurrection when His Spirit would continually live (abide) in union with their new spirit (Ezek. 36:26–27). He wasn't speaking of something they could go in and out of—*abiding—not abiding—abiding—not abiding*—in a moment's notice. Once we are in Him, we are in Him forever (2 Cor. 1:22; Eph. 1:13, 4:30).

If you're still not convinced that Jesus was referring to our eternal spiritual union when He was speaking of abiding, let's hear from one of the eye-witnesses who was knee-deep in grapes with Him that evening. The apostle John clarifies Jesus' meaning when he writes, "By this we know that *we abide in Him* and *He in us*, because *He has given us of His Spirit*" (1 John 4:13). The meaning of abide is crystal clear. If we possess His Spirit (and all believers in Christ do), then we abide in Him and He abides in us. Abiding is a never-ending state for the bride of Christ. It's that simple.

In likening Himself to a vine and His disciples to His branches in John 15:5, Jesus speaks of a wonderful result of our spiritual union with Him. "I am the vine, you are the branches; he who abides in Me and I in him, he bears much fruit, for apart from Me you can do nothing." The one who lives in Jesus and in whom Jesus lives will bear much fruit.

The apostle Paul specifically tells us what this fruit is in his letter to the Galatian church: "The fruit of the Spirit is *love, joy, peace, patience, kindness, goodness, faithfulness, gentleness, self-control*" (Gal. 5:22–23). Please notice that the source of the fruit in this passage is the Spirit. However, you can't have the fruit without the branches. It takes both. It works the same way in the natural realm of childbearing:

> God has given to humankind, male and female, the task, the joy, the privilege of reproducing their own selves. Each mate brings his or her function. That's very important. One implants. The other manifests. There hasn't been a male yet that manifested a child. There hasn't been a female yet that implanted a child. But as one—*as one*—with each performing their God-given function, we reproduce ourselves. He that is joined to the she is one flesh. Out of that physical union comes the life of the seed. The male implants the seed; the female bears the child. He that is joined to the Lord is one spirit … Who provides the seed? God the Spirit. Who provides the life? God the Spirit. Who manifests the offspring? We do.[8]

I love this illustration. A wife cannot bear children *for* her husband *apart from* her husband. By the same token, we cannot bear spiritual fruit for Christ apart from Him. Because we abide in Christ, and He abides in us, we will bear much spiritual fruit—sooner or later. You may be wondering how that statement could include people who accept Jesus on their deathbeds. Take the thief on the cross, for instance. Let's be realistic. There's not much time to bear much fruit this side of eternity when you accept Christ right before you die.

While there are many things we can't fully understand during this time realm, and we won't *know* until we see Him face to face, I believe that we will continue to bear much spiritual fruit in eternity. Our entire being will be saturated with His Spirit, so it only makes sense that we will be expressing His life (fruit)—*forever.*

Part of the definition of abiding in Jesus paints a beautiful picture our intimate union with Him: "to be held, to be kept." We are eternally wrapped in His embrace. We can't wiggle out of His holy hug, even if we were fooled into believing that we wanted to! When our mind is renewed with this truth, and we acknowledge and enjoy our perpetual spiritual union with Him, the fruit that comes forth in our lives is sweet!

And his fruit was sweet to my taste.
When the maiden speaks of her Beloved's fruit as being sweet to her taste, she is referring to her actual experience. In their shared intimacy, she is experiencing His love, kindness, goodness, gentleness, patience, and faithfulness toward her. His joy over her. And the incomprehensible peace of perfect union with Him.

There are two aspects to our spiritual union with our Beloved—the invisible spiritual reality that is imperceptible to our natural senses (John 3:6) and the experiential reality that is discernible to us—also known as *communion*. Simply put, communion is the awareness and enjoyment of our spiritual union with Him. In order to experience the reality of our spiritual union with our Beloved, we need to acknowledge it and grow in our awareness of His love. We need to "taste and see that the Lord is good and that His lovingkindness is everlasting" (Ps. 34:8; 100:5).

My soul aches for those who have never enjoyed sweet intimacy with Jesus. I love this quote from Ruth Myers concerning our communion with Christ:

> Discovering God and His love in actual experience—this is the basis of true joy in life, as well as of true growth in Christ-likeness, which, in turn, brings us still greater joy.[9]

This quote certainly rings true in my own life. To have only a cognitive knowledge of Jesus' love without ever personally experiencing it would be like holding a plate of the ultimate chocolate cake (yes, I love chocolate) in your hands without breathing in its rich aroma and enjoying every delectable morsel.

I can promise you one thing: if you ever get a taste of Jesus' sweet love, you'll go back for seconds, thirds, fourths, and ... well, you get the point. And you will never gain a pound. Instead, the weight of burdens will melt away as you spend sweet time with your Beloved. There is nothing in this world like it, because it is not *of* this world!

I realize that I run the risk of being criticized for stressing the importance of experiential intimacy. There will probably be those who argue that spiritual truth is not something you necessarily will feel. At the other end of the spectrum, there are those who base their truth primarily on their experiences, saying, "I'm not sure I can believe it if I don't feel it." While both sides have valid arguments, one is like eating a great meal without savoring the dessert. And the other is like skipping the nutritious meal and heading straight for the dessert bar. With Jesus, we can enjoy the delicious meal *and* dessert at the same time!

I certainly don't claim to have the market cornered on truth when it comes to experiencing Jesus—I am still in the process of getting my mind renewed, just like you. My desire in this study is to simply express what I believe to be true concerning God's Word and to share some of my personal experiences with you.

Every believer in Christ will experience Him in wonderfully unique ways. I love the diversity in the body of Christ! The point I want to make above all else in this section is this: knowing the truth of our eternal spiritual union with our Beloved is the basis for our experiential communion with Him. We don't need our experiences to tell us what is true; we need truth to be the valid basis for all of our authentic experiences.

> ➢ Please share an example of how your Beloved has revealed His love for you in actual experience and how this experience has impacted your life.

The maiden is in a sweet spot, resting in the shade of her Apple Tree and enjoying the fruit of His presence and His life-giving words. Even though this section focuses on the experiential union (communion) between the bride and her Beloved, I would like to briefly touch on bearing fruit in ministry to others.

Have you ever known a sincere believer who was trying hard to exhibit the fruit of the Spirit (love, joy, peace, patience, kindness, goodness, faithfulness, gentleness, and self-control) toward others, apart from experiencing the delight that comes from communion with Christ? I have. *Me.*

When I reflect on my journey with my Beloved—the times when I consistently soak in His unconditional love, listening to His sweet words of affirmation—I don't have to *try* to be loving, joyful, peaceful, patient, kind, good, faithful, gentle, and self-controlled. All of those fruits are a natural result of experiencing sweet communion with Him.

On the other hand, the times when I get so busy with my to-do list, filling my mind with everything *but* my union with the One who loved me first and loves me most, I find it very difficult to keep from calling a name at the person who just pulled out in front of me on a busy intersection (it just seems to come out of nowhere). I find it challenging to wait patiently in line at the grocery store; to be kind to someone who hurt my feelings; to get my mind to stop going in a thousand different directions when my body is still; to be happy for someone else whose dreams are coming to pass when there's no evidence that mine will *ever* materialize. Can you relate?

If you continue with me on this journey through the entire Song (the next two studies over chapters 3–8), you will find that the first five chapters place a strong emphasis on *experiencing* our Beloved's cherishing love and exuberant life, while the last three chapters emphasize the *expression* of His fruit in ministry to others. You may think it is out of balance—or even selfish—to focus so much on receiving and enjoying His love. But I believe the greater danger lies in trying to minister something to someone that you aren't experiencing yourself.

Let me explain what I mean. When I was growing up, the centerpiece on our dining room table was a brown wooden bowl filled with wooden fruit. I will never forget how real it looked. From far away, you couldn't tell it wasn't the real thing. Upon closer inspection, though, it was obvious that the fruit in that bowl wasn't going to satisfy my need for refreshment. It wasn't real.

While our motives for wanting to minister Christ's love to others may be pure, trying to do this out of our natural resources without regularly experiencing it for ourselves is like handing someone a piece of fake fruit and trying to convince that person that it will satisfy his or her hunger. People are generally more discerning than we give them credit for. They aren't going to buy what we're selling because they know an imitation when they see one.

Although I have a tendency to be idealistic at times, I realize from personal experience that we are not always going to *feel* loving, joyful, peaceful, patient, kind, good, faithful, gentle, and self-controlled when we allow Christ to express Himself through us to others. However, when we personally enjoy the refreshing sweetness of our Beloved's cherishing love and exuberant life, almost everyone in our sphere of influence will also want to experience it. There's no better advertisement than a satisfied customer.

> ➢ What is your Bridegroom speaking to you through today's study? How will you respond?

Day 3

The Shulammite maiden has been feasting on her Beloved's sweet fruit—His love for her; His joy over her; the peace they share in perfect union; the patience, kindness, goodness, faithfulness, and gentleness He has exhibited toward her. While resting in the cool shade of His grace, she has enjoyed the "peaceful fruit of righteousness" He has given to her (Phil. 1:11; Heb. 12:11; 2 Cor. 5:21). After being filled to the brim and overflowing with His abundant provision, she exclaims,

> "He has brought me to his banquet hall,
> And his banner over me is love."
> —Song 2:4

He has brought me to his banquet hall

In response to the maiden's request, *Draw me after you*, the first place the King brought her into was His chambers (Song 1:4). Now, in response to her request for nourishment, He has brought her into His banquet hall—a place of great feasting on His riches (Song 1:7). She knows that *He* is the One who has brought her into these experiences. He has done above and beyond all that she could have imagined or hoped for in response to her requests (Eph. 3:20).

➤ Has your Beloved ever responded to one of your requests in a way far beyond what you could have imagined or hoped for? If so, explain here.

The Hebrew meaning for *banquet hall* is "house of wine."[10] In our discussion of Song 1:4, we learned that wine is a symbol of great joy. The beloved Shepherd-King has brought His maiden into a place of great joy as a result of her feasting on the delicious nourishment of His presence and His words of truth spoken to her.

After Jesus told His disciples about the spiritual union they would one day share with Him, He said, "These things I have spoken to you so that My joy may be in you, and that your joy may be made full" (John 15:11). Notice that Jesus didn't only say, "So that your joy may be made full" but that the prerequisite for their joy being made full would be His joy in them. He wanted them to know that because His Spirit would be one with their spirits, they would have everything they needed, including His joy residing in them. Joy is all about union with Jesus.

Jesus is filled with joy in the union He shares with His Father and the Holy Spirit. As a result, He wants His bride to experience the same. "I want you to know the delight I experience, to find ultimate satisfaction, which is why I am telling you all of this" (John 15:11 VOICE). Jesus wants us to experience ultimate satisfaction in our union with Him—in the holy hug we share with the Triune God.

Hardly a day goes by without our being inundated with advertisements of products that promise ultimate satisfaction. All we have to do is live a few decades on planet earth to conclude that these "things" fall far short of the fulfillment they promote. They just don't deliver the goods.

Because of the fall of man in the garden of Eden, every person born into this world is born spiritually dead—separated from the life of God. As a result, every person's greatest need is to be made spiritually alive through union with life Himself—Jesus Christ (Col. 3:4). The famous French philosopher Blaise Pascal said it well:

> What else does this craving, and this helplessness, proclaim but that there was once in man a true happiness, of which all that now remains is the empty print and trace?
>
> This he tries in vain to fill with everything around him, seeking in things that are not there the help he cannot find in those that are, though none can help, since this infinite abyss can be filled only with an infinite and immutable object; in other words by God himself.[11]

This infinite abyss has also been described as a God-shaped vacuum, void, or a three-pronged electrical socket built into every human heart which will only be satisfied when the life of Christ is plugged into it. Although invisible, we see the effects of this unmet need in unbelievers and believers (with unrenewed minds) alike in the widespread epidemic of addiction. From food, to drugs, to sex, to things, to work, to exercise, to social media, to you name it—whatever people use to try to fill that void.

Most addictions begin as an attempt to meet a need meant to be satisfied through a loving relationship with Jesus Christ. Can you imagine what this world would be like if our only addiction was to Him? Sounds like heaven on earth to me.

In order to experience the banquet hall of Jesus' joy in our lives, we must be convinced that *He* is the Author of true fulfillment. Until we *know that we know that we know* that He is our source for ultimate satisfaction, we will (consciously or subconsciously) continue searching for fulfillment in the things and people of this world.

> ➤ Have you experienced the joy that comes from knowing Jesus as your source of ultimate satisfaction? If yes, explain. If no, where are you still looking to get that need met?

As wonderful as it is to know that Christ's Spirit lives in us and that we have everything we need in Him, our most delightful encounters with Him on this earth are still only a shadow of the intoxicating joys we will experience with Him throughout eternity (Col. 2:17; Heb. 8:5; 10:1; James 1:17). I was reminded of this one day while looking at a grandchild's sticker book.

When I first opened and flipped through it, it wasn't much to look at. Every page contained shadowy shapes. When I reached the end of the book, though, I was delighted to find pages of bright, colorful stickers that were meant to be applied to the matching gray images. You can just imagine the difference throughout the book once all the stickers were applied.

While living on planet earth, we don't see the full picture of our redemption in Christ. Sometimes we have to admit that life looks pretty dismal with all the pain and suffering we see going on in the world—not to mention in our own neck of the woods. Yet as the bride of Christ, we have an incredible hope. When He returns for us, we will get to experience—in living color—the rapturous joy of seeing our Beloved face to face.

Part of the joy we will experience with Him will be at a royal wedding banquet—where He is the Bridegroom and we are the bride. The book of Revelation refers to this banquet as *the marriage supper of the Lamb* (19:9). If you're like me, you may wonder, *When will the marriage supper of the Lamb take place?* While I have done quite a bit of research on the subject of end-time events (eschatology), I certainly do not claim to be an expert. In fact, I *know* that I'm not. The more I study, the more questions I have. I do have an opinion, though, which I will state here.

I believe that the beginning of end-time events will occur when Christ meets His bride in the air to take her home with Him (John 14:2–3; 1 Cor. 15:50–57; 1 Thess. 4:13–18). A common term used to describe this event is the *rapture*, or "catching away" of the saints.

Next, the marriage of the Lamb with His bride (not the marriage supper) will take place

(Rev. 19:7–8). Christ and His bride will then enjoy a seven-year honeymoon period in heaven, while those left on earth will suffer through tribulation (Dan. 9:25–27; 12:1; Matt. 24:21; Mark 13:19; see chapters 6–19 of Revelation). At the end of that seven-year period, Christ will return to the earth with His bride, where He will victoriously defeat the enemies of God in the battle of Armageddon (Ps. 2; Isa. 34:1–16; 63:1–6; Joel 3:1–17; Zech. 12:1–9; 14:1–15; Mal. 4:1–5; Rev. 14:14–20; 16:12–16; 19:19–21).

The marriage supper of the Lamb will occur after this great battle, at the beginning of the one thousand-year reign of Christ and His bride on the earth, also referred to as the *millennial reign* (Isa. 11:1–10; 35:1–10; Jer. 23:5–8; Joel 3:17–21; Zech. 14:9–21, Rev. 19:9; 20:1–7). At the end of this one-thousand-year period, the great white throne judgment of all humanity throughout the ages will take place (Matt. 25:34, 41; Rom. 14:10–12; 1 Cor. 3:10–15; 2 Cor. 5:10; Rev. 20:11–15). Everyone whose name is not found written in the book of life will be thrown into the lake of fire to experience eternal torment along with Satan.

Finally, God will cause the new heaven and new earth to appear—the place where Christ and His bride will dwell together in perfect love, joy, and peace and reign throughout eternity (Isa. 65:17; 66:22; 2 Pet. 3:13; Rev. 21:1–22:5). How's that for happily ever after!

That's my view on end-time events. The fact that several of these events parallel the ancient Jewish marriage customs strengthens my opinion of their order. When a Jewish bridegroom went to his bride's home to retrieve her (the rapture in the air), he brought her back to his father's house to the wedding chamber, where they consummated their marriage (marriage of the Lamb in heaven). After spending seven days alone together (honeymoon in heaven during the tribulation on earth), the Jewish bride and groom emerged from the wedding chamber and joined their guests for a joyous marriage feast (marriage supper of the Lamb on earth). The bridegroom and his bride were given crowns to wear and treated as king and queen during the celebration (millennial reign on earth).

Isn't that fascinating? I encourage you to do your own study of end-time events while trusting your inward Teacher—Christ's Spirit. I believe it will cause you to look forward to your Happily Ever After with your Prince of Peace in a fresh, new way and encourage you in your remaining days on this earth.

I find great rest in the truth that what my Beloved has planned for me is far better than what my finite mind can know or imagine. Disagreement among believers concerning end-time events should not be cause for division. The way things are going to pan out is a nonessential of the Christian faith. The essence of our faith is whether or not the Spirit of Jesus has made us alive through our belief in (into) Him: "He who has the Son has the life; he who does not have the Son of God does not have the life" (1 John 5:12). Eternal union with "the Way and the Truth and the Life" is the only thing that really matters (John 14:6 AMPC).

Now, let's get back to our focal Scripture.

> **"He has brought me to his banquet hall,**
> **And his banner over me is love."**
> **—Song 2:4**

After feasting on her Beloved's presence and His sweet, nourishing words, the maiden joyfully proclaims,

And his banner over me is love.
I believe there should be an exclamation mark instead of a period at the end of her declaration. We have finally arrived at the signature verse of this study. What does it mean that our Beloved has raised a banner of love over us?

Although there were many purposes for banners (flags, ensigns, military standards) in the Old Testament—from rallying troops in war to heralding important events—we will look at the three purposes I believe our Beloved is communicating in this verse.

First, banners display victories won. When a city was captured in wartime, the conquering army raised its native flag over it and declared that it was now part of their country. The banner of love that the maiden's Beloved has raised over her life reveals that she now belongs to Him. He has conquered her heart through expressing His all-encompassing love for her in the midst of her weaknesses. His love for her has absolutely nothing to do with her performance and everything to do with who He is. *He is love* (1 John 4:8).

Our Beloved's love for us is not a generic, one-size-fits-all love. It's private and personal. Exclusive. It's a love that knows us inside and out, that knows all of our favorite things. Our favorite food. Our favorite love song. Our favorite season. Our favorite sport. Our favorite book. Our favorite movie. He knows what moves our hearts, our deepest struggles, and every dark thought we have ever entertained. He knows every unkind word from our mouths and everything about our attitudes and actions that we detest. Yet His love is a love that completely separates our behavior from our identities and looks straight into our hearts and proclaims, "My love, you are pure and lovely. Believe what I say and depend on Me to live My life through you."

His love is a love that never leaves us, not even for a yoctosecond (my new favorite word). It's a love that says, "I will be your sufficiency in everything you need. Just let Me. Just let Me love you out of your mess, out of your sin, out of your addiction. Just let Me love you because *you are the love of My life*, and I will never, *ever* stop loving you." No doubt about it. Our Beloved is the Victor of our hearts.

Second, banners make public declarations. Her Beloved is declaring—for all to see—that everything He does and allows in her life finds its source in His sovereign love and care for her. She can rest in knowing that even though there are times in her life when it looks like everything is out of control, nothing escapes His superintending guidance. He is either in charge of everything, or He is in charge of nothing. Although many verses describe our Beloved as the sovereign Superintendent over all creation, the following are three of my favorites:

- "The Lord has established His throne in the heavens, and His sovereignty rules over all" (Ps. 103:19).
- "Our God is in the heavens; He does whatever He pleases" (Ps. 115:3).
- "He does according to His will in the host of heaven and among the inhabitants of earth; and no one can ward off His hand or say to Him, 'What have You done?'" (Dan. 4:35).

We will experience a peace that passes all understanding when we realize that neither the microscopic nor the macroscopic escapes our Beloved's attention. He is more than able to run the universe, and He is more than able to manage the smallest details of our lives. After all, He created both.

> ➢ Have you ever questioned God's sovereignty? If so, what happened to cause you to believe that He was not in control? What conclusion did you finally reach?

If we live on planet earth long enough, we will be faced with this question: "Is God in control?" In order to experience His peace, we need to relinquish the fleshly desire to have everything figured out, and we must be content in the everlasting arms of the One who has all the answers to life's most troubling questions (Deut. 33:27). If He wants us to know something, He will cause us to hear His voice as we seek Him. We can trust and rest in our sovereign Lover's public declaration over our life:

> "For I know the plans I have for you"—this is the Lord's declaration—"plans for your welfare, not for disaster, to give you a future and a hope." (Jer. 29:11 HCSB)

The third and final purpose for the banner of love that our Beloved has raised over our lives is to draw others together for a common objective. Everything about the maiden's life finds its genesis in His love. She has been so saturated with His all-consuming love that she cannot help but exude it. Although the intensity of her love for her Beloved will undoubtedly make some uncomfortable, it will create longing in others to personally be drawn into His holy embrace. And then *their* lives will draw others in. His love is at the center of all life, and *life is all about His love.*

➢ Have you ever been around someone who was so in love with Jesus that nothing else seemed to matter? If so, how did it make you feel?

If you've ever been head over heels in love, you have no doubt experienced its euphoric effects—intense energy, sleeplessness, loss of appetite, and so on. Scientific research has proven that these effects result when our bodies release the chemicals dopamine and norepinephrine.

Dopamine is responsible for the euphoric feelings of bliss. Norepinephrine is similar to adrenaline, in that it causes excitement and naturally suppresses hunger. When the effects of these chemicals are coupled together long enough, they will inevitably take a toll on the body, resulting in exhaustion.

After an extended period of experiencing her Beloved's extravagant love for her, the maiden is emotionally and physically exhausted from her lovesickness for Him, as evidenced by her next request:

> "Sustain me with raisin cakes,
> Refresh me with apples,
> Because I am lovesick."
> —Song 2:5

Sustain me with raisin cakes

In today's world, we might gulp down an energy drink or inhale a bar of chocolate for a quick boost. Not so in the time of Solomon. The power boost of his day came from natural fruits such as raisin cakes. These were solid cakes of dried grapes pressed together.

King David distributed these nutrient-dense sweets along with bread and meat to the Israelites immediately after the ark of God was brought back to Jerusalem (1 Chron. 16:3). He wanted the people to be strengthened so they could celebrate God's presence being brought back to its rightful place.

These raisin cakes are a picture of the concentrated nourishment (sustenance) that comes from Christ's indwelling Spirit. We need our Beloved's strength to enjoy Him to the fullest. It's just not possible in our natural strength. Whether we are exhausted from experiencing His love or just plain worn out from physical, mental, and emotional stress, all of these natural deficits are springboards for His strength to be demonstrated through our lives.

The apostle Paul learned this principle in the trenches of his ministry. He asked his Beloved three times to remove a "thorn in the flesh" that he was experiencing (2 Cor. 12:7–8). We don't know exactly what the thorn was, since Paul didn't disclose it. Some have suggested that he was experiencing recurring issues with epilepsy. Others have speculated that he was referring to his poor eyesight (Gal. 6:11). Regardless of what Paul's thorn was, the Lord responded by saying, "No. But I am with you; that is all you need. My power shows up best in weak people" (2 Cor. 12:9 TLB).

I believe our Beloved kept Paul's thorn a mystery because it represents personal weakness, in general. And we all experience personal weakness. Just so you don't misunderstand me, I am not suggesting that we shouldn't ask the Lord to heal us when we are hurting. He specifically directs us to pray for healing for ourselves and others (James 5:16). I pray for healing for myself any time I experience sickness or an injury and pray regularly for others who are suffering, asking God to restore and heal them.

When God chooses not to bring physical restoration and healing through specific circumstances, I believe He has a much greater purpose that He wants to accomplish in our lives. He said it Himself: *His power shows up best in weak people.* Above all, He is after our complete dependence on Him and wants to reveal His glory in this world.

Let's look at Paul's somewhat surprising response to the Lord's refusal to remove his thorn.

> Now I am glad to boast about how weak I am; I am glad to be a living demonstration of Christ's power, instead of showing off my own power and abilities. Since I know it is all for Christ's good, I am quite happy about "the thorn," and about insults and hardships, persecutions and difficulties; for when I am weak, then I am strong—the less I have, the more I depend on him. (2 Cor. 12:9–10 TLB)

Amazingly, Paul went from begging God to remove his thorn to *boasting* about how weak it made him. He was glad to be a living demonstration of Christ's power, instead of showing off his natural strength and abilities. He even goes as far as to say that he is quite happy about "the thorn" and any other difficulty that might come his way because all of these things provide the platform for Christ's glory to be showcased through his life.

This passage of Scripture certainly runs cross-current to the deluge of books and programs written by the self-help gurus of this world. While one may certainly find good advice for overcoming natural weaknesses in this vast sea of humanistic methodologies, if our behavior improvement is not based in dependence on the indwelling Spirit of Christ, it is, at best, a temporary fix that lends itself to human pride. Until we experience the personal revelation that *Christ's power shows up best in weak people*, we will continue to be swept away by the currents of self-sufficiency and miss out on the incredible sweetness that comes from complete dependence on our Beloved.

> ➢ Do you have personal weaknesses that you have asked your Beloved to remove, and He has said no? If so, what are they? Have you considered the possibility that He wants you to view these weaknesses as springboards for His power to be demonstrated through your life?

Any time we are faced with personal weakness in any form, we would do well to revisit this passage in order to be reminded that our lives are all about being living demonstrations of Christ's power, rather than our natural strength and abilities. Who knows? Maybe we will even get to the point where we can join with Paul in saying (and meaning) that we are happy about our personal weaknesses—not because we enjoy the difficulties they incur but because we truly understand that they are the incubator for Christ's glory to be revealed to a watching world.

Refresh me with apples, because I am lovesick.
I love the word *refresh*. Just saying words that begin with "re-" does something within my soul. Words like revive, restore, replenish, rejuvenate, and recharge all contain within them a sense of renewal.

The maiden is crying out to her Beloved to refresh her with apples from His very being—the fruit-bearing Apple Tree. The Hebrew root word for *apples* is *naphach*, which means "to breathe or blow on."[12] The Greek root word for the *Spirit* of Christ is *pneo*, which also means "to breathe or to blow."[13] In asking her Beloved to *refresh* her, the maiden is asking Him to fill her entire being with His Spirit. In Ephesians 5:18, Paul exhorts the church to be continually filled with His Spirit: "Do not get drunk with wine, for that is dissipation, but *be filled with the Spirit*."

Within the last few years, my Beloved has caused me to understand the meaning of being *filled with His Spirit* in a fresh, new way. Before, I always thought of being filled with His Spirit from the outside in, much like you would fill a glass with water from a pitcher. Now that I understand my spiritual union with Christ in the core of my being, *Spirit-filled living* takes on a whole new meaning.

I'm convinced that Paul's exhortation in Ephesians 5:18 means "to be filled with the Spirit from the *inside out*." After all, he was the apostle who set forth the doctrine of our spiritual union with Christ in his letter to the Roman church. Further evidence that he is referring to Christ's indwelling Spirit as our wellspring is found just two chapters earlier: "Now to Him who is able to do far more abundantly beyond all that we ask or think, according to the power that works *within* us" (Eph. 3:20).

What could be more refreshing than knowing that Christ's Spirit is flowing through us as we depend on Him? His Spirit being poured out of our new hearts (who we are), into our souls (where we experience conscious thoughts, attitudes, feelings, desires, and choices) and our bodies (where we act) is more than enough to meet all of our needs.

> ➢ What is your Bridegroom speaking to you through today's study? How will you respond?

Day 4

The maiden is faint with love. She has asked her Beloved to refresh and sustain her in the midst of her lovesickness for Him. In response, He makes her even more aware of His intimate embrace. As He does this, she says,

> **"Let his left hand be under my head**
> **And his right hand embrace me."**
> **—Song 2:6**

In general, Song 2:6 is a picture of the intimate communion shared by two hearts deeply in love. If we take a closer look, though, we will find that it also refers to two types of our Beloved's loving activity (handiwork) in our lives.

Let his left hand be under my head

Have you ever seen a couple wrapped in each other's arms on a dance floor, when, all of a sudden, the guy decides to "dip" his girl? With his left hand gently supporting her head and his strong right arm wrapped around her waist, he keeps her from falling to the floor. Even though she can't see either hand, she's more aware of the strength of his right hand holding her up than she is the almost indiscernible support of his left hand behind her head.

Whereas the right hand of our Beloved represents His activity in our lives that we are aware of, His left hand refers to all of His behind-the-scenes work in our lives of which we are unaware. In the gospel of Matthew, Jesus said, "Do not let your left hand know what your right hand is doing" (6:3). Here we see the principle of the perceptible right hand versus the imperceptible left hand.

Many times, the left-hand seasons in our lives are uncomfortable and—let's be honest—sometimes downright painful. Through the gift of hindsight, however, we are often able to see what our Beloved was up to when we look back at a particular season in our lives.

When I first began to experience those health issues (I discussed in day 5 of week 3), I didn't have a clue what my Beloved was up to. *I do now.* He was teaching me about my eternal spiritual union with Him and that He is my life. Through the most difficult left-hand season in my life, He taught me the most important spiritual truth I will ever learn.

While it's nice to be able to reflect on past experiences in our lives and realize how our Beloved was working, there are some things that we just won't understand this side of heaven. Even so, we can rest in knowing that our Beloved is sovereign, all-knowing (omniscient), all-powerful (omnipotent), and all-present (omnipresent). And He has our best interests at heart—at all times. He's got our backs. He's got it all and is never going to let go of us (John 10:28).

> ➤ Describe a time in your life when the left hand of God was at work (you didn't have a clue what He was doing), but now you see more clearly what He was doing.

And his right hand embrace me

As previously mentioned, the right hand of our Beloved refers to His activity in our lives of which we are very much aware. King David referred to the right hand of God as being a place of abundant joy, where he would experience eternal pleasure. "In Your presence is fullness of joy; in Your right hand there are pleasures forever" (Ps. 16:11). The "kisses from the King" that we discussed in week 1 are examples of His right hand at work in our lives. We could also describe these kisses as expressions of His manifest presence that bring great joy.

Whereas His omnipresence refers to His being everywhere at all times, his *manifest presence* is His presence revealed to the human senses. We experience His manifest presence when He chooses to make Himself known and experienced. This aspect of His work in our lives always exhilarates and refreshes us.

Do you know believers who seem to experience the joys of His manifest presence on a regular basis? I don't think it's because they are somehow more special than those who don't have these encounters. I believe they are *intentional* about spending focused time with Him and having their spiritual eyes and ears attuned to His presence and voice. While we cannot control how and when our Beloved chooses to make Himself known, we *can* position ourselves to experience His manifest presence.

Noise, hurrying, and crowds don't typically provide an atmosphere that is conducive to our Beloved's revelation of Himself. On the contrary, silence, stillness, and solitude can help set the thermostat for exhilarating and refreshing encounters with Him. (Can you sense the calming power in these S words just by reading them?)

We all need times when we get alone with Jesus and get still and quiet enough to hear His voice and enjoy His presence. Hopefully, through this study, you have already begun to develop this delightful habit. The more focused time we spend with Him, the more confident and secure we become in hearing His voice and the more time we will want to spend in silence, stillness, and solitude. It is addicting. (Well, it is for me, anyway.)

How long has it been since you experienced your Beloved in quiet stillness, where there were no distractions? Let these words entice you to intentionally set aside time to enjoy just being with Him:

> You are invited to a secret garden which transcends time. Life outside this place will once again clamor for attention. However, for now, none of those things matter in the presence of the Divine Lover. Time seems to stand still before His timeless beauty. This garden is a place to which you are enticed by the Holy Spirit. It is a secret rendezvous in a sacred place shared by two lovers whose greatest joy is to be alone together, reveling in each other's love. It is your own holy hideaway where you and Jesus have the opportunity to celebrate your union together where nothing and nobody can disrupt your intimacy.[14]

Doesn't that sound inviting? While you are on this earth, you can experience your own holy hideaway, where you and Jesus celebrate your union in uninterrupted intimacy. What are you waiting for?

Knowing your primary love language and dominant spiritual temperament (discussed in week 1) will enable you to determine how to get the most out of your focused time with your Beloved. Because I am a words-of-affirmation, physical-touch contemplative, I love being still in His presence and waiting on Him to speak to me through His Word, through thoughts in my mind, and through images of His loving me. I have found that I am most impacted when He gives me motion pictures of us enjoying each other. Enjoying Him comes easy when I see Him enjoying me.

One of the first motion pictures my Beloved gave me was of us dancing together around a campfire on the beach in the moonlight. Talk about romantic! Right after that, the thought ran through my mind, *You just made that up.* That thought made me wonder if the scene had been a figment of my imagination. A few days later while I was reading a new book, the author shared a vision that the Lord had given her, where they were dancing around a campfire together. The word picture she painted was almost identical to the picture Jesus had given me earlier that week! What an incredible kiss! He was confirming the experience in my heart by letting me know that it was genuinely authored by Him.

You and I both know where *You just made that up* came from. It doesn't take a rocket scientist to figure that one out. The enemy despises our communion with our Beloved because our confidence and security in Him are increased as we come to know Him more. When you have impacting encounters with your Beloved, and the enemy tries to accuse you of making them up, dismiss his lies and accusations and continue to enjoy Jesus' intimate embrace. Always deal with enemy interruptions quickly, in dependence on your Beloved (this part is sometimes difficult to remember).

I realize that all of this talk about seeing our Beloved intimately embracing us will be easier for some to digest than others, especially if you are a man. I'm not suggesting that men should picture themselves dancing with Jesus, per se, but let's not forget that it was a man who leaned back on Jesus' breast during the Last Supper (John 13:23, 25). And the same man referred to himself several times as *the disciple whom Jesus loved* (John 19:26; 20:2; 21:7, 20).

One of the men who participated in a class I led on experiencing Jesus was having difficulty (and understandably so) with this concept of dancing with Jesus. One day after church, he came up to me—with a mile-wide grin on his face—and said, "Jesus gave me a picture! We were riding around in my pickup together. I was driving, and He was clipping His toenails!" I couldn't help but laugh—and at the same time thank Jesus for giving this man an up-close-and-personal picture of them spending time together that was tailor-made just for him.

There are also women who have a difficult time picturing themselves dancing with Jesus or being intimately embraced by Him. We all have different perceptions, based on our personalities and life experiences. Everyone is unique. Jesus longs for us to experience Him in ways that are perfectly fitted to our individuality. We just need to *allow* Him to reveal Himself to us in the way that He knows will have the most impact on us.

Experiencing the joyful exhilaration of the right-hand work of our Beloved is much more palatable than the painful confusion and frustration that often accompany His left-hand work. But here is some food for thought: the times when we are not delighting in His manifest presence are what cultivate the fertile ground for the times when we will. Left-hand seasons are powerful motivators to seek Him with all of our heart (Jer. 29:13).

Also consider this: if we experienced His manifest presence all of the time, it wouldn't be as special. It's just like dieting. If we go weeks without eating chocolate (insert your guilty pleasure here), we enjoy it a lot more when we finally allow ourselves to indulge in it than we would if we ate it every day. Am I suggesting that we go weeks where we purposely deprive ourselves of focused time with our Beloved so that the times when we do encounter Him will be more special? No, because *we* don't have to. The busyness and distractions of everyday life automatically do that for us.

I find it interesting that our focal verse concerning our Beloved's left- and right-hand work in our lives has an identical twin tucked away in the last chapter of the Song (8:3). It won't be unpacked until the third and final study. By that point in this unfolding romance, the same words from the maiden tell us that we will experience ups and downs throughout our days on planet earth.

I love to watch older couples who have celebrated the joys and weathered the storms of many years together. Even though they may look like a couple of love-struck teenagers, their love for each other is mature. As we celebrate the joys and weather the storms of life with our Beloved, we will not only fall more in love with Him, but we will also mature in our love for Him. And regardless of whether we are experiencing His left or right hand, *we win*. We are in His arms, at home in His heart—and there's no place like home!

Song 2:6 is the conclusion of the maiden's four-verse response to her Beloved's affirming, endearing words in Song 2:2. *Like a lily among thorns, so is my darling among the maidens.* Now we are going to hear what the beloved Shepherd-King has to say. But this time, He is *not* speaking to His darling maiden. Although what He has to say concerns her, His solemn words are specifically directed to the daughters of Jerusalem:

> **"I adjure you, O daughters of Jerusalem,**
> **By the gazelles or by the hinds of the field,**
> **That you do not arouse or awaken my love**
> **Until she pleases."**
> **—Song 2:7**

I adjure you, O daughters of Jerusalem
The *daughters of Jerusalem* have been a part of the audience of the Shulammite's life, witnessing her lovesickness for her Beloved. He now turns His attention toward them, speaking in a somber tone, *I adjure you, O daughters of Jerusalem …*

The word *adjure* is not a word we commonly use in our interactions with others—at least not in my neck of the woods. It means "to command earnestly and solemnly."[15] We might say instead, *I am dead serious about this …* or *What I'm about to say is super important, so can I have your full attention, please?* What the beloved Shepherd-King is about to say to the daughters of Jerusalem concerning their interaction with the maiden is of paramount importance.

By the gazelles or by the hinds of the field
By the gazelles or by the hinds of the field is another phrase that those of us in the Western Hemisphere would not understand, yet the Hebrew people of Solomon's day were quite familiar with it. Gazelles (small antelope) and hinds (female deer) were highly esteemed

because of their graceful movements, shimmering eyes, and gentleness. They were so valued that the Israelites would often swear by them. Where we might say, "I swear on a stack of Bibles [or my mother's grave]," the Israelites would say instead, "I swear by the gazelles or by the hinds of the field."

When the beloved Shepherd-King says, *I adjure you, O daughters of Jerusalem, by the gazelles or by the hinds of the field*, He wants them to take an oath concerning their interaction with His darling maiden, specifically:

That you do not arouse or awaken my love until she pleases

Another interesting characteristic of the gazelle and the hind is that they are easily stirred up by movement or noise. They are prone to distraction, just like us humans. Because of this tendency, the maiden's Beloved tells the daughters not to *arouse or awaken My love until she pleases*. What He means by this is:

> "You can't hurry love. Do not distract My love by trying to involve her in a lot of activities. She is in a strategic season where she is learning the truths of her identity as My lovely bride. She needs to be still and let Me love her. There are aspects of My heart that she can only learn in the quiet. This is an essential requirement for the next season of her life."

The daughters are puzzled by the maiden's devotion to her Beloved. They don't understand why all she ever talks about is Him and His love for her—why *He* is her magnificent obsession. Their frenzied lifestyles and preoccupation with the things of this world are a radical contrast to the maiden's life. Some even think she is being lazy and apathetic to the problems and needs of those around her and want her to board their "train of busyness" so they can feel better about their panting feverishness.

This is the first of a total of three *Do Not Disturb* signs the beloved Shepherd-King posts over the maiden's life in the Song (Song 2:7; 3:5; 8:4). In each occurrence, we will find that He makes this statement while she is in what could be referred to as a "honeymoon season"—immersed in His lavishing love. He will do whatever He needs to in order to protect her from the distractions that could cause her to be prematurely aborted from that season in her life.

Living in a world where the clarion call is "Do more, be more, have more," it's easy to get caught up in the frenetic pace of those around us. It's like driving the speed limit on a freeway with trucks and cars passing you on all sides, as if you were standing still. Before you know it, you find yourself automatically speeding up to keep up.

Why is everybody in such a hurry? Why is everybody so driven? More important, why are believers blazing down the highway of life at the same speed as the rest of the world, when the yoke promised to us by our Beloved is easy and light? I love the way *The Message* communicates the pace of life that Jesus wants us to keep:

> "Are you tired? Worn out? Burned out on religion? Come to me. Get away with me and you'll recover your life. I'll show you how to take a real rest. Walk with me and work with me—watch how I do it. Learn the unforced rhythms of grace. I won't lay anything heavy or ill-fitting on you. Keep company with me and you'll learn to live freely and lightly." (Matt. 11:28–30)

Jesus wants us to learn *the unforced rhythms of grace*—the free and light pace that He sets for us in our daily living. Don't be deceived. Being a Christian doesn't automatically exempt us from the temptation to live under the tyranny of busyness.

Some have even referred to the word *busy* as an acronym for "Being Under Satan's Yoke." The enemy knows that our effectiveness in the kingdom of God is greatly increased when we get still enough to listen to our Beloved, drown out the cacophony of life, and soak in His lavishing love. It makes complete sense that he would tempt us to join the rest of the world in their race to do more, be more, and have more.

Busyness comes quite naturally to us. For many, it is much easier to work *for* the Lord than it is to enjoy intimacy *with* Him. Perhaps this is because we are operating under the deceptive mind-set that He is more pleased with us when we are doing something for Him rather than our just being with him. This reminds me of the difference in Martha and Mary, Lazarus' sisters, who were good friends with Jesus. You probably know the story:

> Now it happened as they went that He entered a certain village; and a certain woman named Martha welcomed Him into her house. And she had a sister called Mary, who also sat at Jesus' feet and heard His word. But Martha was distracted with much serving, and she approached Him and said, "Lord, do You not care that my sister has left me to serve alone? Therefore tell her to help me."
>
> And Jesus answered and said to her, "Martha, Martha, you are worried and troubled about many things. But one thing is needed, and Mary has chosen that good part, which will not be taken away from her." (Luke 10:38–42 NKJV)

➤ Which sister's pace most characterizes your life: Mary, who sat at Jesus' feet, hanging on His every word, or Martha, who was distracted with much serving?

I don't believe Mary was opposed to hard work or was purposefully insensitive to her older sister's need for help. I believe she was so enamored with the living Word, that she didn't want to miss anything He had to say while He was with them. Don't you think if Jesus had told Mary that He needed something, she would have jumped right up to get it for Him? The point is, how are we going to know unless we are paying attention to Him?

We all go through different seasons of life where one season is busier than the other. I can completely relate to the following quote by an author who sensed the Lord calling him away from the busyness of ministry into quiet intimacy with Him:

> I feel like Lucy Ricardo working on the production line at the candy factory. I can't keep up, and I can't swallow any more. What is God showing me to do? I believe He is redirecting my life and ministry, leading me to focus on the things He has called me to and reminding me to not become distracted by lesser, albeit good things. I need to remember that *bigger* is not necessarily *better*, that to be busier isn't necessarily to be more productive. I need to learn that I don't have to say yes to every "great opportunity" that comes along.
>
> I want to grow in my knowledge of God and His ways. I want to experience greater intimacy with Him. I want to be obsessed with Him, so that the things that don't matter *won't* matter. I want to be inwardly at rest. I want my mind to stop whirling all the time with thoughts, plans, and ideas. I want to be able to relax mentally and to feel an emotional calmness by default. I want to cry with joy over God's manifest presence.[16]

➤ How would your life change if you became so obsessed with your Beloved that the things that don't matter *won't* matter?

When I was experiencing those health issues, I basically dropped out of every area of ministry I was involved in (at the Lord's urging) to get some much-needed rest. One of those areas was a Wednesday evening youth service. Not long after that, a sincere and well-meaning daughter of Jerusalem convinced me that I'd made a wrong decision—that I "belonged" in the Wednesday night service. I respected that daughter's opinion and thought maybe I had heard incorrectly from the Lord. I went back the next Wednesday night. It took all of five minutes for me to figure out that I should have listened to my heart instead of that daughter. (The fact that I sometimes struggle with people-pleasing flesh didn't help either.)

I learned a valuable lesson through that experience. My Beloved was teaching me to trust His voice in my heart, to trust that the desires of my heart were *His heart's desires* because that is where He lives! I also learned that I needed to take more time sitting at His feet and listening to Him so that I would not be so easily swayed by other people's opinions.

All of us have fallen into the deceptive trap of people-pleasing. The apostle Paul warns us of its dangers in his letter to the church at Galatia: "Obviously, I'm not trying to win the approval of people, but of God. If pleasing people were my goal, I would not be Christ's servant" (Gal.1:10 NLT). Any time we are in a decision-making process and thoughts like, *People are going to think …* creep in, we need to see them as red flags. Ask the only One who matters what He wants, and you will be delighted to find that what He wants is what you really want too.

> ➢ Imagine a week in your life where the thought, *People are going to think …* never once enters your mind. How would that week be different from every other week in your life?

Although Galatians 1:10 is a wonderful reminder to reject all forms of people-pleasing, Paul was specifically referring to his disagreement with those who wanted to add works to the gospel of grace. Rather than *Christ alone*, they wanted to preach *Christ plus adherence to the Ten Commandments*, *Christ plus the ceremonial and sacrificial laws*, and so on, in order to be made right with God.

Daughters of Jerusalem will often try to mix law with grace in order to feel more right with God. They have a difficult time believing that they are "the righteousness of God in

Christ" as a free gift, apart from what they do (2 Cor. 5:21). As a result, they adopt a works-based righteousness along with the gospel of grace. They don't realize they cannot mix the two, "But if it is by grace, it is no longer on the basis of works, otherwise grace is no longer grace" (Rom. 11:6). It really is that simple.

In Song 2:7, we find the beloved Shepherd-King's divine intervention on behalf of His darling maiden. He is specifically instructing the daughters *not to distract her* in this season of lovesickness where she is tucked away with Him, receiving and enjoying His love. There will come a day when He calls her out of this particular season. But for now, He wants her to stay put, and He makes no bones about it.

> ➤ What is your Bridegroom speaking to you through today's study? How will you respond?

Day 5

It is uncertain how much time has passed between the beloved Shepherd-King's *Do Not Disturb* sign of Song 2:7 and Song 2:8. In my opinion, this would have been a good place for a chapter break. In the previous verse, the beloved Shepherd-King told the daughters of Jerusalem not to distract His darling maiden in her season of lovesickness with Him. Now, the maiden is speaking, describing her Beloved as being *outside* of their love cottage, as if He has been away from her:

> **"Listen! My beloved!**
> **Behold, he is coming,**
> **Climbing on the mountains,**
> **Leaping on the hills!"**
> **—Song 2:8**

Listen! My beloved!
We know that once we are united with Christ, we can never be separated from Him. However, we go through seasons where we don't hear His voice as often and as clearly as we do in others.

The maiden has just experienced one of these seasons of silence in the gap between Song 2:7 and Song 2:8. We know this because in Song 2:8, she acts as if she hears His voice for the first time in a long time.

Most translations for this verse begin with "The voice of my beloved!" The maiden is hearing the voice of the One whose heart burns for her and is thrilled! She has learned to recognize His voice through enjoying intimate communion with Him.

Behold, he is coming

Any time we see the word *behold* in Scripture, it is a directive to watch and listen closely, as something very important is about to follow. Up to this point in the Song, the maiden has known her Beloved as a gentle Shepherd who has guided her into much-needed rest and nourishment. She has also known Him as a King who laid down His heavenly glory, dying on a cross for her, forgiving all of her sins, and uniting her with Him in His death, burial, resurrection, and ascension.

She previously went through a season of extended focus on Him, getting her mind renewed with the truths of her new identity. Still, she has yet to understand the fullness of these amazing truths. She is in process—as we all are in our journey with Him.

In this verse, the maiden is not only hearing her Beloved's voice but is also seeing Him move toward her as He reveals Himself to her in an unfamiliar light. This reminds me of another scene in the latest film adaptation of Austen's classic *Pride and Prejudice*. Near the end of the movie, Jane Bennett's younger sister, Elizabeth (the heroine of the story and a poor girl of little reputation), realizes that she has fallen head over heels in love with the very wealthy Mr. Darcy. Lady Catherine De Bourgh, Darcy's pompous and condescending aunt, is appalled when she hears rumors of an engagement between her nephew and Elizabeth. So, she decides to pay Elizabeth a late-night visit and confront her about the reported match.

After Elizabeth tells Lady Catherine that the rumors are unfounded, Lady Catherine asks her to promise that she will never marry her nephew. Insulted in the highest degree, Elizabeth refuses to abide by her request and asks her to leave her home immediately.

Unable to sleep after the confrontation, Elizabeth decides to go for an early morning walk. The sun is just beginning to rise, and an ethereal fog blankets the beautiful English countryside. All of a sudden, her breath is stolen as she looks up and sees her beloved Mr. Darcy walking across the meadow toward her. *It is as if she is seeing him for the first time in a new light.* Talk about movies that preach!

In like manner, the maiden's Beloved is revealing Himself to her in a glorious and powerful new light in Song 2:8. He is …

Climbing on the mountains, leaping on the hills!
The maiden is spellbound as she watches her Beloved move effortlessly over the rugged terrain and steep landscape. In Cora Harris Macilravy's exposition of the Song, she writes,

> Suddenly she sees Him leaping upon the mountains; those impassable obstacles, which would prove insurmountable to anyone else, are stepping–places for His feet. He leaps from one to the other with the sure, swift feet of a gazelle or a young stag. It was thus in His first coming, that He came to do His Father's will. As the first rays of the sun in a clear morning glance here and there over the landscape, so Jesus Christ, "The Hind of the Morning," came down to earth leaping upon the mountains and skipping over the hills. He came that He might bring down the high mountains … and build a Highway for the redeemed to pass over as they come rejoicing home. He leaped over the mountains of sin and condemnation to bring salvation to us.
>
> Sometimes, as we see the difficulties in our own lives and the hard things that seem impossible, we wonder if He can surmount them; for we know that we cannot. But He who could surmount the mountains … of man's sin and separation from God's presence, can surmount every mountain and hill that is in your life and mine.[17]

These mountains and hills represent the difficulties and obstacles we encounter in this world that seem impossible to overcome in our own strength. In short, Macilravy is saying that the One who conquered sin and brought us into union with Him by grace through faith is the same One who is more than able to conquer every struggle and adversity we face in our Monday-through-Sunday living.

Song 2:8 paints a splendid picture of our all-powerful, resurrected King. It is true that nothing is too difficult for Him (Jer. 32:17). He is strategically revealing Himself to the maiden in this way and at this time for a specific purpose. He wants her to partner together with Him in expressing His cherishing love and exuberant life in this world in the same way that He partnered with His Father while walking on planet earth in human flesh. "Truly, truly, I say to you, the Son can do nothing of Himself, unless it is something He sees the Father doing; for whatever the Father does, these things the Son also does in like manner" (John 5:19).

Jesus walked in complete dependence on His Father's life in and through Him. Father God showed Jesus what He wanted to do through Him, and then *Jesus let Him.* They shared perfect union. Likewise, because of the maiden's spiritual union with Christ, His resurrection power resides within her to overcome every obstacle in her life as she depends completely on Him. "If the Spirit of Him who raised Jesus from the dead dwells in you, He who raised Christ Jesus from the dead will also give life to your mortal bodies through His Spirit who dwells in you" (Rom. 8:11).

Let's take a closer look at our conquering King who lives *in* us:

- "These things I have spoken to you, so that in Me you may have peace. In the world you have tribulation, but take courage; I have overcome the world" (John 16:33).
- "He put all things in subjection under His feet, and gave Him as head over all things to the church" (Eph. 1:22).
- "When He had disarmed the rulers and authorities, He made a public display of them, having triumphed over them through Him" (Col. 2:15).
- "Thanks be to God, who gives us the victory through our Lord Jesus Christ" (1 Cor. 15:57).
- "Whatever is born of God overcomes the world; and this is the victory that has overcome the world—our faith" (1 John 5:4).

Unbeknownst to the maiden (at this point in their relationship), the conquering King who indwells her is also her courage and her triumph—her victory over the world and every obstacle in it. She has not yet learned how to appropriate His courage to face her greatest fears. But she will.

Because Christ has overcome the world through His victory on the cross, His bride—who is one spirit with Him—has also overcome the world. She is, by nature, an overcomer. She just needs to grow in her awareness of who she *already* is in Him.

- ➤ Are you currently facing hills and mountains in your life? Ask your victorious King for a personal revelation that He has *already* conquered every obstacle in your life, and thank Him for the victory that comes through Him.

The maiden continues to describe her Beloved and then begins to give a play-by-play account of what He does when He reaches their cottage.

> **"My beloved is like a gazelle or a young stag.**
> **Behold, he is standing behind our wall,**
> **He is looking through the windows,**
> **He is peering through the lattice."**
> **—Song 2:9**

My beloved is like a gazelle or a young stag.

The maiden compares her Beloved to a graceful gazelle (antelope) and a strong, young stag (adult male deer) because of the ease in which He leaps over the hills and climbs the mountains. *Gazelle* means "decorated and glorious beauty."[18] *Stag* comes from the Hebrew root word *ayil*, which means "mighty in strength."[19] The maiden's beloved Shepherd-King is revealing Himself to her as the beautiful and glorious mighty One because He wants her to know that she has everything she needs in Him.

Behold, he is standing behind our wall

Here again is a directive to watch or listen closely, indicated by the word *behold*. He is standing behind their wall, as opposed to resting inside on the couch with His darling maiden (Song 1:16). His posture indicates that He is ready to move, and He wants her to join Him. She has been nestled in the security and comfort of their celestial cottage, drinking in the love and affirmation she has desperately needed. Now, He is ready for her to join Him in expressing His cherishing love and exuberant life to the outside world.

He is looking through the windows

Have you ever knocked on someone's door and, after a considerable amount of time with no answer, looked through the windows to see if anyone was at home? She can see Him looking in, waiting for her to respond. The fact that He is not coming inside is her invitation to join Him outside the wall. The windows also signify that she has the outside world in view, but she is not ready to leave the comfortable, safe haven she has grown used to.

He is peering through the lattice.

He is patiently waiting for her to respond to His invitation. Not only is He looking through the windows, but now He is peering through the lattice. *Peering* means "to look searchingly."[20] Lattice is often used for decorative purposes and sometimes as a barrier to keep people on the outside from being able to easily see inside. We typically use blinds and shades on our windows for these reasons.

The lattice signifies the maiden trying to control her circumstances. Have you ever known someone who struggles with controlling flesh? You may be surprised to learn that the root of control is fear—fear of failure. Fear of being hurt. Fear of what other people think. Fear of being ridiculed. Fear of the unknown. The list goes on and on and on.

God repeatedly instructs us in His Word to not be afraid. There are over three hundred references where He tells His people to "fear not" in some form or fashion. He's not telling us that we aren't going to *feel* fear; He's telling us to not let the fear control us.

Even a toddler can learn this. Let me explain. We get to keep our grandchildren on a fairly regular basis. When our grandson, Logan, was two years old, the street that runs alongside the duplex we lived in at that time is the direct route to our city hospital, so the traffic gets pretty busy (and loud) on a fairly regular basis. When we were inside and Logan heard the vehicles go by, it scared him. His eyes got big, and then he would say, *Oh!* and run and jump into my arms. When he did this, I would tell him, "You don't have to be afraid, Logan. The cars are outside, and they can't hurt you."

Logan's fear was unfounded—it was based in deception (falsehood). *Fear* is an acronym for "False Evidence Appearing Real." Logan believed the false evidence that the cars outside the duplex could somehow hurt him while he was inside. Obviously, he was operating from a small child's perspective rather than that of an adult. But he was learning—learning to conquer his fear through experiencing the truth that he was safe inside the house. It was an enlightening process to witness.

As time passed, when he heard the vehicles go by while playing inside with his toys, he made eye contact with me and said out loud, "It's just a car. It's *just* a car. I don't have to be afraid." Logan decided that he wasn't going to let the fear keep him from enjoying his toys, and speaking the truth out loud helped him overcome it. I think we can all learn from his example.

The maiden's feelings of fear indicate that she believes a lie concerning her Beloved's invitation to join Him. She is clearly not convinced that He has her best interests at heart and that she will be safe if she goes with Him.

- Has fear ever kept you from saying yes to your Beloved's invitation to join Him in a specific purpose He has had for your life? If so, briefly describe the situation and what you learned from it.

After waiting patiently outside the wall for the maiden's response, her Beloved finally speaks.

> **"My beloved responded and said to me,**
> **'Arise, my darling, my beautiful one,**
> **And come along.'"**
> —Song 2:10

My beloved responded and said to me, 'Arise, my darling, my beautiful one, and come along.'
He encourages her by reminding her *whose* and *who* she is (My beautiful one, My darling). He always speaks life-giving words into her soul. *Arise* means "to stand up, become powerful, to be established and proven."[21] In other words, He is saying,

> "It is time for you to become in experience who you are in truth, for what is *already* true of you on the inside to be manifested on the outside. It is time for you to let My lavishing, cherishing love and exuberant, resurrection life be expressed through your life."

This is not necessarily a call to vocational ministry. It could be, but most believers aren't in vocational ministry. Think about it. If every believer pursued vocational ministry, there would be no physical expression of Christ's cherishing love and exuberant life in the average workplace. All believers are called to express His love and life to those within their sphere of influence, to let their lights shine for everyone in their corner of the world to see (Matt. 5:16).

Will the maiden say yes to His invitation and join Him, or will she remain inside her comfort zone, safe from the potential hazards of interacting with others? She has had some pretty painful experiences with "porcupine people"[22] in the past, and she's not too excited at the thought of getting poked and pricked again. What she doesn't realize is that while she may be protecting herself from painful situations that could arise from ministering to others, she is also preventing herself from experiencing the joys that come from being a conduit of Christ's love and life.

At this point in the Song, *fear* is the maiden's greatest obstacle. She mistakenly believes that she has to feel courageous and "have it all together" in order to be used by Him. She doesn't understand that if all believers waited until they felt dauntless and perfect before allowing Him to use them, nobody would be living demonstrations of Christ's love and life. All He wants is her trust in Him to do it all through her as she depends on His sufficiency.

In the next verse, her Beloved states the reason why the time is now for her to say yes to His invitation.

> **"For behold, the winter is past,**
> **The rain is over and gone."**
> **—Song 2:11**

For behold
The word *behold* is used a total of four times throughout the Song. This is the first and *only* time the beloved Shepherd-King says it. Please recall that *behold* means "pay close attention, because what follows is very important." What He is about to say to the maiden is of monumental importance.

The winter is past, the rain is over and gone
The Beloved Shepherd is stating the reason that it is now time for the maiden to join Him— *the winter is past, the rain is over and gone.* He is saying that the winter rains of the law—the system of works-based righteousness—is over. Now that the maiden has begun to experience the glorious freedom of the new covenant, He wants her to join Him in sharing with others how they can experience the same freedom. The good news of the gospel is that no one has to earn the righteousness that God freely gives. Jesus paid it all. All they have to do is believe in (into) Him (John 3:16; 19:30; 1 Cor. 6:17; 2 Cor. 5:21).

You may be wondering if I'm suggesting here that everyone go door to door with evangelistic tracts. No. But I'm not discouraging it either. Those who have the gift of evangelism may do this and do this well (Eph. 4:11). What I *am* suggesting is that everyone's life can be a witness of new covenant truth to others. When our lives are an expression of our Beloved's cherishing love and exuberant life, people will be knocking on our doors, asking where they can get some of what we've got. And we will be able to tell them that what we've got is the resurrection life of Christ—also theirs for the receiving.

I find it interesting that *rain* is associated with *winter* in this verse. Snow, sleet, and ice are often constant companions of winters in the Texas Panhandle. Unlike the climates of the United States and Western Europe, Israel basically experiences two seasons: winter and summer. Summer occurs from the end of March to mid-October and is characterized by warm to hot temperatures with virtually no rain. Winter occurs from late October to mid-March, with cool temperatures and light showers in October, followed by colder temperatures and periodic heavy rainfall from November to March. With the exceptions of the upper elevations of Mount Hermon and the Golan Heights, Israel rarely sees snow in the winter months.

I am grateful to live in a part of the world that experiences the four distinct seasons of winter, spring, summer, and autumn. Autumn is my favorite because of the cooler temperatures and the gorgeous foliage. Just as we experience the changing natural seasons, we are also subject to changing experiential seasons in our life with Christ.

It makes perfect sense to talk about the different seasons in a believer's life because throughout Scripture, God's people are metaphorically described as His *garden* (Song 4:12,

15, 16; 5:1; 6:2; Isa. 58:11; Jer. 31:12), *vineyard* (Song 1:6; 8:11–12; Isa. 5:1–10; Matt. 20:1–8; 21:28–41)), or *field* (1 Cor. 3:6–9). We can find great encouragement in identifying which season we are currently experiencing. There is just something about knowing that we are not the only ones who are going (or have gone) through especially difficult times.

We also experience seasons of great joy and celebration. One thing we can know for sure—no matter which season we are in, it will change. Life is not static. Whether we are struggling through a cold and lifeless winter season or a hot and hectic summer season, we can find great hope in knowing that a warm, flourishing spring or a cool, abundant autumn harvest is just around the corner.

The changing seasons of our lives are not haphazard but ordained by our Beloved to accomplish His purposes in our lives: "To everything there is a season, a time for every purpose under heaven" (Eccl. 3:10 NKJV). Regardless of what season we are in, our Beloved wants us to embrace Him, trusting that He will manifest the greatest possible harvest of His fruit in our lives in His perfect timing.

Before we look at the identifying characteristics of each season, I believe it is important to clarify what I mean by "growth." Growth is not a change in our spiritual state. Our new heart is our new spirit united with Christ's Spirit and is complete and unchangeable (Col. 2:10). True growth in believers is measured by the degree to which their minds are renewed with what is *already* true of their new hearts and then manifested through their outward lives (Rom. 12:2). The apostle Peter exhorts believers to "grow in the grace and *knowledge* of our Lord and Savior Jesus Christ" (2 Pet. 3:18).

Knowing which season we are in will not only encourage us to persevere through the difficulties of winter and summer but will enable us to not take for granted the joys of spring and fall. Although we generally prefer one season to another, there are pros and cons within each that bring a nice overall balance to our lives. Let's start with winter.

Winter: The winter season is cold, has fewer daylight hours, and is a time when many plants and trees are dormant. Although they may appear lifeless, their dormancy is actually a part of their growth cycle.

On the downside, the experiential season of winter is characterized by very little sense of our Beloved's love, presence, and activity in our lives (His left hand). Sometimes during this season, it seems as if He has taken a permanent vacation.

The upside to this bleak and barren season is that it creates a hunger to experience our Beloved's presence and will cause us to seek Him to meet our needs.

Spring: The spring season is warmer, has more daylight hours, and is the time for planting new seeds because the ground temperature gets warm enough for germination. Everywhere we turn, we see the emergence of new life in the blooming flowers and the different shades of green in the tree branches, growing grass, leaves, and bushes.

The experiential season of spring is characterized by a greater sense of our Beloved's activity in our lives (His right hand). New seeds of truth are planted in our minds and watered and cultivated through intimacy with Him. This season holds within it great hope—hope that the planted seeds will eventually manifest an abundant harvest.

Summer: The temperatures of summer can range from very warm to unbearably hot. Much attention is given to the growing plants through watering, pulling weeds, and keeping bugs and animals from destroying them.

On the upside, the experiential season of summer symbolizes rapid growth, where we are so energized by what our Beloved has planted in our hearts and minds that we want to share it with everyone.

On the downside, we can become overzealous and get too many irons in the fire. It is important to realize that just because we *see* a need, that doesn't mean our Beloved is calling *us* to meet it. Awareness does not necessarily constitute action on our part. Take time to seek Him. He is an expert at weeding out unnecessary distractions that might keep us from expressing the fullness of His fruit in our lives.

Autumn: In the part of the world where I live, the cooler temperatures of autumn bring refreshing relief from the dog days of summer. Up until the sixteenth century, *harvest* was the term used to refer to this season. Now, it is commonly referred to as *fall* because of the falling leaves of the deciduous trees. (I find it fascinating that their gorgeous hues signify their maturity.)

The experiential season of autumn represents the abundant manifestation of the fruit of our Beloved's Spirit being expressed through our lives. This is a joyous season because this fruit is not the result of our *works*—our trying hard to be more loving, joyful, peaceful, kind, good, faithful, gentle, and self-controlled. It is the delectable, authentic fruit of shared intimacy with our Beloved.

> ➤ What experiential season are you in right now? Describe what you believe your Beloved is doing in your life through this strategic season.

We end week 5 of our study at Song 2:11, where the maiden's Beloved states the reason that the time is *now* to join Him in expressing His cherishing love and exuberant life in this world: The system of works-based righteousness is gone—and people need to know this!

In week 6, He will elaborate on this reason by sharing five more signs that the winter of law is past and the spring of grace has arrived. He will continue to encourage His darling maiden by reminding her who she *already* is in Him. He will also expose the covert strategies used by her enemy in the battle going on in her thought life. Satan would like nothing more than to permanently paralyze her with fear and keep her from bearing the abundant, authentic fruit of her Beloved.

Slowly but surely—as the maiden is made aware of her enemy's deceptive schemes—she will begin to be equipped with the vital ammunition she needs to experience consistent victory over him in her daily living.

> ➤ What is your Bridegroom speaking to you through today's study? How will you respond?

Week 6

REMIND ME WHO I AM

SONG OF SONGS 2:12–2:17

"When I lose my way
and I forget my name
remind me who I am."
—Jason Gray, "Remind Me Who I Am"

Day 1

Week 5 concluded with the maiden's Beloved revealing Himself to her in a new light—as a resurrected conquering King in all His glory. Immediately after that, He invited her to join Him in expressing His love and life to the world, saying, "Arise, my darling, my beautiful one, and come along" (Song 2:10).

Next, He gave her the reason that the time was *now* to join Him: "For behold, the winter is past, the rain is over and gone" (2:11). Everything has changed! The system of works-based righteousness is over. She no longer has to live and work under the cold winter rains of the law to stay in favor with Him. She is free indeed from that oppressive regime, and it's time to tear down the wall of fear that's keeping her from saying yes to her Beloved's call (John 8:36; Gal. 5:1).

Can you hear former President Ronald Reagan's voice in that last line? In the same way that the Berlin Wall was a symbol of Communist oppression in East Germany, the wall of fear in the maiden's life is a symbol of the enemy's oppressive work in her mind. Even though she is hesitating in answering her Beloved's call, He is not giving up. He continues to speak, giving her the first three signs that the old has passed and the new has come.

> "The flowers have already appeared in the land;
> The time has arrived for pruning the vines,
> And the voice of the turtledove has been heard in our land."
> —Song 2:12

The flowers have already appeared in the land

The end of February and beginning of March usher in a radical facelift for Israel's countryside. The emergence of vivid green landscapes, along with the spectacular displays of wildflowers, herald the message of new life. When the beloved Shepherd-King says, "The flowers have already appeared in the land," He is referring to the covenant of grace, where Christ's Spirit would indwell everyone who believed in (into) Him, giving them His righteousness as a gift.

In his letter to the church at Rome, the apostle Paul communicates one of the major benefits of Christ's indwelling Spirit. "If the Spirit of Him who raised Jesus from the dead dwells in you, He who raised Christ Jesus from the dead will also give life to your mortal bodies through His Spirit who dwells in you" (Rom. 8:11). Christ dwells *in* us so that His life can flow *through* our souls and bodies as we choose to walk by His Spirit (See Figure 6: Walking by the Spirit, page 68).

How blessed and privileged we are to be living on this side of the cross! Every person who lived and died before Christ's death and resurrection did not live with the same hope that we do (Heb. 11:39–40). They did not have the extraordinary advantage of containing His indwelling Spirit.

And that's not all. One day, our mortal bodies will be exchanged for new, glorified bodies, and death will be abolished forever:

> When this body that decays is changed into a body that cannot decay, and this mortal body is changed into a body that will live forever, then the teaching of Scripture will come true: "Death is turned into victory!" (1 Cor. 15:54 GW)

This Scripture means more to me as my physical body ages. Our glorified bodies will not be stained by sin, sickness, or aging, so nothing will hinder Christ's glorious light from being expressed through our lives! Oh, what a day that will be when we are no longer influenced by sin! Until then, we have the incredible moment-by-moment privilege to choose by faith to be clothed with Christ's glory.

> ➤ If you do not have a New American Standard Bible, use the Internet (BibleStudyTools.com, BibleGateway.com, and BlueLetterBible.org are my favorite free online Bible study sites) to find Colossians 1:26–27 in that translation. Then, write the passage in the following space:

This passage from Colossians reveals that "Christ *in you*" is the hope of glory. Christ *in me* is the hope of glory. Christ *in us*—is the hope of an unseen God manifesting Himself through our lives to an unbelieving world. When we stop letting fear control us and start allowing Him to express His love and life through us to others, our outward lives will undergo a radical transformation, much like the change we see when the bare landscapes of winter bid their quiet *adieu* and the panoramic vistas of spring shout *hello!*

The significance of flowers appearing on the vines or trees is an indication that fruit is soon to follow. The fruit of the Spirit that is borne through our lives is the result of fixing our eyes on Christ's indwelling Spirit, trusting Him to live through us as we depend on Him.

The beloved Shepherd-King then gives the maiden the next sign that the old has passed and the new has come:

The time has arrived for pruning the vines
Every translation except for the New American Standard Bible renders this phrase as "the time of the singing of the birds has come." All versions carry the same meaning, though. The advent of singing birds and the season for pruning the vines occur at the same time in Israel—at the beginning of summer. Because Israel only has two seasons, the beginning of summer is comparable to our spring season.

Most of my days begin with sitting in my recliner beside the windows in my library spending time with my Beloved. Winter mornings are typically very quiet, with the exception of the occasional howling winds of a cold front blowing through. You can just imagine my ears perking up the first morning that I hear birds singing outside. *Good-bye, winter; hello, spring!*

We know spring has arrived when we hear the singing birds, and we see plants, flowers, potting soil, and fertilizer moving off the shelves of our local discount stores. People begin working in their gardens, diligently preparing the soil. Their cultivation usually includes pruning their perennials—the plants that remain dormant throughout the winter, patiently waiting for the show-and-tell season of spring.

Grapevines are perennials commonly found in Israel. As mentioned in week 5, *God's vineyard* or *garden* is a metaphor for our lives in Christ. In our previous discussion on *abiding*, Jesus used a live grapevine to illustrate our spiritual union with Him and what it meant to bear fruit in His kingdom (John 15:4–5). Let's look at some of the verses surrounding that passage that include Father God's role in the fruit-bearing process.

> "I am the true vine, and My Father is the vinedresser. Every branch in Me that does not bear fruit, He takes away; and every branch that bears fruit, He prunes it so that it may bear more fruit … My Father is glorified by this, that you bear much fruit, and so prove to be My disciples." (John 15:1–2, 8)

Jesus identifies Himself as the vine (the trunk that grows up out of the soil), His Father as the vinedresser (the one who cultivates and prunes the grapevines), and the believer in Christ as the branch (attached to the vine). He goes on to describe two types of branches—those that bear fruit and those that don't—and how His Father interacts with both to cause them to yield a bumper crop of fruit.

When Jesus says, "Every branch in Me that does not bear fruit, He takes away," He does not mean that His Father is separating them from the vine because they can't get their acts together, as some commentaries most unfortunately convey. *Takes away* means "to raise upwards, elevate, lift up."[1]

When grape branches are lying on the ground they are hindered from getting the proper sunlight and air needed to bear much fruit. This is a picture of a believer in Christ continuing to trust in himself (his natural "earthly" abilities and strength) to produce fruit (good works) *for* God. As mentioned previously, it is impossible to bear the authentic fruit of the Spirit through our natural strength (John 15:5). As we look to Jesus, our loving Father will graciously lift us up out of our dark misconceptions and into the light of what it means to "bear fruit for Him" (Rom. 7:4).

Jesus then said, "every branch that bears fruit, He prunes it so that it may bear more fruit." To *prune* branches means to cut stems off them. The stems are the part of the branch where the grapes grow. In his book *Secrets of the Vine*, Bruce Wilkinson shares how he learned the purpose of pruning when he noticed his neighbor shearing off what seemed like large parts of the grapevine rambling along the fence on their shared property line. Thinking his neighbor had gone all Edward Scissorhands on him, Wilkinson walked over to find out what in the world could be motivating him to do such an atrocious thing.

> "You don't like grapes, I guess?" I said, trying to conceal my distress.
>
> "Love grapes," he said.
>
> "Really. Well, I thought maybe we would be sharing the crop from this vine and I …" I hesitated. Maybe it was too late to do any good.
>
> He eyed my shiny shoes. "You're a city boy, aren't ya?" he said.
>
> "Not exactly, but I—"
>
> "Don't know about grapes, do ya?" he broke in, and went back to hacking at the vine.
>
> I told him I knew I liked the taste of them. And I told him I had particularly liked the promising look of this row of grapes when I bought the place.
>
> "You like big, juicy grapes?" he asked over his shoulder.
>
> "Of course! My family does, too," I said.
>
> "Well, son," he said, "We can either grow ourselves a lot of beautiful leaves filling up this whole fence line. Or we can have the biggest, juiciest, sweetest grapes you and your family have ever seen." He looked at me. "We just can't have both."[2]

Lots of leaves *or* big, juicy, sweet grapes. That's a no-brainer. I'll take the big, juicy, sweet grapes! And that's what Jesus wants too.

> God's strategy for coaxing a greater harvest out of His branches ... is to prune, which means to thin, to reduce, to cut off ... The Vinedresser's secret for more is ... less ... For the Christian, a rampant growth represents all those preoccupations and priorities in our lives that ... are keeping us from more significant ministry ... Without pruning, growing Christians will only be able to live up to a fraction of their potential.³

When our lives get filled with so many commitments that we meet ourselves coming and going, the Lord will lovingly let us know what we need to let go of in order to maximize our fruit yield. He used His pruning shears in my life when someone asked me if I wanted to take over his Sunday school class. A desire rose up in me to say yes (because I love teaching and the rewards that come with it), but I told him I would have to pray about it. As it turned out, I didn't even get a chance to pray. When I discussed it with Steven, my Beloved reminded me (through Steven) that He did not want me to get distracted with anything else until I finished writing this study.

Like most believers, I have had to learn God's pruning principles the hard way. In my early years of serving the Lord, my zeal influenced me to say yes to almost every ministry opportunity that surfaced. Then, after the new wore off, I began to burn out because I had so many irons in the fire.

Our passion for a new thing will quickly wane if it is not something God has specifically called us to and wants to do through us. Just because something appears to be a *good* thing does not mean it is necessarily a *God* thing—for you. Those who take on many *good* ministry opportunities often struggle to keep their heads above water and are not bearing much fruit in any area because they are spread too thin. Thankfully, God is patient and gracious and will use His pruning shears to cause us to bear an abundance of fruit in what He has specifically called us to do—that is, *if* we will let Him.

> ➤ Does anything in your life need pruning? If so, agree with God to say no to the things that are keeping you from bearing abundant fruit in the areas He *has* called you to.

And the voice of the turtledove has been heard in our land.

The significance of hearing the voice of the migratory turtledove is yet another sign that the winter of law is over. The turtledove marks the return of spring more noticeably than all of the other birds because it is the *only* bird that sings perpetually from dawn to dusk. From sunup to sundown, they don't shut up!

Jewish expositors often refer to John the Baptist's voice as *the voice of the turtledove*. As mentioned in previous sections, John was a forerunner sent ahead of Jesus to proclaim the extraordinary news of the gospel of grace. His voice sang the praises of a Bridegroom who would take away our sins and give us eternal life (John 1:29; 3:23–36).

If you listen closely, you will hear the cooing turtledoves of our day. God has strategically placed them all over the world to sing of this gospel of grace and the return of "Mr. Grace" Himself for His bride.

> **"The fig tree has ripened its figs,**
> **And the vines in blossom have given forth their fragrance.**
> **Arise, my darling, my beautiful one,**
> **And come along!"**
> **—Song 2:13**

The fig tree has ripened its figs

The ripened figs also signal the end of winter and the beginning of spring. Most fruit trees blossom in early spring, with ripened fruit following. You may be surprised to learn (as I was) that the fig tree blossoms in the winter and bears ripe figs at the beginning of spring (Israel's summer).

Their tiny green blossoms are actually hidden inside a receptacle, and as the winter turns into spring, the receptacle ripens, turns red, and becomes the fruit. The maiden's Beloved is using the example of the fig tree to cause her to realize that she has been blossoming while hidden away with Him, and now it's time to manifest the ripened fruit of His Spirit through her life.

And the vines in blossom have given forth their fragrance

Finally, the maiden's Beloved speaks of the last sign that the winter of law is over and the spring of grace is here—the fragrant, blossoming grapevines. The *vines in blossom* represent the potential for fruitfulness in the maiden's life.

The growth cycle of grapevines begins with the formation of buds, progresses to fragrant blossoms, and culminates with the fruit (grapes). The maiden's life has gone past the budding stage—the early stages in her relationship with her Beloved. She has begun to blossom through experiencing His cherishing love and exuberant life, releasing His fragrance (2 Cor. 2:15). The blossoms of a grapevine emit a scent much like the fruit they will soon become.

In ancient Israel, the vine and the fig tree together represented "spiritual and material well-being" (1 Kings 4:25; Isa. 36:16). "To sit under one's own vine and one's own fig tree became a proverbial expression among the Jews to denote peace and prosperity."[4]

King Solomon's reign was characterized by peace and prosperity and was a foreshadowing of the coming reign of Jesus Christ. When the maiden's Beloved tells her that "the fig tree has ripened its figs, and the vines in blossom have given forth their fragrance," He is also saying, "It's time to let the world know that they too can share in the peace and prosperity of My eternal kingdom."

Just in case you're wondering if I am promoting the popular "prosperity gospel" here, let me assure you that I am not. This "name-it-and-claim-it" theology has several large flies in the ointment. The people of third-world countries would definitely be excluded here. And what about all the saints who were martyred for their faith? And Paul's thorn? The author of two-thirds of the New Testament laid hands on many people who were healed but was denied physical healing for himself. As you can see, the prosperity gospel doesn't "fly" with me.

The truth is—because we live on this fallen earth—we aren't promised that everything is going to work out the way we want it to while we're here. If we believe that, we set ourselves up for disappointment, disillusionment, depression, and all of those other dreaded D words. While it is true that there are those on this earth who may seem to be more blessed than others, all of those outward things are merely temporary. The economy can take a nosedive. People get sick and old. Unspeakable, heart-breaking tragedies happen.

The gospel of grace is the true prosperity gospel. The abundant wealth of life and peace in Christ's eternal kingdom is not of this world. What an incredible hope we have in Him! And it's *forever*.

Arise, my darling, my beautiful one, and come along!

After the beloved Shepherd-King gives the maiden all of the signs that the spring of grace is here and that the time is now to join Him in expressing His cherishing love and exuberant life in this world, she is still not budging. He repeats His invitation from Song 2:10, this time changing the inflection in His voice to that of a sense of urgency (indicated by the exclamation mark): "Arise, my darling, my beautiful one, and come along!"

The maiden needs a revelation that she can do what He calls her to do, regardless of the fear she feels. She does not have to let it paralyze her. Courage is not the *absence* of fear but *acting* in the face of it. To be more specific, courage is allowing Christ's Spirit to be expressed through our lives, regardless of the fleshly feelings of fear that try to hinder us. Christ's resurrection life *in* us is more powerful than anything the enemy could use in his attempt to keep us from glorifying our Beloved. The apostle John puts it this way: "Greater is He who is in you than he who is in the world" (1 John 4:4).

➤ Is there anything currently hindering you from saying yes to what your Beloved is calling you to do? Decide today that *His Spirit though you* can overcome every obstacle. Write a prayer to Him, expressing the desire of your heart to say yes in full dependence on Him.

➤ What is your Bridegroom speaking to you through today's study? How will you respond?

Day 2

The maiden's Beloved has just repeated His invitation to her to rise up out of the fear she is experiencing and join Him in expressing His love and life in this world. Her lack of movement indicates that she has declined His request.

In the next verse, you can almost hear His heartfelt pleading as He continues to remind her *whose* and *who* she is because of their eternal spiritual union. This verse spoken by the beloved Shepherd-King is packed with one of the most comprehensive descriptions of the Shulammite maiden's identity in the entire Song:

> **"O my dove, in the clefts of the rock,**
> **In the secret place of the steep pathway,**
> **Let me see your form,**
> **Let me hear your voice;**
> **For your voice is sweet,**
> **And your form is lovely."**
> **—Song 2:14**

One might say after reading this verse that this is the cry of a *desperate* man! He might even be accused of using flattery to get what He wants. But those who love Him know that is *not* the case. This most sincere Man is head over heels in love with His darling maiden and longs for her to have a personal revelation of her true identity in Him and the supernatural power available within her to overcome every obstacle she faces.

Her greatest obstacle is fear—fear of man, fear of failure, fear of being judged, fear of being hurt again. She has clearly taken her eyes off her Beloved and placed them on all the imaginary scenarios of what *could* happen to her if she says yes. Her predicament is similar to the apostle Peter's in Matthew 14:25–31, where Jesus issued an invitation to him:

> Immediately He made the disciples get into the boat and go ahead of Him to the other side, while He sent the crowds away. After He had sent the crowds away, He went up on the mountain by Himself to pray; and when it was evening, He was there alone.
>
> But the boat was already a long distance from the land, battered by the waves; for the wind was contrary. And in the fourth watch of the night He came to them, walking on the sea. When the disciples saw Him walking on the sea, they were terrified, and said, "It is a ghost!" And they cried out in fear.
>
> But immediately Jesus spoke to them, saying, "Take courage, it is I; do not be afraid." Peter said to Him, "Lord, if it is You, command me to come to You on the water." And He said, "Come!" And Peter got out of the boat, and walked on the water and came toward Jesus.
>
> But seeing the wind, he became frightened, and beginning to sink, he cried out, "Lord, save me!" Immediately Jesus stretched out His hand and took hold of him, and said to him, "You of little faith, why did you doubt?"

Although the maiden's and Peter's circumstances are similar in that they are both afraid, the basis for each one's fear is quite different. Peter's fear was based on what was actually happening at the time. The maiden's fear is coming from past and perceived future hurts. This reminds me of a popular quote by sixteenth-century French philosopher, Michel de Montaigne:

> My life has been filled with terrible misfortune; most of which never happened.[5]

Can you relate? How much of our time do we spend rehearsing the fearful *what-ifs* in our minds? An even better question might be, "How often do the things we fear are going to happen, actually happen?" A fascinating article from the *Huffington Post* says only about

"15 percent" of the time.[6] This means that 85 percent of what we worry about never happens. In light of this astonishing statistic, consider this: an eighty-year-old person who has spent his or her entire life living under the oppression of the *what-ifs*—*What if I can't pay my bills? What if I get cancer? What if my spouse or child dies? What if our country is taken over by terrorists, What if…*—has wasted sixty-eight years worrying about something that has never happened. What a tragedy!

Peter began to sink the very moment he took his eyes off Christ and put them on the storm-ravaged sea surrounding him. As Jesus reached out His hand to save Peter, He said to him, "You of little faith, why did you doubt?" Peter's faith in the storm's ability to destroy him was greater than his faith in Christ's ability to save him.

The apostle Paul tells us in Romans 10:17, "Faith comes from hearing, and hearing by the word of Christ." Peter stepped out of the boat based on the spoken word of Christ ("Come!"), but he began to sink when he listened to the voice of fear ("I'm going to die in this storm!").

Have you ever taken a step of faith based on what you believed Christ was leading you to do, and then you began to sink when you put your eyes on the less-than-favorable circumstances surrounding your decision? I have. And if you're like me, you question if you heard Him correctly—maybe you missed Him somehow. Almost every time this happens to me, He is so faithful to encourage me. He usually speaks gently through a thought in my mind: *Kim, don't question in the dark what I have spoken to you in the light.*

Our Beloved promises to keep those who are "steadfast of mind" in perfect peace because we trust in Him (Isa. 26:3). *Steadfast* means "to lean upon, lay, or rest."[7] Even when our emotions are screaming, we can choose with our will to lean on Him, to rest our minds on Christ and His Word. It may take some time for our emotions to catch up with our choice, but we can experience the perfect peace only *He* can provide when we trust in Him. This is tried-and-true faith in action.

Let's revisit the Amplified Bible, Classic Edition's definition of *faith*: "The leaning of our entire human personality on Him in absolute trust and confidence in His power, wisdom, and goodness." The bride of Christ's desire is to lean entirely on her Beloved, in absolute trust and confidence in His power, wisdom, and goodness. In order to do this, we must keep our eyes fixed on the unseen spiritual realities (communicated to us through God's Word) that are more real than what we can see with our natural eyes (2 Cor. 4:18).

O my dove

In Song 1:15, the beloved Shepherd-King told His darling maiden that she had *eyes like doves*. There, He was specifically referring to her "singleness of vision" in seeking Him alone to meet her need for rest and nourishment. In this phrase, *O my dove*, He is not referring to her focus because her eyes are clearly not fixed on Him at this point. *Fear is blocking her vision.* He is reminding her *who she is* and *Who she belongs to*, so that her *do* will begin to line up with her *true who*.

How often does our *do* line up with our *true who*? As I've previously mentioned, people most generally act like who they think they are. If we see ourselves as fearful, wimpy cowards, trusting in our natural strength and ability, we are going to act like one, even though that is not our true identity. On the other hand, if we see ourselves as courageous, overcoming victors, trusting in Christ's strength in and through us, our behavior will begin to line up with who we really are. Our awareness and acknowledgement of our true identities in Christ pave the way to daily victory.

In the clefts of the rock

When the beloved Shepherd-King refers to His dove as being *in the clefts of the rock*, He's reminding her *where* she is. This is a beautiful portrait of her being *in Christ* (the Rock). *Clefts* symbolize the wounds Christ incurred to obtain His bride. While He hung on the cross, a Roman soldier pierced (cleft) Jesus' side with a spear in order to prove that He was dead (John 19:34). As he did this, both water and blood gushed out:

> Many believe the spear wound in Jesus' side pierced His heart. The wound suggests a picture of the bride of Christ. His betrothed has come from His side like the first woman came from Adam's. Not from His rib, however—from His heart.[8]

As mentioned in the introductory material of this study, Eve's being formed from Adam's rib is an Old Testament foreshadowing of Christ's bride being formed in His death and resurrection. But God planned for us to be *in His Son* even before He created Adam (Eph. 1:4; 1 John 5:11, 20).

Another wonderful Scripture that describes Christ's bride as being safely tucked away *in Him* is Colossians 3:3. "For you have died and your life is hidden with Christ in God." Here we see the holy embrace of the Godhead. Even though it doesn't specifically mention the Spirit, we know He's *in there* because He lives in us.

We are *Christ's dove, hidden with Him in God*. Our old spirit-man was placed into Him and crucified with Him on the cross. Then, we were born again in His resurrection (Rom. 6:6; Gal. 2:20; 1 Pet. 1:3). Our eternal dwelling is *in Him*. The New Testament states over 160 times that Christians are *in Christ, in Jesus, in Him, in whom,* and so on. It's not just some haphazard way to describe a Christian. It's *where we live*—our spiritual location. We were born in Adam; now we are eternally alive in Christ. It's that simple.

Now, let's take a closer look at the second half of our focal phrase: *of the rock*. There are numerous Old Testament Scriptures that refer to God as our *Rock*. In Song 2:14, *rock* means "a stronghold of Jehovah, of security, a refuge safe from foes."[9] The phrase "in the cleft of the rock" is first found in Exodus 33:22, where God responds to Moses' request to see His glory: "It will come about, while My glory is passing by, that I will put you *in the cleft of the rock* and cover you with My hand until I have passed by."

Because God's glory is so powerful, He had to protect Moses from experiencing the fullness of it by hiding him in the cleft of a rock while He passed by. Today, God reveals His glory "in the face of Christ" to hearts hidden in Him (2 Cor. 4:6).

In 1763, Reverend Augustus Montague Toplady wrote "Rock of Ages," the classic Christian hymn that contains the lyrics, "Rock of Ages, cleft for me, let me hide myself in Thee."[10] Contemporary Christian artist Chris Rice has written a modern-day version of this time-honored invitational hymn that holds true to the original lyrics and uses easy-to-understand language. (If you would like to listen to his wonderful rendition, go to YouTube.com and type in "Chris Rice Rock of Ages.")

Every time I hear a hymn of invitation like "Rock of Ages," it reminds me of the one that was playing that crisp autumn evening in 1974 when I accepted Christ's invitation to become His dove (although I didn't know then that I was His dove). The song was "Just As I Am." If you grew up in a Baptist church, you probably know this hymn by heart.

My heart was about to explode inside my chest as I walked down the aisle in a multicolored stripes knit dress. That night, my life was changed forever. And now, after being in Christ, my Rock, for over forty years, I am overwhelmed with thankfulness for His love for me and His faithfulness to me!

In the secret place

The beloved Shepherd-King elaborates on the location of His dove, describing her as being "in the secret place." The definition of *secret place* is "covering, shelter, hiding place"[11] and is also mentioned in the psalms:

- "You hide them in the *secret place* of Your presence from the conspiracies of man; You keep them secretly in a shelter from the strife of tongues" (Ps. 31:20).
- "For in the day of trouble He will conceal me in His tabernacle; in the *secret place* of His tent He will hide me; He will lift me up on a rock" (Ps. 27:5).

There are many wonderful benefits to being hidden in the secret place of our Beloved's presence—from being hidden from the conspiracies of man, to being sheltered from the strife of tongues, to being concealed in the day of trouble. He is our covering, our shelter, and our hiding place!

As I've previously mentioned, movies can stir our souls in ways that mere words on a page cannot. *Quo Vadis* is one of those movies. Set in the time of Rome's evil emperor Nero, this motion picture vividly communicates like no other the unwavering confidence of those who know they are hidden with Christ in God. The images of the early Christians being herded into the Coliseum will be forever burned in my mind.

The most unforgettable part of the movie is near the end, where blood-thirsty spectators are cheering loudly while believers are either being tied to stakes to be burned or left on the ground as prey for hungry lions. All of a sudden, something most unexpected happens. The crowd grows deathly silent as the victims begin singing beautiful songs to the Lord—as if He were standing before them face to face. I couldn't hold back the tears as I sat in front of my television, mesmerized. (There is a lump forming in my throat even now as I recall the scene.)

As you may well imagine, the peaceful countenances and songs of joy coming from the believers astonished and outraged Nero and his maniacal entourage. These captivated martyrs profoundly demonstrated that they knew—even though their physical bodies (houses) were about to be destroyed—*they were safe from harm in the secret place*. And they would soon see Him face to face (2 Cor. 5:1–8).

This scene reminded me of the biblical account of Stephen, a devoted follower of Christ, while he was being stoned by the angry religionists of his day. Acts 7:55 says that right before he died, "he gazed intently into heaven and saw the glory of God, and Jesus standing at the right hand of God." Stephen also knew that no harm could come to him, because he was hidden in the cleft of the Rock, in the secret place.

Of the steep pathway

Steep pathways are difficult and often treacherous to climb in our natural strength. The beloved Shepherd-King describes the secret place in Him as being *of the steep pathway*. Apparently, the pathway to Him is steep—so steep that it's impossible to get to Him in our human strength. Thankfully, He conquered sin and death for us, took us out of Adam, and set us down with Him in heaven—without an ounce of our help (Col. 1:13; Eph. 2:5–6). All we had to do was believe in (into) Him (John 3:16).

There are many who refuse to believe in Christ because it seems too good to be true—too easy. Surely, there is something they must do, some way they can earn their place in heaven.

To think that there is something we can do to save ourselves when Jesus *already* scaled the humanly insurmountable steep pathway for us is the pinnacle of human pride.

Let me see your form, let me hear your voice
In this phrase, the beloved Shepherd-King is pleading with His darling maiden to break through that wall of the fear ("see your form") by speaking ("hear your voice") the truth of who she is in Him. Entire studies have been written on the power of our spoken words (Prov. 12:6; 18:21; Mark 11:23). Words can be either creative or destructive. When we speak the Word of God about who we are in the midst of seemingly formidable circumstances, fear will begin to fall off us, and we will move confidently and courageously forward in the call He has placed on our lives.

For your voice is sweet
When He tells her that her *voice is sweet*, He is reminding her that who she is in Him is sweet (pleasing). Any words she speaks or thoughts she thinks that do not reflect her pure, righteous, and holy identity cannot originate from her pleasant new heart.

And your form is lovely
When He tells her that her *form is lovely*, He is saying, "Who you are is lovely. When you walk by My Spirit—from your new heart—your *behavior* is also lovely and pleasing." Here again, He is reminding her that any motivation to act contrary to His will cannot come from her lovely new heart.

You may be wondering, "If the origin of her refusal to say yes to Him is not coming from her new heart, and her sin nature was crucified with Christ, then where is it coming from, and how is it motivating her to walk by the flesh?" Stay tuned. Days 3 and 4 of this week's study will expose the enemy's strategies for duping believers into walking by the flesh and will offer helpful ways to resist his schemes so that we can consistently walk by Christ's Spirit.

It is important to understand that the maiden is not refusing her Beloved out of blatant rebelliousness but because of fear. The debilitating feelings she is experiencing are not valid, because they are based in deception, rather than the truth. Yes, they are real, but they are not valid. The only way we can overcome invalid feelings of fear is to fill our minds with the truths of who we are in our Beloved.

Contemporary Christian artist Jason Gray has a wonderful music video that encourages believers in Christ to fix their eyes on their true identities. You can go to YouTube.com and type in "Jason Gray Remind Me Who I Am (Official Music Video)" to watch it. If you enjoyed the lyrics to this song, I believe that you will appreciate all of his albums because many of his songs have the believer's true identity in Christ as the underlying theme.

MercyMe's two newest albums, *Lifer* and *Welcome to the New*, are also saturated with the truths of our identity in Christ. I don't think these albums will ever get old to me because the truths in them are timeless. As I dance to, sing along with, and sometimes cry with joy over their liberating lyrics, I am reminded again and again that my voice is sweet and my form is lovely—all because of what my Beloved did for me and in me.

> ➤ Hear your Bridegroom speaking to you. "Let Me see your form, let Me hear your voice; for your voice is sweet, and your form is lovely." Respond by writing a prayer of thankfulness for the realization that who you are *is* your pleasing and lovely new heart.

The beloved Shepherd-King has spent the last five verses (2:10–14) encouraging His darling, beautiful dove to realize who she is, rise up out of her fear, and respond to His invitation to join Him in expressing His cherishing love and exuberant life in this world. The question is, will she finally say yes?

> ➤ What is your Bridegroom speaking to you through today's study? How will you respond?

Day 3

We closed day 2 by listening to the beloved Shepherd-King encouraging His darling, beautiful dove to acknowledge her true identity (*sweet voice* and *lovely form*) in Him and rise up out of the fear that is hindering her from saying yes to His call. At this point, she has not complied.

We also considered the following question concerning the maiden's unresponsiveness: "If the origin of her refusal to say yes to Him is not coming from her new heart, and her sin nature was crucified with Christ, then *where* is it coming from, and *how* is it motivating her to walk by the flesh?" Today's and day 4's study will expose how the enemy works in our minds and will offer practical ways to resist his schemes so that we can consistently walk by Christ's Spirit.

I have to admit that these two days of study are probably my favorites. They blow the enemy's cover in a way that can bring incredible freedom to anyone who is struggling with his or her thought life (Eph. 5:11). Do you know *any* Christian who hasn't struggled with his or her thought life? Sure, there may be some who display a persona that might suggest otherwise, but it's just a facade. They live inside a fleshly body that has not yet been redeemed and is subject to the influence of sin (see Romans 7). And I'm not talking about the verb *sin* but the noun *sin*. Stay tuned for day 4.

Let's begin this exposé by reading a story about a princess named Annaleigh.

> Once upon a time, in a beautiful kingdom, there lived a princess named Annaleigh. A great king ruled the kingdom. He resided in a palace in the center of the land, surrounded by many princes and princesses. All of his children were welcome to come see him at the palace anytime they wished. The Princess Annaleigh went often to visit with the king. She'd sit on his lap while he told her stories. Sometimes they'd sing together. When she wasn't in the palace, the princess loved to be outdoors. She'd splash in the stream running around the edge of the kingdom, climb the giant trees, and dance barefoot in the lush green meadows.
>
> However, the Nidgits also lived in the kingdom. The Nidgits wanted to overthrow the Great King so they could rule the kingdom themselves. But they knew the Great King was too wise, too strong, and too powerful to be beaten. So they decided the best way to attack him was through his children, and Princess Annaleigh became one of their targets. The Nidgits knew that if the princess saw them, she'd pay no attention to them or what they said, so they decided to hide in the bushes while she waded in the river, climbed the trees, and danced in the meadow and tell her Lies.

Beginning the following day, when Princess Annaleigh went out to play, she began to hear the whispered Lies. As she waded, she'd hear, "You're stupid and ugly. You aren't worth much." As she climbed, she'd hear, "The Great King doesn't really love you." As she danced, she'd hear, "The other princesses are prettier than you." Sadly, Annaleigh began to believe the words. She felt worthless, unloved, and ugly. And she soon stopped wading, climbing, and dancing. But the words continued to ring in her head. She heard them over and over again. And they became more and more true to her. She also stopped visiting the Great King—after all, she thought, why would he want to see stupid, ugly, worthless me?

One day, Princess Annaleigh heard a knock on the door. She'd hoped it wasn't one of the other princesses or princes asking her to play again. She was so tired of giving excuses. Maybe I'll just ignore it, she thought. But the knocking persisted, and she finally opened the door—just a crack. There, on her stoop, stood the Great King. "Where have you been?" he asked, his voice soft and sad.

The Great King? Here to see me? But why? She shrugged in response. She was ashamed to say that she wasn't worth it. That he had no reason to love her. That the other princesses were prettier than she. But he seemed to know anyway. "My sweet Annaleigh, don't believe the Lies you hear whispered by the Nidgits. They are not true. They only tell you those things to get you away from me."

The princess began to weep. And the Great King drew her into his magnificent arms and assured her of his love for her and her immense value to him. The more she heard his voice, the more ridiculous the Lies seemed. Of course, they weren't true. She was precious. She was loved. She was beautiful.

The Great King looked solemn for a moment. "Annaleigh, the Lies will always be there. They will continue to be whispered around you. But you must come to me in order to know the truth."

The next day, Princess Annaleigh went to wade in the sparkling streams, climb the towering oak trees, and dance barefoot in the lush green meadows. The whispers still came. And the Lies seemed to make sense again. So she ran to the palace to see the Great King. And as he held her on his lap and stroked her hair, he spoke Truth to her until the Lies faded away, and once more she knew how much the King adored her. And Princess Annaleigh and the Great King lived happily ever after.[12]

➤ What strategy did the Nidgits use to attack Princess Annaleigh, and how was it so effective?

➤ Could you see yourself in this story? If so, what lies are you believing that keep you from enjoying your life and spending time with your Beloved King?

The Nidgets' *hiddenness* caused Princess Annaleigh to believe their whispered lies and kept her from enjoying her life and her relationship with the Great King. More than likely, she believed they were her own thoughts because she could not see where they were coming from. And after all, if she was thinking them, wouldn't they have to be true?

Real? Yes.

True? Not necessarily.

This poignant fairy tale resembles what is happening in the Song. The maiden cannot see the culprits behind the paralyzing fear she is experiencing, but her Beloved can (He's omniscient). In the same way that the Great King exposed the Nidgits' lies, the beloved Shepherd-King exposes the *real* culprits behind the maiden's unresponsiveness and tells her exactly what to do with them.

> **"Catch the foxes for us,**
> **The little foxes that are ruining the vineyards,**
> **While our vineyards are in blossom."**
> **—Song 2:15**

Catch the foxes for us

An entire library could be written on the importance of following our Beloved's command to catch the foxes. These foxes are the lies being fed to our minds by our enemy, and it is our responsibility to catch them.

A New Testament parallel to this verse is found in Paul's second letter to the Corinthian church. In this epistle, he was responding to the accusations of false teachers who had infiltrated the church and were attacking his integrity and authority as an apostle. Rather than viewing this conflict as a battle against flesh and blood, Paul recognized that it was a *spiritual* battle and described it in the language of military warfare.

> ➤ If you do not have a New American Standard Bible, use the Internet (BibleStudyTools.com, BibleGateway.com, or BlueLetterBible.org) to find 2 Corinthians 10:3–5 in that translation. Then, write the passage in the following space.

Please notice that Paul is not referring to walking *by* the flesh (in dependence on the flesh), but walking *in* the flesh in this passage. This means that we live in a physical realm experienced through our physical senses of sight, hearing, taste, touch, and smell. Paul is pointing out that the battle he is experiencing is one in which the real culprits are hidden from his natural radar. His battle is against unseen spiritual fortresses.

> ➤ In verse 5, what does Paul say these fortresses are made up of?

The Greek words used for *speculations* and *every lofty thing raised up against the knowledge of God* refer to thoughts that are hostile or antagonistic to Christ and His Word. These thoughts can rightfully be described as *enemies of Christ* because they oppose Him and His Word.

> ➤ What does Paul instruct us to do with these unseen enemy thoughts?

Practically speaking, what does it mean for us to take these enemy thoughts *captive to the obedience of Christ*? First, the obvious must be stated. Soldiers capture their enemies, not their fellow soldiers. These enemy thoughts cannot originate within the new heart of a believer. They are introduced through sources outside the new heart. In week 2 of our study, we described one of these sources as the flesh—the patterns stored in our physical brains that are rooted in deception and interfere with our dependence on Christ's Spirit. Let's revisit our diagram of "The Flesh."

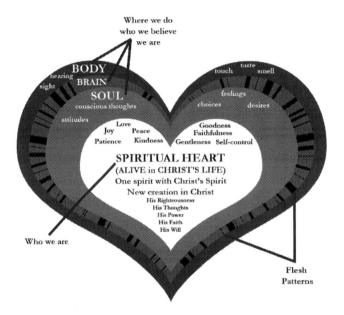

Figure 4: The Flesh

Please notice that these patterns are not part of but are *outside* our new man (our spiritual hearts). A commonly held misconception is that the thoughts of man are generated in the brain. Yet Scripture describes them as being formed in the heart or spirit (Matt. 15:19; Mark 7:21; Luke 1:51; Heb. 4:12).

Our brain is a computer where information is received, processed, and stored. Information received from our environment through our physical senses of sight, hearing, taste, smell, and touch will either reflect truth or lies, depending on its original source. Information that comes from our new hearts (the union of our new spirit with Christ's Spirit) will always reflect truth. All truth ultimately finds its origin in Jesus (John 14:6). At the opposite end of the spectrum is Satan, the father of lies (John 8:44). The Greek word for *father* is *pater*, which means "generator."[13] All lies are generated by our enemy.

Information, whether in the form of truth or lies, enters our brains as thoughts. These thoughts could be classified as godly (truth), neutral (factual truth), or ungodly (lies). The believer's brain can receive ungodly thoughts from outside sources, but ungodly thoughts cannot be generated in his or her new heart. Further evidence of this can be found when we examine what it means to take ungodly enemy thoughts captive to the obedience of Christ. Let's look at Philippians 2:8 to find out what the "obedience of Christ" was:

> Being found in appearance as a man, He humbled Himself by becoming obedient to the point of death, even death on a cross.

➢ What was the obedience of Christ?

Now let's look at Romans 5:19 to see what the obedience of Christ accomplished.

> For as through the one man's disobedience the many were made sinners, even so through the obedience of the One the many will be made righteous.

➢ What did the obedience of Christ accomplish?

Through Christ's humble obedience in laying down His life on the cross, He caused all who would believe in (into) Him to become the righteousness of God through their co-crucifixion and co-resurrection with Him (2 Cor. 5:21; Gal. 2:20; Rom. 6:6; 1 Pet. 1:3). Those who are "the righteousness of God in Jesus Christ" *cannot generate* unrighteous (ungodly) thoughts. They have "the mind of Christ," which means they possess His thoughts, feelings, and purposes (1 Cor. 2:16 AMPC). To "take every thought captive to the obedience of Christ," then, means to judge the thoughts we experience in light of the truth of our righteous identity in Christ.

If the thoughts we experience are ungodly, they didn't come from our new hearts but from sources outside of it, which ultimately find their genesis in Satan. If they are godly, they either came from our new hearts (new spirits united with Christ's Spirit) or godly outside sources, such as the Bible. If they are neutral, they came from factual outside sources.

When we first become aware of an ungodly thought, we must acknowledge that it did not come from us but from Satan, the generator of all lies. Then, we need to take it captive by saying out loud, "That is not my thought! I refuse to own it, meditate on it, or act on it! I am the righteousness of God in Jesus Christ, and I have the thoughts, feelings, and purposes of His heart."

If we could actually see the face of the one speaking these ungodly thoughts into our minds, we would be much less likely to accept them as our own. The following is an enlightening illustration of this concept:

> I was once counseling a man who battled with this problem. Periodically, blasphemous thoughts would cross his mind. This led him to believe that he had committed the unpardonable sin. Yet the man was a Christian. I attempted to explain to him that not all his thoughts were his own, but he didn't understand.
>
> There was another person in the room with us observing our meeting. I leaned toward the man with the problem and motioned for him to lean toward me. I then whispered in his ear, "Do you see Jim sitting there beside you?" He nodded.
>
> "Slap him in the face as hard as you can," I said. The man looked at Jim and then looked at me, bewildered. I waited. He sat there for a moment, looking back and forth. Again I motioned for him to lean toward me, then whispered, "With an open hand, slap Jim in the face so hard that you knock him off the chair!" (Jim didn't know his vulnerable position at this moment!) Then I sat back. The man looked confused, unsure of what to do.
>
> Finally, I asked him aloud, "Are you going to do it?" "No!" he answered. "Well, are you at least going to confess to God that you had such a terrible thought?" I asked. "No," he said. "Why not?" I persisted. "Because *you* said it!" he responded. "That's right," I said. "And somebody else is saying things to you sometimes, too, but you've been taking the blame for it."[14]

Somebody else is saying things to you sometimes, but you've been taking the blame for it. Satan's power lies in his deception, his duping us into believing that these ungodly thoughts originated with us. In this battle going on in our minds, it is vital that we understand that it is not a sin to *hear* (become aware of) an ungodly thought. Sin is conceived in our minds when we accept the ungodly thought as our own and meditate on it. It then comes to full fruition when we act on it.

In one of the sessions I teach at our "Your Bridegroom Awaits" women's retreats, I share how the enemy works in our thought lives by feeding us ungodly thoughts. My daughter-in-law, Katie, attended our last fall retreat and was hearing this for the first time. She said out loud (during the session), "I feel so violated!" The knowledge of how the enemy works in her thought life made her mad! And rightly so.

If this information of how the enemy works in your thought life is also new to you, dear bride, I pray that you will rise up in holy and righteous anger (in Christ's strength) and make a commitment to refuse Satan's garbage. If the thoughts you are experiencing are ungodly, Satan is throwing his trash in your yard, and you don't have to put up with it. Pick it up and throw it right back at him!

Satan's greatest weapon is deception (Rev. 12:9). Our greatest weapons are the Word of God and the Spirit of Christ living in us. First John 4:4 tells us, "Greater is He who is in you than he who is in the world." Through the power of Christ and His Word, we can successfully take these ungodly thoughts captive. We can *catch the foxes* that are ruining our vineyards.

So far, we have been discussing defensive strategies in the battle going on in our thought lives—what we do in response to Satan's infiltrating our minds with his ungodly thoughts. Let's get real here. If we tried to analyze and deal with every ungodly thought we experience, it would likely drive us nuts. The picture that comes to mind is the arcade game where moles pop up out of their holes and our job is to bop all of them on the head with a hammer so they will go back inside. There's no way we're getting a perfect score on that one! And there's no way that we could possibly deal with every sinful thought we experience.

Let's hang up our hammer and play a different game. Let's go on the offensive and be proactive in the battle going on in our minds. After all, someone said, "The best defense is a good offense." One of the ways we can be proactive is to allow Christ to captivate our minds to the point that there is room for little else. Just like Annaleigh sat on the Great King's lap and listened to Him tell her truth until the lies faded away, we can fill our minds with new covenant truth—the gospel of grace. We can intentionally acknowledge and enjoy our Beloved's affection, practice His presence through worshiping Him, and trust Him on a moment-by-moment basis to think His thoughts and live His life through us.

I mentioned in an earlier section that we can use sticky notes to keep our minds filled with the truth concerning our pure, holy, and righteous identities in Christ. These tangible reminders posted in places we frequent throughout the day will enable us to focus on unseen spiritual truth.

If you want to be reminded on a regular basis that ungodly thoughts don't come from you, post a sticky note on your bathroom mirror that reads, "I have the mind of Christ—His thoughts, feelings, and purposes." You can also post notes on your vehicle visor, your desk at work, your refrigerator, and your coffee table that read, "Christ lives in me to think His thoughts and live His life through me." This will remind you that Christ is your life, and apart from Him you can do nothing of eternal value.

There are so many ways that we can be intentional about keeping our minds on Christ. When you get thirsty and reach for a bottle of water, let this be a reminder that you need to take time each day to acknowledge and enjoy Christ's refreshing love. Ask Him to reveal His love for you *to* you in personal ways. He delights in doing this! So keep your eyes open.

When you see sunrises and sunsets, take a moment to acknowledge and worship the Artist who paints them new for you every day. When you breathe in the fragrance of fresh flowers and behold their exquisite beauty, thank their Creator for giving you pleasure through them. When you hear a song on the radio that you needed to hear at that moment in time, praise your Beloved for being so personal. Keeping our minds fixed on Christ is the only way to live! Have fun, and be creative in how you plan to do this.

Just as sure as the sun rises in the morning, you can be certain that there will be days when you realize you have gone hours without having Christ on your mind. When this happens, thank Him for the nudge and don't beat yourself up. For someone to think about Christ every second of every day, while living in a world filled with distractions, would be nothing short of miraculous.

> ➤ What changes are you going to make—beginning today—in order to be proactive in the battle going on in your mind? Be specific.

> ➤ What is your Bridegroom speaking to you through today's study? How will you respond?

Day 4

In day 3, we began our discussion of Song 2:15, where the beloved Shepherd-King reveals the culprits behind the paralyzing fear the maiden is experiencing—the ungodly thoughts (the foxes) introduced into her mind by the enemy. He implores her to take action against ("catch") these despicable, destructive creatures:

> **"Catch the foxes for us,**
> **The little foxes that are ruining the vineyards,**
> **While our vineyards are in blossom."**
> **—Song 2:15**

The little foxes that are ruining the vineyards, while our vineyards are in blossom.
Foxes, moles, gophers, groundhogs, prairie dogs, and rabbits are all, by nature, burrowers that make their homes in underground tunnels. Of all of these dirt dwellers, foxes are the most cunning and deceptive, skilled at using hiddenness to their advantage. People who are known for their underhandedness and trickery are often referred to as "sly foxes."

The foxes that are ruining the vineyards in the Song are not full-grown foxes that are typically seen eating the fruit but the *little foxes*. The maiden's Beloved is telling her that these little foxes are responsible for destroying her fruit-bearing capacity (blossoming vineyards). These ungodly thoughts are hindering her from expressing His cherishing love and exuberant life.

You might ask, "How can something so small ruin an entire vineyard?" The answer lies in where they do their dirty work. While full-grown foxes can wipe out entire crops by eating the fruit off the vine, the little foxes often remain unseen while they dig their tunnels and holes and spoil the roots of the grapevines. They also gnaw on the branches until they are severed from the vine, completely destroying their fruit-bearing capacity.

I'm not suggesting that the ungodly thoughts we hear in our minds have the ability to sever us from the life of Christ. Nothing can do that (John 10:28; 2 Tim. 2:13; Heb. 13:5). They can, however, dupe us into walking by the flesh, which will keep the fruit of the Spirit—love, joy, peace, patience, kindness, goodness, faithfulness, gentleness, and self-control—from being expressed through our lives (Gal. 5:22–23).

If we want our fruit yield maximized and our Beloved glorified, our role is clear: catch the foxes. Take the ungodly thoughts (lies) that Satan feeds to us captive by refusing to own, meditate on, or act on them. While our role in this battle going on in our minds is clear, that doesn't always mean it's easy to do. Our enemy is cunning.

As mentioned in day 3, the fact that we cannot see Satan inject these ungodly thoughts into our minds gives him an advantage. It is easy to believe they came from us because we are the only one hearing them in our minds. And when we believe they came from us, it feels like there is a civil war going on inside—a "good me" fighting against a "bad me."

Let's face it. Feelings can be very strong motivators. That's why it is so important to know the truth. Truth always trumps feelings in this faith walk. And the simple truth is the "bad you" was exterminated. Annihilated. Eliminated. Obliterated. Eradicated. Decimated. (See Rom. 6:6; Gal. 2:20; Col. 3:3.) There is no way that these ungodly thoughts are coming from the new you!

Our battle is not against ourselves but against unseen spiritual forces, often working through the familiar flesh patterns stored in our brains. The apostle Paul shares specifically what these unseen powers are in his letter to the Ephesian church:

> Our fight is not against people on earth but against *the rulers and authorities* and *the powers of this world's darkness*, against *the spiritual powers of evil in the heavenly world*. (Eph. 6:12 NCV)

The enemy is thrilled when he is able to trick us into thinking that our battle is against ourselves or other people (flesh and blood). As long as he remains undercover as our real opponent, he has more power to wield over us. The opposite is also true. Once his schemes are exposed, his power to do damage in our lives is greatly diminished.

Although I have no personal knowledge of what it is like to be a soldier in the military, doing battle against a real, physical enemy, I did learn to do full-court battle with various opponents when I played basketball in junior high and high school. In practices, we would run through different defensive and offensive strategies because our goal was to win the upcoming game.

Can you imagine how differently I would have played if I'd been able to sit in the locker room of the opposing team and hear their strategy for winning the game before it started? Whether we realize it or not, Satan's game plan for defeating us in the battle going on in our minds is to trap us into doing "his will" (2 Tim. 2:26). He is a thief whose job description is "to steal and kill and destroy" (John 10:10). Although Satan cannot touch us spiritually, he can greatly hinder our effectiveness in expressing our Beloved's cherishing love and exuberant life if he can trick us into owning the ungodly thoughts he serves up to us.

Even though history was one of my least favorite subjects in school, I have been highly motivated to learn about military war strategies due to the battle going on in my thought life. We can learn a great deal about how the master deceiver does battle in our minds from one of his most nefarious pawns, Adolf Hitler.

Much of Hitler's power was amassed through covert operations. After World War I—and in complete violation of the Treaty of Versailles—he secretly began rearming Germany, building tanks and planes in large factories disguised as elementary school buildings. While many of the countries hit hard by the war were rebuilding their economies, Germany was rebuilding its military strength, all the while going unseen. Clandestine operations like this helped Hitler and his forces gain tremendous military advantage at the beginning and through much of World War II.

One operation in particular caught my attention because of its likeness to the way the enemy works in our thought lives. Operation Greif was used by German forces during the Battle of the Bulge near the end of the war. Its purpose was to capture one or more of the bridges over the Meuse River before Allied forces could destroy them.

Hitler informed the commander of the operation that his mission could be accomplished more quickly and with fewer losses if he and his men disguised themselves in U.S. and British uniforms and traveled in captured Allied tanks. These men also needed to know how to speak fluent English and have knowledge of the American dialect in order to ensure the success of this highly covert operation.

Hitler's aim was for the small units disguised as Allies to cause great confusion by giving false orders, upsetting communications, and misdirecting troops. Although his plan failed in achieving its original aim of securing the Meuse bridges, it wrought much havoc before the American and British forces caught wind of it. Once they were made aware of their enemy's schemes, however, the Allied forces became vigilant in their defense, on the lookout for any impostors.

Operation Greif mirrors how Satan hoodwinks us in our thought lives. He dresses up his thoughts as our own in order to delude and discombobulate us in our walk with Christ. And if we allow these impostors to set up camp in our minds, they can do untold amounts of damage.

In war, the more our enemy can remain hidden in his schemes, the more wreckage he can cause. Had another one of Hitler's surreptitious plans been fully realized before the end of World War II, the final outcome could have been very different.

In an effort to reduce the visibility of his military air power, Hitler collaborated with aviation specialists to develop stealth aircraft—much like the bombers we see today. *Stealth* means "the act or characteristic of moving with extreme care and quietness, especially so as to avoid detection."[15] These aircraft were being designed in a way that would hinder their detection by enemy radar. If they would have been completely developed and mass produced before the end of the war, the Axis powers might have triumphed. Thank God they weren't!

Even though our Beloved has *already* secured the eternal spiritual victory for us, if we are going to consistently express His love and His life in this world, we need to know how the enemy works in our minds. So far, we have learned that the believer in Christ cannot generate ungodly thoughts—Satan is introducing them into our minds, disguising them as our own. The question is, how exactly does he dress up his suggestions to trick us into believing they came from us?

Satan's thoughts are disguised in a way that is highly undetectable by our own radar. But his cover is about to be blown. Once you get this revelation—once his primary disguise is revealed—your life will never be the same. I know, because mine hasn't been, not since Bill Gillham taught me how the enemy works in my thought life.[16]

The Spirit revealed this to Bill, he communicated it to me (through his books), and the Spirit has confirmed it in my heart. Thank you, Bill (if you are listening from heaven), for sharing this liberating knowledge! I am so blessed to take this baton of truth and, through this study, pass it on to other believers in their race to the finish line of faith (1 Cor. 9:24; 2 Tim. 4:7; Heb. 12:1). Because of this teaching, my race has been so much more enjoyable, and I pray the same for everyone participating in this study.

First, it is important for us to acknowledge that Satan has no direct (inside) access to us (our new spiritual heart). We are protected and sealed eternally in Christ. But he is able to influence our choices from the outside in. And he does his dirty work through an invisible, rogue agent. Let's look at Romans 7:15–24, where the apostle Paul shares his personal struggle with this entity (italics added for emphasis).

> For what I am doing, I do not understand; for I am not practicing what I would like to do, but I am doing the very thing I hate. But if I do the very thing I do not want to do, I agree with the Law, confessing that the Law is good. So now, *no longer am I the one doing it, but sin which dwells in me.*
>
> For I know that nothing good dwells in me, that is, in my flesh; for the willing is present in me, but the doing of the good is not. For the good that I want, I do not do, but I practice the very evil that I do not want. But if I am doing the very thing I do not want, *I am no longer the one doing it, but sin which dwells in me.* I find then the principle that evil is present in me, the one who wants to do good.
>
> For I joyfully concur with the law of God in the inner man, but *I see a different law in the members of my body, waging war against the law of my mind and making me a prisoner of the law of sin which is in my members.* Wretched man that I am! Who will set me free from the body of this death?

In this passage, there are two participants, Paul and sin. Paul is the one who "wants to do good," and sin is the one who is influencing Paul "to do the very evil that he does not want to do." According to Paul, where does sin reside? Verse 23 clearly states that sin dwells in the members of Paul's body (his physical house), not in his new heart.

Most of the time, we think of the word sin as an action verb, but in this context and in other places in the Word of God, sin is a noun, not a verb. In fact, sin is personified in these verses. Satan's covert agent, sin, works through the members of our physical bodies (which include the flesh patterns in our brains) in an attempt to control us through deception.

The first place in Scripture this personified entity rears its ugly head is Genesis 4:7, where we find God warning Cain, "If you do well, will not your countenance be lifted up? And if you do not do well, *sin is crouching at the door; and its desire is for you, but you must master it.*" The King James Version actually uses the personal pronouns *his* and *him* in referring to this power called sin.

We also find several references to sin (the personified noun) in the chapter just prior to the account of Paul's struggle:

> Therefore *do not let sin reign in your mortal body so that you obey its lusts, and do not go on presenting the members of your body to sin as instruments of unrighteousness;* but present yourselves to God as those alive from the dead, and your members as instruments of righteousness to God. For *sin shall not be master over you,* for you are not under law but under grace … Do you not know that *when you present yourselves to someone as slaves for obedience, you are slaves of the one whom you obey, either of sin resulting in death, or of obedience resulting in righteousness?* (Rom. 6:12–14, 16)

In the above passage, sin is described as trying to influence us to offer our bodies as instruments of unrighteousness. We could think of this agent of Satan that dwells in our physical bodies as the antithesis of Christ's Spirit, who dwells in our new spirit. Whereas Christ's Spirit positively influences us (from the inside out) to offer our bodies as tools for expressing righteousness, sin negatively influences us (from the outside in) to offer our bodies as tools for expressing unrighteousness. So yes, there is an unmistakable battle going on in our minds. But it is not between a good you and a bad you. It is between your new heart and Satan's rogue agent, sin, which resides in your physical body.

When we believed in (into) Christ, nothing changed in our physical bodies. We got spiritual heart transplants and became brand-new persons, but we still live inside the same old earth suits. One morning, the Lord gave me a picture that helped me understand the relationship between my new heart, soul, and body, and this invisible agent of Satan called sin.

He used Andrew Farley's book *God without Religion* to do this. In his book, Farley compares sin in our physical bodies to a rat living inside the walls of our house.[17] Let's take a look at that picture.

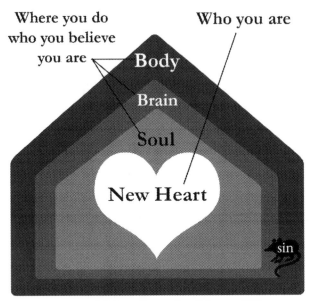

Figure 8: The Rat in Your House

My prayer is that this diagram will help you understand that the bad you no longer exists. Please notice that you are not the house you live in. Second Corinthians 5:1 clarifies that our bodies are where we live, not who we are. "We know that if our earthly house, this tent, is destroyed, we have a building from God, a house not made with hands, eternal in the heavens" (NKJV).

Your body (which includes your brain) is represented by the walls of this house. Your new heart—who you are now—lives inside the walls. Your soul and body are where you do who you believe you are. Satan's undercover agent, sin, which resides in your physical body, is like a rat that lives inside the walls of your house.

Have you ever heard a rat inside the walls of your house? One night after Steven and I had gone to bed, we heard scratching noises. We got up and turned on the light to see if we could figure out where the noise was coming from, but we couldn't see anything. We had a pretty good idea it was a rat, though. (Okay, it was probably just a mouse, but they're all *rats* to me!) Even though we couldn't see it, we knew it was there, hidden inside the walls of our house.

In Farley's book, he shares a true story of how a real rat did more than just make noise at his house. Unbeknownst to him and over a considerable amount of time, this ruinous rodent ate through the tubing in his heating unit and a bathtub pipe, costing him $3,500 in damages!

Unseen varmints clearly have the capability of making noise and wreaking all kinds of havoc in our lives—especially sin. Unbeknownst to us, Satan has been working through his covert agent, sin, to try to destroy our effectiveness in the kingdom of God (John 10:10).

Before exposing sin's primary disguise in the battle going on in our minds, it is important to point out that even though sin resides in our physical bodies, the body itself is not evil. It is a tool that can be used for righteousness or unrighteousness, depending on our choices (Rom. 6:16). A can of spray paint isn't evil, but it can be used for evil purposes, such as vandalism. Alternately, it can be used for good to refresh a piece of furniture. God designed our bodies to be effective tools for accomplishing His purposes in this world.

Now, are you ready to find out exactly how this rogue rat causes damage in our lives, all the while going unseen? We are going to blow his cover by looking at your written response from page 165 of this study. There, you were asked to write down the ungodly thoughts you experience on a regular basis that cause negative feelings.

> ➢ Please rewrite your response here. If your answer is blank, please take some time (before moving on) to write down the ungodly thoughts you experience on a regular basis that cause negative feelings.

> ➢ Which specific words within these thoughts would lead you to believe they originated with you?

If you answered the question with first-person pronouns (I, me, myself, mine), then you have uncovered Satan's primary disguise in influencing you to own, meditate on, and act on the ungodly thoughts he introduces to you through his personified agent called sin. He feeds thoughts to you in first person so you will believe that you thought them!

I saw the perfect example of this while watching a superhero movie (I love superhero movies). In this particular scene, the antagonist made himself invisible to the people he was in the room with. Then, he spoke a first-person thought into the ear of a very influential man. Immediately, the man parroted the thought. Of course, he thought it was *his* own suggestion. He couldn't see his enemy! That suggestion set in motion a very destructive turn of events that cost a lot of lives.

While Satan certainly cannot read our minds (he is not omniscient), he has access to our thought lives through this personified entity called sin. He whispers ungodly thoughts into our minds in first person and makes us think they are our thoughts. If we could see that Satan was the original source of these thoughts—thoughts like, *I'm such a loser! I can't do anything right!*—we wouldn't even give them the time of day. But when we are convinced that these thoughts originated with us, we have a difficult time believing we are the new creation that Christ unquestionably declares us to be in His Word, and our spoken words and actions ultimately reflect what we believe. In short, we become a pawn in the enemy's hands when we take his bait.

Knowledge of our righteous identity in Christ and how the enemy feeds us unrighteous thoughts can help us experience daily victory in the battle going on in our thought lives. However, if we own and act on these ungodly thoughts, we will experience sure defeat.

By the way, just in case you're wondering, Satan also feeds us thoughts in second and third person—condemning thoughts like, *You've really done it this time. You've really made a mess of things*; and judgmental thoughts like, *They think they're really something special, don't they?* The point is that Satan will feed us thoughts through his agent, sin, using all kinds of personal pronouns to get us to believe that we are the persons thinking those thoughts. It just happens to be the first-person thoughts that seem to pack the most convincing punch.

In exposing Satan's primary disguise in this battle going on in our minds, I don't want you to get the wrong impression that we can put all the blame on Satan when we sin. What I am saying is that we are not responsible for generating the original sinful thoughts. Romans 6:12 clearly communicates our responsibility in the battle going on in our thought lives: "Do not let sin reign in your mortal body." In other words, Satan's not the boss of you! Don't let him tell you what to do!

If we choose to own the thoughts injected by Satan through sin, they become our thoughts, and we are responsible for them. Most of the time this happens so fast, it seems as if they come out of nowhere. And they sound so much like something *we* would think—regional accent and all! This is how he dupes us into walking by the flesh.

The following testimony was written by one of my precious sisters in Christ, Doris Kear. In it, she shares how God revealed to her that the thoughts she was experiencing weren't her own thoughts.

Last summer, I was involved in a Bible-based book study called *The Confident Woman* by Anabel Gillham. There was a chapter that explained to us how Satan talks to us and puts thoughts in our minds when we don't even realize it. I thought that was interesting, but I really did not think about what we had discovered until a few weeks later.

I was asked to work my first Walk to Emmaus. There are a number of meetings that the team had to attend before the Walk. Well, I had arrived at my first team meeting. I did not know anyone and I felt really out of place. A speaker began to talk and give a message. I was starting to get a bad attitude about the whole thing. I was having thoughts like, *I do not care for this speaker. They don't speak like what I'm used to hearing.* Then I thought, *This is not going to be any fun. I feel weird around all of these ladies I don't know.*

All of a sudden, I remembered that Satan was the one putting these thoughts in my head. I could choose to accept these thoughts as my own or rebuke them. So I rebuked them and went on. After that, I was able to listen to the rest of the message. I ended up loving that speaker and the message they shared. I got to know some of the ladies that day and really bonded with them. Being able to work that Walk was one of the biggest blessings that I have ever received. It was my choice whether to let Satan steal it or not. Thank God for the knowledge that we receive through His Word, Bible studies, and other Christians.[18]

When Doris wrote, "All of a sudden, I remembered that Satan was the one putting these thoughts in my head," that was the Spirit's revelation of the enemy's activity in her mind. And we can learn a lot from her simple response to these insidious impostors: "So I rebuked them and went on." Isn't that good! The same goes for all of us in Christ. We can choose to accept ungodly thoughts as our own, be miserable, and look like the rest of the world, or we can simply rebuke them, be happy, and go on with our Christ-glorifying lives!

➢ What are you going to do with ungodly thoughts, now that you understand they are not coming from *you*?

The Shulammite maiden is obviously being influenced by Satan through his personified agent, sin, feeding her fear-filled thoughts in first person—thoughts like, I *can't go with you! I'm not ready.* Thoughts like, *If I put myself out there, I will just get hurt again.* Thoughts like, *If you really knew me, you wouldn't be asking me to go with you.* Thoughts like, *I'm afraid I will fail you.* Thoughts like, *You'd be better off without me.* Until she, like Doris, gets a revelation that it is the foxes (fear-filled, ungodly thoughts coming from an outside enemy) that are hindering her, she will remain unresponsive to her Beloved and miss out on the adventure-filled life He has designed especially for her to walk in (Eph. 2:10; 5:9).

> ➤ What is your Bridegroom speaking to you through today's study? How will you respond?

Day 5

We have arrived at the final day of our journey through the first two chapters of the Song of Solomon—the divine romance between Christ and His lovely bride. My first greatest hope for you as this premier study comes to a close is that your mind has begun to be renewed with the wonderful truths of who you are as Christ's pure, holy, and righteous bride.

If you have lived years as a Christian, believing lies about your true identity, please be patient with yourself as you learn to walk in the extraordinary truths of the gospel of grace. If you're like me, you'll have to do some major *unlearning* of false concepts and ideas when you begin to understand the difference between law-based living and grace-based living. I found that a lot of my erroneous beliefs were steeped in religious tradition, rather than in new covenant truth.

My second greatest hope for you is that you have begun to experience greater intimacy with your Beloved as a result of getting your mind renewed in grace. He is a Bridegroom whose name is Faithful and True—the perfect One who is head over heels in love with you (Rev. 19:11). As you continue to allow Him to love you without condition, you will fall more deeply in love with Him, and the fruit of His Spirit will be consistently expressed through your life (Gal. 5:22–23; Eph. 5:9).

Now, let's wrap up our discussion of Song 2:15, and then we will unpack the last two verses of the chapter to conclude this study.

> **"Catch the foxes for us,**
> **The little foxes that are ruining the vineyards,**
> **While our vineyards are in blossom."**
> **—Song 2:15**

The little foxes have been at work in the maiden's mind, effectively hindering her from responding to her Beloved's repeated invitation to rise up out of her fear and join Him in the plans He has for their life together. These plans are for her greatest good and designed to cause her to live an abundantly fruitful life (Jer. 29:11; Gal. 5:22–23; Eph. 2:10; 5:9).

In order to say yes to her Beloved's invitation, the maiden must capture the little foxes that are ruining their blossoming vineyards. These little foxes are the ungodly thoughts introduced to us through Satan's rogue agent, sin, which resides in our physical bodies, where we do life. When we are deceived into owning, meditating on, and acting on these ungodly thoughts, the fruit of our Beloved's Spirit is successfully aborted.

Interestingly, the Hebrew root word for *little* is *quwt*, which means "to loathe oneself, to be cut off."[19] Have you ever loathed yourself for hearing an ungodly thought in your mind? (Notice I said *hearing*, not *thinking* because *you* didn't generate it.) I have. I lived as a defeated Christian for over thirty years because of lack of knowledge of my identity as Christ's pure, righteous, and holy bride and the way Satan works in my thought life.

In the past, when I owned these deceptive thoughts, I believed that I was a bad person, loathed myself, and cut myself off from enjoying the unconditional love of my Beloved. But now that I have knowledge of the enemy's schemes, I experience and express Christ's cherishing love and exuberant life much more often than I used to! Jesus didn't tell us that the *truth* alone would set us free; He said that *knowing truth* would cause us to experience the freedom He died to give us (John 8:32).

As long as we live in this earthly house (our physical body), it is *our* responsibility to take the enemy thoughts captive to the obedience of Christ, judging them in light of the truth of our pure, holy, and righteous identity in our Beloved.

In many ways our mind is like our e-mail inboxes. Every day, messages pour in. Some of these messages are good. These can be from friends and family members or just personal reminders. However, some of these are unwanted spam. Do you know what "spam" stands for? "Satan's Plan of Attack on my Mind." To be proactive in managing this daily influx of messages, we need to have knowledge of the three primary sources for the thoughts we experience.

- **Our new hearts:** Our new hearts are our new spirits, joined with Christ. Because our spirits are one with His, these messages will always agree with the Word of God and will be *good*. This is why it is important to aggressively put God's Word into our minds.
- **Satan, through his agent, sin:** These messages are disguised as our own thoughts. Sin often operates through the familiar flesh patterns in our brains. Satan was instrumental in helping to build those patterns and is aware of our weaknesses. Of course, all messages from sin are bad, even though much of the time they are disguised as good (2 Cor. 11:14).
- **The world:** These messages come through our five senses of sight, hearing, touch, smell, and taste. These messages can be good or bad, depending on their original source. Most of the time, we have control over which messages come into our minds through who we associate with and what we read, watch, and listen to.

We need to be effective managers of the messages that pour into our inboxes, or we will get distracted and waste a lot of time. When Satan floods our inboxes with sinful thoughts, we would do well to remember to "Submit therefore to God. Resist the devil and he will flee from you" (James 4:7). That is exactly what Jesus did when He was faced with the temptation to sin in the wilderness. He was fully submitted to and dependent upon His Father, and He resisted every one of Satan's temptations by speaking truth (Luke 4:1–13). We need to follow our Beloved's lead and remain fully submitted to and dependent on His indwelling Spirit, replacing the lies we hear in our minds with truth.

As previously mentioned, the most effective offensive strategy in this battle going on in our thought lives is to allow Christ to captivate our minds by giving Him our full attention—to become so obsessed with Him that the things that *don't* matter *won't* matter. The following are three of my favorite Scriptures that exhort us to do this:

> We are surrounded by a great cloud of people whose lives tell us what faith means. So let us run the race that is before us and never give up. We should remove from our lives anything that would get in the way and the sin that so easily holds us back. *Let us look only to Jesus*, the One who began our faith and who makes it perfect. He suffered death on the cross. But he accepted the

shame as if it were nothing because of the joy that God put before him. And now he is sitting at the right side of God's throne. (Heb. 12:1–2 NCV)

In conclusion, my friends, *fill your minds* with those things that are *good* and that *deserve praise*: things that are *true, noble, right, pure, lovely,* and *honorable*. (Phil. 4:8 GNT)

Since you were brought back to life with Christ, focus on the things that are above—where Christ holds the highest position. *Keep your mind on things above, not on worldly things.* You have died, and your life is hidden with Christ in God. *Christ is your life.* When he appears, then you, too, will appear with him in glory. (Col. 3:1–4 GW)

As we keep our eyes fixed on Christ, *who is our life*, and fill our minds with what is true, all that is ungodly will be crowded out, and we will consistently experience and express His cherishing love and exuberant life. While it is true that it's humanly impossible to think about Christ all of the time, every minute spent focused on and in dependence on Him is a minute well-invested and to His glory.

At this point in the Song, the maiden is obviously not investing her focus on her Beloved, but instead she is fixating on the paralyzing fear that is keeping her from saying yes to His repeated invitation to join Him in His purposes for their life together. After His five-verse discourse, she finally responds:

> **"My beloved is mine, and I am his;**
> **He pastures his flock among the lilies."**
> **—Song 2:16**

My beloved is mine, and I am his

She is pondering the wonderful truth of her eternal spiritual union with her Beloved—He belongs to her, and she belongs to Him. He is the One she has been searching for her whole life! This phrase can also be rendered as, "My Beloved is *for* me, and I am *for* Him."[20] He is on my side—not against me (Rom. 8:31).

Contemporary Christian music singer and songwriter Kari Jobe has written and recorded a song called "You Are for Me," which beautifully expresses her intimate knowledge of her Beloved being *for* her. (If you have Internet access, go to YouTube.com and type in "Kari Jobe: You Are for Me Behind the Song" to watch the story behind the song. Then, type in "Kari Jobe: You Are for Me" to listen to it.)

➤ Are you at a place in your life where you need to continually remind yourself, *I know that He is for me*? If not, have you ever been? Describe what you are currently going through or your past experience. When you go through difficult times, it is important to acknowledge the truth that *He* is for you … He *is* for you … He is *for* you … He is for *you*.

The maiden's proclamation of her possession of her Beloved (*My Beloved is mine and I am His*) is the third one she has made thus far in the Song. The first two occurred in chapter 1:

- "My beloved is to me a pouch of myrrh which lies all night between my breasts" (verse 13).
- "My beloved is to me a cluster of henna blossoms in the vineyards of Engedi" (verse 14).

Verse 13 focused on her personal experience of Christ's cherishing love and exuberant life through His indwelling presence, and verse 14 focused on the outward expression of His cherishing love and exuberant life through her life. This third declaration, "My Beloved is mine, and I am his," reveals that she is progressing from focusing on the benefits of His meeting all of her needs ("My Beloved is to me" and "My Beloved is mine") to focusing on the benefits that He will enjoy because she belongs to Him ("I am his"). But she is not there yet. Her possession of Him is still at the forefront of her mind because she says, "My Beloved is mine" first and "I am his" last.

Through her immersion into grace, the maiden still believes that even though she has twice refused Him, He is for her. His faithful track record has proven to her that her actions could never cause Him to be unfaithful to her. Second Timothy 2:13 says, "If we are faithless, He remains faithful, for He cannot deny Himself."

He pastures His flock among the lilies.
In declaring that her Beloved "pastures His flock among the lilies," the maiden is speaking of His work and where He can be found faithfully doing it. He provides nourishment, rest, and guidance for His flock—the church—among (together with) the lilies. The maiden views the

lilies as those believers who have joined the beloved Shepherd-King in expressing His cherishing love and exuberant life in this world. Even though she is—in truth—a lily, she doesn't fully see herself as one and is allowing fear to keep her from realizing it in her experience.

There will come a day, though, when she fully grasps the truth of her identity in Him. She will *know that she knows that she knows* that His Spirit—His resurrection power—is within her and is all she needs to say yes to any request He makes of her. She has "the strength to face all conditions by the power that Christ gives" to her (Phil. 4:13 GNT).

Now, let's look at the maiden's final words to her Beloved in response to His request.

> **"Until the cool of the day when the shadows flee away,**
> **Turn, my beloved, and be like a gazelle**
> **Or a young stag on the mountains of Bether."**
> —Song 2:17

Until the cool of the day when the shadows flee away
The coolest part of the day typically occurs right before and during sunrise, when the shadows of the night are swallowed up by the dawn of a new day. The maiden is telling her Beloved that she will not be able to join Him until the "shadows flee away"—until she stops being afraid. She has yet to understand that His light within her has the power to drive away the dark fear she is currently experiencing (1 John 1:5).

Turn, my beloved, and be like a gazelle or a young stag on the mountains of Bether.
In telling her Beloved to "turn and be like a gazelle or a young stag on the mountains of Bether," she is saying, "Go ahead and do your work in this world without me." *Bether* means "division."[21] The maiden has chosen to walk by the flesh rather than her Beloved's Spirit. Even though it may appear that she is being rebellious, she is not. She honestly believes that she cannot do what He's asking her to do. And in a sense, she is right. *She* can't do it in her natural strength, but *He* can—through her. All He wants from her is to depend on Him to express His cherishing love and exuberant life through her as she offers the members of her body to Him as "instruments of righteousness" (Rom. 6:13).

Dear bride, it is extremely important that you do not interpret Song 2:17 as a *spiritual* division or separation. The spirit of the believer in Christ is forever joined in union with His Spirit (1 Cor. 6:17). We will never again be separated from Him because of the new covenant He made with us in His blood (Matt. 26:28).

The Hebrew root word for *Bether* is *bathar*[22]—the same word found in the Genesis account where God promised Abram that he would be the father of many nations. Because both

Abram and Sarai were well past their childbearing years, Abram asked God for confirmation that His promise would come to pass. And God responded to him in the language of covenant:

> So He said to him, "Bring Me a three year old heifer, and a three year old female goat, and a three year old ram, and a turtledove, and a young pigeon."
> Then he brought all these to Him and cut (*bathar*) them in two, and laid each half opposite the other; but he did not cut the birds. (Gen. 15:9–10)

In Abram's day, covenants between two parties were made by cutting (separating) animal sacrifices in half. Both halves were then placed with enough space between them to form a pathway for the two parties to walk through in order to ratify the covenant. Walking between the sacrifices represented each person's commitment to fulfill his part of the covenant. But that's not what happened between God and Abram:

> Now when the sun was going down, a deep sleep fell upon Abram; and behold terror and great darkness fell upon him ... It came about when the sun had set, that it was very dark, and behold, there appeared a smoking oven and a flaming torch which passed between these pieces. (Gen. 15:12, 17)

When the time came to establish the covenant, God caused Abram to fall into a deep sleep. Knowing that Abram could do nothing to cause Him to fulfill His commitment, nor could he do anything to prevent Him from bringing it to completion, God entered into covenant with Himself:

> When God made his promise to Abraham, since there was no one greater for him to swear by, he swore by himself ... God did this so that, by two unchangeable things (His promise and His oath to keep His promise) in which it is impossible for God to lie, we who have fled to take hold of the hope set before us may be greatly encouraged. We have this hope as an anchor for the soul, firm and secure. (Heb. 6:13, 18–19 NIV)

God was faithful in His promise to Abraham through the covenant He made with Himself. Isaac was born and through his bloodline, Abraham, to this day, has "descendants as numerous as the stars in the sky and as countless as the sand on the seashore" (Gen. 15:5; 22:17; 32:12; Heb. 11:12). Likewise, our Beloved—*the One whose heart burns for us*—will remain forever faithful to His covenant of eternal spiritual union with His bride (John 10:28; 2 Tim. 2:13; Heb. 13:5).

Even though the maiden is walking by the flesh in her refusal to join her Beloved in His purposes for their life together, she *still* belongs to Him. Our Happily Ever After is a sure (firm and secure) thing! While our hearts' desire is to walk by His Spirit, twenty-four/seven, as long as we live on this earth in these mortal bodies, it will be impossible. But we can depend on *His* faithfulness toward us, twenty-four/seven. We can experience great rest and peace in His promise to never leave us nor forsake us (Heb. 13:5). We will *never* be separated from our Beloved, regardless of what we do or don't do:

> For I am convinced that neither death, nor life, nor angels, nor principalities, nor things present, nor things to come, nor powers, nor height, nor depth, *nor any other created thing*, will be able to separate us from the love of God, which is in Christ Jesus our Lord. (Rom. 8:38–39)

No created thing (that includes ourselves) will be able to separate us from our Bridegroom's cherishing love and exuberant life. Our union with Him will never end.

While the second chapter of the Song closes on a somber note, we know that this is not the end of the Song, nor the end of our story. The maiden's journey in her Beloved is just beginning.

If you enjoyed this study, stay tuned for *His Banner Over Me Is Sustaining Love* (over chapters 3–5) to find out what happens next. In the meantime, I want to encourage you to go back through this one on a regular basis. As you meditate on the truths of your new identity in Christ, fixing your eyes on Him, you will consistently experience and express His cherishing love and exuberant life. And there is nothing more fulfilling or satisfying than for the pure, righteous, and holy bride of Christ to live in this way!

> ➤ What is your Bridegroom speaking to you through today's study? How will you respond?

If this study has blessed or encouraged you in any way, I would love to hear from you!

Kim K. Francis
PO Box 357
Perryton, Texas 79070
kim@kimkfrancis.com

You can also Like/Follow my author page, *Kim K Francis*, on Facebook and/or subscribe to my blog, *A Happy Christian's Secret Life*, at http://www.kimkfrancis.com to stay current on my publishing journey.

SONG LIST

1. "Alabaster Box," CeCe Winans
2. "True Love's Kiss," Amy Adams and James Marsden
3. "Let Me Love You," Dennis Jernigan
4. "You Are More," Tenth Avenue North
5. "You Call Me Yours," Prelude
6. "Flawless," MercyMe
7. "(Everything I Do) I Do It for You," Bryan Adams
8. "It Is Well with My Soul," your artist of choice
9. "Finally Home," Kerrie Roberts
10. "More than Ashes," Tim Reimherr/Merchant Band
11. "Rock of Ages," Chris Rice
12. "Remind Me Who I Am," Jason Gray
13. "You Are for Me," Kari Jobe

ANCIENT JEWISH MARRIAGE RESOURCE LIST

1. Calhoun, Rhonda, *Song of Solomon Verse by Verse Study* (Holden, Mo.: Heart Publishing, 2005).
2. Calhoun, Rhonda, *Song of Solomon Verse by Verse Study, 19 Audio CD Set* (Holden, Mo.: Heart Publishing, 2005).
3. Ethridge, Shannon, *Completely His: Loving Jesus Without Limits* (Colorado Springs, Co.: WaterBrook Press, 2007).
4. Greenwood, R. Glenn and Latayne C. Scott, *The Shout of the Bridegroom: Understanding Christ's Intimate Love for His Church* (Webb City, Mo.: Covenant Publishing, 2002).
5. Lash, Jamie, *The Ancient Jewish Wedding … and the Return of Messiah for His Bride* (Ft. Lauderdale, Fl.: Jewish Jewels, 1997).
6. Lash, Neil and Jamie, *The Ancient Jewish Wedding … and the Return of Messiah for His Bride* (Ft. Lauderdale, Fl.: Jewish Jewels, 1997), Video.
7. Lawley, Martha, *Attending the Bride of Christ: Preparing for His Return* (Nashville, Tn.: LifeWay Press, 2005), Bible study.
8. Rountree, Anna, *Heaven Awaits the Bride* (Lake Mary, Fl.: Charisma House, 2007).
9. Smith, Laura, *Embracing Unity as the Bride of Christ* (2004), *www.xulonpress.com*.

"WHO I AM IN CHRIST IS WHO I AM!" SCRIPTURES

Jeremiah 31:31–34 (NASB) "'Behold, days are coming,' declares the Lord, 'when I will make a new covenant with the house of Israel and with the house of Judah, not like the covenant which I made with their fathers in the day I took them by the hand to bring them out of the land of Egypt, My covenant which they broke, although I was a husband to them,' declares the Lord. 'But this is the covenant which I will make with the house of Israel after those days,' declares the Lord, 'I will put My law within them and on their heart I will write it; and I will be their God, and they shall be My people. They will not teach again, each man his neighbor and each man his brother, saying, "Know the Lord," for they will all know Me, from the least of them to the greatest of them,' declares the Lord, 'for I will forgive their iniquity, and their sin I will remember no more.'"

Ezekiel 11:19 (GW) "I will give them a single purpose and put a new spirit in them. I will remove their stubborn hearts and give them obedient hearts."

Ezekiel 16:8 (MSG) "I came by again and saw you, saw that you were ready for love and a lover. I took care of you, dressed you and protected you. I promised you my love and entered the covenant of marriage with you. I, God, the Master, gave my word. You became mine."

Ezekiel 36:25–27 (MSG) "I'll pour pure water over you and scrub you clean. I'll give you a new heart, put a new spirit in you. I'll remove the stone heart from your body and replace it with a heart that's God-willed, not self-willed. I'll put my Spirit in you and make it possible for you to do what I tell you and live by my commands."

Hosea 2:19–20 (MSG) "'At that time'—this is God's Message still—'you'll address me, "Dear husband!" Never again will you address me, "My slave-master!" … And then I'll marry you for good—forever! I'll marry you true and proper, in love and tenderness. Yes I'll marry you and neither leave you nor let you go. You'll know me God, for who I really am.'"

Mark 12:30–31 (NASB) "'You shall love the Lord your God with all your heart, and with all your soul, and with all your mind, and with all your strength.' The second is this, 'You shall love your neighbor as yourself.' There is no other commandment greater than these."

Luke 22:20 (GNT) "He gave them the cup after the supper, saying, 'This cup is God's new covenant sealed with my blood, which is poured out for you.'"

John 1:12 (NCV) "To all who did accept him and believe in him he gave the right to become children of God."

John 1:29 (NLT) "The next day John saw Jesus coming toward him and said, 'Look! The Lamb of God who takes away the sin of the world!'"

John 3:3–6 (GNT) "Jesus answered, 'I am telling you the truth: no one can see the Kingdom of God without being born again.' 'How can a grown man be born again?' Nicodemus asked. 'He certainly cannot enter his mother's womb and be born a second time!' 'I am telling you the truth' replied Jesus, 'that no one can enter the Kingdom of God without being born of water and the Spirit. A person is born physically of human parents, but is born spiritually of the Spirit.'"

John 3:16 (NASB) "God so loved the world, that He gave His only begotten Son, that whoever believes in Him shall not perish, but have eternal life."

John 3:17–18 (NCV) "God did not send his Son into the world to judge the world guilty, but to save the world through him. People who believe in God's Son are not judged guilty. Those who do not believe have already been judged guilty, because they have not believed in God's one and only Son."

John 3:36 (NIV) "Whoever believes in the Son has eternal life, but whoever rejects the Son will not see life, for God's wrath remains on them."

John 4:14 (NLT) "Those who drink the water I give will never be thirsty again. It becomes a fresh, bubbling spring within them, giving them eternal life."

John 4:24 (GNT) "God is Spirit, and only by the power of his Spirit can people worship him as he really is."

John 5:24 (NCV) "I tell you the truth, whoever hears what I say and believes in the One who sent me has eternal life. That person will not be judged guilty but has already left death and entered life."

John 6:28–29 (NLT) "They replied, 'We want to perform God's works, too. What should we do?' Jesus told them, 'This is the only work God wants from you: Believe in the one he has sent.'"

John 6:47 (GNT) "I am telling you the truth: he who believes has eternal life."

John 7:38–39 (NCV) "'If anyone believes in me, rivers of living water will flow out from that person's heart, as the Scripture says.' Jesus was talking about the Holy Spirit. The Spirit had not yet been given, because Jesus had not yet been raised to glory. But later, those who believed in Jesus would receive the Spirit."

John 10:4–5 (NASB) "The sheep follow him because they know his voice. A stranger they simply will not follow, but will flee from him, because they do not know the voice of strangers."

John 10:10 (GNT) "The thief comes only in order to steal, kill, and destroy. I have come in order that you might have life—life in all its fullness."

John 10:27–28 (GNT) "My sheep listen to my voice; I know them, and they follow me. I give them eternal life, and they shall never die. No one can snatch them away from me."

John 11:25–26 (MSG) "You don't have to wait for the End. I am, right now, Resurrection and Life. The one who believes in me, even though he or she dies, will live. And everyone who lives believing in me does not ultimately die at all. Do you believe this?"

John 13:5–8, 10 (NASB) "Then He poured water into the basin, and began to wash the disciples' feet and to wipe them with the towel with which He was girded. So He came to Simon Peter. He said to Him, 'Lord, do You wash my feet?' Jesus answered and said to him, 'What I do you do not realize now, but you will understand hereafter.' Peter said to Him, 'Never shall You wash my feet!' Jesus answered him, 'If I do not wash you, you have no part with Me … He who has bathed needs only to wash his feet, but is completely clean; and you are clean, but not all of you.'"

John 14:6 (AMPC) "Jesus said to him, I am the Way and the Truth and the Life; no one comes to the Father except by (through) Me."

John 14:12–14 (NCV) "I tell you the truth, whoever believes in me will do the same things that I do. Those who believe will do even greater things than these, because I am going to the Father. And if you ask for anything in my name, I will do it for you so that the Father's glory will be shown through the Son. If you ask me for anything in my name, I will do it."

John 14:15 (NCV) "If you love me, you will obey my commands."

John 14:16–17 (AMPC) "I will ask the Father, and He will give you another Comforter (Counselor, Helper, Intercessor, Advocate, Strengthener, and Standby), that He may remain with you forever—The Spirit of Truth, Whom the world cannot receive (welcome, take to its heart), because it does not see Him or know and recognize Him. But you know and recognize Him, for He lives with you [constantly] and will be in you."

John 14:19–21 (CEV) "In a little while the people of this world won't be able to see me, but you will see me. And because I live, you will live. Then you will know that I am one with the Father. You will know that you are one with me, and I am one with you. If you love me, you will do what I have said, and my Father will love you. I will also love you and show you what I am like."

John 14:26 (AMPC) "The Comforter (Counselor, Helper, Intercessor, Advocate, Strengthener, Standby), the Holy Spirit, Whom the Father will send in My name [in My place, to represent Me and act on My behalf], He will teach you all things. And He will cause you to recall (will remind you of, bring to your remembrance) everything I have told you."

John 14:27 (AMPC) "Peace I leave with you; My [own] peace I now give *and* bequeath to you. Not as the world gives do I give to you. Do not let your hearts be troubled, neither let them be afraid. [Stop allowing yourselves to be agitated and disturbed; and do not permit yourselves to be fearful and intimidated and cowardly and unsettled.]"

John 15:3–5 (GW) "You are already clean because of what I have told you. Live in me, and I will live in you. A branch cannot produce any fruit by itself. It has to stay attached to the vine. In the same way, you cannot produce fruit unless you live in me. I am the vine. You are the branches. Those who live in me while I live in them will produce a lot of fruit. But you can't produce anything without me."

John 15:11 (AMPC) "I have told you these things, that My joy *and* delight may be in you, and that your joy *and* gladness may be of full measure *and* complete *and* overflowing."

John 15:11 (VOICE) "I want you to know the delight I experience, to find ultimate satisfaction, which is why I am telling you all of this."

John 15:15 (VOICE) "I don't call you servants any longer; servants don't know what the master is doing, but I have told you everything the Father has said to Me. I call you friends."

John 15:26–27 (GNT) "The Helper will come—the Spirit, who reveals the truth about God and who comes from the Father. I will send him to you from the Father, and he will speak about me. And you, too, will speak about me, because you have been with me from the very beginning."

John 16:7 (CEB) "I assure you that it is better for you that I go away. If I don't go away, the Companion won't come to you. But if I go, I will send him to you."

John 16:13–15 (NASB) "When He, the Spirit of truth, comes, He will guide you into all the truth; for He will not speak on His own initiative, but whatever He hears, He will speak; and He will disclose to you what is to come. He will glorify Me, for He will take of Mine and will disclose it to you. All things that the Father has are Mine; therefore I said that He takes of Mine and will disclose it to you."

John 16:23–24 (NCV) "In that day you will not ask me for anything. I tell you the truth, my Father will give you anything you ask for in my name. Until now you have not asked for anything in my name. Ask and you will receive, so that your joy will be the fullest possible joy."

John 16:33 (NCV) "I told you these things so that you can have peace in me. In this world you will have trouble, but be brave! I have defeated the world."

John 17:3 (NASB) "This is eternal life, that they may know You, the only true God, and Jesus Christ whom You have sent."

John 17:13–15 (GW) "Father, I'm coming back to you. I say these things while I'm still in the world so that they will have the same joy that I have. I have given them your message. But the world has hated them because they don't belong to the world any more than I belong to the world. I'm not asking you to take them out of the world but to protect them from the evil one."

John 17:19–21 (NASB) "For their sakes I sanctify Myself, that they themselves also may be sanctified in truth. I do not ask on behalf of these alone, but for those also who believe in Me through their word; that they may all be one; even as You, Father, are in Me and I in You, that they also may be in Us, so that the world may believe that You sent Me."

John 17:22–23 (NLT) "I have given them the glory you gave me, so they may be one as we are one. I am in them and you are in me. May they experience such perfect unity that the world will know that you sent me and that you love them as much as you love me."

John 17:26 (NASB) "I have made Your name known to them, and will make it known, so that the love with which You loved Me may be in them, and I in them."

John 19:30 (NASB) "When Jesus had received the sour wine, He said, 'It is finished' And He bowed His head and gave up His spirit."

Acts 1:5, 8 (AMPC) "John baptized with water, but not many days from now you shall be baptized with (placed in, introduced into) the Holy Spirit … But you shall receive power (ability, efficiency, and might) when the Holy Spirit has come upon you, and you shall be My witnesses in Jerusalem and all Judea and Samaria and to the ends (the very bounds) of the earth."

Acts 11:9 (CEB) "The voice from heaven spoke a second time, 'Never consider unclean what God has made pure.'"

Acts 15:8–9 (NCV) "God, who knows the thoughts of everyone, accepted them. He showed this to us by giving them the Holy Spirit, just as he did to us. To God, those people are not different from us. When they believed, he made their hearts pure."

Acts 15:11 (NLT) "We believe that we are all saved the same way, by the undeserved grace of the Lord Jesus."

Acts 17:24–28 (NASB) "The God who made the world and all things in it, since He is Lord of heaven and earth, does not dwell in temples made with hands; nor is He served by human hands, as though He needed anything, since He Himself gives to all people life and breath and all things; and He made from one man every nation of mankind to live on all the face of the earth, having determined their appointed times and the boundaries of their habitation, that they would seek God, if perhaps they might grope for Him and find Him, though He is not far from each one of us; for in Him we live and move and exist, as even some of your own poets have said, 'For we also are His children.'"

Romans 1:16 (NLT) "I am not ashamed of this Good News about Christ. It is the power of God at work, saving everyone who believes—the Jew first and also the Gentile."

Romans 3:21–24 (NCV) "God has a way to make people right with him without the law, and he has now shown us that way which the law and the prophets told us about. God makes people right with himself through their faith in Jesus Christ. This is true for all who believe in Christ, because all people are the same: Everyone has sinned and fallen short of God's glorious standard, and all need to be made right with God by his grace, which is a free gift. They need to be made free from sin through Jesus Christ."

Romans 4:3–50 (GNT) "The scripture says, 'Abraham believed God, and because of his faith God accepted him as righteous.' A person who works is paid wages, but they are not regarded as a gift; they are something that has been earned. But those who depend on faith, not on deeds, and who believe in the God who declares the guilty to be innocent, it is this faith that God takes into account in order to put them right with himself."

Romans 4:17 (CEV) "God … gives life to the dead and … creates something out of nothing."

Romans 5:1 (CEB) "Since we have been made righteous through his faithfulness combined with our faith, we have peace with God through our Lord Jesus Christ."

Romans 5:5 (VOICE) "Hope will never fail to satisfy our deepest need because the Holy Spirit that was given to us has flooded our hearts with God's love."

Romans 5:8–10 (CEB) "God shows his love for us, because while we were still sinners Christ died for us. So, now that we have been made righteous by his blood, we can be even more certain that we will be saved from God's wrath through him. If we were reconciled to God through the death of his Son while we were still enemies, now that we have been reconciled, how much more certain is it that we will be saved by his life?"

Romans 5:15 (GW) "There is no comparison between God's gift and Adam's failure. If humanity died as the result of one person's failure, it is certainly true that God's kindness and the gift given through the kindness of one person, Jesus Christ, have been showered on humanity."

Romans 5:17 (CEB) "If death ruled because of one person's failure, those who receive the multiplied grace and the gift of righteousness will even more certainly rule in life through the one person Jesus Christ."

Romans 5:19 (NASB) "Through the one man's disobedience the many were made sinners, even so through the obedience of the One the many will be made righteous."

Romans 5:20 (VOICE) "When the law came into the picture, sin grew and grew; but wherever sin grew and spread, God's grace was there in fuller, greater measure. No matter how much sin crept in, there was always more grace."

Romans 6:3–4 (NASB) "Do you not know that all of us who have been baptized into Christ Jesus have been baptized into His death? Therefore we have been buried with Him through baptism into death, so that as Christ was raised from the dead through the glory of the Father, so we too might walk in newness of life."

Romans 6:6 (NASB) "Knowing this, that our old self was crucified with Him, in order that our body of sin might be done away with, so that we would no longer be slaves to sin."

Romans 6:7 (NASB) "He who has died is freed from sin."

Romans 6:11 (NASB) "Consider yourselves to be dead to sin, but alive to God in Christ Jesus."

Romans 6:12–13 (NASB) "Do not let sin reign in your mortal body so that you obey its lusts, and do not go on presenting the members of your body to sin as instruments of unrighteousness; but present yourselves to God as those alive from the dead, and your members as instruments of righteousness to God."

Romans 6:14 (NASB) "Sin shall not be master over you, for you are not under law but under grace."

Romans 6:17–18 (NASB) "Thanks be to God that though you were slaves of sin, you became obedient from the heart to that form of teaching to which you were committed, and having been freed from sin, you became slaves of righteousness."

Romans 6:22 (AMPC) "Since you have been set free from sin and have become the slaves of God, you have your present reward in holiness and its end is eternal life."

Romans 6:23 (NASB) "The wages of sin is death, but the free gift of God is eternal life in Christ Jesus our Lord."

Romans 7:4 (NCV, NASB) "My brothers and sisters, your old selves died, and you became free from the law through the body of Christ, so that you might be joined to another, to Him who was raised from the dead, in order that we might bear fruit for God."

Romans 7:6 (NCV) "In the past, the law held us like prisoners, but our old selves died, and we were made free from the law. So now we serve God in a new way with the Spirit, and not in the old way with written rules."

Romans 8:1 (NCV) "Those who are in Christ Jesus are not judged guilty."

Romans 8:2 (GNT) "The law of the Spirit, which brings us life in union with Christ Jesus, has set me free from the law of sin and death."

Romans 8:6 (NASB) "The mind set on the flesh is death, but the mind set on the Spirit is life and peace."

Romans 8:8–9 (NASB) "Those who are in the flesh cannot please God. However, you are not in the flesh but in the Spirit, if indeed the Spirit of God dwells in you. But if anyone does not have the Spirit of Christ, he does not belong to Him."

Romans 8:11 (NLT) "The Spirit of God, who raised Jesus from the dead, lives in you. And just as God raised Christ Jesus from the dead, he will give life to your mortal bodies by this same Spirit living within you."

Romans 8:14–15 (GNT) "Those who are led by God's Spirit are God's children. For the Spirit that God has given you does not make you slaves and cause you to be afraid; instead, the Spirit makes you God's children, and by the Spirit's power we cry out to God, 'Father! my Father!'"

Romans 8:17 (CEV) "His Spirit lets us know that together with Christ we will be given what God has promised. We will also share in the glory of Christ, because we have suffered with him."

Romans 8:26–27 (NASB) "The Spirit also helps our weakness; for we do not know how to pray as we should, but the Spirit Himself intercedes for us with groanings too deep for words; and He who searches the hearts knows what the mind of the Spirit is, because He intercedes for the saints according to the will of God."

Romans 8:28 (NASB) "We know that God causes all things to work together for good to those who love God, to those who are called according to His purpose."

Romans 8:31–32 (NASB) "If God is for us, who is against us? He who did not spare His own

Son, but delivered Him over for us all, how will He not also with Him freely give us all things?"

Romans 8:38–39 (NASB) "I am convinced that neither death, nor life, nor angels, nor principalities, nor things present, nor things to come, nor powers, nor height, nor depth, nor any other created thing, will be able to separate us from the love of God, which is in Christ Jesus our Lord."

Romans 10:4 (NASB) "Christ is the end of the law for righteousness to everyone who believes."

Romans 10:9–10 (NASB) "If you confess with your mouth Jesus as Lord, and believe in your heart that God raised Him from the dead, you will be saved; for with the heart a person believes, resulting in righteousness, and with the mouth he confesses, resulting in salvation."

Romans 10:17 (NCV) "Faith comes from hearing the Good News, and people hear the Good News when someone tells them about Christ."

Romans 11:6 (NLT) "Since it is through God's kindness, then it is not by their good works. For in that case, God's grace would not be what it really is—free and undeserved."

Romans 11:16 (GW) "If the root is holy, the branches are holy."

Romans 11:29 (NCV) "God never changes his mind about the people he calls and the things he gives them."

Romans 12:1–2 (VOICE) "In light of all I have shared with you about God's mercies, I urge you to offer your bodies as a living and holy sacrifice to God, a sacred offering that brings Him pleasure; this is your reasonable, essential worship. Do not allow this world to mold you in its own image. Instead, be transformed from the inside out by renewing your mind. As a result, you will be able to discern what God wills and whatever God finds good, pleasing, and complete."

Romans 13:14 (NASB) "Put on the Lord Jesus Christ, and make no provision for the flesh in regard to its lusts."

Romans 15:7 (GNT) "Accept one another, then, for the glory of God, as Christ has accepted you."

Romans 16:20 (NASB) "The God of peace will soon crush Satan under your feet."

1 Corinthians 1:2 (GW) "God's church … was made holy by Christ Jesus and called to be God's holy people."

1 Corinthians 1:30 (GNT) "God has brought you into union with Christ Jesus, and God has made Christ to be our wisdom. By him we are put right with God; we become God's holy people and are set free."

1 Corinthians 2:12 (NLT) "We have received God's Spirit (not the world's spirit), so we can know the wonderful things God has freely given us."

1 Corinthians 2:16 (NASB) "We have the mind of Christ."

1 Corinthians 3:16–17 (CEB) "Don't you know that you are God's temple and God's Spirit lives in you? … God's temple is holy, which is what you are."

1 Corinthians 3:23 (GW) "You belong to Christ, and Christ belongs to God."

1 Corinthians 6:11 (NLT) "You were cleansed; you were made holy; you were made right with God by calling on the name of the Lord Jesus Christ and by the Spirit of our God."

1 Corinthians 6:17 (NASB) "The one who joins himself to the Lord is one spirit with Him."

1 Corinthians 6:19 (NASB) "Do you not know that your body is a temple of the Holy Spirit who is in you, whom you have from God, and that you are not your own?"

1 Corinthians 6:20 (VOICE) "You have been purchased at a great price, so use your body to bring glory to God!"

1 Corinthians 7:23 (VOICE) "A high price has been paid for your freedom, so don't devalue God's investment by becoming a slave to people."

1 Corinthians 10:13 (NLT) "The temptations in your life are no different from what others experience. And God is faithful. He will not allow the temptation to be more than you can stand. When you are tempted, he will show you a way out so that you can endure."

1 Corinthians 12:27 (CEV) "Together you are the body of Christ. Each one of you is part of his body."

1 Corinthians 15:56–57 (MSG) "It was sin that made death so frightening and law-code guilt that gave sin its leverage, its destructive power. But now in a single victorious stroke of Life, all three—sin, guilt, death—are gone, the gift of our Master, Jesus Christ. Thank God!"

2 Corinthians 1:21–22 (NASB) "He who establishes us with you in Christ and anointed us is God, who also sealed us and gave us the Spirit in our hearts as a pledge."

2 Corinthians 2:14–15 (NASB) "Thanks be to God, who always leads us in triumph in Christ, and manifests through us the sweet aroma of the knowledge of Him in every place. For we are a fragrance of Christ to God among those who are being saved and among those who are perishing."

2 Corinthians 3:5–6 (NLT) "It is not that we think we are qualified to do anything on our own. Our qualification comes from God. He has enabled us to be ministers of his new covenant. This is a covenant not of written laws, but of the Spirit. The old written covenant ends in death; but under the new covenant, the Spirit gives life."

2 Corinthians 3:17 (NLT) "The Lord is the Spirit, and wherever the Spirit of the Lord is, there is freedom."

2 Corinthians 3:18 (VOICE) "All of us, with our faces unveiled, reflect the glory of the Lord as if we are mirrors; and so we are being transformed, metamorphosed, into His same image from one radiance of glory to another, just as the Spirit of the Lord accomplishes it."

2 Corinthians 4:7 (GW) "Our bodies are made of clay, yet we have the treasure of the

Good News in them. This shows that the superior power of this treasure belongs to God and doesn't come from us."

2 Corinthians 4:16 (CEV) "We never give up. Our bodies are gradually dying, but we ourselves are being made stronger each day."

2 Corinthians 4:17–18 (CEV) "These little troubles are getting us ready for an eternal glory that will make all our troubles seem like nothing. Things that are seen don't last forever, but things that are not seen are eternal. That's why we keep our minds on the things that cannot be seen."

2 Corinthians 5:6 (AMPC) "We are always full of good *and* hopeful *and* confident courage; we know that while we are at home in the body, we are abroad from the home with the Lord [that is promised us]."

2 Corinthians 5:7 (CEV) "We live by faith, not by what we see."

2 Corinthians 5:14 (NASB) "The love of Christ controls us, having concluded this, that one died for all, therefore all died."

2 Corinthians 5:16 (CEB) "From this point on we won't recognize people by human standards. Even though we used to know Christ by human standards, that isn't how we know him now."

2 Corinthians 5:17 (GNT) "Anyone who is joined to Christ is a new being; the old is gone, the new has come."

2 Corinthians 5:18–19 (CEB) "All of these new things are from God, who reconciled us to himself through Christ and who gave us the ministry of reconciliation. In other words, God was reconciling the world to himself through Christ, by not counting people's sins against them. He has trusted us with this message of reconciliation."

2 Corinthians 5:21 (GNT) "Christ was without sin, but for our sake God made him share our sin in order that in union with him we might share the righteousness of God."

2 Corinthians 10:3–5 (VOICE) "Though we walk in the world, we do not fight according to this world's rules of warfare. The weapons of the war we're fighting are not of this world but are powered by God and effective at tearing down the strongholds erected against His truth. We are demolishing arguments and ideas, every high-and-mighty philosophy that pits itself against the knowledge of the one true God. We are taking prisoners of every thought, every emotion, and subduing them into obedience to the Anointed One."

2 Corinthians 11:2 (NLT) "I am jealous for you with the jealousy of God himself. I promised you as a pure bride to one husband—Christ."

2 Corinthians 12:9 (NLT) "Each time he said, 'My grace is all you need. My power works best in weakness.' So now I am glad to boast about my weaknesses, so that the power of Christ can work through me."

Galatians 1:10 (GNT) "Does this sound as if I am trying to win human approval? No indeed! What I want is God's approval! Am I trying to be popular with people? If I were still trying to do so, I would not be a servant of Christ."

Galatians 2:16 (CEB) "We know that a person isn't made righteous by the works of the Law but rather through the faithfulness of Jesus Christ. We ourselves believed in Christ Jesus so that we could be made righteous by the faithfulness of Christ and not by the works of the Law—because no one will be made righteous by the works of the Law."

Galatians 2:20 (CEB) "I have been crucified with Christ and I no longer live, but Christ lives in me. And the life that I now live in my body, I live by faith, indeed, by the faithfulness of God's Son, who loved me and gave himself for me."

Galatians 3:26–27 (GNT) "It is through faith that all of you are God's children in union with Christ Jesus. You were baptized into union with Christ, and now you are clothed … with the life of Christ himself."

Galatians 3:28–29 (GNT) "There is no difference between Jews and Gentiles, between slaves and free people, between men and women; you are all one in union with Christ Jesus. If you belong to Christ, then you are the descendants of Abraham and will receive what God has promised."

Galatians 4:6–7 (NLT) "Because we are his children, God has sent the Spirit of his Son into our hearts, prompting us to call out, 'Abba, Father.' Now you are no longer a slave but God's own child. And since you are his child, God has made you his heir."

Galatians 5:1 (CEV) "Christ has set us free! This means we are really free. Now hold on to your freedom and don't ever become slaves of the Law again."

Galatians 5:16 (NASB) "Walk by the Spirit, and you will not carry out the desire of the flesh."

Galatians 5:22–23 (CEV) "God's Spirit makes us loving, happy, peaceful, patient, kind, good, faithful, gentle, and self-controlled. There is no law against behaving in any of these ways."

Galatians 5:24 (NASB) "Those who belong to Christ Jesus have crucified the flesh with its passions and desires."

Ephesians 1:3 (GNT) "Let us give thanks to the God and Father of our Lord Jesus Christ! For in our union with Christ he has blessed us by giving us every spiritual blessing in the heavenly world."

Ephesians 1:4 (GNT) "Even before the world was made, God had already chosen us to be his through our union with Christ, so that we would be holy and without fault before him."

Ephesians 1:5–6 (NCV) "Because of his love, God had already decided to make us his own children through Jesus Christ. That was what he wanted and what pleased him, and it brings praise to God because of his wonderful grace. God gave that grace to us freely, in Christ, the One he loves."

Ephesians 1:7–9 (NCV) "In Christ we are set free by the blood of his death, and so we have forgiveness of sins. How rich is God's grace, which he has given to us so fully and freely. God, with full wisdom and understanding, let us know his secret purpose. This was what God wanted, and he planned to do it through Christ."

Ephesians 1:13–14 (NASB) "In Him, you also, after listening to the message of truth, the gospel of your salvation—having also believed, you were sealed in Him with the Holy Spirit of promise, who is given as a pledge of our inheritance, with a view to the redemption of God's own possession, to the praise of His glory."

Ephesians 2:4–7 (MSG) "Immense in mercy and with an incredible love, he embraced us. He took our sin-dead lives and made us alive in Christ. He did all this on his own, with no help from us! Then he picked us up and set us down in highest heaven in company with Jesus, our Messiah. Now God has us where he wants us, with all the time in this world and the next to shower grace and kindness upon us in Christ Jesus."

Ephesians 2:8–9 (MSG) "Saving is all his idea, and all his work. All we do is trust him enough to let him do it. It's God's gift from start to finish! We don't play the major role. If we did, we'd probably go around bragging that we'd done the whole thing!"

Ephesians 2:10 (GNT) "God has made us what we are, and in our union with Christ Jesus he has created us for a life of good deeds, which he has already prepared for us to do."

Ephesians 2:13 (GNT) "Now, in union with Christ Jesus you, who used to be far away, have been brought near by the blood of Christ."

Ephesians 2:19 (NASB) "You are no longer strangers and aliens, but you are fellow citizens with the saints, and are of God's household."

Ephesians 3:6 (NLT) "This is God's plan: Both Gentiles and Jews who believe the Good News share equally in the riches inherited by God's children. Both are part of the same body, and both enjoy the promise of blessings because they belong to Christ Jesus."

Ephesians 3:12 (CEB) "In Christ we have bold and confident access to God through faith in him."

Ephesians 4:24 (NASB) "Put on the new self, which in the likeness of God has been created in righteousness and holiness of the truth."

Ephesians 4:32 (NLT) "Be kind to each other, tenderhearted, forgiving one another, just as God through Christ has forgiven you."

Ephesians 5:8 (NASB) "You were formerly darkness, but now you are Light in the Lord; walk as children of Light."

Philippians 2:13 (NLT) "God is working in you, giving you the desire and the power to do what pleases him."

Philippians 3:20–21 (NLT) "We are citizens of heaven, where the Lord Jesus Christ lives. And we are eagerly waiting for him to return as our Savior. He will take our weak mortal bodies and change them into glorious bodies like his own, using the same power with which he will bring everything under his control."

Philippians 4:6–7 (GNT) "Don't worry about anything, but in all your prayers ask God for what you need, always asking him with a thankful heart. And God's peace, which is far beyond human understanding, will keep your hearts and minds safe in union with Christ Jesus."

Philippians 4:13 (GNT) "I have the strength to face all conditions by the power that Christ gives me."

Philippians 4:19 (NLT) "This same God who takes care of me will supply all your needs from his glorious riches, which have been given to us in Christ Jesus."

Colossians 1:13–14 (NLT) "He has rescued us from the kingdom of darkness and transferred us into the Kingdom of his dear Son, who purchased our freedom and forgave our sins."

Colossians 1:22 (NLT) "He has reconciled you to himself through the death of Christ in his physical body. As a result, he has brought you into his own presence, and you are holy and blameless as you stand before him without a single fault."

Colossians 2:9–10 (NLT) "In Christ lives all the fullness of God in a human body. So you also are complete through your union with Christ, who is the head over every ruler and authority."

Colossians 2:12 (NASB) "Having been buried with Him in baptism, in which you were also raised up with Him through faith in the working of God, who raised Him from the dead."

Colossians 2:13–14 (NASB) "When you were dead in your transgressions and the uncircumcision of your flesh, He made you alive together with Him, having forgiven us all our transgressions, having canceled out the certificate of debt consisting of decrees against us, which was hostile to us; and He has taken it out of the way, having nailed it to the cross."

Colossians 3:1–4 (GW) "Since you were brought back to life with Christ, focus on the things that are above—where Christ holds the highest position. Keep your mind on things above, not on worldly things. You have died, and your life is hidden with Christ in God. Christ is your life. When he appears, then you, too, will appear with him in glory."

Colossians 3:5 (NASB) "Consider the members of your earthly body as dead to immorality, impurity, passion, evil desire, and greed, which amounts to idolatry."

Colossians 3:12–14 (NCV) "God has chosen you and made you his holy people. He loves you. So you should always clothe yourselves with mercy, kindness, humility, gentleness, and patience. Bear with each other, and forgive each other. If someone does wrong to you, forgive that person because the Lord forgave you. Even more than all this, clothe yourself in love. Love is what holds you all together in perfect unity."

Colossians 3:15 (NCV) "Let the peace that Christ gives control your thinking, because you were all called together in one body to have peace. Always be thankful."

Colossians 3:16 (NASB) "Let the word of Christ richly dwell within you, with all wisdom teaching and admonishing one another with psalms and hymns and spiritual songs, singing with thankfulness in your hearts to God."

Colossians 3:17 (AMPC) "Whatever you do—no matter what it is—in word or deed, do everything in the name of the Lord Jesus *and* in dependence upon His Person, giving praise to God the Father through Him."

Colossians 3:23–24 (NASB) "Whatever you do, do your work heartily, as for the Lord rather than for men, knowing that from the Lord you will receive the reward of the inheritance. It is the Lord Christ whom you serve."

1 Thessalonians 5:5 (NLT) "You are all children of the light and of the day; we don't belong to darkness and night."

2 Timothy 1:7 (VOICE) "You see, God did not give us a cowardly spirit but a powerful, loving, and disciplined spirit."

2 Timothy 1:9 (CEB) "God is the one who saved and called us with a holy calling. This wasn't based on what we have done, but it was based on his own purpose and grace that he gave us in Christ Jesus before time began."

2 Timothy 2:13 (NIV) "If we are faithless, he remains faithful, for he cannot disown himself."

Titus 2:11–12 (GNT) "God has revealed his grace for the salvation of all people. That grace instructs us to give up ungodly living and worldly passions, and to live self-controlled, upright, and godly lives in this world."

Hebrews 1:3 (NLT) "The Son radiates God's own glory and expresses the very character of God, and he sustains everything by the mighty power of his command. When he had cleansed us from our sins, he sat down in the place of honor at the right hand of the majestic God in heaven."

Hebrews 2:11 (NCV) "Jesus, who makes people holy, and those who are made holy are from the same family. So he is not ashamed to call them his brothers and sisters."

Hebrews 3:1 (NCV) "All of you holy brothers and sisters, who were called by God, think about Jesus, who was sent to us and is the high priest of our faith."

Hebrews 4:3 (NASB) "We who have believed enter that rest."

Hebrews 8:10–12 (GW) "'This is the promise that I will make to Israel after those days, says the Lord: I will put my teachings inside them, and I will write those teachings on their hearts. I will be their God, and they will be my people. No longer will each person teach his neighbors or his relatives by saying, "Know the Lord." All of them from the least important to the most important will all know me because I will forgive their wickedness and I will no longer hold their sins against them.'"

Hebrews 9:14 (GW) "The blood of Christ, who had no defect, does even more. Through the eternal Spirit he offered himself to God and cleansed our consciences from the useless things we had done. Now we can serve the living God."

Hebrews 9:25–26 (NCV) "The high priest enters the Most Holy Place once every year with blood that is not his own. But Christ did not offer himself many times. Then he would have had to suffer many times since the world was made. But Christ came only once and for all time at just the right time to take away all sin by sacrificing himself."

Hebrews 10:2 (NLT) "If they could have provided perfect cleansing, the sacrifices would have stopped, for the worshipers would have been purified once for all time, and their feelings of guilt would have disappeared."

Hebrews 10:10 (GNT) "Because Jesus Christ did what God wanted him to do, we are all purified from sin by the offering that he made of his own body once and for all."

Hebrews 10:14 (GNT) "With one sacrifice, then, he has made perfect forever those who are purified from sin."

Hebrews 10:16–17 (GW) "'This is the promise that I will make to them after those days, says the Lord: 'I will put my teachings in their hearts and write them in their minds.' Then he adds, 'I will no longer hold their sins and their disobedience against them.'"

Hebrews 10:22 (CEB) "Let's draw near with a genuine heart with the certainty that our faith gives us, since our hearts are sprinkled clean from an evil conscience and our bodies are washed with pure water."

Hebrews 12:1–2 (NCV) "We are surrounded by a great cloud of people whose lives tell us what faith means. So let us run the race that is before us and never give up. We should remove from our lives anything that would get in the way and the sin that so easily holds us back. Let us look only to Jesus, the One who began our faith and who makes it perfect. He suffered death on the cross. But he accepted the shame as if it were nothing because of the joy that God put before him. And now he is sitting at the right side of God's throne."

Hebrews 13:5 (GW) "Don't love money. Be happy with what you have because God has said, 'I will never abandon you or leave you.'"

1 Peter 1:3–5 (NASB) "Blessed be the God and Father of our Lord Jesus Christ, who according to His great mercy has caused us to be born again to a living hope through the resurrection of Jesus Christ from the dead, to obtain an inheritance which is imperishable and undefiled and will not fade away, reserved in heaven for you, who are protected by the power of God through faith for a salvation ready to be revealed in the last time."

1 Peter 1:23 (NLT) "You have been born again, but not to a life that will quickly end. Your new life will last forever because it comes from the eternal, living word of God."

1 Peter 2:5 (NLT) "You are living stones that God is building into his spiritual temple. What's more, you are his holy priests. Through the mediation of Jesus Christ, you offer spiritual sacrifices that please God."

1 Peter 2:9–10 (GW) "You are chosen people, a royal priesthood, a holy nation, people who belong to God. You were chosen to tell about the excellent qualities of God, who called you out of darkness into his marvelous light. Once you were not God's people, but now you are. Once you were not shown mercy, but now you have been shown mercy."

1 Peter 5:8 (CEV) "Be on your guard and stay awake. Your enemy, the devil, is like a roaring lion, sneaking around to find someone to attack."

2 Peter 1:3–4 (NASB) "Seeing that His divine power has granted to us everything pertaining to life and godliness, through the true knowledge of Him who called us by His own glory and excellence. For by these He has granted to us His precious and magnificent promises, so that by them you may become partakers of the divine nature, having escaped the corruption that is in the world by lust."

1 John 2:12 (GW) "I'm writing to you, dear children, because your sins are forgiven through Christ."

1 John 3:1 (VOICE) "Consider the kind of extravagant love the Father has lavished on us—He calls us children of God! It's true; we are His beloved children. And in the same way the world didn't recognize Him, the world does not recognize us either."

1 John 3:9 (NASB) "No one who is born of God practices sin, because His seed abides in him; and he cannot sin, because he is born of God."

1 John 4:4 (NLT) "You belong to God, my dear children. You have already won a victory over those people, because the Spirit who lives in you is greater than the spirit who lives in the world."

1 John 4:9 (NCV) "This is how God showed his love to us: He sent his one and only Son into the world so that we could have life through him."

1 John 4:15 (GW) "God lives in those who declare that Jesus is the Son of God, and they live in God."

1 John 4:17 (GNT) "Love is made perfect in us in order that we may have courage on the Judgment Day; and we will have it because our life in this world is the same as Christ's."

1 John 4:19 (NASB) "We love, because He first loved us."

1 John 5:4 (GW) "Everyone who has been born from God has won the victory over the world. Our faith is what wins the victory over the world."

1 John 5:11 (VOICE) "This is the truth: God has given us the gift of eternal life, and this life is in His Son."

1 John 5:12 (CEB) "The one who has the Son has life. The one who doesn't have God's Son does not have life."

1 John 5:13 (GW) "I've written this to those who believe in the Son of God so that they will know that they have eternal life."

1 John 5:14–15 (NCV) "This is the boldness we have in God's presence: that if we ask God for anything that agrees with what he wants, he hears us. If we know he hears us every time we ask him, we know we have what we ask from him."

1 John 5:18 (NASB) "We know that no one who is born of God sins; but He who was born of God keeps him, and the evil one does not touch him."

1 John 5:20 (GW) "We know that the Son of God has come and has given us understanding so that we know the real God. We are in the one who is real, his Son Jesus Christ. This Jesus Christ is the real God and eternal life."

Revelation 5:9 (GW) "They sang a new song, 'You deserve to take the scroll and open the seals on it, because you were slaughtered. You bought people with your blood to be God's own. They are from every tribe, language, people, and nation.'"

Revelation 19:7–9 (JUB) "Let us be glad and rejoice and give glory to him; for the marriage of the Lamb is come, and his bride has made herself ready. And to her was granted that she should be arrayed in fine linen, clean and bright: for the fine linen is the righteousness of the saints. And he said unto me, Write, Blessed are those who are called unto the marriage supper of the Lamb. And he said unto me, These are the true words of God."

Revelation 21:2–3 (NASB) "I saw the holy city, new Jerusalem, coming down out of heaven from God, made ready as a bride adorned for her husband. And I heard a loud voice from the throne, saying, 'Behold, the tabernacle of God is among men, and He will dwell among them, and they shall be His people, and God Himself will be among them.'"

LEADER'S GUIDE

Thank you for your willingness to lead a group for *His Banner Over Me Is Pursuing Love*. It is both an honor and a blessing to partner together with you in this noble endeavor. As a group leader, you can rest in the sufficiency of your Beloved—the One who lives in you and will lead through you as you trust Him.

This study can be experienced with groups of women or men only, mixed groups, or married couples. The advantage of having a mixed or married couples group is that you will get both gender perspectives. However, when you have a mixed group there are obviously more dynamics involved that should be prayerfully considered.

This leader's guide will help you facilitate seven group sessions—the introductory session and sessions 1 through 6 (for each of the six weeks of study). You may want to slow the pace and take thirteen weeks (introductory session and two weeks for each of the six weeks of study) instead. Prayerfully consider which option would best suit you as the group leader/facilitator.

The goal of this study is to help each group member renew his or her mind with the truths of Christ as his or her Spiritual Bridegroom and his or her identity as His pure, righteous, and holy bride (Rom. 12:1–2). To meet this goal, each group member will need to set aside time to complete the five days of the interactive study before meeting together as a group. As with any study, group members will get out of it what they invest into it. Through practically experiencing Christ's cherishing love and exuberant life, they will begin to express it more consistently in their lives (John 17:3; 1 Cor. 6:20).

You do not have to complete every activity in the introductory session or go over every question from each of the six weeks of study. Be flexible and open to the leading of Christ's Spirit, taking into consideration the unique needs of your group, as well as your own personal preferences. As you depend on His leading, you will be amazed at how He will work in your own life as well as your group members' lives.

As the group leader, it is important that you set a good example by being prepared for each week's meeting. Complete the study and spend time each week praying for the members of your group. Encourage them throughout the study and contact anyone who misses a session to let that person know he or she was missed. Make it your goal to build up your group members as you learn together what it means to experience Jesus as your Spiritual Bridegroom and to see yourself as His pure, righteous, and holy bride.

Getting Started

1. If you plan to conduct *His Banner Over Me Is Pursuing Love* at your church, make sure you have the support of your pastor. Look at your church's calendar, prayerfully taking into consideration other activities before you set the dates for the study. Your pastor and/or church secretary can help you with this.
2. Advertise at least one month before you want to begin the study through your church website, video announcements at your church, church bulletins, and social networking tools.
3. You will need a sign-up sheet available before and after your church's weekly worship services. List your contact information (name, address, phone number, e-mail) on the first line. You could also create an event through social media to invite people to sign up for the study.
4. Once your group is established, you may want to create a group page on your social media network of choice where the members can interact concerning the material presented in the study. The use of technology can greatly enhance group participation.
5. Obtain a copy of *His Banner Over Me Is Pursuing Love* for each group member who signed up. It would be wise to have a few extra books for last-minute sign-ups at the introductory session.
6. At least one week before the introductory session, have each participant pick up and pay for his or her book. Instruct them to read through page xxix in preparation for the session.

Introductory Session

Before the Session

1. Familiarize yourself with the layout of *His Banner Over Me Is Pursuing Love*.

   - As you begin the study, pray and ask your Beloved for insight on how to best lead your group.
   - Review the table of contents (page vii) for an overview of the study. Each week's title is the name of a song relevant to its content.
   - Read the introductory material and day 1 of week 1 (pages xi–7), completing the interactive questions/directives from day 1. Feel free to

highlight, underline, and write notes in the margins. This study is designed for you to interact with it.

2. Optional: Create a handout titled "Getting to Know You." On it, have the group members write their names and ages and answer the following questions/directives: Why did you choose to be a part of this study? Tell me a little about yourself to help me know you better. If you could describe yourself with one word, what would it be? What do you believe is the greatest obstacle/hindrance (if any) in your relationship with Christ?

3. Gather pens, name tags and markers, and a basket or wire tray for collecting book money.

4. Pray for each group member, asking God to use this study to help them renew their minds with the truths of Christ as their Spiritual Bridegroom and their identities as His pure, righteous, and holy bride.

5. Plan to arrive at your group's meeting place early. Arrange the furniture in a circle or U-shape to enhance group interaction.

During the Session (90 minutes)

1. Greet members as they arrive. For those who did not sign up prior to the introductory session, ask them to add their contact information to the sign-up sheet and give them their books (they can wait until after the session to pay for them). Have every member fill out and put on their name tags and find a seat. Ask them to complete the "Getting to Know You" questionnaire (optional) and collect them when everyone is finished.

2. Begin on time and ask group members to silence and put away their cell phones.

3. Introduce yourself and briefly tell your group why you chose to lead this study. Ask if anyone else would like to share why he or she chose to be a part of this study.

4. Explain that each group session will consist of discussion of their answers to the interactive questions/directives and will close by having group members share their prayer requests and praying.

5. If group members get behind, encourage them to not let that keep them from attending the group session. Regardless of whether or not they completed the prior week's study, they will benefit from listening to the insights of others during the sessions.

6. Discuss the importance of group confidentiality. Have group members turn to the Group Covenant (page 291) and follow along as you read it out loud. Tell them that a covenant is "an agreement between one or more parties where each person agrees to do their part, regardless of what anyone else does." Ask the group if they would like to add anything else to the covenant (in the blanks on number 6). If so, and a consensus is reached concerning the addition, have each group member write it in. Finally, have each one pass around his or her book so everyone in the group can sign it.

7. Introduce the study by asking this question (depending on how tech savvy you are, you may want to use media to display discussion questions during the sessions): "What comes to mind when you hear the word *bride*?" Allow group members to answer the question. Then say, "Dictionary.com defines *bride* as "a newly married woman or a woman about to be married."[1] Explain that in the ancient Jewish marriage customs, once a couple was betrothed (or what we think of as *engaged*), they were considered legally married under Jewish law. If a betrothed Jewish man changed his mind about the marriage, he had to obtain a divorce (a Jewish woman could not obtain a divorce). The word *betroth* means "thoroughly" and "truth, a pledge."[2] As the bride of Christ, we are thoroughly pledged to our Bridegroom, Jesus Christ, in truth.

8. The following are group discussion topics based on the introductory material found on pages xi–xxix.

   a) Read this paragraph from page xii: "Man (humanity in general) is a spiritual being who lives inside a physical body, not a physical being who houses a spirit. In order to understand our relationship with God, we need to see with spiritual eyes. Being *sons of God* refers to our new birth in Christ (the Son of God) and our role as spiritual children of our Father, God. Being the *bride of Christ*, however, refers to our spiritual union with Christ and our role of experiencing and expressing His cherishing love and exuberant life. Just as a husband and wife in the natural realm share a physical union and bear the fruit of children, Christ and His bride share a spiritual union where He has implanted His bride with His life and, with her cooperation, causes her to manifest the fruit of His Spirit (Rom. 7:4; Gal. 5:22–23; Eph. 5:9)."

Ask the following questions:

- Does this paragraph give you a clearer understanding of what it means for you to be the bride of Christ? If so, please comment. If not, what do you find confusing about it?

b) Read this paragraph from page xii: "Deeply cherished bride of Christ, your Beloved longs for you to understand that you are the love of His life. I could tell you this again and again, sounding like a broken record, but until His Spirit gives you revelation of this truth, it will not affect you personally. You might agree that this is true information because the Bible says Christ's church is His bride, but you will not experience the enjoyment of truly *knowing* you are the object of His extravagant affection until it becomes personal revelation."

Ask the following questions:

- Do you agree that the statement "You are the love of His life" is true information? Have you ever experienced the enjoyment of truly knowing you are the object of Christ's extravagant affection through personal revelation? If so, describe the experience and how it affected you. If not, this study is designed to help you do just that.

c) Read and discuss this statement from page xiii: "Your increasing desire to experience Christ as your Spiritual Bridegroom will be your greatest asset, because the bottom line is that most people find a way to do what they *want* to do."

d) On page xv, the author shared that the sinful woman in Luke 7:36–50 was the person in the Bible she most closely related to. She also shared a song that reflected that woman's (and her own) thankfulness for her Savior's incredible gift of love and forgiveness.

Ask the following questions:

- Which person in the Bible do you most closely relate to and why? Is there a particular song that you closely relate to? How can music enhance our intimacy with Christ?

e) On page xix, the author shares Scriptures of the bride of Christ's future co-reigning with Him (Dan. 7:18, 22, 27; Rev. 5:9–10; 20:4, 6; 22:5).

Ask the question:

- What do you think it will be like to rule alongside Jesus, your Bridegroom King, throughout eternity?

f) Read this paragraph from page xxv: "This highly symbolic and poetic book has more than one interpretation. Its literal interpretation celebrates love in an earthly marriage and has only existed within the last one hundred years. Many marriages have been strengthened through studies based on the Song's literal interpretation, but earthly marriage is not the focus of this study. The focus of this study is the Song's allegorical interpretation, which, in fact, is its most ancient interpretation."

Ask the following questions:

- Does it surprise you to learn that the most ancient interpretation of the Song of Solomon is its allegorical interpretation—the interpretation that describes the divine romance between Christ and His bride? Explain your answer.

g) Read this statement found on page xxvi: "Due to its numerous exchanges of words of affection between King Solomon and the Shulammite maiden, the Song could have been rightly named Terms of Endearment."

Ask the following questions:

- Out of all the terms of endearment listed on page xxvi, which of Jesus' terms of endearment for His bride means the most to you? Why?

h) Read this paragraph from pages xxvi–xxvii: "The following is a list of character profiles of the individuals and groups of people represented in the Song. Please keep in mind that these are *spiritual* rather than *physical* representations. They are defined primarily by their spiritual state (believer in Christ or unbeliever in Adam). In addition, the believers in Christ are described secondarily by the extent to which their minds have been renewed with the truths of their identity and the extent to which their true identity is being expressed through their daily lives."

In his second letter to the Corinthian church, the apostle Paul exhorts them to view one another with spiritual eyes, rather than physical eyes: "Therefore from now on we recognize no one according to the flesh" (2 Cor. 5:16). Discuss the importance and challenge of following his exhortation.

i) Look together with your group through week 1, pages 1–35. Explain that the study will last six (or twelve) weeks, each week containing five days, and each day averaging five to six pages in length. Throughout each week's study, there will be opportunities for the group members to interact with the study. These places of interaction are indicated by a bullet point (arrow). Point out each of these in day 1 of the study.

j) Discuss the importance listening to the songs, even though they may be tempted to skip them to save time.

k) Recommend that your group members do their study in the morning before their day gets busy. Read over the Scriptures below, which indicate that the quiet of the morning is a prime time to hear our Beloved's voice, and pick two or three to share with your group.

- "In the morning, O Lord, You will hear my voice; in the morning I will order my prayer to You and eagerly watch" (Ps. 5:3).
- "As for me, I shall sing of Your strength; yes, I shall joyfully sing of Your lovingkindness in the morning, for You have been my stronghold and a refuge in the day of my distress" (Ps. 59:16).
- "God, You are my God; early will I seek You; my soul thirsts for You; my flesh longs for You in a dry and thirsty land where there is no water" (Ps. 63:1 NKJV).
- "But I, O Lord, have cried out to You for help, and in the morning my prayer comes before You" (Ps. 88:13).
- "Satisfy us in the morning with Your lovingkindness, that we may sing for joy and be glad all our days" (Ps. 90:14).
- "Let me hear Your lovingkindness in the morning; for I trust in You; teach me the way in which I should walk; for to You I lift up my soul" (Ps. 143:8).

- "The Lord God has given Me the tongue of disciples, that I may know how to sustain the weary one with a word. He awakens Me morning by morning, He awakens My ear to listen as a disciple" (Isa. 50:4).
- "In the early morning, while it was still dark, Jesus got up, left the house, and went away to a secluded place, and was praying there" (Mark 1:35).

As a group leader, it is important that you realize some people are naturally morning people and some are not. Although you can recommend the quiet of the mornings to do their study, be careful not to make a law out of it. Each member would do well to follow the advice of Hudson Taylor, a British missionary to China in the late nineteenth century and early twentieth century: "Whatever is your best time in the day, give that in communion with God."[3]

1) Point out that at the end of each day's study the same two questions appear:

> What is your Bridegroom speaking to you through today's study?
> How will you respond?

Many believers struggle with confidence in hearing God's voice. Encourage them with the encouragement of our Beloved Shepherd from the tenth chapter of John's Gospel:

- "But he who enters by the door is a shepherd of the sheep. To him the doorkeeper opens, and *the sheep hear his voice*, and *he calls his own sheep by name* and leads them out. When he puts forth all his own, he goes ahead of them, and *the sheep follow him because they know his voice*. A stranger they simply will not follow, but will flee from him, because *they do not know the voice of strangers*" (John 10:2–5).
- "*I am the good shepherd, and I know My own and My own know Me*, even as the Father knows Me and I know the Father; and I lay down My life for the sheep" (John 10:14–15).
- "*My sheep hear My voice, and I know them, and they follow Me*" (John 10:27).

9. Remind each participant that you will be praying for him or her by name throughout the week as they seek to know their Bridegroom more intimately. Close the introductory session in prayer, asking your Beloved to enable each group member to experience the romance of His amazing love throughout the study.

After the Session
1. Reflect on the session, noting any concerns that may have arisen. Take time to read through your group member's "Getting to Know You" questionnaires (optional). This could help you to better understand them. Remember that you are not in a leadership position to judge but to lead and encourage. Ask your Beloved to give you discernment on how best to pray for each group member.
2. Obtain any additional books and deliver them as quickly as possible to the members (or have the members pick them up), so that they will have ample time to complete the first week's study before the next group meeting.
3. Send thank-you e-mails or notes to those who provided their addresses. Tell them how excited you are to have them in your group and that you pray they will be blessed and encouraged in their relationship with their Beloved through the study. Also encourage them to communicate any concerns that they may have throughout the course of the study.
4. Group size adds to the dynamic of participation. If there are more than ten people in your group, you may want to divide them into smaller groups of no more than six and designate one person each week to facilitate the discussion for weeks 1 through 6.

Sessions 1–6

Before each Session
1. Pray and ask your Beloved to give you insight on how to facilitate your unique group in a way that is most beneficial to them. You will be surprised and delighted at what He shows you.
2. Complete the prior week's material. Highlight facts and insights that are especially meaningful to you. You may want to prioritize the questions you feel are most important for the group discussion. Cover those first, and if time remains, go over the skipped questions.

During Each Session (90 minutes)
1. Welcome members as they arrive.
2. Begin on time, silence and put away cell phones, and open with prayer, asking Christ's Spirit to lead the group time.
3. Have group members turn to the first interactive question/directive for that week and begin your discussion by reading the question and sharing your answer. Then invite your group to do the same. Be careful not to allow individual members to monopolize the group discussion. This way, each group member will have an opportunity to contribute.
4. If time remains after going over interactive questions/directives, ask if there was any other part of the material they covered that week that they would like to discuss as a group.
5. (10–15 minutes before the end of class) Allow group members to share their prayer concerns and commit to pray for one another throughout the following week.
6. Close in prayer and dismiss the group.
7. (Optional) At your last group meeting, provide refreshments and encourage members to stay in touch. Tell them, if they are interested, that you will notify them when *His Banner Over Me Is Sustaining Love* (over chapters 3–5 of the Song of Solomon) is available.

After Each Session
1. Pray for each group member and send notes of encouragement through e-mail or regular mail.

Group Covenant

I, _____ , covenant with my Bible study group to do the following:

1. Complete the five days of interactive study before the group meeting.
2. Pray consistently for my fellow group members and leader.
3. Attend all group meetings, barring any unexpected circumstances which would interfere with my ability to attend.
4. Remember and abide by: "What is shared in the group meeting *stays* in the group meeting."
5. Be patient with my fellow group members, remembering that we are all in the process of getting our minds renewed and walking in the truths of our identity as Christ's lovely Bride.

6. _____

Signed: _____   Date: _____

Group Members' Signatures

NOTES

Author's Background
1. Janice Sjostrand. *Alabaster Box*. CeCe Winans. © 1999 by Wellspring Gospel. MP3.

Looking at Scripture through a Bridal Lens
1. Rhonda Calhoun, *Song of Solomon Verse by Verse Study* (Holden, Mo.: Heart Publishing, 2005), Session 1, CD 1.
2. type. Dictionary.com. *Dictionary.com Unabridged*. Random House, Inc. http://www.dictionary.com/browse/type (accessed: March 27, 2017).
3. His Heart's Desire Ministries website page: http://www.hhdministries.com/#/living-loved/womens-retreats.

Overview of the Song of Solomon
1. allegory. Dictionary.com. *Dictionary.com Unabridged*. Random House, Inc. http://www.dictionary.com/browse/allegory (accessed: March 27, 2017).
2. Quotation from Mishnah Yadayim 3:5, translated by Herbert Danby, The Mishnah. Oxford: Clarendon Press, 1933. As quoted in Barry L. Bandstra, *Reading the Old Testament, 4th Edition*. Belmont: Wadsworth Cengage, 2009; page 418.

Week 1—This Kiss
Quote on title page by Watchman Nee also in Day 1 of Week 1 and cited in note 4.
1. "H7965 - shalowm - Strong's Hebrew Lexicon (NASB)." *Blue Letter Bible*. Accessed 27 Mar, 2017. https://www.blueletterbible.org//lang/lexicon/lexicon.cfm?Strongs=H7965&t=NASB.
2. "G1515 - eirēnē - Strong's Greek Lexicon (NASB)." *Blue Letter Bible*. Accessed 27 Mar, 2017. https://www.blueletterbible.org//lang/lexicon/lexicon.cfm?Strongs=G1515&t=NASB
3. "H5400 - nasaq - Strong's Hebrew Lexicon (NASB)." *Blue Letter Bible*. Accessed 27 Mar, 2017. https://www.blueletterbible.org//lang/lexicon/lexicon.cfm?Strongs=H5400&t=NASB.
4. Watchman Nee, *The Song of Songs: The Divine Romance Between God & Man* (Anaheim: Living Stream Ministry, 1993), 12.

5. Adapted from *Falling in Love with Jesus: Abandoning Yourself to the Greatest Romance of Your Life*. Copyright © 2001 by Dee Brestin and Kathy Troccoli. Published by W. Publishing Group, a Division of Thomas Nelson, Nashville. Secondary source: Jamie Lash, *A Kiss a Day* (Hagerstown, Md.: Ebed, 1996), 17.

6. "H1730 - dowd - Strong's Hebrew Lexicon (NASB)." *Blue Letter Bible*. Accessed 27 Mar, 2017. https://www.blueletterbible.org//lang/lexicon/lexicon.cfm?Strongs=H1730&t=NASB.

7. Gary Chapman, *God Speaks Your Love Language: How to Feel and Reflect God's Love* (Chicago, Ill.: Northfield Publishing, 2009).

8. Taken from *Sacred Pathways* by Gary Thomas. Copyright © 1996 by Gary L. Thomas. Used by permission of Zondervan. *www.zondervan.com*.

9. Calhoun, *Song of Solomon Verse by Verse Study*, Session 1, CD 2.

10. Mike Bickle, *The Pleasures of Loving God* (Lake Mary, Fla.: Charisma House, 2000), 111.

11. "H5197 - nataph - Strong's Hebrew Lexicon (NASB)." *Blue Letter Bible*. Accessed 27 Mar, 2017. https://www.blueletterbible.org//lang/lexicon/lexicon.cfm?Strongs=H5197&t=NASB.

12. "H7826 - shachal - Strong's Hebrew Lexicon (NASB)." *Blue Letter Bible*. Accessed 27 Mar, 2017. https://www.blueletterbible.org//lang/lexicon/lexicon.cfm?Strongs=H7826&t=NASB.

13. "H2459 - cheleb - Strong's Hebrew Lexicon (NASB)." *Blue Letter Bible*. Accessed 27 Mar, 2017. https://www.blueletterbible.org//lang/lexicon/lexicon.cfm?Strongs=H2459&t=NASB

14. "H3835 - laban - Strong's Hebrew Lexicon (NASB)." *Blue Letter Bible*. Accessed 27 Mar, 2017. https://www.blueletterbible.org//lang/lexicon/lexicon.cfm?Strongs=H3835&t=NASB.

15. "H4843 - marar - Strong's Hebrew Lexicon (NASB)." *Blue Letter Bible*. Accessed 27 Mar, 2017. https://www.blueletterbible.org//lang/lexicon/lexicon.cfm?Strongs=H4843&t=NASB.

16. "H7076 - qinnamown - Strong's Hebrew Lexicon (NASB)." *Blue Letter Bible*. Accessed 27 Mar, 2017. https://www.blueletterbible.org//lang/lexicon/lexicon.cfm?Strongs=H7076&t=NASB.

17. "H7069 - qanah - Strong's Hebrew Lexicon (NASB)." *Blue Letter Bible*. Accessed 27 Mar, 2017. https://www.blueletterbible.org//lang/lexicon/lexicon.cfm?Strongs=H7069&t=NASB.

18. "H6915 - qadad - Strong's Hebrew Lexicon (NASB)." *Blue Letter Bible*. Accessed 27 Mar, 2017. https://www.blueletterbible.org//lang/lexicon/lexicon.cfm?Strongs=H6915&t=NASB.

19. "G5547 - Christos - Strong's Greek Lexicon (NASB)." *Blue Letter Bible*. Accessed 27 Mar, 2017. https://www.blueletterbible.org//lang/lexicon/lexicon.cfm?Strongs=G5547&t=NASB.

20. "H8034 - shem - Strong's Hebrew Lexicon (NASB)." *Blue Letter Bible*. Accessed 27 Mar, 2017. https://www.blueletterbible.org//lang/lexicon/lexicon.cfm?Strongs=H8034&t=NASB.

21. "H7324 - ruwq - Strong's Hebrew Lexicon (NASB)." *Blue Letter Bible*. Accessed 27 Mar, 2017. https://www.blueletterbible.org//lang/lexicon/lexicon.cfm?Strongs=H7324&t=NASB.

22. pour. Dictionary.com. *Online Etymology Dictionary*. Douglas Harper, Historian. http://www.dictionary.com/browse/pour (accessed: March 28, 2017).

23. "H5959 - `almah - Strong's Hebrew Lexicon (NASB)." *Blue Letter Bible*. Accessed 27 Mar, 2017. https://www.blueletterbible.org//lang/lexicon/lexicon.cfm?Strongs=H5959&t=NASB.

24. Nee, *The Song of Songs: The Divine Romance Between God & Man*, 13.

25. Nee, *The Song of Songs: The Divine Romance Between God & Man*, 12.

Week 2—Flawless

Song lyric source on title page: MercyMe, David Garcia, Ben Glover, Solomon Olds. "Flawless." MercyMe. © 2014 by Fair Trade/Columbia. MP3.

1. *Song of Songs: Unveiling the Mystery of Passionate Intimacy with Christ* by Watchman Nee, © 1965 by CLC Publications. Used by permission of CLC Publications. May not be further reproduced. All rights reserved. 28.

2. Vine, W. "Death, Death-Stroke (See Also Die) - Vine's Expository Dictionary of New Testament Words." *Blue Letter Bible*. Last Modified 24 Jun, 1996, Accessed 28 Mar, 2017, https://www.blueletterbible.org/search/Dictionary/viewTopic.cfm.

3. Rhonda Calhoun, *The Great I AM* (Holden, Mo.: Heart Publishing, 2007), 127–128.

4. exult. Dictionary.com. *Dictionary.com Unabridged*. Random House, Inc. http://www.dictionary.com/browse/exult (accessed: March 28, 2017).

5. "H2142 - zakar - Strong's Hebrew Lexicon (NASB)." *Blue Letter Bible*. Accessed 28 Mar, 2017. https://www.blueletterbible.org//lang/lexicon/lexicon.cfm?Strongs=H2142&t=NASB.

6. Taken from: *What God Wishes Christians Knew About Christianity*. Copyright © 1998 by Bill Gillham. Published by Harvest House Publishers. Eugene, Oregon 97402. *www.harvesthousepublishers.com*. Used by Permission. 82.

7. Adapted from Jamie Lash's *Freedom in Christ* seminar. Used by permission. Accessed March 29, 2017, http://www.lifegivingwords.com/audio_materials.htm.

8. Abraham Lincoln, "House Divided Speech," *Speeches & Writings. Abraham Lincoln Online*, accessed March 28, 2017, http://www.abrahamlincolnonline.org/lincoln/speeches/house.htm.

9. Andrew Wommack, *Spirit, Soul & Body* (Colorado Springs: Andrew Wommack Ministries, 2005), 2–3.

10. Adapted from Jamie Lash's *Freedom in Christ* seminar. Used by permission. Accessed March 29, 2017, http://www.lifegivingwords.com/audio_materials.htm.

11. Rick Howard and Jamie Lash, *This Was Your Life! Preparing to Meet God Face to Face* (Grand Rapids, Mich.: Chosen Books, 2002), 43–44. Original quote from Hannah Whitall Smith, *The Unselfishness of God* (Princeton, N.J.: Littlebrook, 1987), 136–139.

12. "The Holy Materials – Typology," *Bible History Online*, accessed March 29, 2017, http://www.bible-history.com/tabernacle/TAB4Preparing_for_the_Tabernacle.htm.

Week 3—You Are More

Song lyric source on title page: Tenth Avenue North. "You Are More." Tenth Avenue North. © 2010 by Reunion. MP3.

1. Taken from *Present Perfect* by Gregory A. Boyd. Copyright © 2010 by Gregory A. Boyd. Used by permission of Zondervan. *www.zondervan.com*. 122.

2. Reprinted by permission. (*The Search for Significance*), Robert S. McGee, 1998, 2003, Thomas Nelson. Nashville, Tennessee. All rights reserved. 7–8.

3. McGee, *The Search for Significance*, 11.

4. Adapted from Jamie Lash's *Freedom in Christ* seminar. Used by permission. Accessed March 29, 2017, http://www.lifegivingwords.com/audio_materials.htm

5. Howard and Lash, *This Was Your Life! Preparing to Meet God Face to Face*, 70.

6. Reprinted by permission. *Deadly Emotions*, Don Colbert, M.D., 2003, Thomas Nelson. Nashville, Tennessee. All rights reserved. 139. Adapted from V. E. Frankl, *Man's Search for Meaning* (New York: Washington Press, 1963).

7. Nee, *Song of Songs: Unveiling the Mystery of Passionate Intimacy with Christ*, 33.

8. C. S. Lewis, *The Problem of Pain* (copyright CS Lewis Pte Ltd 1940).

9. Nee, *Song of Songs: Unveiling the Mystery of Passionate Intimacy with Christ*, 33.

10. "H157 - 'ahab - Strong's Hebrew Lexicon (NASB)." *Blue Letter Bible*. Accessed 28 Mar, 2017. https://www.blueletterbible.org//lang/lexicon/lexicon.cfm?Strongs=H157&t=NASB.

11. despair. Dictionary.com. *Dictionary.com Unabridged*. Random House, Inc. http://www.dictionary.com/browse/despair (accessed: March 28, 2017).

12. "G2570 - kalos - Strong's Greek Lexicon (NASB)." *Blue Letter Bible*. Accessed 28 Mar, 2017. https://www.blueletterbible.org//lang/lexicon/lexicon.cfm?Strongs=G2570&t=NASB.

13. "G3173 - megas - Strong's Greek Lexicon (NASB)." *Blue Letter Bible*. Accessed 28 Mar, 2017. https://www.blueletterbible.org//lang/lexicon/lexicon.cfm?Strongs=G3173&t=NASB.

14. mega. Dictionary.com. *Collins English Dictionary - Complete & Unabridged 10th Edition*. HarperCollins Publishers. http://www.dictionary.com/browse/mega (accessed: March 28, 2017).

15. ruminate. Dictionary.com. *Dictionary.com Unabridged*. Random House, Inc. http://www.dictionary.com/browse/ruminate (accessed: March 28, 2017).

16. "G3784 - opheilō - Strong's Greek Lexicon (NASB)." *Blue Letter Bible*. Accessed 28 Mar, 2017. https://www.blueletterbible.org//lang/lexicon/lexicon.cfm?Strongs=G3784&t=NASB.

17. "G5055 - teleō - Strong's Greek Lexicon (NASB)." *Blue Letter Bible*. Accessed 28 Mar, 2017. https://www.blueletterbible.org//lang/lexicon/lexicon.cfm?Strongs=G5055&t=NASB.

18. convict. Dictionary.com. *Dictionary.com Unabridged*. Random House, Inc. http://www.dictionary.com/browse/convict (accessed: March 28, 2017).

19. "H3302 - yaphah - Strong's Hebrew Lexicon (NASB)." *Blue Letter Bible*. Accessed 29 Mar, 2017. https://www.blueletterbible.org//lang/lexicon/lexicon.cfm?Strongs=H3302&t=NASB.

20. "H7474 - ra`yah - Strong's Hebrew Lexicon (NASB)." *Blue Letter Bible*. Accessed 29 Mar, 2017. https://www.blueletterbible.org//lang/lexicon/lexicon.cfm?Strongs=H7474&t=NASB.

21. darling. Dictionary.com. *Dictionary.com Unabridged*. Random House, Inc. http://www.dictionary.com/browse/darling (accessed: March 29, 2017).

22. Taken from *The Zondervan NASB Study Bible*. Copyright © 1999 by the Zondervan Corporation. Used by permission of Zondervan. *www.zondervan.com*. 949.

23. "H6960 - qavah - Strong's Hebrew Lexicon (NASB)." *Blue Letter Bible*. Accessed 9 Apr, 2017. https://www.blueletterbible.org//lang/lexicon/lexicon.cfm?Strongs=H6960&t=NASB.

24. "H2498 - chalaph - Strong's Hebrew Lexicon (NASB)." *Blue Letter Bible*. Accessed 9 Apr, 2017. https://www.blueletterbible.org//lang/lexicon/lexicon.cfm?Strongs=H2498&t=NASB.

25. Taken from *The Confident Woman*. Copyright © 1993 by Anabel Gillham. Published by Harvest House Publishers. Eugene, Oregon 97402. *www.harvesthousepublishers.com*. Used by Permission. 122–123.

Week 4—Everything I Do

1. "H3895 - lĕchiy - Strong's Hebrew Lexicon (NASB)." *Blue Letter Bible*. Accessed 29 May, 2017. https://www.blueletterbible.org//lang/lexicon/lexicon.cfm?Strongs=H3895&t=NASB.

2. "H4998 - na'ah - Strong's Hebrew Lexicon (NASB)." *Blue Letter Bible*. Accessed 29 Mar, 2017. https://www.blueletterbible.org//lang/lexicon/lexicon.cfm?Strongs=H4998&t=NASB.

3. "H8446 - tuwr - Strong's Hebrew Lexicon (NASB)." *Blue Letter Bible*. Accessed 29 Mar, 2017. https://www.blueletterbible.org//lang/lexicon/lexicon.cfm?Strongs=H8446&t=NASB.

4. Gillham, *What God Wishes Christians Knew About Christianity*, 126.

5. "H8447 - towr - Strong's Hebrew Lexicon (NASB)." *Blue Letter Bible*. Accessed 29 Mar, 2017. https://www.blueletterbible.org//lang/lexicon/lexicon.cfm?Strongs=H8447&t=NASB.

6. "The Holy Materials – Typology," *Bible History Online*, accessed March 29, 2017, http://www.bible-history.com/tabernacle/TAB4Preparing_for_the_Tabernacle.htm.

7. "The Holy Materials – Typology," *Bible History Online*, accessed March 29, 2017, http://www.bible-history.com/tabernacle/TAB4Preparing_for_the_Tabernacle.htm.

8. redeem. Dictionary.com. *Dictionary.com Unabridged*. Random House, Inc. http://www.dictionary.com/browse/redeem (accessed: March 29, 2017).

9. R. Glenn Greenwood & Latayne C. Scott, *The Shout of the Bridegroom—Understanding Christ's Intimate Love for His Church* (Webb City, Mo.: Covenant Publishing, 2002), 61–62.

10. "H4524 - mecab - Strong's Hebrew Lexicon (NASB)." *Blue Letter Bible*. Accessed 29 Mar, 2017. https://www.blueletterbible.org//lang/lexicon/lexicon.cfm?Strongs=H4524&t=NASB.

11. This short story is the author's retelling of the subject matter in Peter Lord's *Turkeys & Eagles*. Copyright © MCMLXXXVII by Peter Lord. Published by Christian Books Publishing House. Auburn, Maine 04210.

12. Wikipedia contributors, "Spikenard," *Wikipedia, The Free Encyclopedia*, https://en.wikipedia.org/w/index.php?title=Spikenard&oldid=763823623 (accessed March 29, 2017).

13. Wikipedia contributors, "Spikenard," *Wikipedia, The Free Encyclopedia*, https://en.wikipedia.org/w/index.php?title=Spikenard&oldid=763823623 (accessed March 29, 2017).

14. Adapted from Dana Candler's audio teaching series *Deep unto Deep - The Journey of His Embrace*. Used by permission. Accessed August 19, 2017, https://archive.org/details/SeriesDeepUntoDeep-TheJourneyOfHisEmbrace/DarkYetLovely.mp3.

15. "H6887 - tsarar - Strong's Hebrew Lexicon (NASB)." *Blue Letter Bible*. Accessed 29 Mar, 2017. https://www.blueletterbible.org//lang/lexicon/lexicon.cfm?Strongs=H6887&t=NASB.

16. bundle. Dictionary.com. *Dictionary.com Unabridged*. Random House, Inc. http://www.dictionary.com/browse/bundle (accessed: March 29, 2017).

17. cluster.Biblestudytools.com. *Gill's Exposition of the Entire Bible*, accessed March 29, 2017, http://www.biblestudytools.com/commentaries/gills-exposition-of-the-bible/song-of-solomon-1-14.html.

18. "H3724 - kopher - Strong's Hebrew Lexicon (NASB)." *Blue Letter Bible*. Accessed 29 Mar, 2017. https://www.blueletterbible.org//lang/lexicon/lexicon.cfm?Strongs=H3724&t=NASB.

19. Cora Harris Macilravy, "Christ and His Bride," *Joanna May.org*, accessed March 29, 2017, http://stage.joannamay.org/files/ChristHisBridechap1-10.pdf, 46–47. This work was published in 1916; therefore, it is in the public domain (works published before 1922).

20. "H5872 - `Eyn Gediy - Strong's Hebrew Lexicon (NASB)." *Blue Letter Bible*. Accessed 29 Mar, 2017. https://www.blueletterbible.org//lang/lexicon/lexicon.cfm?Strongs=H5872&t=NASB.

21. "Family Tragedy: The American Colony in Jerusalem," *A Library of Congress Exhibition*, accessed March 29, 2017, http://www.loc.gov/exhibits/americancolony/amcolony-family.html.

22. "Family Tragedy: The American Colony in Jerusalem," *A Library of Congress Exhibition*, accessed March 29, 2017, http://www.loc.gov/exhibits/americancolony/amcolony-family.html.

23. "Family Tragedy: The American Colony in Jerusalem," *A Library of Congress Exhibition*, accessed March 29, 2017, http://www.loc.gov/exhibits/americancolony/amcolony-family.html.

24. Brother Lawrence, *The Practice of the Presence of God* (Grand Rapids, Mich.: Baker Publishing Group, 1967), 44.

25. "H5276 - na`em - Strong's Hebrew Lexicon (NASB)." *Blue Letter Bible*. Accessed 19 Aug, 2017. https://www.blueletterbible.org//lang/lexicon/lexicon.cfm?Strongs=H5276&t=NASB.

26. "H7488 - ra`anan - Strong's Hebrew Lexicon (NASB)." *Blue Letter Bible*. Accessed 29 Mar, 2017. https://www.blueletterbible.org//lang/lexicon/lexicon.cfm?Strongs=H7488&t=NASB.

27. "Symbols in Christian Art & Architecture: A Resource for Learning the Sign Language of Faith – Flowers, Plants, and Trees," *Planetgast.net*, accessed March 29, 2017, http://www.planetgast.net/symbols/plants/plants.html.

28. "Symbols in Christian Art & Architecture: A Resource for Learning the Sign Language of Faith – Flowers, Plants, and Trees," *Planetgast.net*, accessed March 29, 2017, http://www.planetgast.net/symbols/plants/plants.html.

29. "H7799 - shuwshan - Strong's Hebrew Lexicon (NASB)." *Blue Letter Bible*. Accessed 29 Mar, 2017. https://www.blueletterbible.org//lang/lexicon/lexicon.cfm?Strongs=H7799&t=NASB.

30. "Sand Lily Photo," *TrekNature*, accessed March 29, 2017, http://www.treknature.com/gallery/Middle_East/Israel/photo2072.htm.

31. "H5959 - `almah - Strong's Hebrew Lexicon (NASB)." *Blue Letter Bible*. Accessed 29 Mar, 2017. https://www.blueletterbible.org//lang/lexicon/lexicon.cfm?Strongs=H5959&t=NASB.

32. "H1323 - bath - Strong's Hebrew Lexicon (NASB)." *Blue Letter Bible*. Accessed 29 Mar, 2017. https://www.blueletterbible.org//lang/lexicon/lexicon.cfm?Strongs=H1323&t=NASB.

33. "Symbols in Christian Art & Architecture: A Resource for Learning the Sign Language of Faith – Flowers, Plants, and Trees," *Planetgast.net*, accessed March 29, 2017, http://www.planetgast.net/symbols/plants/plants.html.

34. "Calla Lily Flower: Its Meaning & Symbolism," *Flowermeaning.com*, accessed March 29, 2017, http://www.flowermeaning.com/calla-lily-meaning.

35. Taken from: *Daily in Christ*. Copyright © 1993 by Neil T. Anderson. Published by Harvest House Publishers. Eugene, Oregon 97402. *www.harvesthousepublishers.com*. Used by Permission. May 3rd.

Week 5—Welcome to the New

Quote on title page by Dr. Martyn Lloyd-Jones also in Day 1 of Week 5 and cited in note 3.

1. "H8598 - tappuwach - Strong's Hebrew Lexicon (NASB)." *Blue Letter Bible*. Accessed 7 Apr, 2017. https://www.blueletterbible.org//lang/lexicon/lexicon.cfm?Strongs=H8598&t=NASB.
2. "Know Your Etrog," *Judaism 101*, accessed April 7, 2017, http://www.jewfaq.org/etrog.htm.
3. Dr. Martyn Lloyd-Jones, *Roman's 6:1–The New Man* (Carlisle, Pa: Banner of Truth Trust, 1972), 8.
4. "The Westminster Shorter Catechism," *The Westminster Presbyterian*, accessed April 7, 2017, http://www.westminsterconfession.org/confessional-standards/the-westminster-shorter-catechism.php.
5. Chris Adsit, "The Measure of a Ministry," posted January 1, 2011, *Discipleship Revolution, January–February 2011 issue, Mission Frontiers*, accessed April 7, 2017, http://www.missionfrontiers.org/issue/article/the-measure-of-a-ministry.
6. "H3427 - yashab - Strong's Hebrew Lexicon (NASB)." *Blue Letter Bible*. Accessed 7 Apr, 2017. https://www.blueletterbible.org//lang/lexicon/lexicon.cfm?Strongs=H3427&t=NASB.
7. "G3306 - menō - Strong's Greek Lexicon (NASB)." *Blue Letter Bible*. Accessed 7 Apr, 2017. https://www.blueletterbible.org//lang/lexicon/lexicon.cfm?Strongs=G3306&t=NASB.
8. Dan Stone and David Gregory, *The Rest of the Gospel* (Corvallis, Ore.: One Press, 2000), 83–84.
9. Ruth Myers, *The Satisfied Heart* (Colorado Springs, CO: WaterBrook Press, 1999), book jacket.
10. "H3196 - yayin - Strong's Hebrew Lexicon (NASB)." *Blue Letter Bible*. Accessed 7 Apr, 2017. https://www.blueletterbible.org//lang/lexicon/lexicon.cfm?Strongs=H3196&t=NASB, "H1004 - bayith - Strong's Hebrew Lexicon (NASB)." *Blue Letter Bible*. Accessed 7 Apr, 2017. https://www.blueletterbible.org//lang/lexicon/lexicon.cfm?Strongs=H1004&t=NASB.
11. Blaise Pascal. *Penses* (New York: Penguin Books, 1966), 75.
12. "H5301 - naphach - Strong's Hebrew Lexicon (NASB)." *Blue Letter Bible*. Accessed 7 Apr, 2017. https://www.blueletterbible.org//lang/lexicon/lexicon.cfm?Strongs=H5301&t=NASB.

13. "G4154 - pneō - Strong's Greek Lexicon (NASB)." *Blue Letter Bible*. Accessed 7 Apr, 2017. https://www.blueletterbible.org//lang/lexicon/lexicon.cfm?Strongs=G4154&t=NASB.

14. Taken from: *A Divine Invitation: Experiencing the Romance of God's Amazing Love*. Copyright © 2002 by Steve McVey. Published by Harvest House Publishers. Eugene, Oregon 97402. Out of print. Used by Author's Permission. 145–146.

15. adjure. Dictionary.com. *Dictionary.com Unabridged*. Random House, Inc. http://www.dictionary.com/browse/adjure (accessed: April 7, 2017).

16. McVey, *A Divine Invitation: Experiencing the Romance of God's Amazing Love*, 13.

17. Cora Harris Macilravy, "Christ and His Bride," *Joanna May.org*, accessed March 29, 2017, http://stage.joannamay.org/files/ChristHisBridechap1-10.pdf, 5–6. This work was published in 1916; therefore, it is in the public domain (works published before 1922).

18. "H6643 - tsĕbiy - Strong's Hebrew Lexicon (NASB)." *Blue Letter Bible*. Accessed 7 Apr, 2017. https://www.blueletterbible.org//lang/lexicon/lexicon.cfm?Strongs=H6643&t=NASB.

19. "H352 - 'ayil - Strong's Hebrew Lexicon (NASB)." *Blue Letter Bible*. Accessed 7 Apr, 2017. https://www.blueletterbible.org//lang/lexicon/lexicon.cfm?Strongs=H352&t=NASB.

20. peering. Dictionary.com. *Dictionary.com Unabridged*. Random House, Inc. http://www.dictionary.com/browse/peering (accessed: April 8, 2017).

21. "H6965 - quwm - Strong's Hebrew Lexicon (NASB)." *Blue Letter Bible*. Accessed 7 Apr, 2017. https://www.blueletterbible.org//lang/lexicon/lexicon.cfm?Strongs=H6965&t=NASB.

22. Author Lee Ezell coined the phrase in her book *Porcupine People: Learning to Love the Unloveable* (Ventura, Calif.: Vine Books, 1998).

Week 6—Remind Me Who I Am

Song lyric source on title page: Jason Gray and Jason Ingram. "Remind Me Who I Am." Jason Gray. © 2011 by Centricity Music. MP3.

1. "G142 - airō - Strong's Greek Lexicon (NASB)." *Blue Letter Bible*. Accessed 8 Apr, 2017. https://www.blueletterbible.org//lang/lexicon/lexicon.cfm?Strongs=G142&t=NASB.

2. Bruce Wilkinson, *Secrets of the Vine: Breaking Through to Abundance* (Sisters, Ore.: Multnomah Publishers, 2001), 56–57.

3. Wilkinson, *Secrets of the Vine: Breaking Through to Abundance*, 57–60.

4. William Smith, "Fig, Fig tree," *Smith's Bible Dictionary Online, 1901*, accessed April 8, 2017, http://www.biblestudytools.com/dictionaries/smiths-bible-dictionary/fig-fig-tree.html.

5. "Michael de Montaigne > Quotes > Quotable Quotes," *Goodreads.com*, accessed April 8, 2017, http://www.goodreads.com/quotes/489558-my-life-has-been-filled-with-terrible-misfortune-most-of.

6. Don Joseph Goewey, "85 Percent of What We Worry About Never Happens," last modified August 25, 2016, *The Huffington Post*, accessed April 8, 2017, http://www.huffingtonpost.com/don-joseph-goewey-/85-of-what-we-worry-about_b_8028368.html.

7. "H5564 - camak - Strong's Hebrew Lexicon (NASB)." *Blue Letter Bible*. Accessed 8 Apr, 2017. https://www.blueletterbible.org//lang/lexicon/lexicon.cfm?Strongs=H5564&t=NASB.

8. Beth Moore, *Jesus, the One and Only* (Nashville, TN: Broadman & Holman Publishers, 2002). Reprinted and used by permission. 332–333.

9. "H5553 - cela` - Strong's Hebrew Lexicon (NASB)." *Blue Letter Bible*. Accessed 8 Apr, 2017. https://www.blueletterbible.org//lang/lexicon/lexicon.cfm?Strongs=H5553&t=NASB.

10. Augustus Montague Toplady, "Rock of Ages," Thomas Hastings, comp. First published in 1775 in The *Gospel Magazine*.

11. "H5643 - cether - Strong's Hebrew Lexicon (NASB)." *Blue Letter Bible*. Accessed 8 Apr, 2017. https://www.blueletterbible.org//lang/lexicon/lexicon.cfm?Strongs=H5643&t=NASB.

12. Kathy Buchanan, "Annaleigh and the Nidgets," *Want More Love? (Brio Devotional Series)* (Wheaton, Ill.: Tyndale House, 2004), 22–23.

13. "G3962 - patēr - Strong's Greek Lexicon (NASB)." *Blue Letter Bible*. Accessed 16 Aug, 2017. https://www.blueletterbible.org//lang/lexicon/lexicon.cfm?Strongs=G3962&t=NASB.

14. Taken from *Grace Rules*. Copyright © 1998 by Steve McVey. Published by Harvest House Publishers. Eugene, Oregon 97402. *www.harvesthousepublishers.com*. Used by Permission. 134–135.

15. stealth. Dictionary.com. *Dictionary.com Unabridged*. Random House, Inc. http://www.dictionary.com/browse/stealth (accessed: April 8, 2017).

16. Bill shares extensively how the enemy operates in our thought life in his books *Lifetime Guarantee* and *What God Wishes Christians Knew About Christianity*. Bill's wife, Anabel, also shares this teaching in her book *The Confident Woman*.

17. Andrew Farley, *God Without Religion* (Grand Rapids, Mich.: Baker Books, 2011), 155–157.
18. Doris Kear, 2006. Used by permission.
19. "H6962 - quwt - Strong's Hebrew Lexicon (NASB)." *Blue Letter Bible.* Accessed 8 Apr, 2017. https://www.blueletterbible.org//lang/lexicon/lexicon.cfm?Strongs=H6962&t=NASB.
20. Jamieson, Fausset & Brown, "Commentary on Song of Solomon 2 by Jamieson, Fausset & Brown." *Blue Letter Bible.* Last Modified 19 Feb, 2000. https://www.blueletterbible.org/Comm/jfb/Sgs/Sgs_002.cfm.
21. "H1335 - bether - Strong's Hebrew Lexicon (KJV)." *Blue Letter Bible.* Accessed 8 Apr, 2017. https://www.blueletterbible.org//lang/lexicon/lexicon.cfm?Strongs=H1335&t=KJV.
22. "H1334 - bathar - Strong's Hebrew Lexicon (NASB)." *Blue Letter Bible.* Accessed 18 Aug, 2017. https://www.blueletterbible.org//lang/lexicon/lexicon.cfm?Strongs=H1334&t=NASB.

Leader's Guide

1. bride. Dictionary.com. *Dictionary.com Unabridged.* Random House, Inc. http://www.dictionary.com/browse/bride (accessed: April 9, 2017).
2. betroth. Dictionary.com. *Online Etymology Dictionary.* Douglas Harper, Historian. http://www.dictionary.com/browse/betroth (accessed: April 9, 2017).
3. "27 Hudson Taylor Quotes," *Christian Quotes*, accessed April 9, 2017, https://www.christianquotes.info/quotes-by-author/hudson-taylor-quotes/#axzz4dllYNg2h.

Printed in the United States
By Bookmasters